America, the Vietnam War, and the World

COMPARATIVE AND INTERNATIONAL PERSPECTIVES

This book presents new perspectives on the Vietnam War, its global repercussions, and the role of this war in modern history. The volume reveals "America's War" as an international event that reverberated all over the world: in domestic settings of numerous nation-states, combatants and noncombatants alike, as well as in transnational relations and alliance systems. The volume thereby covers a wide geographical range – from Berkeley and Berlin to Cambodia and Canberra. The chapters address political, military, and diplomatic issues no less than cultural and intellectual consequences of "Vietnam." The contributors also set the Vietnam War in comparison to other major conflicts in world history; they cover more than three centuries and develop general insights into the tragedies and trajectories of military conflicts as phenomena of modern societies in general. For the first time, "America's War" is thus depicted as a truly global event whose origins and characteristics deserve an interdisciplinary treatment.

Andreas W. Daum is currently Professor of History at the University at Buffalo, State University of New York. He is the author of *Wissenschaftspopularisierung im 19. Jahrhundert* (1998) and *Kennedy in Berlin: Politik, Kultur und Emotionen im Kaltern Krieg* (2003).

Lloyd C. Gardner is the Charles and Mary Beard Professor of History at Rutgers University. His recent publications include *Pay and Price* (1995) and *Spheres of Influence* (1993).

Wilfried Mausbach is Assistant Professor of History at the John F. Kennedy Institute, Free University of Berlin, and a Research Fellow of the Volkswagen Foundation. He is the author of *Zwischen Morgenthau und Marshall* (1996).

PUBLICATIONS OF THE GERMAN HISTORICAL INSTITUTE,
WASHINGTON, D.C.

Edited by Christof Mauch
with the assistance of David Lazar

The German Historical Institute is a center for advanced study and research whose purpose is to provide a permanent basis for scholarly cooperation among historians from the Federal Republic of Germany and the United States. The Institute conducts, promotes, and supports research into both American and German political, social, economic, and cultural history; into transatlantic migration, especially in the nineteenth and twentieth centuries; and into the history of international relations, with special emphasis on the roles played by the United States and Germany.

Recent books in the series

Norbert Finzsch and Dietmar Schirmer, editors, *Identity and Intolerance: Nationalism, Racism, and Xenophobia in Germany and the United States*

Susan Strasser, Charles McGovern, and Matthias Judt, editors, *Getting and Spending: European and American Consumer Societies in the Twentieth Century*

Carole Fink, Philipp Gassert, and Detlef Junker, editors, *1968: The World Transformed*

Roger Chickering and Stig Förster, editors, *Great War, Total War: Combat and Mobilization on the Western Front*

Manfred F. Boemeke, Gerald D. Feldman, and Elisabeth Glaser, eds., *The Treaty of Versailles: A Reassessment After 75 Years*

Manfred Berg and Martin H. Geyer, editors, *Two Cultures of Rights: The Quest for Inclusion and Participation in Modern America and Germany*

Manfred F. Boemeke, Roger Chickering, and Stig Förster, editors, *Anticipating Total War: The German and American Experiences, 1871–1914*

Roger Chickering and Stig Förster, editors, *The Shadows of Total War: Europe, East Asia, and the United States, 1919–1939*

Elisabeth Glaser and Hermann Wellenreuther, editors, *Bridging the Atlantic: The Question of American Exceptionalism in Perspective*

America, the Vietnam War, and the World

COMPARATIVE AND INTERNATIONAL PERSPECTIVES

Edited by

ANDREAS W. DAUM
University at Buffalo, State University of New York

LLOYD C. GARDNER
Rutgers University

WILFRIED MAUSBACH
John F. Kennedy Institute, Free University of Berlin

GERMAN HISTORICAL INSTITUTE
Washington, D.C.
and

 CAMBRIDGE
UNIVERSITY PRESS

PUBLISHED BY THE PRESS SYNDICATE OF THE UNIVERSITY OF CAMBRIDGE
The Pitt Building, Trumpington Street, Cambridge, United Kingdom

CAMBRIDGE UNIVERSITY PRESS
The Edinburgh Building, Cambridge CB2 2RU, UK
40 West 20th Street, New York, NY 10011-4211, USA
477 Williamstown Road, Port Melbourne, VIC 3207, Australia
Ruiz de Alarcón 13, 28014 Madrid, Spain
Dock House, The Waterfront, Cape Town 8001, South Africa

http://www.cambridge.org

First published 2003

Printed in the United States of America

Typeface Bembo 11/13 pt.   *System* LATEX 2_ε [TB]

A catalog record for this book is available from the British Library.

Library of Congress Cataloging in Publication Data

America, the Vietnam War, and the world / edited by Andreas W. Daum,
Lloyd C. Gardner, Wilfried Mausbach.
p.   cm. – (Publications of the German Historical Institute)
Includes bibliographical references and index.
ISBN 0-521-81048-5 – ISBN 0-521-00876-X (pb.)
1. Vietnamese Conflict, 1961–1975.   2. Vietnamese Conflict, 1961–1975 – United States.
3. World politics – 20th century.   I. Daum, Andreas W.   II. Gardner, Lloyd C., 1934–
III. Mausbach, Wilfried, 1964–   IV. Series.
DS557 .A87   2003
909.82′6–dc21   2002074045

ISBN 0 521 81048 5 hardback
ISBN 0 521 00876 X paperback

Contents

Contributors

Michael Adas is a professor of history at Rutgers, the State University of New Jersey.

Sabine Behrenbeck is Programmdirektorin for Sonderforschungsbereiche at the Deutsche Forschungsgemeinschaft in Bonn.

Andreas W. Daum is a professor of history, University at Buffalo, State University of New York.

Peter Edwards is a visiting professor at the School of Politics of the University of New South Wales at the Australian Defence Force Academy, Canberra.

Lloyd C. Gardner is a professor of history at Rutgers, the State University of New Jersey.

Fabian Hilfrich is a researcher at the Institut für Zeitgeschichte, Auswärtiges Amt, Berlin.

T. Christopher Jespersen is a professor of history at North Georgia College and State University.

Jeffrey Kimball is a professor of history at Miami University of Ohio.

Arne Kislenko is a professor of history at Ryerson University, Toronto.

Fredrik Logevall is a professor of history at the University of California at Santa Barbara.

Wilfried Mausbach is an assistant professor of history at the John F. Kennedy Institute, Free University of Berlin, and a Research Fellow of the Volkswagen Foundation.

Leopoldo Nuti is a professor in the Department of Political Institutions and Social Sciences of the University of Rome.

John Prados is an analyst compiling the Vietnam Documentation Collection for the National Security Archives in Washington, D.C.

Eva-Maria Stolberg is an assistant professor of history at the University of Bonn.

Barbara L. Tischler teaches at the Horace Mann School in Riverdale, New York.

Günter Wernicke is an assistant professor at the Institute for the Historical Sciences at the Humboldt University of Berlin.

Hubert Zimmermann is an assistant professor of history at the University of Bochum.

Preface

"The whole world is watching," went the rousing chant of demonstrators at the Democratic National Convention in Chicago in August 1968. Directed primarily at the unfolding violence of the police and National Guard, the slogan also applied to the very American actions in Vietnam that the protesters wanted Democratic delegates to confront. But people around the world were not merely passive observers of the American war in Southeast Asia and its repercussions within the United States. As this book vividly demonstrates, the Vietnam War, in affecting governments and ordinary citizens way beyond the principal belligerents, represented in fact nothing less than a global event.

In presenting international and comparative perspectives on an important subject in American and – as it turns out – world history, this book dovetails nicely with the research agenda of the German Historical Institute (GHI) in Washington, D.C. Committed to the study of cultural, economic, political, and societal interaction between the United States, Germany, and Europe, the GHI has found it rewarding to take a global perspective on occasion. Most recently, the success of *1968: The World Transformed* (edited by Carole Fink, Philipp Gassert, and Detlef Junker) has been a prime example of the scholarly merits of such endeavors. The present collection continues on this path.

America, the Vietnam War, and the World grew out of an international conference held at the GHI on November 19–22, 1998. I extend my warmest thanks to all those colleagues who participated in the conference as chairpersons, contributors, or discussants. Although the lively discussions following each session could not be included here, numerous remarks and comments are reflected in the published essays. The staff of the GHI did a superb job of assuring that yet another scholarly meeting at 1607 New Hampshire Avenue would be a smooth and enjoyable affair. For this, I particularly thank

xi

Christa Brown, Dieter H. Schneider, and Bärbel Thomas. During the conference, the conveners were also able to rely on the unwavering support of Uta Balbier.

Turning a collection of papers into a book is always a challenge. Several colleagues helped to meet this challenge. At the GHI, Thomas Goebel and Annette Marciel carefully read the manuscript. As always, a special thank you must go to Daniel S. Mattern, the series editor at the Institute, whose expertise in creating chapters out of conference papers and then molding them into a concise and readable book manuscript remains unsurpassed. Outside of the GHI, I thank the two anonymous reviewers for reading the entire manuscript and for providing valuable comments and criticism. Last but not least, I would like to thank Frank Smith, the Institute's editor at Cambridge University Press, for his support of this project from the start and for expertly guiding the manuscript through to publication.

Detlef Junker
Heidelberg, Germany
July 2001

Introduction

America's War and the World

ANDREAS W. DAUM, LLOYD C. GARDNER,
AND WILFRIED MAUSBACH

I

Wars are undeniable events in history, and – as constantly reported in the daily news – they still occur all over the world, even in an age that has produced more legal and political mechanisms to avoid war and has drafted more manifestos to decry violent conflict than any other epoch in history. As soon as we embark on scrutinizing the meaning of wars more closely, questions arise that trigger heated disputes: Why are wars fought? What reasons justify the conduct of war? In which military, political, and ideological categories do belligerents couch their strategies and experiences? What impact does war have on the politics, societies, and cultures of combatants and noncombatants? How do wars affect the international community and international relations beyond the immediate events on the battlefields? Why do we label some military conflicts wars but not others?

The answers to these questions are highly contested; this holds especially true for one of the most dramatic conflicts in modern history: the American war in Vietnam, as it took shape with the deployment of U.S. combat troops to South Vietnam and the bombing of North Vietnam in the mid-1960s, and concluded with the Paris agreements between the United States and the Socialist Republic of Vietnam in 1973. Accordingly, it is not surprising that the shelves of libraries and bookstores groan under the weight of a burgeoning literature on the topic. There can be no doubt that the Vietnam War is one of the most widely discussed, researched, and documented events in recent history.[1] Why then yet another book on this subject?

---

1 The most comprehensive, partly annotated, and continuously updated compilation of primary and secondary sources – although it lists primarily books and only a few articles – is Edwin E. Moïse, *Vietnam War Bibliography* (http://hubcap.clemson.edu/~eemoise/bibliography.html). See also Anton Legler and Kurt Hubinek, *Der Krieg in Vietnam: Bericht und Bibliographie*, 5 vols. (Frankfurt am Main, 1969–79); Ronald Spector, *Researching the Vietnam Experience* (Washington, D.C., 1983); Richard Dean

Although both popular imagination and academic research on the Vietnam War continue to flourish, there is no consensus in sight. Only the U.S. Civil War rivals the power of the Vietnam War to divide and inflame generation upon generation of Americans. The still-growing body of research on the Vietnam War nearly forms an independent subdiscipline within the historiography of American foreign relations. But it still mirrors a seemingly "unending debate"[2] that constantly produces new cycles of orthodoxy, revisionism, and postrevisionism. At the same time, the Vietnam War and its legacies have elicited new questions that provoke unexpected answers and allow new perspectives. This book attempts to present such perspectives. Its fundamental concern is to link together three dimensions of the Vietnam War – the war as America's war, as an international event, and as a starting point for historical comparisons – and to analyze the interconnectedness of these dimensions. With this approach we attempt to shed light not only on the history of the Vietnam conflict, but also on the meaning of wars in modern history in general and on the relevance of strategies to cope with war beyond what we know about the case of Vietnam.

The Vietnam War as America's war serves as the book's crucial point of reference. The United States undoubtedly dominated the course of events in Vietnam from the late 1950s and until the South Vietnamese defeat in 1975. By contrast, and given the universality of the American-Soviet confrontation during the Cold War, no other external conflict besides Vietnam had such an unprecedented and profound effect on the conduct of American foreign policy and on American domestic affairs. This small, curved country at the edge of Southeast Asia and the events that took place in the region greatly

Burns and Milton Leitenberg, *The Wars in Vietnam, Cambodia, and Laos, 1945–1982: A Bibliographic Guide* (Santa Barbara, Calif., 1984); Lester H. Brune and Richard Dean Burns, *America and the Indochina Wars, 1945–1990: A Bibliographical Guide* (Claremont, Calif., 1992); and James S. Olson, ed., *The Vietnam War: Handbook of the Literature and Research* (Westport, Conn., 1993).

2 Gary R. Hess, "The Unending Debate: Historians and the Vietnam War," in Michael J. Hogan, ed., *America in the World: The Historiography of American Foreign Relations Since 1941* (New York, 1995), 358–94. See also Joe P. Dunn, "In Search of Lessons: The Development of a Vietnam Historiography," *Parameters* 9 (1979): 28–40; John M. Gates, "Vietnam: The Debate Goes On," *Parameters* 14 (1984): 15–24; George C. Herring, "America and Vietnam: The Debate Continues," *American Historical Review* 92 (1987): 350–62; David L. Anderson, "Why Vietnam? Postrevisionist Answers and a Neorealist Suggestion," *Diplomatic History* 13 (1989): 419–29; Herbert Shapiro, "The Vietnam War and the American Historical Profession," in John Drumbell, ed., *Vietnam and the Antiwar Movement: An International Perspective* (Aldershot, U.K., 1989), 7–33; Robert K. Brigham and Martin J. Murray, "Conflicting Interpretations of the Vietnam War, 1945–1975," *Bulletin of Concerned Asian Scholars* 26 (1994): 111–18; David W. Levy, *The Debate over Vietnam*, 2d ed. (Baltimore, 1995); Marc Frey, "Der Vietnam-Krieg im Spiegel der neueren amerikanischen Forschung," *Neue Politische Literatur* 42 (1997): 29–47; and Jonathan Mirsky, "The Never-Ending War," *New York Review of Books*, May 25, 2000, 54–63.

influenced and, in many ways, fundamentally changed American politics and culture.

America's war, however, was not just an issue of and for the United States. As much as Vietnam reverberated in American society and embodied "many wars" for the United States,[3] it also radiated into world politics and permeated the domestic political settings and cultural discourses in many countries to a surprising degree. Several chapters in this book trace these reverberations in Europe, Asia, and the South Pacific. They look at the multiple cultural and political conflicts that Vietnam triggered in the domestic arenas of several of America's key allies.[4] Other contributors analyze the impact of the Vietnam conflict on international organizations and structures, and on the dynamics of alliance politics and bilateral relations.[5] A comparative approach, seldom utilized with regard to Vietnam, complements this approach by setting America's war and the world in relation to each other. Some of the chapters use Vietnam as the starting point to compare problems that seem to be specific to post–World War II America with those that the United States and other countries have encountered at different times in history. This way of looking at the Vietnam War produces exciting diachronic analogies that discuss aspects of warfare, ideological war preparation, war termination, and war's domestic effects.[6]

In pursuing this agenda, the editors seek to do justice to the fundamental ambiguity that characterized the Vietnam War: Vietnam was undoubtedly America's war, but at the same time the struggle for Vietnam had a deep impact on many other areas of the world and on the domestic settings of many noncombatants. The interconnections among the United States, the Vietnam War, and the wider world are therefore the focus of this undertaking, which is an attempt to internationalize the interpretation of one of the most dramatic and tragic events in contemporary history.

II

Not surprisingly, most of the literature on the Vietnam War has been written by Americans and has been devoted to the American experience, its origins and aftermath. From the mid-1960s to this day, debate – both public and scholarly – has revolved around a core set of questions: Why did the United

---

3 See Lloyd C. Gardner's chapter in this book and Marilyn B. Young, *The Vietnam Wars, 1945–1990* (New York, 1991).
4 See the chapters by Arne Kislenko, Peter Edwards, Leopoldo Nuti, and Wilfried Mausbach in this book.
5 See the chapters in Part Two and Günter Wernicke's chapter in this book.
6 See the chapters in Part One of this book.

States get involved? Was the American commitment politically and morally necessary?[7] What were the crucial factors for the eventual outcome, and was defeat indeed inevitable? The latter question in particular provoked a lively debate on military strategy, the supposed failure of the civilian leadership to understand the conflict, and the impact of ever-worsening public sentiment on policy makers and combatants alike, culminating in a sort of stab-in-the-back theory not unlike the one Germany experienced after World War I.[8]

But diplomatic and military historians were far from the only ones to grapple with America's involvement in Southeast Asia and its enduring legacy. Political scientists, sociologists, and scholars in the fields of cultural and literary studies have examined almost every facet of America's entanglement with Vietnam, from its digestion in film and fictional literature to the plight of returning veterans, from its impact on gender roles to its treatment in comic books.[9]

7 The most powerful recent addition to this literature and the first to place American decision-making in a wider international context on the basis of extensive research in U.S. and overseas archives is Fredrik Logevall, *Choosing War: The Lost Chance for Peace and the Escalation of War in Vietnam* (Berkeley, Calif., 1999). For an opposing view, see the essayistic account by Michael Lind, *Vietnam, the Necessary War: A Reinterpretation of America's Most Disastrous Military Conflict* (New York, 1999). Other important studies with different answers to these questions include David Halberstam, *The Making of a Quagmire: America and Vietnam During the Kennedy Era* (New York, 1964); George McT. Kahin and John W. Lewis, *The United States in Vietnam* (New York, 1967); Arthur M. Schlesinger, *The Bitter Heritage: Vietnam and American Democracy*, rev. ed. (Greenwich, Conn., 1968); Guenter Lewy, *America in Vietnam* (New York, 1978); Norman Podhoretz, *Why We Were in Vietnam* (New York, 1982); and George McT. Kahin, *Intervention: How America Became Involved in Vietnam* (New York, 1986). For a useful compilation of diverse perspectives, see Jeffrey P. Kimball, ed., *To Reason Why: The Debate About the Causes of U.S. Involvement in the Vietnam War* (Philadelphia, 1990).

8 Leslie H. Gelb and Richard K. Betts, *The Irony of Vietnam: The System Worked* (Washington, D.C., 1978); Harry G. Summers, *On Strategy: A Critical Analysis of the Vietnam War* (Novato, Calif., 1982); Andrew F. Krepinevich, *The Army and Vietnam* (Baltimore, 1986); Gary R. Hess, "The Military Perspective on Strategy in Vietnam," *Diplomatic History* 10 (1986): 91–106; Warren I. Cohen, "Vietnam: New Light on the Nature of the War?" *International History Review* 9 (1987): 108–16; Jeffrey P. Kimball, "The Stab-in-the-Back Legend and the Vietnam War," *Armed Forces and Society* 14 (1988): 433–58; William Colby with James McCargar, *Lost Victory* (Chicago, 1989); David H. Hackworth and Julie Sherman, *About Face* (New York, 1989); and Jeffrey Record, *The Wrong War: Why We Lost in Vietnam* (Annapolis, Md., 1998). For the German case, see Heide Barmeyer, "Geschichte als Überlieferung und Konstruktion – Das Beispiel der Dolchstosslegende," *Geschichte in Wissenschaft und Unterricht* 28 (1977): 257–71; and Gerd Krumeich, "Die Dolchstoss-Legende," in Etienne François and Hagen Schulze, eds., *Deutsche Erinnerungsorte*, vol. 1 (Munich, 2001), 585–99.

9 Robert Buzzanco, *Vietnam and the Transformation of American Life* (Malden, Mass., 1999); Arnold R. Isaacs, *Vietnam Shadows: The War, Its Ghosts, and Its Legacy* (Baltimore, 1997); Linda Dittmar and Gene Michaud, eds., *From Hanoi to Hollywood: The Vietnam War in American Film* (New Brunswick, N.J., 1990); Kevin Hillstrom and Laurie Collier Hillstrom, *The Vietnam Experience: A Concise Encyclopedia of American Literature, Songs, and Films* (Westport, Conn., 1998); Philip D. Beidler, *American Literature and the Experience of Vietnam* (Athens, Ga., 1982); Sandra M. Wittman, *Writing About Vietnam: A Bibliography of the Literature of the Vietnam Conflict* (Boston, 1989); Philip H. Melling, *Vietnam in American Literature* (Boston, 1990); John Newman et al., *Vietnam War Literature: An Annotated Bibliography of Imaginative Works About Americans Fighting in Vietnam*, 3d ed. (Lanham, Md., 1996); Arthur Egendorf, *Healing from the War: Trauma and Transformation After Vietnam* (Boston, 1985); Wilbur J. Scott, *The Politics of Readjustment: Vietnam Veterans Since the War* (New York, 1993); Chuck Lawrence, *Tears of*

The various interpretations have been marked by a peculiar homogeneity in a focus on, if not an obsession with, the American role in this conflict and its resonance in the United States. If the political-military decisions of the Johnson administration in the spring and summer of 1965 transformed the conflict in Indochina into America's war,[10] then the vitality and fertility of scholarship in the United States has also, and inevitably, led to the Americanization of the historiography of the Vietnam War. There can be no doubt that this process has been fueled by a democratic system that allows early and comparatively broad access to archival material, and by the thriving publishing sector of a capitalist consumer society. All this has helped to make the Vietnam War a remarkable, rare, and perhaps the most striking exception to Winston Churchill's observation that history is written by the victors.

The intensity of public debate arising from America's twentieth-century trauma has almost turned the Vietnam War into an example of what could be called negative exceptionalism. The uniqueness of the American national experience as an escape from European corruption and the seizure of a pristine continent through the relentless pushing of spatial and human frontiers by the American "Adam" has been irretrievably besmirched by the dirty war in Southeast Asia.[11] Vietnam balks at figuring as merely one of a very few missing pieces in the otherwise heroic jigsaw puzzle of American history. Unable to explain Vietnam as an aberration, some have seen it instead as the culmination of an American exceptionalism inherently problematic from its inception.[12] Probably more common, though, have been the righteous anger and helpless despair produced by the feeling that American actions in Indochina were especially loathsome precisely because they deviated so starkly from earlier innocence.[13] Whatever shape this

Blood: The Betrayal of America's Veterans (Auburn, Wash., 1998); Susan Jeffords, *The Remasculinization of America: Gender and the Vietnam War* (Bloomington, Ind., 1989); and Bradford Wright, "The Vietnam War and Comic Books," in Olson, ed., *Vietnam War*, 427–54.

10 Logevall, *Choosing War*, 333–75; Brian VanDeMark, *Into the Quagmire: Lyndon Johnson and the Escalation of the Vietnam War* (New York, 1991); and Larry Berman, *Planning a Tragedy: The Americanization of the War in Vietnam* (New York, 1982).

11 On the founding of the United States as an escape from Europe, see John Higham, "The Future of American History," *Journal of American History* 80 (1994): 1289–309, esp. 1292. For a good recent survey of American exceptionalist thinking, see Seymour Martin Lipset, *American Exceptionalism: A Double-Edged Sword* (New York, 1996). A good deal of the scholarly work on the phenomenon is reviewed by Michael Kammen, "The Problem of American Exceptionalism: A Reconsideration," *American Quarterly* 45 (1993): 1–43.

12 John Hellmann, *American Myth and the Legacy of Vietnam* (New York, 1986); Milton J. Bates, *The Wars We Took to Vietnam: Cultural Conflict and Storytelling* (Berkeley, Calif., 1996), 9–47.

13 The present inattention to the nation-state in many quarters of the American scholarly community and the predilection of social and cultural historians for the inarticulate and marginalized perhaps also represent the yearning for a cast that has not yet lost its innocence. This is suggested by

negative exceptionalism takes on, however, it remains mired in a peculiar self-referentiality.

To be sure, the Americanization of the conflict's historiography did not result in a single grand narrative. This war has always meant and still means different things to different Americans. There are, indeed, at least two major narratives within the American public discourse. The first puts the conflict squarely into a Cold War framework in which the South Vietnamese national liberation movement, abetted by Moscow, Beijing, and Hanoi, appears as part of a global pattern of communist expansion. Here, any distinction between communism and anticolonialism is lost, and the struggle in Indochina becomes "a communist 'war of liberation.'"[14] The Cold War narrative was predominant until the mid-1960s, and it survived the American defeat in Vietnam, propagated most prominently by former policy makers and their successors. Thus, former president Richard M. Nixon maintained in 1980 that the real war facing the United States was the war against Soviet expansionism and that Vietnam was just one battle in this third world war.[15] With the end of the East-West conflict, then, Vietnam became merely a lost battle in an ultimately victorious war. The battle was not even a futile sacrifice because, as Walt Rostow, President Lyndon B. Johnson's national security adviser from 1966 to 1969, tells us, it bought time for the rest of Asia to prosper behind a barrier that held aggression at bay.[16]

The second major narrative began to seriously challenge the standard interpretation of American involvement in Vietnam by the mid-1960s and eventually replaced it — at least in academic and intellectual circles — by the early 1970s. Its framework was not the Cold War but the hot wars of decolonization fought in the Third World. In this other epic struggle of the twentieth century, America ended up on the losing side because it had decided to follow in the footsteps of the European colonial powers. The last U.S. chopper that left Saigon in 1975 did not, therefore, signal defeat in a single battle but in the war itself. In contrast to the Cold War narrative, the decolonization narrative stresses the distinction between communism and anticolonialism. In this view, North Vietnamese leader Ho Chi Minh was more of a nationalist than a communist, and the struggle in Vietnam

---

Dorothy Ross, "Grand Narrative in American Historical Writing: From Romance to Uncertainty," *American Historical Review* 100 (1995): 651–77.

14 Memorandum from the secretary of defense (McNamara) to the president, Mar. 16, 1964, in U.S. Department of State, ed., *Foreign Relations of the United States* (hereafter FRUS) 1964–1968, 1:153–67, here 154.

15 Richard M. Nixon, *The Real War* (New York, 1980).

16 Walt W. Rostow, "The Case for the War: How American Resistance in Vietnam Helped Southeast Asia to Prosper in Independence," *Times Literary Supplement,* June 9, 1995, 3–5.

appeared as a civil war rather than an externally masterminded communist insurgency.[17] Thus, when it comes to the Vietnam conflict, America alone knows at least two histories.[18]

This should come as no surprise. Wars have always stood at the center of a multiplicity of narratives. Even the seemingly simple and neutral act of naming a war turns out to be highly prejudiced. Naming reflects how different people – be they participants in a war or neutrals – perceive the same war in many different ways. The military campaigns between 1756 and 1763, for example, stretching from Europe to America and from Western Africa to India, were known in Prussia as the Seven Years' War, whereas colonists overseas experienced them as the French and Indian War or the British-French War. The American Civil War is still remembered in some southern U.S. states as the War of Northern Aggression. The British think of World War I as the Great War, a term more or less unknown in Germany. Many Russians still subscribe to the official Soviet term "Great Patriotic War," whereas most of the rest of the world speaks of World War II. And finally, of course, the Vietnam War remains the "American War" in Vietnamese memory, the successor to the French War of the 1940s and 1950s, and it is therefore dubbed by others as the Second Indochina War.

The Vietnam conflict in fact encompasses numerous wars, some of which involved the United States only indirectly and most of which have so far been neglected.[19] First and foremost among these are, of course, the wars within Vietnamese society. One of the first Vietnamese memoirs written in English reminded Americans that the overarching struggle for independence and the conflict between Buddhists and Catholics – only sporadically acknowledged by the West – were merely the tip of the iceberg.

Behind the religious war came the battle between city people and country people – the rich against the poor – a war fought by those who wanted to change Vietnam and those who wanted to leave it as it had been for a thousand years. Beneath all that, too, we had vendettas: between native Vietnamese and immigrants (mostly

---

17 See, e.g., Michael H. Hunt, *Lyndon Johnson's War: America's Cold War Crusade in Vietnam, 1945–1968* (New York, 1996). A classic in this respect is Frances FitzGerald, *Fire in the Lake: The Vietnamese and Americans in Vietnam* (Boston, 1972). For a comprehensive biography of the North Vietnamese leader, see now William J. Duiker, *Ho Chi Minh* (New York, 2000).

18 It has been suggested that the real Vietnam syndrome was the realization that there are alternatives to the heroic metanarrative of U.S. history. See Marilyn B. Young, "Dangerous History: Vietnam and the 'Good War,'" in Edward T. Linenthal and Tom Engelhardt, eds., *History Wars: The Enola Gay and Other Battles for the American Past* (New York, 1996), 199–209. More generally, see also Charles S. Maier, "Consigning the Twentieth Century to History: Alternative Narratives for the Modern Era," *American Historical Review* 105 (2000): 807–31.

19 This is also acknowledged by the standard account of America's experience in Vietnam; see George C. Herring, *America's Longest War, 1950–1975*, 3d ed. (New York, 1996), 335.

Chinese and Khmer) who had fought for centuries over the land. Many of these wars go on today. How could you hope to end them by fighting a battle so different from our own?[20]

Although historians have finally begun to explore the war stories of America's counterparts in Vietnam,[21] the experiences of Washington's South Vietnamese ally are still getting short shrift.[22] There is considerable merit to Shawn McHale's recent proposition that "the full history of the Vietnam War, one which combines the U.S. view of the war with a nuanced appreciation of the Vietnamese social, political, and cultural context, is yet to be written."[23]

However, this book contends that even a synthesis of American and Vietnamese narratives would still not constitute "a full history" of the Vietnam War. As necessary as it is to proceed on this path, and as much as the reverberations of Vietnam in American culture and society deserve further analysis, the time is also ripe to acknowledge that America's war had even wider geographical, political, and cultural ramifications.[24] Moreover,

20 Le Ly Hayslip, *When Heaven and Earth Changed Places: A Vietnamese Woman's Journey from War to Peace* (New York, 1989), xv.
21 See, e.g., David Chanoff and Doan Van Toai, *Portrait of the Enemy* (New York, 1986); Michael Lee Lanning and Dan Cragg, *Inside the VC and the NVA: The Real Story of North Vietnam's Armed Forces* (New York, 1992); Hy V. Luong with Nguyen Dac-Bang, *Revolution in the Village: Tradition and Transformation in North Vietnam, 1925–1988* (Honolulu, 1992); Mark Bradley and Robert K. Brigham, *Vietnamese Archives and Scholarship on the Cold War Period: Two Reports*, Cold War International History Project Working Paper no. 7 (Washington, D.C., 1993) (cwihp.si.edu/publications.htm); Mark Bradley et al., *The Vietnam War: Vietnamese and American Perspectives*, in Jayne S. Werner and Luu Doan Huynh, eds. (Armonk, N.Y., 1993); William J. Duiker, *The Communist Road to Power in Vietnam*, 2d ed. (Boulder, Colo., 1996); Kevin Ruane, *War and Revolution in Vietnam, 1930–75* (London, 1998); and Robert K. Brigham, *Guerrilla Diplomacy: The NLF's Foreign Relations and the Vietnam War* (Ithaca, N.Y., 1998). Even some former policy makers have started to listen – at least perfunctorily – to North Vietnamese perspectives. See Robert S. McNamara, James G. Blight, and Robert K. Brigham, *Argument Without End: In Search of Answers to the Vietnam Tragedy* (New York, 1999).
22 Almost an exception is Gabriel Kolko, *Anatomy of a War: Vietnam, the United States, and the Modern Historical Experience* (New York, 1985). See also Douglas C. Dacy, *Foreign Aid, War, and Economic Development: South Vietnam, 1955–1975* (New York, 1986); George C. Herring, "'Peoples Quite Apart': Americans, South Vietnamese, and the War in Vietnam," *Diplomatic History* 14 (1990): 1–23; and David Chanoff and Doan Van Toai, *Vietnam: A Portrait of Its People at War* (London, 1996).
23 Shawn McHale, "'Colonial' Scholarship On the Vietnam War," *Washington Post*, July 31, 1999, A20.
24 Scattered attempts to portray the relationship of such countries to the war have been confined mostly to diplomatic and military matters. See Lloyd C. Gardner and Ted Gittinger, eds., *International Perspectives on Vietnam* (College Station, Tex., 2000); R. B. Smith, *An International History of the Vietnam War*, 3 vols. (New York, 1983–91); Daniel S. Papp, *Vietnam: The View from Moscow, Peking, Washington* (Jefferson, N.C., 1981); Douglas Pike, *Vietnam and the Soviet Union: Anatomy of an Alliance* (Boulder, Colo., 1987); Keith L. Nelson, *The Making of Détente: Soviet-American Relations in the Shadow of Vietnam* (Baltimore, 1995); Ilya V. Gaiduk, *The Soviet Union and the Vietnam War* (Chicago, 1996); Jian Chen, "China's Involvement in the Vietnam War, 1964–1969," *China Quarterly* 142 (1995): 356–89; Qiang Zhai, "Opposing Negotiations: China and the Vietnam Peace Talks, 1965–1968," *Pacific Historical Review* 68 (1999): 21–49; Odd Arne Westad et al., *77 Conversations Between Chinese and Foreign Leaders on the Wars in Indochina, 1964–1977*, Cold War International History Project Working Paper no. 22 (Washington, D.C., 1998); Thomas R. Havens, *Fire Across the Sea: The Vietnam War and*

we must acknowledge Akira Iriye's insight that international history is much more than the sum total of national histories.[25] The international dimension of this book therefore is complemented by transnational and comparative approaches.

To be sure, the chapters in this book, which are concerned with differences and commonalities between the American entanglement with Vietnam and earlier events in American history as well as experiences in other countries, do not aspire to be an attempt at comparative history in any systematic way. Rather, they employ – in George Fredrickson's words – "exotic analogy as a way of shedding additional light on some phenomenon in a single nation or society."[26] Moreover, Seth Koven rightly remarked that although "transnational and transchronological comparative history is enormously difficult, especially for historians trained to pay close attention to the contingent, local, and peculiar nature of their subject, . . . nonetheless, one reward of this kind of inquiry is the opportunity to discover patterns and structures which are invisible when viewed from the perspective of parochial, national histories."[27] Thus, several chapters embark on comparisons rather pragmatically, either to suggest general models or to highlight and bring into focus specific aspects by throwing them against the backdrop of some other time and/or place. To internationalize the history of the Vietnam War and put it into comparative perspective dovetails with recent calls to test the paradigm and the ideological premises not only of American exceptionalism but of a nation-centered historiography per se.[28] In this vein,

Japan (Princeton, N.J., 1987); Robert M. Blackburn, *Mercenaries and Lyndon Johnson's "More Flags": The Hiring of Korean, Filipino and Thai Soldiers in the Vietnam War* (Jefferson, N.C., 1994); Kil J. Yi, "Alliance in the Quagmire: The United States, South Korea, and the Vietnam War, 1964–1968," Ph.D. diss., Rutgers University, 1997; Glen St. J. Barclay, *A Very Small Insurance Policy: The Politics of Australian Involvement in Vietnam, 1954–1967* (St. Lucia, 1988); Peter Edwards, *A Nation at War: Australian Politics, Society and Diplomacy During the Vietnam War, 1965–75* (Sydney, 1997); Douglas A. Ross, *In the Interest of Peace: Canada and Vietnam, 1954–1973* (Toronto, 1984); Victor Levant, *Quiet Complicity: Canadian Involvement in the Vietnam War* (Toronto, 1986); John Dumbrell, "The Johnson Administration and the British Labour Government: Vietnam, the Pound and East of Suez," *Journal of American Studies* 30 (1996): 211–31; Rolf Steininger, "Grossbritannien und der Vietnamkrieg 1964/65," *Vierteljahrshefte für Zeitgeschichte* 45 (1997): 589–628; Joachim Arenth, *Johnson, Vietnam und der Westen: Transatlantische Belastungen 1963–1969* (Munich, 1994); Fredrik Logevall, "De Gaulle, Neutralization, and American Involvement in Vietnam," *Pacific Historical Review* 61 (1992): 69–102; and Fredrik Logevall, "The Swedish-American Conflict over Vietnam," *Diplomatic History* 17 (1993): 421–45.

25 Akira Iriye, "The Internationalization of History," *American Historical Review* 94, no. 2 (1989): 1–10.
26 George M. Fredrickson, "Comparative History," in Michael Kammen, ed., *The Past Before Us: Contemporary Historical Writing in the United States* (Ithaca, N.Y., 1980), 457.
27 Seth Koven, "Revisioning Reconstructions," in Norbert Finzsch and Jürgen Martschukat, eds., *Different Restorations: Reconstruction and "Wiederaufbau" in Germany and the United States: 1865, 1945, and 1989* (Providence, R.I., 1996), 230.
28 Ian Tyrrell, "American Exceptionalism in an Age of International History," *American Historical Review* 96 (1991): 1031–55. More generally, Jürgen Osterhammel has argued for looking beyond national histories: "Transnationale Gesellschaftsgeschichte: Erweiterung oder Alternative?" *Geschichte*

our endeavor can be understood as part of an effort – in Michael Geyer's and Charles Bright's words – "to historicize the United States, robbing this nation of its sublime presence as history entirely of and for itself."[29]

In so doing, the following chapters travel along several avenues that sometimes intersect. They represent an exercise in international history in that they respond to the fact that after World War II "the amount of attention to and concern about the United States on the part of governments, elite groups, and mass populations in other parts of the world" increased dramatically.[30] There is no single event to illustrate this more forcefully than the history of the Vietnam War. On a geopolitical level, this war can serve as an illuminating example of the relationships between hegemonic centers and less powerful regions; it can explore patterns of support and delimitation; and it can demonstrate how the repercussions of hegemonic action began to affect the world as a whole in the second half of the twentieth century.[31] However, there is more to this than only a geopolitical story.

In fact, the chapters of this book also show that Vietnam readily lends itself to inquiries that transcend national boundaries. Scholars of race, class, gender, immigration, and social movements increasingly stress the transnational characteristics of their subjects.[32] The worldwide political, social,

und Gesellschaft 27 (2001): 464–79, and *Geschichtswissenschaft jenseits des Nationalstaats: Studien zu Beziehungsgeschichte und Zivilisationsvergleich* (Göttingen, 2001). See also Prasenjit Duara, *Rescuing History from the Nation: Questioning Narratives of Modern China* (Chicago, 1995).

29 Michael Geyer and Charles Bright, "World History in a Global Age," *American Historical Review* 100 (1995): 1039.

30 Ernest R. May, "Writing Contemporary International History," *Diplomatic History* 8 (1984): 106.

31 See the essays by Fredrik Logevall, Christopher Jespersen, John Prados, Arne Kislenko, Peter Edwards, and Leopoldo Nuti in this book. For an analysis of the nature of such strategic repercussions a decade before Vietnam took center stage, see William Stueck, *The Korean War: An International History* (Princeton, N.J., 1995).

32 To name just a few: Philip D. Curtin, *The Rise and Fall of the Plantation Complex: Essays in Atlantic History*, 2d ed. (Cambridge, 1998); Michelle A. Stephens, "Black Transnationalism and the Politics of National Identity: West Indian Intellectuals in Harlem in the Age of War and Revolution," *American Quarterly* 50 (1998): 592–608; Sean Wilentz, "Against Exceptionalism: Class Consciousness and the American Labor Movement, 1790–1920," *International Labor and Working Class History* 26 (1984): 1–24; Frederick Cooper et al., eds., *Confronting Historical Paradigms: Peasants, Labor, and the Capitalist World System in Africa and Latin America* (Madison, Wis., 1993); Donald Meyer, *Sex and Power: The Rise of Women in America, Russia, Sweden, and Italy*, 2d ed. (Middletown, Conn., 1989); Ian Tyrell, *Woman's World/Woman's Empire: The Woman's Christian Temperance Union in International Perspective* (Chapel Hill, N.C., 1991); Seth Koven and Sonya Michel, *Mothers of a New World: Maternalist Politics and the Origins of the Welfare States* (New York, 1993); Leila Rupp, *Worlds of Women: The Making of an International Women's Movement* (Princeton, N.J., 1997); Philip D. Curtin, *Death by Migration: Europe's Encounter with the Tropical World in the Nineteenth Century* (Cambridge, 1989); Walter Nugent, *Crossings: The Great Transatlantic Migrations, 1870–1914* (Bloomington, Ind., 1992); Nina Glick Schiller, Linda Blasch, and Cristina Blanc-Szanton, eds., *Towards a Transnational Perspective on Migration: Race, Class, Ethnicity, and Nationalism Reconsidered* (New York, 1992); Mark Wyman, *Round-Trip to America: The Immigrants Return to Europe, 1880–1930* (Ithaca, N.Y., 1993); Donna R. Gabaccia, "Liberty, Coercion, and the Making of Immigration Historians," *Journal of American History* 84 (1997): 570–5; David G. Gutiérrez, "Migration, Emergent Ethnicity, and the 'Third Space': The

cultural, and economic upheavals that surround the history of the Vietnam War and were to a considerable extent provoked and fueled by this conflict represent rich fields for transnational approaches.[33] Examples include an analysis of how the war affected the world economic system, the study of antiwar protests, and an investigation of women's liberation, which found both opportunity and frustration within the peace movement.[34]

Another trajectory to follow is the complicated procedures by which people construct their own meanings out of foreign discourses, appropriating and recontextualizing them on the basis of their own social, cultural, and national experiences.[35] An example is the way in which the Vietnam War was suddenly transformed into a battleground of contested German history and identity, and the peculiar role that the philosopher Herbert Marcuse played in this process as an avid border-crosser.[36] Historians might well be able to find similarly creative manipulations of American or Vietnamese actions and their representation in other countries.

III

The first part of this book concentrates on comparing America's war with other conflicts that occurred at different times and in different geographical areas. Reframing the Vietnam War by putting it into comparative perspective has at least two consequences that, at first glance, seem paradoxical but, in fact, complement each other.[37] On the one hand, the Vietnam War loses

Shifting Politics of Nationalism in Greater Mexico," *Journal of American History* 86 (1999): 481–517; Marcus Rediker, *Between the Devil and the Deep Blue Sea: Merchant Seamen, Pirates, and the Anglo-American Maritime World, 1700–1750* (Cambridge, 1987); Doug McAdam and Dieter Rucht, "The Cross-National Diffusion of Movement Ideas," *The Annals of the American Academy of Political and Social Science* 528 (1993): 56–74; and George Katsiaficas, *The Imagination of the New Left: A Global Analysis of 1968* (Boston, 1987).

33 See Carole Fink, Philipp Gassert, and Detlef Junker, eds., *1968: The World Transformed* (New York, 1998).

34 See the chapters by Günter Wernicke, Barbara Tischler, and Hubert Zimmermann in this book.

35 The process of Americanization has recently been increasingly understood in this way. See Richard F. Kuisel, *Seducing the French: The Dilemma of Americanization*, 2d ed. (Berkeley, Calif., 1996); Alf Lüdtke, Inge Marsszolek, and Adelheid von Saldern, eds., *Amerikanisierung: Traum und Alptraum im Deutschland des 20. Jahrhunderts* (Stuttgart, 1996); Rob Kroes, *If You've Seen One, You've Seen the Mall: Europeans and American Mass Culture* (Urbana, Ill., 1996); Konrad Jarausch and Hannes Siegrist, eds., *Amerikanisierung und Sowjetisierung in Deutschland, 1955–1970* (Frankfurt am Main, 1997); Richard Pells, *Not Like Us: How the Europeans Have Loved, Hated, and Transformed American Culture Since World War II* (New York, 1997); and Anselm Doering-Manteuffel, *Wie westlich sind die Deutschen? Amerikanisierung und Westernisierung im 20. Jahrhundert* (Göttingen, 1999).

36 See Wilfried Mausbach's chapter in this book. On the concept of borderlands and border crossings, see David Thelen, "Of Audiences, Borderlands, and Comparisons: Toward the Internationalization of American History," *Journal of American History* 79 (1992): 432–62.

37 On the use of comparisons as a methodological tool in historiography, see Theodor Schieder, "Möglichkeiten und Grenzen vergleichender Methoden in der Geschichtswissenschaft," *Historische Zeitschrift* 200 (1965): 529–51; C. Vann Woodward, ed., *The Comparative Approach to American History*

some of its unique character when set in relation to comparable historical phenomena. The American conduct of war, its underlying ideological assumptions, and the overall strategic setting of a confrontation between a great power and a far-away small power are seen here as expressions of "typical" problems rather than outcomes of specific challenges. In fact, as the contributions in this volume point out, many features of the Vietnam conflict can be generalized to a certain degree. Among these are problems of imperial overstretch and the underestimation of adversaries on the part of great powers, misperceptions – often imbued with racial stereotypes and national clichés – of so-called peripheral states, and tendencies to evaluate economic and security threats according to long-standing idiosyncrasies rather than on the basis of concrete, up-to-date assessments of the diversity of causes that may underlie a given conflict. Indeed, as Robert Schulzinger has aptly written, Americans "were [always] preoccupied with something – be it domestic politics, containment, the Cold War, or credibility – other than what was actually happening in Vietnam."[38]

In elaborating on systematic patterns of great-power behavior and their ideologies, many of the volume's contributors make a strong plea for analyzing Vietnam against the backdrop of long-term processes. The most important of these might be summarized under the rubrics of colonialism, decolonization, and "recolonization" (Michael Adas). Certain ideological constructs that show a remarkable persistence, such as the variations of the so-called domino theory,[39] are also part of what might be called patterns of *longue durée* in the history of international relations.

On the other hand, the Vietnam War also gains a more specific profile by comparison. For example, comparing the behavior of great powers shows that they tend to commit the same mistakes over and over again but also commit new mistakes or revise old patterns. Here, the comparative approach serves to distinguish elements of continuity from those of discontinuity and to sharpen our understanding of the contingent elements of historical processes. This also means to acknowledge that comparisons based

(New York, 1968); Hans-Ulrich Wehler, *Modernisierungstheorie und Geschichte* (Göttingen, 1975); Fredrickson, "Comparative History," passim; Raymond Grew, "The Case for Comparing Histories," *American Historical Review* 85 (1980): 763–78; Erich Angermann, *Challenges of Ambiguity: Doing Comparative History, with comments by Carl N. Degler and John A. Garraty* (New York, 1991); Heinz-Gerhard Haupt and Jürgen Kocka, eds., *Geschichte und Vergleich: Ansätze und Ergebnisse international vergleichender Geschichtsschreibung* (Frankfurt am Main, 1996); and Hartmut Kaelble, *Der historische Vergleich: Eine Einführung zum 19. und 20. Jahrhundert* (Frankfurt am Main, 1999).

38 Robert D. Schulzinger, *A Time for War: The United States and Vietnam, 1941–1975* (New York, 1997), 327.

39 See Fabian Hilfrich's chapter in this book.

on analogies or similarities in character, which in themselves are condensed into ideal-types to make this character comparable, can and shall not lead to historical determinism.

Within this general comparative framework and with a sensitivity to continuities as well as to discontinuities of behavior and ideologies in time, the authors of Part One of this book have chosen specific foci. Michael Adas begins by placing Vietnam in the history of colonial wars. Not only did the Cold War lead the United States to quickly discard its criticism of European colonial practices, American foreign policy itself acquired a colonial touch and revitalized the tendency to perceive peripheral areas as battlegrounds for great-power rivalries. Economic considerations, in particular the concern to secure zones for capitalist expansion, enhanced this process and made its driving forces quite similar to those that pushed imperialist and colonial behavior during the nineteenth century. Several differences, however, should be kept in mind. The "Imperial Age" (Eric Hobsbawm) did not know "imperialism by proxy," as practiced by the American support for Japan as a bulwark against communism.[40] Also, nineteenth-century imperial claims often followed rather uncoordinated regional actions by men on the spot, which simply created facts that would trigger governmental action. The American decision to intervene heavily in Vietnam, however, resulted from deliberate considerations in the center and on the highest level of political decision-making. Finally, the United States had not been a participant in the initial struggle in Indochina but only followed in the footsteps of French failure. This new and ironic twist, as Adas argues (touching on observations Michael Hunt has made elsewhere),[41] reflects specific American prejudices against Latin, and particularly French, people and statecraft. It differs remarkably from the United States' stance regarding the dissolution of the British Empire.

Fabian Hilfrich follows up on the hierarchical structures inherent in American foreign-policy thinking. He delineates the analogies between American assessments of the Philippines around 1900 and Vietnam in the 1960s. In both cases, what was perceived as "peripheral," that is, the societies and state organizations of the Philippines and Vietnam, remained

---

40 On the peculiar arrangement that placed Japan and Germany at the center of economic integration in Asia and Europe after World War II while having them at the same time entrust their security to American-led alliance structures, see the essays in the first part of Gustav Schmidt and Charles F. Doran, eds., *Amerikas Option für Deutschland und Japan: Die Position und Rolle Deutschlands und Japans in regionalen und internationalen Strukturen: Die 1950er und 1990er Jahre im Vergleich* (Bochum, 1996).

41 Michael H. Hunt, *Ideology and U.S. Foreign Policy* (New Haven, Conn., 1987).

insignificant in its own right and was evaluated primarily in its assumed meaning for the power struggles at the "center" – above all, for the American interests in these struggles. American visions of the Asian periphery, as Hilfrich demonstrates, have not only been conditioned by strategic considerations but were heavily permeated with a lasting mixture of Darwinian, racist, and ethnocentric ideas. Hilfrich develops this line of argumentation along the history of two discursive constructions: the domino theory and the notion of "civilization." Both have served as vehicles for American diplomacy to deal with Asia at the fin-de-siècle as well as in the 1960s. The domino theory always consisted of a bundle of military, political, and psychological moments to describe chain reactions that would not only express a decline in American influence and a direction toward an evil political system but also assumed a positive meaning when being read as the path toward the opening of the Chinese market or toward regional modernization.

Vietnam finds its place in an even wider chronological framework in Christopher Jespersen's chapter. He addresses the character of the Vietnam conflict as a revolutionary struggle for national liberation that eventually created a new social and political order, the unified Socialist Republic of Vietnam. This process affected the international system as much as it was, reversibly, codetermined by the position of the international powers. Thus, the Vietnamese revolution resembles the American struggle for independence and the founding of the United States. In both cases, the leading and technologically most advanced international power – Great Britain in the eighteenth century and the United States in the 1960s – sought a military solution to suppress a national liberation movement (given, of course, the fundamental difference that the American colonists were, indeed, part of the British Empire and, at least in the beginning, did not form an indigenous nationalist movement). These attempts failed but did not shatter the dominance of the leading power in the long run. On the contrary, and quite remarkably, Great Britain and the United States survived their defeats abroad, retained positions of international leadership, and – to a different degree – succeeded for some time in isolating the new national state in the international arena. At the same time, those powers who supported the national movements – France during the American War of Independence and the Soviet Union during the Vietnam War – strained their economies considerably.

Undoubtedly, military measures and the way a war is conducted reveal much of the rationale of the combatants, and military mistakes reflect strategic shortcomings as well as political miscalculations. In this respect, the case of Japan's military intervention in China during the 1930s is no less revealing than the American involvement in Vietnam, as John Prados demonstrates. Both Japan and the United States had to embark on a mixture of conventional operations and counterguerilla actions to pursue their military aims. Both wars increasingly undermined the actual strength of the great powers and diverted them from their key interests. The "peripheral wars" absorbed military and economic energies to an extent that shattered the great powers' resources and undermined their capabilities to act firmly in other and more central areas of conflict. Prados distills a "recipe for disaster" from studying the Japanese invasion of Manchuria: Japan got caught up in the temptation to dominate China and its southern neighbors at the expense of its ability to wage war against Russia and the United States. Moreover, although the Japanese tried to limit manpower and spending for the "peripheral war," it proved extremely difficult to handle the war as a sideshow because it increasingly diverted important energies. The United States would experience the same twenty years later in Vietnam. During the early Cold War, American national security planning had been devoted primarily to Europe and Korea, and – like Japan – the American government began and executed its Southeast Asian intervention without clearly formulating its overall policy and war aims. The Vietnam War soon led to a general shortage of munitions, equipment, and experienced personnel, all of which would have been necessary if there had been a major contingency in Europe or Korea, the two main crisis spots.

Miscalculations, however, occur not only at the beginning of wars; they also influence their endings. Jeffrey Kimball takes a closer look at this phenomenon. He distinguishes three ideal types of war termination: a decisive victory of a power that can then dictate an unconditional surrender; the imposition of peace from outside; and negotiations leading to an armistice. The protracted process to end the Korean War, after a military stalemate had been reached, is a telling example of how negotiations are dragged out by the inability of the combatants to solve a single, crucial question – in this case the repatriation of prisoners of war, a problem that stalled talks for one-and-a-half years. To be sure, serious negotiating is required to end a war, and Vietnam is certainly a case in point. Because of domestic pressures as well as military setbacks, the Nixon administration was gradually forced to confront the bitter truth that a favorable ending of the war – to say nothing of victory – was impossible. However, the Paris agreements between the United States and North Vietnam would only be the prelude to the final chapter of the war that took shape along the lines of Kimball's first ideal-type: a disastrous defeat of the South Vietnamese regime.

Whereas victories on the battlefield, international pressure, and negotiations can put an end to combat and armed hostilities, they do not necessarily terminate wars in the minds of those people affected by them. Coming to terms with war can be a lengthy process, as Sabine Behrenbeck shows in her comparison of the place of the Vietnam conflict in American collective memory and the end of World War I on Germany's mental map after 1918, encapsulated in the term *Versailles*.[42] In both countries, discussions about war memorials and the eventual selection of specific artistic solutions, which expressed certain political attitudes, reflected the intricate challenge of integrating military defeats and traumatic experiences into collective memory. During the years immediately following the signing of the Treaty of Versailles, war memorials of various kinds – abstract, Christian, or heroic – were created in Germany. Discussions about a national war memorial aroused bitter controversy, leading to the construction of three different memorials at three separate sites. One of these was the so-called Neue Wache in Berlin, which, in its minimalist contours, assumed a seemingly apolitical character but in fact alluded to a well-known iconography of patriotic symbols. Increasingly after 1925, Germany witnessed a revival of heroic and tragic narratives, a process that was vigorously exploited by the National Socialists.

In contrast, the United States witnessed relatively few attempts to memorialize the Vietnam War before a national memorial was commissioned. Maya Lin's "Vietnam Wall," as many visitors to Washington refer to the Vietnam Veterans Memorial on the National Mall, immediately elicited worldwide attention and admiration because of its dignity based on respect for the individual victims and its refrain from any political statement about the war itself. This alone, however, was not sufficient for some conservatives who preferred a more traditional and naturalistic expression of the war experience. What turned out as a compromise – the addition of a sculpture of three American soldiers by Frederic Hart – did not, however, create a retrospective heroism. It might have allowed an even wider array of people to make their peace with the Vietnam War.

IV

Leaving the field of historical comparisons, Part Two of this book shifts the focus onto the multilateral and systemic dimensions of the Vietnam

---

42 On the significance and aftermath of the Versailles treaty, see Manfred F. Boemeke, Gerald D. Feldman, and Elisabeth Glaser, eds., *The Treaty of Versailles: A Reassessment After 75 Years* (New York, 1998).

War. In particular, the role of conflict in international relations and alliance politics comes under scrutiny. Hubert Zimmermann widens our view by embarking on a *tour d'horizon* of the international monetary system and the impact that the United States's preoccupation with Southeast Asia had on the global economy. After World War II, American economic dominance and the coherence of the Western alliance under American leadership had been based on the financial system created at Bretton Woods. This system had made the dollar the world's principle reserve currency. At the same time, however, the Americans had committed themselves to the conversion of dollars into gold at a fixed rate of $35 an ounce. This system came under increasing pressure when the U.S. balance-of–payments situation deteriorated during the 1960s, not least due to the growing expenditures for Vietnam. When the United States turned to its allies for economic support – in short, asking them to support the Vietnam War indirectly – the allies became increasingly critical. This was especially true of France, which, under Charles de Gaulle, became the principal opponent of American monetary policies and advocated a return to a strict gold standard. Vietnam became the rallying point for European criticism of American monetary policy. Even Germany, which was completely dependent on U.S. security guarantees and had thus become Washington's most steadfast ally, expressed misgivings. This was particularly unsettling because the economically powerful Federal Republic was a key factor in stabilizing the U.S.-led international monetary system. The American war in Vietnam ultimately contributed to the breakdown of the Bretton Woods system. Perhaps even more important, those Europeans who had long held inflated dollars in order to stabilize that system, thus effectively co-financing the Vietnam War, now had the gold window slammed shut in their faces – an experience that convinced them of the necessity for a more independent European monetary policy.

What developed as a clear divergence of monetary interests between the United States and the countries of Western Europe was accompanied by different political and military assessments of Vietnam and America's war. Fredrik Logevall analyzes the increasing isolation of the United States within the Western alliance during the mid-1960s, when American efforts to mobilize direct and indirect support for the war in the international arena generated only desultory responses and met with more and more opposition. With the notable exception of Australia,[43] America's key allies not only refused to join any military efforts but also distanced themselves from the

43 See Peter Edwards's chapter in this book.

very idea that South Vietnam – a country whose government was seen as incompetent and corrupt – really mattered to Western security. France took the most radical stand in advocating a neutralization of Vietnam, but Canada, Germany, and Great Britain – all influenced by growing domestic protests against the war – remained noncommittal. In fact, they harbored major reservations without openly conveying them to Washington. Even France did not press the matter with U.S. officials, so that President Lyndon Johnson could claim rhetorical support and maintain the façade of anticommunist unity. In terms of actual allied support, however, his "More Flags" campaign failed miserably.

The causes, extent, and consequences of America's international isolation during the Vietnam conflict still represent largely unexamined fields. Further research is needed that focuses on particular regional settings and on the impact of the Vietnam War on individual countries and their bilateral relations with the United States. This book contains several case studies that might offer some remedy. Arne Kislenko looks at Thailand, a regional middle power keenly interested in a status quo that blocked communist infiltration from outside and, above all, prevented China, Thailand's ancient enemy, from encroaching further on the Southeast Asian continent. In this respect, the United States' involvement in Vietnam and direct American military and intelligence support offered welcome protection. The United States tried to integrate Thailand into its own strategic plans because the Asian ally formed an important barrier against an unstable Laos; Thailand even sent troops into South Vietnam in September 1967 to support American efforts. But there were obvious limits to this alliance: The influx of American consumer goods and entertainment commodities produced fear of an "Americanization" of Thai culture. Eventually, the Thai government also realized that it could not count on any prospects for an American victory but would have to be able to accommodate even a communist neighbor. Thailand's spectacular re-evaluation of its position in 1969, which called for American disengagement, stands in the tradition of the country's great flexibility in foreign policy for the sake of maintaining regional security in its own national interest.

Against the background of the attitudes toward the Vietnam War in Western Europe and Thailand, where national interests soon began to deviate from the course that the United States would have liked its allies to follow, it is interesting to look at the case of Australia. Peter Edwards investigates the unique support Australia offered for America's war in Vietnam, where eventually all three Australian armed services and altogether 50,000 Australian soldiers were involved. Until Australia's new labor government attained power in 1972, the ruling class had been committed to an American military presence in Southeast Asia. The Australian strategic policy had two objectives: peace and a balance of powers to the north plus good relations with Great Britain and the United States. This dual strategy put considerable strains on the country when it embarked on pacifying two regional conflicts, in Malaysia (1948–60) and Indonesia (1963), and was at the same time asked by the United States to support the latter's policy in Vietnam. As a "willing ally," the Australian government soon became the target of a homegrown antiwar movement. The growing opposition increasingly circumscribed Canberra's willingness and ability to close ranks with the United States. As Edwards points out, this growing restraint in Australia (and in New Zealand) contributed to the decision by U.S. Secretary of Defense Clark Clifford to pursue a strategy of de-escalation in the late 1960s.

But the waves created within the Western alliance by disagreements over Vietnam were ripples compared to the fierce rivalry that the war generated within the communist camp. In her essay, Eva-Maria Stolberg depicts the changing history of Sino-Soviet relations after 1949 with regard to Vietnam and its quest for national unity. For China and the Soviet Union, supporting the Vietnamese liberation movement served a triple purpose: It enabled these great powers to validate or attack certain ideological concepts; it was part of Chinese and Soviet strategy vis-à-vis the United States as their primary global antagonist; and, last but not least, it was a vehicle to pursue interests within domestic party structures. In the People's Republic of China, Mao Zedong became the advocate of the concept of "people's warfare," which centered around guerilla tactics and the political mobilization of the rural population. People's warfare was envisioned as a global model for the anticapitalist struggle. The Vietnamese national liberation movement fit this model well and thus enjoyed Chinese support. At the same time, however, China restrained itself from direct involvement on account of its own national security interests. Moreover, Mao Zedong repeatedly instrumentalized the idea of people's warfare in order to gain support for radical domestic measures such as the "Great Leap Forward." Meanwhile, Nikita Khrushchev's Soviet Union pursued the concept of "peaceful cooperation" that would have implied accepting the division of Vietnam – a threatening idea for China. Only after Khrushchev's removal from office did the Soviet Union embark on a more active Southeast Asian policy that entailed support for the North Vietnamese. This proxy war also permitted Moscow to test the latest Soviet military technology. In terms of concrete military support, the leaders of both communist countries for the most part followed pragmatic reasoning, especially after 1965 when Sino-Soviet relations rapidly deteriorated.

V

The cases of America's allies in Europe, Asia, and the Pacific, as well as the attitudes of China and the Soviet Union, collectively demonstrate that diplomatic positions and international policies of states were intrinsically linked to domestic issues during the Vietnam era. As Part Three shows, international and national politics were profoundly interrelated. Here, several case studies focus on the impact of America's war on the domestic scenes of individual countries.

In his essay on Italy, Leopoldo Nuti explores a particularly telling example. Because of Italy's peculiar post–World War II development, the Vietnam War had a disproportionate relevance for its domestic and foreign policy. After 1945, the United States had begun to stabilize Italian politics, an attempt that included efforts to bring Italy's Socialist Party (PSI) into the democratic camp and into a coalition with the Christian Democrats (DC). Christian Democratic politicians indeed undertook the experiment of an "opening to the left," and after November 1963 the Socialists fully participated in the national government. However, this participation created a paradoxical situation. As the new center-left government – supported by the Kennedy and Johnson administrations – was taking shape, America's escalation of the war in Vietnam threatened its chances of survival. Polarized by harsh criticism of the Vietnam War from the far left, the Italian Socialists found themselves between a rock and a hard place. The ruling coalition repeatedly tried to extricate itself from this difficult position by endorsing a number of peace efforts. These attempts included the rather bizarre exertions of Florence's former mayor Giorgio La Pira and two more serious initiatives, code-named "Marigold" (via Polish channels and supported by Italy's ambassador in South Vietnam, Giovanni d'Orlandi) and "Kelly" (through Romanian channels).[44] These peace initiatives did nothing, however, to save the Socialists from defeat in the 1968 elections. The opening to the left eventually failed, and the Italian public's concerns about the conflict in Vietnam turned into massive criticism of the United States.

---

44 See also George C. Herring, ed., *The Secret Diplomacy of the Vietnam War: The Negotiating Volumes of the Pentagon Papers* (Austin, Tex., 1983); James G. Hershberg, "Who Murdered 'Marigold'? New Evidence on the Mysterious Failure of Poland's Secret Initiative to Start U.S.–North Vietnamese Peace Talks, 1966," Cold War International History Project, Working Paper no. 27 (Washington, D.C., 2000).

As in Italy, the public in West Germany paid increasing attention to the Vietnam War in the second half of the 1960s. One consequence, Wilfried Mausbach argues, was that Vietnam became a symbolic tool in an attempt to refashion the collective identity of West Germans. Undermining the official American line of argument, which claimed that defending Saigon was defending Berlin, critics of the war began to draw parallels between the American and South Vietnamese conduct of the war and the Holocaust. By invoking Vietnam as a contemporary representation of Auschwitz, they sought to alter the way Germans confronted their own National Socialist past. New conceptual frameworks that focused on the consequences of capitalist aggression in the Third World suggested a new Auschwitz was a real possibility. The Vietnam-Auschwitz analogy found its place in ideological concepts on the left, which claimed that protesting the Vietnam War also meant opposing fascist tendencies at home. It contributed to the notion of a necessary ideological and political struggle in the capitalist center. Student radicalization shifted the emphasis from protest to resistance and allowed the critics at home to assume an actual function in what they saw as a global struggle against imperialism.

In contrast to West Germany, the German Democratic Republic (GDR) had always taken anti-imperialism as part of its official state ideology. The East German government and the ruling Socialist Unity Party (SED) thus took an active role in cultivating opposition to the Vietnam War. Authorities in East Berlin established the German Peace Council (GPC) as a chapter of the communist-backed World Peace Council (WPC) to promote their anti-imperialist stance in the international arena. As Günter Wernicke demonstrates, the GPC soon found itself enmeshed in numerous controversies. Almost immediately, the Sino-Soviet rivalry left a deep imprint on the socialist peace movement, splitting the membership of the WPC and sometimes even individual national chapters along ideological lines. Beyond the communist camp, efforts to forge alliances with Western peace movements often required the GPC to walk a thin line between expectations in East Berlin and the need to demonstrate institutional independence and ideological flexibility. In the international as well as domestic arenas, there seemed to have been a lingering ambivalence in the GPC's task. On the one hand, the German Peace Council aimed to rally a mass movement behind the anti-imperialist cause of peace. On the other, the bureaucracy in East Berlin was indeed wary of the potential of such movements to become uncontrollable. Finally, East Germany's Vietnam policy was conflated with more important foreign-policy goals. Thus, in February 1968 East German organizations withdrew from the International Vietnam Congress being held in West Berlin when they grew concerned that the meeting would be critical of a lack of Soviet support for the Vietnamese cause. However, the SED tried to enlist the North Vietnamese in its propaganda campaign against the Federal Republic, an effort that was on a par with the GPC's ultimate goal of winning diplomatic recognition for the East German regime.

What we see here, then, is yet another example of the Vietnam War being recast in a discourse – in this case a complicated German-German one – quite alien to Americans and Vietnamese. Foreign-policy considerations like those noted above also confronted individual activists with the problem of being torn between loyalty to their own country and its inescapable alliance with the Soviet Union, on the one hand, and, on the other, a deep humanitarian impulse discernible in large donations for the suffering Vietnamese.

Many antiwar protest movements found themselves in dual roles as participants in a global effort and as elements in processes of societal reform or upheaval that easily transcended the Vietnam issue. Some of these domestic issues even created divisions among the protesters themselves. Barbara Tischler focuses on this aspect of antiwar activism and emergent feminism. There was no simple shift from one movement to the other: Women did not abandon the antiwar cause to take up feminist concerns. In fact, by being a major part of the antiwar movement, women gained valuable organizational and ideological experience. However, because many in the New Left failed to appreciate the female contribution to their common cause and to recognize continued patterns of male dominance, women often had to choose between continuing protest alliances with men and their desire to put feminist issues on the political agenda. This difficult process of feminist self-organization unfolded gradually. Triggered to a large extent by experiences of female marginalization in the American antiwar movement, it was also part of an international wave of feminist mobilization that had many counterparts abroad.

In the final chapter of the book, Lloyd C. Gardner returns to the key questions raised at the beginning. The Vietnam War cannot be described in a linear narrative and does not relate to an "epic tale." This war encompasses many wars, at home and abroad. It has always been possible to read America's war in many different and often contradictory ways. Certainly, for many years Vietnam served as a prime example of the validity of the Truman Doctrine and the domino theory, which are in fact two sides of the same coin, namely, America's foreign policy during the Cold War. But Vietnam was more: The Asian country threatened by communism (as the story was told) was seen as part of a campaign to spread America's global vision of the world order.[45] This vision incorporated the capitalist idea of creating free markets to allow economic expansion and prosperity, and it simultaneously absorbed the idea of progressive modernization. After 1961, intellectuals sympathetic to the Kennedy and Johnson administrations depicted Vietnam as a test case for modernization theories, transplanting ideas of the Great Society into an arena that turned out to be structurally incompatible with this concept. Be it these visions or succeeding ones, such as Nixon's concept of Asia after Vietnam – all were marked by an amazing degree of abstraction insofar as they reflected America's own ideological premises much more than the indigenous issues of Vietnam. Indeed, as Gardner argues, the commitment to Vietnam, so vehemently and emphatically repeated by American officials, was always a commitment to America itself. The kind of revolution the United States would have welcomed in the Third World, one that was congenial to the American experience, was not to happen. Instead, the North Vietnamese eventually succeeded in what was not only their familiar geographical realm but also their own cultural ground on which American diplomats, soldiers, and intellectuals would always remain strangers.

VI

This book, in short, argues for viewing the multitude of conflicts and struggles encapsulated in the term *Vietnam War* from a variety of perspectives that take account of the international ramifications of this war and its comparability with other conflicts. In doing so, the character of the Vietnam War itself becomes more fluid. As the chapters demonstrate, for some countries the Vietnam War led to direct military involvement and was perceived in the domestic political arena as a more immediate event than in other regions of the world. Immediacy, however, does not necessarily depend on military entanglement, as the case of the Federal Republic of Germany illustrates. The war in Vietnam could be incorporated in many different forms – as a military challenge no less than a cultural and economic event or a political argument – into many different narratives of different regions. It circulated around the globe, was transmitted by the modern media, and acquired new meanings in different places. The Vietnam conflict could also assume a place in temporal processes other than those marked by the chronology of this war's events. Vietnam might be seen as part of such long-term developments

---

45 See also Emily Rosenberg, *Spreading the American Dream: American Economic and Cultural Expansion, 1890–1945* (New York, 1982); and Tony Smith, *America's Mission: The United States and the Worldwide Struggle for Democracy in the Twentieth Century* (Princeton, N.J., 1994).

as the rise of the nation-state, decolonization, and modernization; it can be seen as part of enduring conflicts between central and peripheral states; and, as a cultural event, it can be analyzed on regional and local levels in settings such as peace movements and discourses about the commemoration of war. From this point of view, seemingly simple questions about the beginning and the end of the war become much more intricate and subtle than normally assumed.

In shedding additional light on the Vietnam War by exposing its history to questions that arise from non-American perspectives, our aim is not to diminish the role of the United States but to relocate the Vietnam War in a more comprehensive setting. This will allow historians to be more specific about the place of America's war not only in the "American Century"[46] but in the history of modern state and societal conflicts in general.

"The whole world is watching" was the famous slogan that antiwar protesters shouted in 1968 when they rallied on the occasion of the Democratic National Convention in Chicago. This slogan not only ar- ticulated a warning to the Democratic delegates but also reflected the international interest in and the globalization of concerns about the Vietnam conflict. Today, a generation later, it might be appropriate to reverse the spotlight and look through the lens of America's war at the world and at those who closely followed the fate of Vietnam from the sidelines but nevertheless took a stance in this conflict, who incorporated the Vietnam War into their own cultural and political landscapes and ascribed new meanings to it.

46 See "The American Century: A Roundtable," *Diplomatic History* 23 (1999): 157–370, 391–537.

PART ONE

Relocating Vietnam: Comparisons in Time and Space

1

A Colonial War in a Postcolonial Era

The United States' Occupation of Vietnam

MICHAEL ADAS

I

The available accounts of the exchanges among the leaders of the grand alliance against the Axis powers in World War II make it clear that Franklin D. Roosevelt rarely passed up a chance to debunk European-style colonialism. Although Roosevelt explicitly rejected the idealistic moralizing that had earlier pervaded Woodrow Wilson's dealings with the other great powers, allies and enemies alike,[1] he evinced a good deal more concern than Wilson had for the condition and future of the colonized peoples of Africa and Asia. Wilson was undoubtedly convinced that the principle of self-determination – and the ideals of justice, open diplomacy, and democratization it enshrined – was a vital component of the new world order that he sought to fashion from the wreckage of the Great War. But as African and Asian leaders as diverse as Ho Chi Minh and the members of the Egyptian delegation (*wafd*) to the Versailles peace conference soon learned, Wilson intended self-determination for Poles and Czechs at best, and certainly not Vietnamese and Arabs.[2] In sharp contrast, Roosevelt was convinced that the war had accelerated the demise of an obsolescent European colonial order and that the forces unleashed by decolonization movements were bound to shape the postwar global order in major ways.[3]

---

1 Warren F. Kimball, *Forged in War: Roosevelt, Churchill, and the Second World War* (New York, 1997), esp. chap. 7.
2 Robert Lansing, *The Peace Negotiations: A Personal Narrative* (Boston, 1921), chap. 7; David Fromkin, *A Peace to End All Peace* (New York, 1989), chap. 41; Jean Lacouture, *Ho Chi Minh: A Political Biography* (New York, 1968), 24–5; and P. J. Vatikiotis, *The History of Egypt from Muhammad Ali to Mubarak* (Baltimore, 1985), 260–70.
3 Lloyd C. Gardner, *Approaching Vietnam: From World War II Through Dienbienphu* (New York, 1988), 30–6; Kimball, *Forged in War*, 138–40, 199, 208, 300–5; and Stein Tonneson, *The Vietnamese Revolution of 1945: Roosevelt, Ho Chi Minh and de Gaulle in a World at War* (London, 1991), esp. 62–6.

Roosevelt quibbled intermittently with Winston Churchill and other
European leaders over the colonial question, but he reserved his harshest
and most unrelenting criticisms for the French, particularly the legacy of
their rule in Indochina. Although some of his statements make it clear
that Roosevelt actually knew little about conditions in the Vichy-Japanese–
controlled colonies there, he dismissed the French as incompetent and ex-
ploitative overlords whose century of rule had impoverished the peoples of
the area and done little to prepare them for self-rule. The stunning Nazi
defeats of the French military in Europe and the puppet status of the French
colonial functionaries left in Japanese-occupied Indochina obviously influenced Roosevelt's assessment in major ways. His views were consistent with
a broader skepticism on the part of American diplomats and military leaders,
both during and after the war, regarding the capacity of the French in politics and making war. Perhaps consciously seeking to deflect American barbs
aimed at the British imperium, Churchill resoundingly seconded Roosevelt's
conviction that the French had made a mess of things both at home and
in the colonies. But predictably the British war leader stridently contested
Roosevelt's broader conclusion that the failures of the French confirmed
the inevitability of the European retreat from overseas empire.[4]

The views of Roosevelt and other American policy makers regarding
the French as colonizers in Indochina appeared to have been translated –
however tenuously – into actual wartime policy by the assistance provided by the Office of Strategic Services (OSS) and other allied agencies to
the Viet Minh and other Vietnamese nationalist groups openly resisting the
Japanese overlords and their Vichy puppets.[5] Ho Chi Minh's quite deliberate
paraphrases from and references to the American Declaration of Independence in his proclamation of Vietnamese nationhood in September 1945
were simply the most striking manifestations of a more general Vietnamese
determination to depict the United States as an ally in their freedom
struggle.[6] It is impossible to know whether or not their hopes would have

4 Gardner, *Approaching Vietnam*, 30–9, 138, 149, 300–2; Kimball, *Forged in War*, 298–305; Walter
  Lefeber, "Roosevelt, Churchill, and Indochina: 1942–1945," *American Historical Review* 80, no. 5
  (1975): 1277–80, 1285; and for a British perspective on the standoff over Indochina, see Christopher
  Thorne, *Allies of a Kind: The United States, Britain, and the War Against Japan, 1941–1945* (New York,
  1978).
5 Ronald Spector has provided considerable evidence to demonstrate that American military commanders and OSS operatives continued to push Roosevelt's anticolonial stance long after it had
  been explicitly abandoned at higher levels. See his "Allied Intelligence and Indochina, 1943–45,"
  Pacific Historical Review 51, no. 1 (1982): 23–50.
6 For an American view of Allied–Viet Minh wartime contacts and cooperation, see esp. Archimedes
  Patti, *Why Vietnam? Prelude to America's Albatross* (Berkeley, Calif., 1980), 45–58, 69–71, 82–8, 124–9,
  144–7; on Vietnamese references to American historical precedents and expectations of postwar
  U.S. backing for decolonization, see Mark Bradley, "Imagining Vietnam: The United States in

been more fully realized had Roosevelt lived, particularly because he himself appeared to retreat from them in the last months of his life. But Harry S. Truman and his inner circle of advisers began to distance themselves from the Viet Minh and prepare the way for the reoccupation of Indochina by the French months before the Pacific War was brought to its unsettling end in the fall of 1945.[7]

In the following years, driven by the imperatives of a rapidly globalizing Cold War, the United States quickly dropped all pretense of championing decolonization, particularly in Southeast Asia. American policy makers not only encouraged, they actively intervened to facilitate France's return to colonial domination in Indochina. By the early 1950s, the United States had become a vital source of military supplies and had assumed a major share of the costs for that failed endeavor.[8] In the next decade, three American presidents presided over an escalating political and military involvement in Indochina that had most of the main attributes of colonial interventions in the preceding centuries of European global domination. Defying the decidedly anticolonial rhetoric of the Roosevelt years, they committed the United States to a massive colonial occupation in a postcolonial era.

II

The Cold War calculations that were used to justify the increasingly costly American commitment were mainly a mix of the same sort of strategic and prestige concerns that had motivated European statesmen in the era of high imperialism. As communist China came to be seen by the late 1950s as a threat to a decolonizing Southeast Asia, independent of and even more menacing than the Soviet Union, the multipolar great-power rivalries that had driven the late-nineteenth-century scramble for overseas colonies provided much of the impetus for the prolonged Cold War contest over hegemony in Indochina. As was the case in American responses to peasant insurgencies in other formerly colonized areas of Latin America, Vietnam and Indochina were more generally viewed as zones of insta-bility on the periphery of an expanding capitalist world system. In the

---

Radical Vietnamese Anti-Colonial Discourse," *Journal of American–East Asian Relations* 4, no. 2 (1995): 299–329.

7 The extent of Roosevelt's abandonment of his vision of a postcolonial world order and the respon-sibility of Truman and his advisers for the shift to support for the French have been the subject of a protracted debate. The differing positions are superbly laid out by Stein Tonnesson, who provides a cogent, alternative interpretation of his own. See *Revolution of 1945*, 13–19, and chap. 7.

8 Patti, *Why Vietnam?*, 415–35; Ellen Hammer, *The Struggle for Indochina, 1940–1955: Vietnam and the French Experience* (Stanford, Calif., 1966), 313–14.

late nineteenth century, colonial expansion was frequently linked to the disintegration of client and comprador linkages between the industrial powers and indigenous political and mercantile elites that had been established earlier through informal modes of domination.[9] In the years after the end of World War II, these ties and the extractive systems that had been established in Indochina in the decades of French colonial rule were perceived by American policy makers to be threatened by the revolutionary insurgency led by the Viet Minh. Thus, the escalating American intervention in the Indochina wars was prompted in part by the need to stabilize a peripheral area in turmoil.

If falling dominoes and the need to bolster wavering allies, both Asian and European, figured prominently in the thinking of American policy makers, they also responded to other strategic and economic considerations reminiscent of those that provoked late-nineteenth-century European expansion. As D. C. M. Platt cogently argued some decades ago,[10] Britain's late-nineteenth-century commitment to low tariffs and free trade pushed it to imperialist interventions to deny rival powers control over areas of potential investment, market opportunity, or raw material extraction. Although some post–World War II American policy makers noted that South Vietnam was one of the "rice bowls" of Asia,[11] few seriously contended that the fall of such a small and impoverished region to the communists would in itself significantly reduce economic opportunities for the United States and its capitalist allies. But they feared that the "loss" of South Vietnam to the communist camp might provide the impetus for an economic domino effect that would mean the constriction of investment and market options throughout Southeast Asia. Similar concerns had informed the decisions of nineteenth-century European expansionists who acceded to territorial acquisitions of little apparent strategic worth and dubious resource potential because they feared that these areas would be colonized by rival powers, thereby rendering their future market and resource potential inaccessible. Given the protectionist policies pursued by the continental powers and

9 The most influential conceptualization of these processes has proved to be Ronald Robinson's "Non-European Foundations of European Imperialism: Sketch for a Theory of Collaboration," in Roger Owen and Bob Sutcliffe, eds., *Studies in the Theory of Imperialism* (London, 1972), 117–40. For a fine recent survey of the history of the African epicenter of the "scramble," see H. L. Wesseling, *Divide and Rule: The Partition of Africa, 1880–1914* (London, 1996); and for a superb analysis of these patterns in one of the most pivotal zones that was an object of the scramble, see Anthony Hopkins, *An Economic History of West Africa* (New York, 1973), chap. 4.

10 D. C. M. Platt, *Finance, Trade and Politics in British Foreign Policy, 1814–1914* (Oxford, 1968). For rather different French approaches to these issues with similar annexationist outcomes, see Jacques Marseilles, *Empire colonial et capitalisme français: Histoire d'un divorce* (Paris, 1984).

11 Gardner, *Approaching Vietnam*, 79.

the United States in the decades of the scramble, these anxieties were not unfounded.[12]

American concerns to secure zones for capitalist expansion were particularly pronounced with regard to Japan, then struggling to recover from the devastation inflicted by the Allies in World War II. Like Germany in the West, Japan was increasingly seen by American strategists as the most critical bulwark against the advance of communism in Asia. A number of American policy makers argued that South Vietnam's potential as a market for Japanese products and investment was a compelling reason for denying it to the communist North,[13] although this was not a rationale that was likely to rally American public opinion in support of the Vietnam venture. This exercise in imperialism by proxy had no counterpart in the great power contests for colonial territories in the nineteenth century.

Another important contrast between the patterns of colonial expansion exhibited by the industrial powers in the late nineteenth century and by the United States after 1945 in Indochina was the level at which effective decisions for advance were made. In the era of the scramble, military adventurers, explorers, and commercial agents spearheaded the extension of colonial territories throughout much of Asia and Africa. The speed of communication between European or North American metropoles and areas where colonial claims were being asserted had greatly improved after telegraphic, rail, and steamship connections were extended into Asia and Africa after the middle decades of the nineteenth century. But once British, French, and German explorers and merchant- or military-adventurers set off from European-controlled coastal enclaves into the interior of Africa and Southeast Asia, or steamed out to remote islands in the Pacific, they could be out of contact with even local officials for months and in some cases years at a time. Through timely alliances with threatened or aspiring indigenous potentates, bogus treaties, and limited expeditionary assaults, these "men-on-the-spot," as they came to be known in the historiography of European overseas expansion, often concluded their expeditions by presenting rulers and parliaments in the metropoles with what in effect were faits accomplis. Faced with the prospect of being vilified in the popular press and pummeled by their political rivals – both domestic and foreign – European statesmen frequently concluded that they had little choice but to ratify locally initiated

---

12 Hans-Ulrich Wehler has aptly termed the psychological reflex behind this rash of preemptive colonial annexations as *Torschlusspanik* or "fear of the closing door." See his *Bismarck und der Imperialismus* (Cologne, 1969), 437.

13 Andrew Rotter, *The Path to Vietnam: Origins of the American Commitment to Southeast Asia* (Ithaca, N.Y., 1987), chap. 2; and Gardner, *Approaching Vietnam*, 16, 81, 96ff, 108–14, 294–5.

territorial annexations or treaties in which unsuspecting local potentates acceded to European overlordship.[14]

By contrast, escalating American involvement in Vietnam and Indochina more generally was charted by a succession of presidents and their civilian and military advisers at the highest levels in Washington. The vastly increased speed and greatly enhanced geographical reach of command and control communications networks – both civilian and military – in the second half of the twentieth century, in comparison with the last decades of the nineteenth, meant that the escalation of American involvement in Vietnam could be meticulously planned in Washington and directed from Saigon as well as the military headquarters of the tactical zones into which South Vietnam had been divided. Special inquiries, classified reports, and interminable debates in the National Security Council preceded each step into the quagmire. Lyndon Johnson, who presided over the greatest expansion by far of America's war in Indochina, personally plotted the targets for bombing sorties against North Vietnam in the mid-1960s.[15]

III

Beyond motivations for direct intervention, the American occupation of South Vietnam resembled earlier patterns of Western overseas colonization in important ways. It also exhibited what appear to be variations on nineteenth-century approaches to colonization that were in fact characteristic of the rather belated entry of the United States into the competition for overseas possessions. The most striking of these seeming deviations was the American assumption of the role of colonizer that the French had formerly played in Indochina. Although the Western powers often squabbled over the same colonial turf during the decades of the scramble, European statesmen displayed considerable skill at negotiating divisions of the spoils that were far from satisfactory to all of the parties but agreeable enough to prevent open warfare between the rivals in question. As a general rule, territories already colonized by European states – even militarily weak ones, such as

---

14 Jean Stengers has made a compelling case for the predominance of this dynamic through the end of the nineteenth century. See his "L'impérialisme colonial de la fin du XIXe siècle: Mythe ou réalité?" *Journal of African History* 3 (1961): 469–91. For German and British examples, see respectively, Wehler, *Bismarck und Imperialismus*, chap. 5; and Ronald Robinson and John Gallagher, *Africa and the Victorians* (London, 1961), esp. chaps. 7, 13.

15 Of the rather extensive literature on the centralization and personalization of decision making in the escalation of America's involvement in Indochina, rather different but revealing perspectives can be found in Loren Baritz, *Backfire* (New York, 1985); Larry Berman, *Planning a Tragedy: The Americanization of the War in Vietnam* (New York, 1982); and Lloyd C. Gardner, *Pay Any Price: Lyndon Johnson and the Wars for Vietnam* (Chicago, 1995).

Portugal and The Netherlands – were excluded from the real estate that the industrial powers sought to include in their growing empires.

On all counts, the American venture in Indochina appeared to be setting new precedents. Given Roosevelt's summary judgment that French rule in the region had been an utter failure and the disdain evinced by wartime American statesmen for colonialism in general, the American recolonization of Vietnam following the French retreat appeared to be not only a new departure but supremely ironic. But the Cold War situation in which Roosevelt's successors made their incremental decisions for escalating American involvement in Indochina were very different from those of the World War II years, when communist and capitalist states were allied in the great antifascist crusade. Less obviously, the American takeover from the French had ample precedent, both in the history of the relations between the two nations and in broader but equally enduring American assessments of the political and military aptitudes of peoples of "Latin" descent.

Michael Hunt has usefully surveyed the diverse permutations in the long history of American prejudice against Latinos, the Iberian-descended peoples of the Western Hemisphere.[16] He also perceptively grounds disparaging American attitudes toward the Latinos in deep-rooted hostility to the Spanish themselves, which in the form of the "black legend" provided the basis for the original Anglo-American censures of a colonial rival in the sixteenth and seventeenth centuries. In the nineteenth century, champions of America's continental manifest destiny deployed ethnic and increasingly racial stereotypes of Latinos as slothful, incompetent, corrupt, and effeminate to rally support for territorial acquisitions from Florida to the Pacific littoral. At the end of the nineteenth century, the sorry record of Spanish misrule proved a persuasive justification for the Spanish-American war and America's first round of overseas annexations in the Caribbean and the Philippines.[17] But similar stereotypes had long been applied to the French as well.

From the bitter hostility English settlers felt toward the Catholic French to the anomalous position in American society of the French Creoles of Louisiana that persisted well into the twentieth century,[18] the French have been represented in elite discourse and popular American culture as languid, emotional, politically inept, and incurably sentimental. Thus, Roosevelt's

16 Michael Hunt, *Ideology and U.S. Foreign Policy* (New Haven, Conn., 1987), 58–62.
17 For representative assessments of the Spanish as colonizers by American officials at the time of the annexation, see Jacob G. Shurman, *Philippine Affairs* (New York, 1902), 26–7; and Luke Wright, "The Situation in the Philippines," *The Outlook*, Sept. 12, 1903, 114–15.
18 Daniel H. Usner, "Between Creoles and Yankees: The Discursive Representation of Colonial Louisiana in American History," unpublished working paper, Seminar on Comparative History, Cornell University, Feb. 1999.

harsh assessment of the legacy of French colonial rule drew on deeply rooted sentiments and a long history of summary dismissals. The fact that America had to rescue the French in World War I and liberate them in the global conflict that followed only served to fix these representations more firmly in American discourse. There even was an obvious precedent to buttress the American determination to repair the damage done by a century of French colonial rule in Indochina: The French had, after all, failed miserably in their attempts to construct a canal across the isthmus of Panama. The later American success in this Herculean undertaking left little doubt about their superiority to the French in energy, ingenuity, persistence, and organizational acumen – all qualities that Latins in general were seen as lacking. That the French earlier had succeeded in building the Suez Canal did little to moderate American assessments of their ineptitude; rather, they routinely dismissed Suez as a far less challenging enterprise.[19] It is noteworthy in this regard that though the Americans and British continued to quarrel over postwar policy regarding many of the areas that came to be collectively known as the Third World, the British were in most instances left in charge of their own colonial retreat, and the Americans never sought to politically or militarily reoccupy the territories the British turned over to indigenous nationalist leaders.[20]

IV

Like their nineteenth-century European counterparts and earlier American colonizers, the United States' political and military leaders who escalated American involvement in the civil wars of postcolonial Indochina were confident that the organizational and technological advantages they possessed over what were deemed "primitive" Third World adversaries assured eventual victory. Although again and again both the Viet Cong and the North Vietnamese proved more resilient adversaries than expected, American planners refused to even entertain the possibility that a small, poor, underdeveloped society could resist the richest, most technologically advanced, industrial colossus humankind had ever produced. When periodic crises over "the price America was willing to pay" occurred because the insurgents

19 David McCullough, *The Path Between the Seas: The Creation of the Panama Canal, 1870–1914* (New York, 1977), 313–14; and Joseph Bucklin Bishop, *The Panama Gateway* (New York, 1913), esp. chap. 25.
20 As studies such as W. Roger Louis's *Imperialism at Bay: The United States and the Decolonization of the British Empire, 1941–1945* (New York, 1978) amply illustrate, this does not mean that the Americans did not meddle in British colonial affairs or try in often disconcerting ways to shape the contours of their global withdrawal.

refused to yield, the Rostows and McNamaras insisted that ratcheting up the level of the technowar unleashed against the peoples of Indochina would bring victory.[21]

Historically, American colonizers had placed even greater reliance than the Europeans on their assumed technological and organizational superiority, both to crush resistance to their political and military dominance and to provide the impetus for social and economic "development" in areas brought under their sway.[22] The success of the guerrilla warfare mounted by the communist insurgents against the French provided both further evidence of French ineptitude and an additional motive for U.S. intervention. As was the case earlier in Panama, the Americans were confident that their superior technology, engineering skills, and managerial abilities would allow them to succeed where the French had failed. Responding to Johnson's challenge to his fellow Americans to produce both guns and butter, American planners simultaneously plotted the defeat of the Viet Cong and the North Vietnamese, and drew up schemes for massive public works projects, such as a Tennessee Valley Authority–style refashioning of the Mekong Delta.[23]

In a global context rife with peasant uprisings sustained by guerrilla warfare, the defeat of communist-style insurgency in Vietnam proved to be one of the more pressing rationales for escalating intervention. American policy makers insisted that the tactics of counterinsurgency worked out in Vietnam could be applied to suppress guerrilla resistance throughout the Third World.[24] Here again the contrast between American responses to the French and British is instructive. Although some in the U.S. military realized that French officers had useful lessons to share, most dismissed the French approach as a dismal failure that could provide little in the way of guidance for the American effort. But the British defeat of the 1950s communist insurgency in Malaya was seen as a model for antiguerrilla warfare. Excepting rare academic specialists, few policy makers pointed out that Malaya was a very different place from Vietnam.[25]

Nineteenth-century Western colonizers had, of course, to contend with guerrilla warfare. In fact, from Algeria and across central Africa to

---

21 Baritz, *Backfire*, 110, 137, 164; James Gibson, *The Perfect War: Technowar in Vietnam* (Boston, 1986), 98–103.

22 For late-nineteenth-century comparisons, see Michael Adas, "Improving on the Civilising Mission? Assumptions of United States Exceptionalism in the Colonisation of the Philippines," *Itinerario* 22, no. 4 (1998): 44–66.

23 Gardner, *Pay Any Price*, 6, 52–3, 191–7; and Baritz, *Backfire*, 167–8.

24 Gibson, *Perfect War*, 21–2, 78–80; and Michael Klare, *War Without End: American Planning for the Next Vietnams* (New York, 1972).

25 But academics like Michael Osborne argued this in considerable detail in *Strategic Hamlets in Vietnam* (Ithaca, N.Y., 1965).

Afghanistan and Vietnam, guerrilla tactics proved the most effective counter to the repeating rifles and field guns of European and European-trained armies. Resistance leaders such as Abd al-Qadir in Algeria and Mahmadou Lamine and Samori in West Africa, who were quick to recognize the suicidal nature of set-piece battles and direct assaults on European forces, were able to prolong resistance to colonial domination for years, and in some cases decades, through the skillful use of guerrilla tactics.[26] At times stunning victories were won by African and Asian adversaries who led their forces to victory in conventional battles through the use of surprise tactics or simply overwhelming numerical superiority. But peoples who persisted in conventional warfare invariably met with appalling casualties and demoralizing defeats, such as those that marked the suppression of the Maji Maji uprisings in German East Africa, the defeat of the vaunted Zulu *impis* by a small British force at Rorke's Drift, and the annihilation of the Madhist cavalrymen by Kitchener's Maxim guns at Omdurman.[27]

Like those of their European counterparts, the designs of American settler expansionists had been the most effectively and persistently frustrated by indigenous peoples whose modes of warfare incorporated the guerrilla principles of deception, surprise, and hit-and-run assaults. Revealingly, their main foray into overseas colonization in the Philippines had begun with a campaign of repression that was prolonged for years in some areas by the Filipino nationalists' resort to guerrilla warfare.[28]

V

No historical precedents could have prepared the expansionist industrial powers for the more sophisticated brand of guerrilla resistance they increasingly encountered in the mid-twentieth century. Quite consciously responding to the growing organizational and technological gap between dominant industrialized and colonized, nonindustrialized peoples, revolutionary theorists/practitioners, such as Mao Zedong and Vo Nguyen Giap, melded ancient traditions of guerrilla warfare with cadre indoctrination and

---

26 Charles-André Julien, *Histoire de l'Algérie contemporaine, 1827–1871* (Paris, 1964); Olatunji Oloruntimehin, "Senegambia-Mahmadou Lamine," and Yves Person, "Guinea-Samori," both in Michael Crowder, ed., *West African Resistance: The Military Response to Colonial Occupation* (New York, 1971), 80–110, 111–43.

27 Respectively, Gilbert Gwassa, "African Methods of Warfare During the Maji Maji War, 1905–1907," in B. A. Ogot, ed., *War and Society in Africa* (London, 1972), 123–48; Donald R. Morris, *The Washing of the Spears: The Rise and Fall of the Zulu Nation* (New York, 1965), 389–420; and P. M. Holt, *The Mahdist State in the Sudan, 1881–1898* (Oxford, 1970), chap. 12.

28 Stuart Creighton Miller, *Benevolent Assimilation: The American Conquest of the Philippines, 1899–1903* (New Haven, Conn., 1982), chaps. 9–12.

discipline, communist ideological incentives, and a (necessarily) selective application of modern weaponry. This "modernized" version of what was an ancient approach to warfare and violent resistance against stronger adversaries greatly improved the survival potential of peasant recruits, provided a clearly delineated organizational chain of command and ladder of career advancement, and stressed ways of winning support from the great majority of the rural population in contested and base areas. It meshed political objectives, military targets, and programs aimed at social and economic reform. As formulated by Mao and Giap, revolutionary guerrilla warfare was also conceived as a sequence of interlocking stages – strategic defensive, tactical offensive, counteroffensive – that committed successful insurgent forces to an eventual transition to conventional warfare. As the communist victories over the Guomindang in the late 1940s and the Vietnamese humiliation of the French at Dien Bien Phu in 1954 demonstrated, this highly directed and decision-oriented mode of guerrilla strategy made it possible to win total victory over what were deemed more powerful adversaries and to seize political power in the name of the revolutionary cause.[29]

As had long been the case with sustained resistance to European colonial expansion, the new style of guerrilla warfare mounted by communist nationalists in China and Vietnam made it possible to mobilize substantial insurgent forces for protracted conflict with adversaries who were reliant on industrial technology. When directed against village populations that supported guerrilla forces or struggled to remain neutral, the campaigns of suppression launched by Western colonizers and indigenous regimes backed by them, served to alienate peasants and urban workers and increase support for the insurgents. The technowar the United States waged in sharply escalating increments against the peoples of Indochina proved highly counterproductive in this regard – paradoxically increasingly so as more sophisticated weapons and ever greater amounts of ordinance were employed.

The American reliance on high-tech responses to counter the guerrilla tactics of the Viet Cong and their North Vietnamese backers meant that the casualties inflicted on the civilian population vastly exceeded those in any of the wars of resistance to colonization fought in the nineteenth or early twentieth centuries. The difficulty in telling friendly from hostile peasants had long been one of the key principles of successful guerrilla mobilization. The casualties that resulted were magnified many times by the Americans' impersonal, distanced, and massive application of bombing, strafing, and chemical

---

29 Mao Zedong, *Selected Military Writings, 1928–1949* (Beijing, 1963); Vo Nguyen Giap, *People's War, People's Army* (New York, 1962); and George K. Tanham, *Communist Revolutionary Warfare: From the Vietminh to the Viet Cong* (New York, 1967).

saturation against elusive guerrilla forces. But perhaps even more devastating were the losses inflicted on villagers deemed friendly to the enemy and, as often, those who simply had the misfortune to be in the way. The tech-nowar was also increasingly directed against the physical environment in large swaths of rural Indochina.[30]

The overkill and appalling level of civilian casualties that almost invari-ably resulted from the routinized high-tech responses of the American and South Vietnamese military undermined the already constricted base of the client regimes in the South and pushed the bulk of the peasantry to support the North Vietnamese–backed guerrilla insurgency, which offered them at the very least a fighting chance for survival. The increasing and eventually overwhelming American determination to pursue the technowar also meant that the ambitious development agenda for South Vietnam, which Johnson and his advisers in particular had advanced at least rhetorically, was neglected and deprived of essential resources from the outset. From grandiose visions of the transformation of the Mekong Delta, the development components of the anticommunist crusade devolved rather rapidly into poorly funded schemes for village schools and community centers, and, even more reveal-ingly, "strategic hamlet"–oriented programs that were more about denying communist guerrillas access to the rural population than raising standards of living.[31]

VI

Beyond a determined and skillful application of a style of guerrilla warfare adapted to the industrial age, communist insurgents in post–World War II Vietnam enjoyed a number of marked advantages over their counterparts in resistance to colonialism in the late nineteenth and early twentieth centuries. Although routinely labeled communist by the Americans to obfuscate its nationalist credentials, the Viet Minh–led Vietnamese insurgency had, over the course of the middle decades of the twentieth century, established itself as the single most viable movement for decolonization and the establishment of an independent nation. Despite numerous false starts and outright disas-ters, most notably the peasant uprisings in Nghe-An and Ha-Tinh in 1930, the communist leadership had survived while rival movements, such as the

---

30 Gibson, *Perfect War*, esp. chaps. 5, 8, 15; John Lewallen, *Ecology of Devastation: Indochina* (Baltimore, 1971); and Jeffrey Race, *War Comes to Long An* (Berkeley, Calif., 1972).

31 On the increasing neglect of the development side of the American intervention, see Robert L. Sansom, *The Economics of Insurgency in the Mekong Delta of Vietnam* (Cambridge, Mass., 1970); and Neill Sheehan, *A Bright Shining Lie: John Paul Vann and America in Vietnam* (New York, 1988), book 6.

Vietnamese Nationalist Party (Viet Nam Quoc Dan Dong or VNQDD), were co-opted or brutally suppressed by the French regime. As the main impetus for ever-expanding resistance to both the French and Japanese colonizers during the early 1940s, the Viet Minh strengthened its nationalist credentials vis-à-vis its rivals by both its modest successes in the anticolonial struggle and the programs it developed for the uplift of the hard-pressed Vietnamese peasantry. By the late 1940s, when resistance to French reoccupation grew into a full-fledged war of independence, the Viet Minh had seized the mantle of national leadership. Their leader, Ho Chi Minh, proclaimed the independent Republic of Vietnam in October 1945; they set to work establishing a government over the territories they controlled in northern and central Vietnam; and they began to receive international support for their struggles to build a new nation in an age when the colonial powers were in full retreat in South and Southeast Asia.[32]

With the possible exception of the Koreans, the Vietnamese were the only people formally colonized in the industrial age who possessed a strong sense of ethnic and cultural identity and who historically aspired to an ideal of political unity. But from the mid-nineteenth century onward, an alienated peasantry and divided elite largely canceled out any advantages they might have derived from what in effect was a preexisting sense of nationalism in their long struggles to check the advance of French colonial rule. Ironically, by discrediting the imperial dynasty and the Chinese-derived system of absolutist rule that had held sway in Vietnam for millennia, the French conquest helped to open the way for a Marxist-inspired movement to emerge as the most compelling proponent of the Vietnamese national cause. The puppet status to which the Nguyen emperors had been reduced in the last half of the nineteenth century rendered futile French efforts to legitimize their rule through association with the dynasty. Thus, the surrogate option that virtually all the industrial colonizers had exercised from West Africa to Cambodia had never been very persuasive in Vietnam. After the upheavals of two world wars and a global depression, French and later (and more tentative) American attempts to gain legitimacy by backing the surviving Nguyen emperor, Bao Dai, stood little chance of success. A heightened sense of national identity and the increasing mobilization of the Vietnamese peasantry and workers in the struggles for decolonization meant that it no longer was possible for foreign colonizers to exploit dynastic squabbles as their entrée for conquest and to buttress their control by toppling recalcitrant princes in favor of more pliable ones.

32 Huýnh Kim Khánh, *Vietnamese Communism, 1925–1945* (Ithaca, N.Y., 1982).

VII

Despite all the lessons U.S. policy makers might have learned from earlier forays into overseas colonization, and particularly the experience of the French in Vietnam, successive decisions to escalate America's participation in the Indochina wars were made with little knowledge of or even concern to master the history of the peoples and societies of the region. As a consequence, little notice was taken of the long Vietnamese tradition of fierce resistance to domination by outsiders. Of special relevance to the managers of America's technowar was the David and Goliath mindset with which the Vietnamese had for millennia approached foreign invaders as a result of their long struggle to retain their independence from the Chinese colossus to the north. The fact that the Vietnamese had long employed pre-Maoist guerrilla tactics against the more powerful military forces of Chinese or Mongol invaders was also of obvious importance to American planners.[33] But beyond a handful of academic specialists and journalists, many of whom at this point were French, these vital aspects of Vietnamese history were virtually ignored. And despite Roosevelt's wartime antipathy toward the old European empires, post-1945 American planners and statesmen were for the most part oblivious to the sorry history of Indochina in the French colonial period. A consequence of their oversight was the fact that they never seriously addressed the extent to which the American recolonization of Vietnam transferred to the United States the hostility and implacable spirit of resistance that decades of exploitation and repression by the French had aroused in the great majority of the Vietnamese people.

The historical perspectives that informed American decision making were those of the then trendy modernization theorists – most prominently Walt W. Rostow – who lumped the Third World together in constructing highly abstract and generalized propositions about non-Western, underdeveloped, undemocratic, peasant-based societies.[34] As had been the case earlier in the Philippines and the Caribbean,[35] development theory had much more to do with the American experience than the history and culture of the peoples the United States had colonized. In any case,

33 Le Thanh Khoi, *Le Viet-Nam: Histoire et civilisation* (Paris, 1955), 92–134, 180–9; and Truong Buu Lam, *Patterns of Vietnamese Response to Foreign Intervention, 1858–1900* (New Haven, Conn., 1967).
34 The most perceptive critique of modernization ideology remains Dean Tipps, "Modernization Theory and the Comparative Study of Societies: A Critical Perspective," *Comparative Studies in Society and History* 15, no. 2 (1973). For a provocative exploration of the impact of 1960s development presuppositions in Vietnam, see D. Michael Shafer, *Deadly Paradigms: The Failure of U.S. Counterinsurgency Policy* (Princeton, N.J., 1988), chap. 9.
35 Glenn May, *Social Engineering in the Philippines* (Westport, Conn., 1980); and Hans Schmidt, *The United States Occupation of Haiti, 1915–1934* (New Brunswick, N.J., 1995).

U.S. policy was premised on the assumption that the sooner the "natives" were Americanized, the better off they would be. Because communism was assumed to be antithetical to the American way, its resonance in Vietnamese society was ignored, and the claims of the Viet Minh or the leaders of North Vietnam to nationalist legitimacy were rejected out of hand. Despite highly publicized rhetoric about the importance of the conflict in Indochina as a school for counterinsurgency, U.S. military responses to Vietnamese (or Laotian) guerrilla resistance were overwhelmingly of the high-tech, maximum-scale sort that had long been hallmarks of the American way of waging war.

VIII

We may never know the full cost in terms of human casualties and environmental degradation of the decades-long Indochinese wars against Western colonialism. But the tens of millions of people maimed and killed, thousands of neighborhoods and villages destroyed, and hundreds of thousands of acres defoliated or cratered in the Indochina conflicts alone call into question John Gaddis's characterization of the post-1945 decades as the era of "the Long Peace."[36] His analysis of the structural factors that obviated direct conflict between the superpowers in the era of the Cold War is perceptive and cogent. But it marginalizes the numerous and often bloody interventions by the industrial powers and the fifty-five to sixty (depending on who is counting and how) major wars that have raged since 1945 in the Orwellian zone collectively known as the Third World. Although Gaddis notes in passing the endemic violence and persistent warfare of the Cold War decades, his equation of peace with the absence of nuclear war is superpower-centric in the extreme. It not only glosses over the very substantial psychic price and the massive economic and environmental costs of the nuclear standoff, it also obfuscates the horrors inflicted by protracted conflicts on a clear majority of the Earth's peoples in the post-1945 period. Some of these wars were in part at least proxy wars of the superpowers. But many others – perhaps a majority – were precipitated and sustained primarily by global processes, such as decolonization and ethnic and cultural rivalries, that were every bit as much hallmarks of the age as the clash of the superpowers.

More than anything else, Gaddis's vision of the "Long Peace" calls to mind the myth of the "Little England" era that British historians John Gallagher

36 John Lewis Gaddis, "The Long Peace: Elements of Stability in the Postwar International System," *International Security* 10 (1986): 99–142.

and Ronald Robinson so thoroughly debunked decades ago.[37] As in the mid-nineteenth century, great-power meddling has touched off or magnified a sizable portion of the wars that have devastated nonindustrial nations. The gunboat diplomacy of the "age of high imperialism" has been superseded by the vastly more lethal, and impersonal, B-52 retaliations of the Cold War era and, more recently, by the cruise missile retribution unleashed by the Bush and Clinton administrations, presumably as portents of the "new world order." Formal colonization has inevitably dwindled in an era of deliberate, internationally sanctioned decolonization. But as the Russian invasion of Afghanistan in the 1980s and the American occupation of Vietnam in the 1960s emphatically demonstrate, the temporal boundaries of the end of the age of imperialism have been as blurred and porous as those of its onset.

---

37 John Gallagher and Ronald Robinson, "The Imperialism of Free Trade," *Economic History Review*, 2d ser., 4, no. 1 (1953): 1–15.

2

Visions of the Asian Periphery

Vietnam (1964–1968) and the Philippines (1898–1900)

FABIAN HILFRICH

"I once drew a map for Dean Rusk and said, 'This is your map of the world.' I had a tiny United States with an enormous Vietnam lying right off our coast." With this ironic image, George Ball, in-house critic of the Johnson administration, described the enormous importance with which his government had endowed the peripheral Asian nation.[1] For the most part, this skewed vision, verging on obsession, has been analyzed in the context of Cold War bipolarity. Because a direct confrontation between the central powers – the United States and the Soviet Union – no longer was an option in the nuclear age, it was transferred to the periphery in wars between client states or in limited wars in which one or both superpowers more or less directly intervened. The periphery thus did not matter so much in its own right as in relation to the power struggle at the center.

A diachronic approach to American foreign policy, juxtaposing the discursive construction of the Asian periphery in the Vietnam War with that in the conflict over Philippine annexation following the Spanish–American War, reveals that such a symbolic sublimation of the periphery's importance has been a perennial feature in American worldviews and that it therefore was conditioned not solely by the particular constellation of the Cold War. In both cases, the interventionist discourse on the periphery was guided by two rhetorical strategies that may at first seem contradictory but that were actually mutually supportive. First, the importance of the Philippines and Vietnam was vastly exaggerated; second, racist or cultural stereotypes fixed the periphery in a hierarchical relationship to the center. On closer inspection, however, the elevation of Asian countries to a place of importance was denigrating in itself because their value was deduced from extrinsic rather

---

1 George W. Ball, Oral History (hereafter OH), Lyndon Baines Johnson Presidential Library, Austin, Tex. (hereafter LBJL).

than intrinsic factors. In other words, the Philippines and Vietnam emerged as crucial symbols in a larger American worldview and understanding of global power politics.

Although we may explain this phenomenon with the aid of Philip Darby's typology of imperial worldviews – that is, each center's view of the periphery – American views were also anchored in something innately American, namely, the idea of exceptionalism.[2] This conviction of uniqueness as a result of the country's democratic founding entailed a universal democratic mission, be it by force or passive example, that, on a discursive level, did not discriminate between regions or countries. In a redemptive vision, the world was America's concern, whereas particular American experiences as well as American concepts of society and world order were assumed to be applicable to and naturally shared by the rest of the world. In this respect, the periphery figured mainly as the proving ground for American ideas and ideals. Concepts such as the domino theory and the discourse on Western civilization, which have been singled out for the purpose of this study, reified and simplified these ideas, which helps to explain why the periphery was so vital to the victory of American ideals and even to national security. By the same token, the advocates of intervention in both the Philippines and Vietnam employed rationalizations that internalized the external struggles on the periphery, turning them into American morality plays or demonstrations of willpower and stamina. In both instances, then, the concept of America, and not only the power struggle between the central states, was the referent for comprehending events on the periphery.

This fundamental similarity of perspectives on the periphery should not be understood to imply that there were no crucial differences between the 1890s and the 1960s, or that this was the only determining feature of the debates on imperialism and on the Vietnam War. The discursive construction of the periphery remained largely constant, however, and this constancy was largely conditioned by the continuity of certain elements of the American worldview. Concentrating on discourse, moreover, is not inconsequential to an analysis of history and politics. Discourses are not "mere rhetoric" but rather are symbolic patterns that reflect and *form* societal ideals and views of the international environment. That they can also have

---

2 Philip Darby compares nineteenth-century British imperialism and American policies during the Cold War in *Three Faces of Imperialism: British and American Approaches to Asia and Africa, 1870–1970* (New Haven, Conn., 1987).

a bearing on policy making itself was perfectly illustrated by the rhetoric of credibility and commitment in the 1960s.[3]

I

Within this broad sweep, Asia occupied a prominent place. Having built the New World in opposition to the Old, Americans had long believed that their future lay in the west, a conviction strongly supported by the ancient idea of a *translatio imperii*, the westward course of empires. In this narrative, Asia was the cradle of civilization, passing the torch to successive empires further west until finally the imperial (although not necessarily imperialist) role fell to the United States. America's special destiny thus was not only religiously or democratically sanctioned but also historically and geographically justified.[4] In the 1890s, this notion was strongly supported by the closing of the frontier, the official completion of America's continental westward movement, which prompted many imperialists to demand a "natural" continuation even farther west. With the opportunities offered in the Pacific and in Asia, imperialists argued, the United States had the unique opportunity to complete the circle and bring about a global millennium. "Westward the Star of Empire takes its way," was Senator Albert J. Beveridge's rousing call, whereas Ernest Fenollosa believed that Americans were completing Columbus's dream "and carry[ing] the Aryan banner of his caravels where he aimed to plant it – on the heights of an awakened East."[5] Such redemptionist triumphalism was more muted in the 1960s, but many observers still believed in a special relationship between the United States and Asia. In an editorial half-jokingly entitled "Westward,

---

3 On discourse, Gail Bederman has noted that it "does not differentiate between intellectual ideas and material practice." This definition is not intended to flatten all differences between reality and language, but it establishes the crucial importance of rhetoric in the construction of reality, an importance which historians not usually associated with postmodernism have also recognized. Gail Bederman, *Manliness & Civilization: A Cultural History of Gender and Race in the United States, 1880–1917* (Chicago, 1995), 24. Frank Ninkovich, "No Post-Mortems for Postmodernism, Please," *Diplomatic History* 22 (summer 1998): 451–66, demonstrates the value of discourse analysis for international relations, but is also sensibly cautious in too general an application. Michael H. Hunt has also emphasized that rhetoric is crucial rather than "empty" because it has to reflect societal values and patterns in order to be successful and sustainable; *Ideology and U.S. Foreign Policy* (New Haven, Conn., 1987), 15–16. For Michel Foucault's definition of discourse, see his more easily accessible *Power/Knowledge: Selected Interviews & Other Writings, 1972–1977*, ed. Colin Gordon (New York, 1980).

4 For the concept of a *translatio imperii*, see Ernest Lee Tuveson, *Redeemer Nation: The Idea of America's Millennial Role* (Chicago, 1968), 91–7.

5 Beveridge, "The Star of Empire," in Beveridge, *The Meaning of the Times and Other Speeches* (Indianapolis, 1908), 143; Ernest F. Fenollosa, "The Coming Fusion of East and West," *Harper's Monthly Magazine* 98 (December 1898): 122. On the frontier and its connection to imperialism, compare David M. Wrobel, *The End of American Exceptionalism: Frontier Anxiety from the Old West to the New Deal* (Lawrence, Kans., 1993), chap. 5.

Ho," the *National Review* congratulated President Lyndon B. Johnson on traveling to Asia before going to Europe because the editor considered Asia more important to the United States than the Old World.[6]

In both the 1890s and the 1960s, moreover, China figured prominently in American thinking about the Asian periphery. The sheer size of its population either fascinated or terrified American policy makers and the public. In the 1890s, fascination was embodied in the myth of the China market, which envisioned the country's countless millions as potential customers for American goods. Seventy years later, after China had "gone communist," however, and particularly after the experiences in the Korean War, the large Chinese population was a cause for concern. Many Americans feared that, in a possible confrontation, the Chinese would be willing to sacrifice millions of their own, employing "the human wave strategy – the triumph of numbers over our technologically advanced tools of defense."[7]

II

Although these notions served to set the Asian periphery apart from, say, the African, most rhetorical strategies that interventionists used to dramatize the importance of this periphery extended beyond the regional to the global level. I have chosen to examine the domino theory and the discourse on civilization because they were central to both debates and because they contained assumptions and experiences that facilitate a comparison between the imperialist period and the Vietnam War.

The domino theory was given a name in the 1950s, but the ideas that went into it were by no means new nor particularly American. Worrying about the loss of his American colonies in the late eighteenth century, for example, King George III had warned that "[s]hould America succeed, the West Indies must follow them... Ireland would soon follow... then this Island [Great Britain] would be reduced to itself and soon would be a poor

---

6 *National Review* 18 (Nov. 1, 1966): 1083–4.
7 Anthony Harrigan, "Our War with Red China," *National Review* 18 (Mar. 8, 1966): 204–6. President Johnson (hereafter LBJ) uttered this fear in his election campaign in 1964 when he still insisted on never sending American troops to Asia; "Remarks in Manchester," Sept. 28, 1964, in *Public Papers of the Presidents of the United States – Lyndon Baines Johnson, 1963–64* (Washington, D.C., 1965), 2: 1160–8 (hereafter *PPP*). On a presumed Asian indifference toward human lives, see John Roche, "Containing China," *Commentary* 41 (May 1966): 26; William Bundy, "Asian Reaction to a Major US Force Increase," first draft, Mar. 1, 1968, box 48, National Security Council History (hereafter NSCH), National Security File (hereafter NSF), LBJL. More generally, on images of China in the 1960s, see F. M. Kail, *What Washington Said: Administration Rhetoric and the Vietnam War, 1949–1969* (New York, 1973), 30.

Island indeed."[8] President Harry S. Truman employed similar apocalyptic shibboleths in his advocacy of American assistance to Greece and Turkey in the late 1940s, but President Dwight D. Eisenhower was the first to relate it to Vietnam. In essence, the domino theory served as a rhetorical "condensation symbol," an abstraction that reduced complex events and eventualities to an easily accessible game metaphor. It represented an interconnected international system in which the loss of a peripheral area could be seen as a threat to the national security of the United States.[9]

As James Burnham explained in the 1960s, the consequence of South Vietnam's fall "would be the loss of all bases and friendly ports in the western Pacific and South Seas, and the foldback of our basic line of defense to our own Pacific coast."[10] Although this simplistic idea fell into increasing disrepute, the Johnson administration continued to affirm its contents even if it rejected the precise term. Thus, in 1967 Johnson focused on the word "theory" and added that "the threat of Communist domination is not a matter of theory for Asians. Communist domination for Asians is a matter of life and death."[11] Concentrating instead on the game aspect, Secretary of State Rusk emphasized that "these matters are not games played with little wooden blocks with dots on them." The essence of the metaphor, he asserted, was still valid because it was borne out by the fact of "communist aggression" throughout Southeast Asia.[12]

"Domino thinking" – if not in name, then in substance – was also invoked by the imperialists at the turn of the century, with the significant difference that the United States did not yet hold any "game pieces" in Asia. Focusing on unclaimed or recently deserted "dominoes," most notably Hawaii and the

---

8 King George III, quoted in Estelle and Saul Gilson, "A Curiosity of History," *American Scholar* 40 (spring 1971): 270.

9 J. Justin Gustainis, *American Rhetoric and the Vietnam War* (Westport, Conn., 1993), 5. For Eisenhower's original conception, see "Dwight D. Eisenhower Explains the 'Domino Theory,' 1954," in Thomas G. Paterson, ed., *Major Problems in American Foreign Policy: Documents and Essays*, 2 vols., 2d ed. (Lexington, Mass., 1984), 478–9.

10 Burnham, "The Weakest Front," *National Review* 17 (June 15, 1965): 499.

11 LBJ, "Remarks to the Foreign Policy Conference for Business Executives," Dec. 4, 1967, in *PPP – 1967*, 2: 1096. Among those who have pointed out the less frequent use of the simplistic domino theory are Frank Ninkovich, *Modernity and Power: A History of the Domino Theory in the Twentieth Century* (Chicago, 1994), 303; Darby, *Three Faces of Imperialism*, 165.

12 Dean Rusk, "American Purposes and the Pursuit of Human Dignity," Address before the American Legion National Convention, Boston, Aug. 29, 1967, *Department of State Bulletin* 57 (Sept. 18, 1967): 347. As Stein Tonneson has recently shown, America's communist adversaries were equally certain about the essential validity of the theory, although Tonneson insists that this does not necessarily mean that the domino theory was indeed an adequate representation of reality; "Tracking Multi-Directional Dominoes," in Odd Arne Westad et al., *77 Conversations between Chinese and Foreign Leaders on the Wars in Indochina, 1964–1977*, Cold War International History Project, Working Paper no. 22 (Washington, D.C., 1998), 34–45.

Philippines, imperialists asserted that other powers would immediately seize these territories should America fail to claim them. Japan was considered the most likely competitor in Hawaii, and Germany emerged as the potential opponent in the Philippines not only because it had already clashed with the United States over Samoa but also because its naval squadron was sailing off the Manila coastline during the Spanish-American War. John Hay, who later became secretary of state, wrote to Senator Henry Cabot Lodge: "*Voila l'ennemi* in the present crisis. The jealousy and animosity felt toward us in Germany is something which can hardly be exaggerated.... They want the Philippines, the Carolines, and Samoa – they want to get into our markets and keep us out of theirs."[13] Given their perception of having competitors in the Pacific realm, the imperialists described the consequences of their nation's hesitation with regard to annexation in terms similar to those of 1960s interventionists. Arguing for the annexation of Hawaii, Senator George F. Hoar, otherwise a staunch anti-imperialist, warned that if the islands were annexed "by any powerful foreign government [there] will be a great military and naval danger to our western coast."[14] Once again, then, peripheral territories emerged as pawns in a great power game, and their "loss" was viewed as a potential danger to the United States.

Nevertheless, this invocation of an eventual threat to American national security did not play the decisive part in the controversy over expansion. To the extent that the domino theory was influential in the debate, it was a reverse or positive reading that came to influence the arguments of annexationists. Much more than their ideological descendants did in the 1960s, turn-of-the-century imperialists argued with promises of a bountiful future rather than with warnings of imminent disaster. As in the Vietnam debate, however, it was the extrinsic, not the intrinsic worth of territories like Hawaii or the Philippines that came to dominate arguments for their acquisition. In essence, these islands were described as "stepping-stones" on the way to the fabled China market, as strategic coaling stations and bulwarks that would facilitate the promotion of U.S. commercial interests in Asia.[15]

13 See, for example, Hay to Lodge, July 27, 1898; Lodge to Hay, Aug. 17, 1898, box 13, General Correspondence, Lodge papers, Massachusetts Historical Society, Boston (hereafter MHS). In his letter, Lodge concurred that "Germany is the hostile spot and we must keep a look-out on William the Wild."

14 Hoar in *Congressional Record*, 55th Cong., 2nd sess., 1898: 6662; Albert Shaw in *Review of Reviews* 18 (Aug. 1898): 126. For these strategic threats perceived by annexationists since 1893, see Thomas J. Osborne, *"Empire Can Wait": American Opposition to Hawaiian Annexation, 1893–1898* (Kent, Ohio, 1981), 40–4.

15 The concept of the "stepping-stone" has been developed in Thomas McCormick, "Insular Imperialism and the Open Door: The China Market and the Spanish-American War," *Pacific Historical Review* 32 (May 1963): 155–70. The second quotation is from Albert Jeremiah Beveridge, *Congressional*

This strategy had been formulated prior to the Spanish-American War, most notably by Alfred Thayer Mahan. In fact, his preference for strategic bases over formal colonies was so strong that, in 1898, he initially exhibited great skepticism toward the proposal to annex the entire Philippine archipelago.[16] However, most imperialists found no difficulty in using Mahan's originally limited reasoning to advocate the annexation of entire countries. In this vein, Senator Lodge emphatically proclaimed the Philippines "the great strategic and commercial point of the East. We hold one side of the Pacific and with Manila we have our foothold on the other."[17] Moreover, the archipelago was described as the "key to the whole eastern situation," the vantage point from which to access "China's illimitable markets."[18]

Events seemed to confirm the imperialists' theoretical reasoning. The military campaign against Spain in the Philippines had proved the strategic value of Hawaii as a supply station en route to Asia. Hawaiian annexation thus emerged as a "military necessity," and some who had previously been opposed to its annexation were now convinced that "we *must* have Hawaii because we must have Manila," thereby reversing the order of the dominoes in the Pacific.[19] Whereas events in the Philippines aided the case for the acquisition of Hawaii, subsequent events in China seemed to underscore the strategic importance of the Philippines. The other great powers' positive response to John Hay's "Open Door" notes in relation to China was frequently attributed to the fact that America could back up its demands with the tangible power at its disposal in the Philippines.[20] More importantly, the dispatch of American troops from the archipelago to participate in the quelling of the Boxer uprising "serve[d] to prove how useful the

Record, 56th Cong., 1st sess., 1900: 704. For background on the China market, see Marilyn Blatt Young, *The Rhetoric of Empire: American China Policy, 1895–1901* (Cambridge, Mass., 1968).

16 On Mahan's ideas and their influence on contemporaries, see Walter LaFeber, *The New Empire: An Interpretation of American Expansion, 1860–1898* (Ithaca, N.Y., 1963), 80–95.

17 Lodge to George Lyman, May 4, 1898, box 37, bound volumes, Lodge papers, MHS.

18 Spencer Borden to President McKinley, June 10, 1898, reel 3, series 1, William McKinley papers (microfilm ed.), Manuscript Division, Library of Congress, Washington, D.C. (hereafter LC); Albert Jeremiah Beveridge in *Congressional Record*, 56th Cong., 1st sess., 1900: 704, where the speaker also provided detailed descriptions of commercial possibilities in the Philippines. As a note of caution, however, it must be added that commercial and strategic arguments did not occupy the most important place in imperialist oratory, because the anti-imperialist opponents frequently charged that annexationists were only motivated by the sordid desire for pecuniary gain. In most imperialist texts, therefore, the promise of such gain was muted.

19 George H. Lyman to Lodge, Mar. 26, 1898, box 12, General Correspondence, Lodge papers, MHS. Compare also Representative Freeman Knowles in *Congressional Record*, 55th Cong., 2nd sess., 1898: 5989–91. On Hawaiian annexation as a "military necessity," see Lodge to Anna Cabot Lodge, May 29, 1898, box 103, Family Correspondence, Lodge papers, MHS.

20 For the open door notes, see Hay to White; Hay to Choate, Sept. 6, 1899, U.S. Department of State, ed., *Foreign Relations of the United States* (hereafter *FRUS*), *1899*, 129–33; Hay to Herdliska, July 3, 1900, *FRUS, 1900*, 299.

Philippines are likely to be to us in the event of any future difficulties with China and how useful they are now."[21] Thus, imperialists proceeded with perfect, domino-like, step-by-step reasoning, arguing that the annexation of the Philippines required that of Hawaii, and that the mythical China market could only be exploited from a local base like the Philippines. With this domino theory in reverse, imperialists confirmed their domestic opponents' worst fear, namely, that one territorial acquisition would lead to another, that "the appetite will grow with the eating."[22]

In their supreme confidence that Hawaii and the Philippines would open the markets of Asia, imperialists were as optimistic about what these additions would bring as 1960s interventionists were gloomy about the possible consequences of the loss of South Vietnam. Notwithstanding the fact that other powers held exclusive spheres of influence in China, American imperialists asserted that simply by occupying outposts on the Asian periphery the United States would soon assume the "command of the East" or even become the "first power" in the Pacific. Senator Beveridge, undoubtedly the fiercest imperialist, made an even bolder prediction for the future: "The power that rules the Pacific . . . is the power that rules the world. And, with the Philippines, that power is and will forever be the American Republic."[23] To Beveridge, holding the Philippines thus was not only the "key" to Asia but also to world domination. Just as in the Cold War version of the domino theory, the periphery was described as the key to the center. Once again, however, the periphery's value was deduced from extrinsic rather than intrinsic factors.

In sum, around 1900 the United States began to put up some of the domino pieces that new enemies would try to topple after World War II. This is not to say that the 1960s did not witness its own positive version of the domino theory. Roughly coinciding with Walt Rostow's appointment to the post of national security adviser in mid-1966, the Johnson administration began to emphasize that American involvement in Vietnam – more than merely protecting that country – provided "the dam behind which a dramatic turn for the better is taking place in Asia and the world." In the wake of the Manila Conference of October 1966, this approach was publicly introduced as "regionalism." It emphasized the progress toward

---

21 White to Lodge, June 25, 1900, box 16; also Lodge to Hay, June 23, 1900, box 15, General Correspondence, Lodge papers, MHS. Similarly Mahan, "Effects of Asiatic Conditions upon International Policies," *North American Review* 171 (Nov. 1900): 609–28.
22 Carl Schurz, "Manifest Destiny," *Harper's Monthly Magazine* 87 (Oct. 1893): 739.
23 General Lawton to Theodore Roosevelt, Aug. 28, 1899, reel 3, series 1, Theodore Roosevelt papers (microfilm ed.), LC; John Barrett, "America in the Pacific and Far East," *Harper's Monthly* 99 (Nov. 1899): 926; Beveridge in *Congressional Record*, 56th Cong., 1st sess., 1900: 704.

regional modernization and cooperation, as well as the increasing ability of Asian countries to stand on their own without excessive U.S. aid.[24] As a rhetorical device in the inner-American debate on the war, this new theme had several tangible benefits. First, it substituted for the lack of concrete progress in the Vietnamese theater of war. Second, regionalism served as an answer to those critics who charged the administration with indiscriminate globalism and overcommitment. As American aid and protection progressively strengthened its regional allies, so the reasoning went, the latter would be able to assume more responsibility for their own defense, thus relieving the United States of its solitary duty to defend freedom. Regionalism, in Rostow's words, thus emerged as a convenient "middle way" between "overcommitment and isolation."[25] For our purposes it is important to observe that "regionalism" added a positive spin to the otherwise fatalistic domino theory: America was not only engaged in Vietnam to prevent the fall of that domino but also to strengthen the adjacent game pieces. Because few dominoes toppled after the fall of South Vietnam, regionalism even allowed defenders of the war effort to claim victory retrospectively. In their eyes, the United States had been successful in its "effort to hold and organize Southeast Asia, which the contentious war was ultimately about."[26] One has, of course, to believe in the validity of the domino theory in the first place to make such an assertion.

Regionalism seemed to create an autonomous place for the periphery because it envisioned the periphery's eventual capacity to defend itself against outside threats. Nor can it be denied that some regional powers did have a genuine interest in the American defense of Vietnam. From the American point of view, however, regionalism implied an a priori congruity of interest that closely circumscribed the autonomy of regional powers. Significantly, the theme was introduced at a time of intense criticism in the United States

24 Walt W. Rostow, Memorandum to Bill Moyers et al., June 27, 1966, box 8, Memos to the President, NSF, LBJL. Significantly, Rostow noted that his staff did not share his optimism at the time. For the president's recollections of the beginnings of "regionalism," see LBJ, *The Vantage Point: Perspectives of the Presidency, 1963–1969* (New York, 1971), 357–9. This theme was most prominently reiterated during the president's speeches on his trip to and from Manila; Department of State, ed., *The Promise of the New Asia: United States Policy in the Far East as Stated by President Johnson on his Pacific Journey* (Washington, D.C., 1966). For this positive twist on the domino theory see also F. M. Kail, *What Washington Said*, 91.

25 Rostow, OH, LBJL. This approach of course re-emerged in Nixon's slogan of "Vietnamization."

26 Rostow, comment on his book *The Diffusion of Power: An Essay in Recent History, 1957–1972* (New York, 1972), personal communication to the author. Apart from the fact that one has to believe in the validity of the domino theory to make the assertion that America's endeavor in Vietnam prevented the fall of further game pieces, this version of success also omits the long-stated goal of guaranteeing the independence of South Vietnam itself. Furthermore, for the conclusion that subsequent events in Southeast Asia actually disproved the domino theory, compare George C. Herring, *America's Longest War: The United States and Vietnam, 1950–1975*, 2d. ed. (New York, 1986), 269–70.

about the lack of substantive allied contributions to the war, and as such, regionalism was very much designed for public consumption to dispel the notion that other regional powers – the dominoes – did not feel the threat articulated by the American government. As the war progressed, however, it became obvious to many "that the other troop-contributing countries no longer shared our degree of concern about the war in South Viet Nam," and it was this development that finally moved some decision makers to curtail the U.S. effort there.[27]

III

The notion that America was providing a buffer for the Southeast Asian periphery by its intervention in Vietnam underlined the symbolic character of its investment and introduced what George Ball poignantly referred to as the "psychological domino theory."[28] In this interventionist narrative, neatly summarized as "commitment" and "credibility," the United States sent troops to South Vietnam to honor the security guarantees that successive administrations had promised. Standing by these guarantees, the interventionists continued, was an important signal to allies worldwide that the United States would not abandon them in the face of communist aggression. A withdrawal, by the same token, would spell incalculable global disaster because, as President Johnson insisted, "no nation can ever again have the same confidence in American promises, or in American protection."[29] Combining the predictions of the mechanistic domino theory with those of the "psychological" one, Secretary Rusk spelled out the importance of remaining in Vietnam: "Not only would SEA [Southeast Asia] be overrun, but the fidelity of the United States under its security treaties all over the world would be brought into question.... The credibility of the President of the United States at a moment of crisis and the fidelity of the United States to its security treaties are both of the utmost importance in maintaining the peace of the world."[30] In short, an American withdrawal from Vietnam would not only result in the loss of the Southeast Asian periphery but also in a loss of confidence in American security guarantees on the part

---

27 This was how Clark Clifford, describing his observations on a mid-1967 trip to Asia, justified his reappraisal and his subsequent decision to wind down the war; "A Viet Nam Reappraisal: The Personal History of One Man's View and How It Evolved," *Foreign Affairs* 47 (July 1969): 606–8. Compare also Herring, *America's Longest War*, 195–9. For the noticeable and contradictory increase in official U.S. claims of regional support in 1967, see Kail, *What Washington Said*, 93.

28 Ball, *The Past Has Another Pattern* (New York, 1982), 386–7.

29 LBJ, "The President's News Conference of July 28, 1965," *PPP – 1965*, 2: 794.

30 Rusk, OH, LBJL.

of U.S. allies. Such a loss of trust would supposedly make the allies more "accommodationist" and less willing to stand up to communist threats. In 1965, for example, National Security Adviser McGeorge Bundy believed such a development to be one of the main problems in South Vietnam. He insisted that the South Vietnamese elites "feel that we are unwilling to take serious risks." Insecure about its future, the allied government thus was not proceeding as forcefully against the communists as was desired. Bundy therefore recommended an increased American military commitment.[31]

As much as America's allies would be disheartened by a U.S. withdrawal from Vietnam, moreover, the administration warned that the nation's enemies would be emboldened. Thus, President Johnson told the congressional leadership after the Gulf of Tonkin incident: "We can tuck our tails and run, but if we do these countries will feel all they have to do to scare us is to shoot the American flag." Beyond the regional enemy's perceptions, the American obsession with being considered a "paper tiger" extended to the entire communist camp. As Richard Nixon explained: "A Communist victory in Vietnam would be the green light for Communist instigation and support of Vietnam-type 'wars of national liberation' all over the world."[32] This interpretation was based on the interventionist assertion that Vietnam was not a civil war but a "war of national liberation" instigated and supported by the great communist powers in an effort to subvert unstable peripheral nations. Vietnam thus emerged as a test case in which the United States had to prove before the court of world opinion that it could cope with this novel challenge. Otherwise, similar wars would erupt all over the world's periphery, ultimately threatening to unleash World War III. Credibility therefore was no empty obsession but a crucial factor, as Rusk answered his critics in a press conference, because its loss could result in "a catastrophe for all mankind."[33] Ball undoubtedly was right when he described this version of the domino theory as vastly more pervasive than the mechanistic one. Whereas the latter covered regional threats, the province of the psychological

---

31 McGeorge Bundy, memorandum for the president, Jan. 27, 1965, box 40, NSCH, NSF, LBJL.
32 LBJ in Jenkins, summary of leadership meeting, Aug. 4, 1964, box 38, NSCH, NSF, LBJL; Nixon, The Choice in Vietnam, March 15, 1965, Speech Manuscript of Address at Republican Clubs, box 215, Ex ND19/CO312, White House Central File (hereafter WHCF), LBJL. On decision makers' obsessions that their country not be regarded as a "paper tiger," see Lloyd C. Gardner, *Pay Any Price: Lyndon Johnson and the Wars for Vietnam* (Chicago, 1995), 204.
33 "Secretary Rusk's News Conference of October 12," *Department of State Bulletin* 57 (Oct. 30, 1967): 555. For the concept of "world opinion," cf. Ninkovich, *Modernity and Power*, xiv. In this context, the arguments about credibility tied in neatly with the notorious Munich analogy, the lesson that, like Adolf Hitler, no aggressor could be successfully appeased. For an analysis of the Munich analogy and its uses, see Yuen Foong Khong, *Analogies at War: Korea, Munich, Dien Bien Phu, and the Vietnam Decisions of 1965* (Princeton, N.J., 1992).

version was the world, where all peripheral dominoes could fall virtually simultaneously after the loss of American credibility in Vietnam.

Similar to the imperialist step-by-step reasoning, the Johnson administration built its case for intervention in concentric circles. In the inner circle, it predicted that South Vietnam would fall if the United States failed to act. By virtue of the mechanistic domino theory, this event would lead to the "loss" of Southeast Asia and the Pacific region. In the outer circle, the psychological domino theory extended the significance of a defeat in South Vietnam to the world, for it spelled the loss of confidence in the United States and, by encouraging the enemies of the United States, the onset of a wider war. For each of these levels of argument, moreover, the administration singled out the appropriate enemy. On the lowest level, this was North Vietnam, whereas in Southeast Asia, China was considered the appropriate foe. On the last, global level the enemy was, predictably, world communism. The psychological domino theory thus emerged as the proper representation of American universalism and the ubiquity of the United States' concern for the farthest reaches of the periphery. The latter, however, figured only in symbolic and extrinsic contexts as a proving ground for America's resolve and its capability to resist the challenges presented by its strategic opponents.

Even to establishment critics like Ball, however, American credibility was a crucial factor in the international arena, and this was precisely why, from the very beginning, he urged his colleagues to de-escalate their rhetorical investment in an effort that Ball and others considered hopeless. The loss of credibility, Ball argued, was a self-fulfilling prophecy because the war in Vietnam could not be won and, hence, because "the more grandiloquent our verbal encouragement of the South Vietnamese was, the more costly was any disengagement."[34] On the discursive level, therefore, Vietnam presents a perfect case of how important rhetoric – far from being mere blustering – can actually be. The Johnson administration had exaggerated Vietnam's significance to such an extent that extrication became increasingly difficult, particularly if one did not want to risk the credibility one had rhetorically staked there in the first place.

---

34 Ball, OH, LBJL. Compare also id. in his famous October 5, 1964 memorandum, rpt. as "Top Secret: The Prophecy the President Rejected," *Atlantic Monthly* 230 (July 1972): 43. Although some critics angrily pointed out that it was the personal prestige of policy makers rather than the prestige of the nation that American troops had to protect with their lives, most conceded that a negotiated solution had to be found because a precipitate withdrawal would indeed hurt the United States' standing in the world. Compare Hans J. Morgenthau, "Johnson's Dilemma," *New Republic* 154 (May 28, 1966): 15. For the charge that Americans were fighting "to save the professional reputation of policy planners," see George McGovern, "Vietnam Address," Goshen College, Ind., Apr. 21, 1967, speech manuscript, box 30, Processed Collection, McGovern papers.

Although such pervasive global thinking was in its infancy around the turn of the twentieth century, imperialists invariably celebrated the victory over Spain as the United States' "awakening" to world-power status.[35] Now, however, Americans had to prove themselves worthy of their new role and accept the responsibilities it carried. In this context, the advocates of annexation insisted that the peace treaty regulating the cession of the Philippines would have to be ratified because a failure to do so would be "humiliating in the eyes of the world."[36] Retrospectively, President William McKinley recalled how crucial world opinion had been in his decision to demand the entire archipelago:

[O]ne of the best things we ever did was to insist upon taking the Philippines and not a coaling station or an island, for if we had done the latter we would have been the *laughing stock of the world*. And so it has come to pass that in a few short months we have become a world power; and I know, sitting here in this chair, with what added respect the nations of the world now deal with the United States, and it is vastly different from the conditions I found when I was inaugurated.[37]

Imperialists also believed that they had to prove themselves in the eyes of the world, or to be more precise, in the eyes of the other great powers. Once again, the periphery emerged as the proving ground for national will, capability, and stamina.

Presumably, the victory over Spain and the status of world power entailed duties and responsibilities on the periphery that had to be performed not only for the sake of the Filipinos but also for the whole of mankind.[38] Failing to accomplish these tasks, then, would be tantamount to failing mankind and the exceptional promise with which America had been endowed since its inception. Archbishop John Ireland intoned this challenge in the form of a prayer: "America, the eyes of the world are upon thee. Thou livest for the world. The new era is shedding its light upon thee, and through thee upon the world. Thy greatness and thy power daze me – I would say affright me.

35 Fenollosa, "The Coming Fusion of East and West," *Harper's Monthly Magazine* 98 (Dec. 1898): 115–22. The view of America's sudden emergence on the global scene was most noticeably propounded in the various peace jubilees between October 1898 and May 1899; see Robert I. Fulton and Thomas C. Trueblood, eds., *Patriotic Eloquence: Relating to the Spanish-American War and Its Issues* (New York, 1900).

36 Lodge to Anna C. Lodge, Jan. 22, 1899, box 103, Family Correspondence; Mahan to Lodge, Feb. 7, 1899, Box 14, General Correspondence, Lodge papers, MHS.

37 The president in conversation with James Boyle and Charles G. Dawes, according to his private secretary George B. Cortelyou, diary entry, Sept. 17, 1899, box 52, diaries, Cortelyou papers, LC (emphasis added).

38 On the important discourse of "duty" and "destiny," see the rather dated but still unsurpassed Albert K. Weinberg, *Manifest Destiny: A Study of Nationalist Expansionism in American History* (Baltimore, 1935; reprint, Chicago, 1963), chap. 9.

America, thou failing, democracy and liberty fail throughout the world."[39]
World opinion and historical destiny supposedly demanded that the United
States take up its share of the "white man's burden," the center's civilizing
mission at the periphery.

Although the pursuit of credibility never achieved quite the obsessive
character it had in the Vietnam War, the imperialist discourse of civilization
possessed a determinism of its own. The term *civilization* itself was never un-
equivocally defined but rather used as "an unstable mixture of fact and value"
in which elements of democracy, modernization, gender, and Darwinism
were quite freely arranged and reshuffled.[40] Civilization represented the
center, whereas "barbarism" was portrayed as its irreconcilable antagonist
on the periphery. Barbarism, for which the Philippines served as an example,
equaled war, disorder, and regression, whereas civilization stood for peace,
progress, and liberty. "Every expansion of civilization," Theodore Roosevelt
confidently asserted, "makes for peace," for if barbarism meant incessant war,
the American annexation and intervention, much like that in Vietnam,
could be paradoxically understood as the only way to real peace.[41] At the
same time, American expansion was rationalized as something inherently
unselfish because it contributed to the betterment of the world.

Imperialists differed only slightly in the extent to which the role of
the United States in this type of progress was preordained or voluntary.
Beveridge, for instance, was adamant that "[t]he movement has even a biological basis. It is merely the disappearance of a decaying race and inferior
civilization before higher types and a nobler society."[42] Biological metaphors
were frequently stretched so far as to demonstrate that a nation was a living
organism that, like "animal, vegetable and moral life," had to grow and
expand or wither and die. In this narrative, the United States had no choice
but to "accept" its preordained role in the Philippines.[43] Such Darwinian
rhetoric obviously established a determinism far more sweeping than that
of the domino theory. Regarding the specific role of the United States,

39 John Ireland, "Speech Extracts from Chicago Peace Jubilee, Oct. 18, 1898," in Fulton and Trueblood,
    eds., *Patriotic Eloquence*, 172–3.
40 Ninkovich, *Modernity and Power*, xi–xii. For a more detailed analysis of the term *civilization*, see
    Bederman, *Manliness & Civilization*, 23–31.
41 Roosevelt, "Expansion and Peace," *The Independent* 51 (Dec. 21, 1899): 3401–5. This idea had
    previously been formulated by the immensely popular John Fiske; "Manifest Destiny," *Harper's New
    Monthly Magazine* 70 (Mar. 1885): 578–90.
42 Beveridge to John Temple Graves, July 13, 1898, vol. 1: Letterbooks, Beveridge Papers, LC. Con-
    sidering the date of this letter, Beveridge was probably referring to the Spanish, but the view also fits
    perfectly with his convictions on the Philippine question.
43 John D. Long, "Speech at the Banquet of the Merchants' and Manufacturers' Association,"
    Milwaukee, Oct. 16, 1899, reel 83, series 4, McKinley papers (microfilm ed.), LC.

however, Roosevelt emphasized the conscious choice his countrymen had to make in the matter, although he left no doubt that civilization would march on in any event. Should Americans renege on their part in the process, "the bolder and stronger peoples will pass us by and will win for themselves the domination of the world."[44]

This would be all the more unfortunate, imperialists reasoned, because they believed that their country possessed exceptional qualifications for a civilizing mission, given the democratic ideals on which its polity was founded. Thus, Congressman Charles H. Grosvenor claimed in 1900 that the "government . . . has done more in the last two years to disseminate, among the fallen and the suffering, the blessings of liberty and democracy, than has been done by all the other countries of the world for a quarter of a century!"[45] The future shape of world order, John Procter warned, would be decided by which kind of civilizing mission ultimately triumphed. He poignantly juxtaposed the democratic, open-door expansionism of the "Anglo-Saxon" countries with the authoritarian, exclusionary version of the continental European powers.[46] Despite Roosevelt's assurance that future wars would not be waged between civilized powers, the imperialists took into account the global race for colonies. Their worldview, however, remained anchored in the monumental conflict between barbarism and civilization, much as the domino theory relied on the binary opposition of democracy and communism. Both conceptions were zero-sum games in which any loss to the enemy would spell the beginning of the end, although imperialists admittedly focused more on promise than disaster, as Franklin MacVeagh's grandiose expectations for the future demonstrated:

Democracy, in short, has seriously begun to rule humanity; and the illuminating truth is that democracy's ideals are not the ideals of isolation. Its concern is mankind. We are the greatest exponent of democracy, and we are appointed to live up to its ideals. And we must realize that a new democratic development is advancing which is characterized by broader demands of the democratic spirit – not demands for mere political institutions, important as they are, but for democratic civilization that shall reach all mankind, and for democratic human progress that shall include every corner of our earth.[47]

Thus, at the turn of the century Americans saw themselves as the missionaries of democratic civilization, whereas their 1960s descendants claimed

---

44 Roosevelt, "The Strenuous Life," speech before the Hamilton Club, Chicago, Apr. 10, 1899, in State of New York, ed., *Public Papers of Theodore Roosevelt, Governor, 1899* (Albany, N.Y., 1899), 307.
45 Charles H. Grosvenor, "A Republican View of the Presidential Campaign," *North American Review* 171 (July 1900): 48–9.
46 John Procter, "Isolation or Imperialism?" *Forum* 26 (Sept. 1898), 14–26.
47 MacVeagh, Address at the Jubilee Banquet, *Chicago Tribune*, Oct. 20, 1898.

the role of defensive guardian against the onslaught of barbaric, totalitarian enemies.[48] There was thus no fundamental difference in what imperialists and Vietnam-era interventionists sought to accomplish with respect to the periphery and the world at large. Rather, their different emphases on promise and warning, offensive and defensive roles, reflected the change in America's concrete power status that had taken place in the seventy intervening years. What imperialists strove for, Vietnam-era interventionists had already achieved and now tried to safeguard.

IV

Although all these conceptions symbolically enhanced the importance of the periphery, rendering any point potentially crucially important, they also functioned as "wide-angle lens[es] which, while enlarging the field of vision, at the same time scale[d] down the objects in view."[49] The periphery's importance was deduced from extrinsic, symbolic constructs, but intrinsically and autonomously the countries were deemed to be of little consequence.

Policy makers in the 1960s asserted their nation's selfless desire to preserve South Vietnamese independence and democracy, but their larger strategic designs alone already overrode these goals. Nowhere was this more obvious than in John McNaughton's notorious memorandum that calculated the proportional importance of the American war aims: "To avoid a humiliating U.S. defeat," that is, the psychological version of the domino theory, figured as the most important goal by far at 70 percent, whereas South Vietnam's right to self-determination was rated at only 10 percent. In 1968, Senator Gale McGee even resorted to a paradox: "To understand Vietnam, it is necessary to understand that the issue is not Vietnam."[50] This was precisely the notion of what Frank Ninkovich has called "symbolic interventionism": The United States was not defending a specific country but rather the abstract principles of democracy, world order, and civilization.[51] Moreover, although the administration claimed that it was defending the right of each nation to live in freedom from aggression, this principle only made sense if one understood "aggression" as communist aggression. Presidential adviser

---

48 James Burnham emphasized America's "imperial and conserving role on behalf of its civilization"; "The Antidraft Movement," *National Review* 19 (June 13, 1967): 629.

49 Darby, *Three Faces of Imperialism*, 186.

50 The remaining 20 percent were attributed to the containment of Chinese expansionism; McNaughton to McNamara, Mar. 24, 1965, U.S. Congress, Senate, Subcommittee on Public Buildings and Grounds, *The Pentagon Papers (The Senator Gravel Edition)*, 4 vols. (Boston, 1971), 3:695. McGee, quoted in Darby, *Three Faces of Imperialism*, 162.

51 Ninkovich, *Modernity and Power*, xv.

Harry McPherson admitted as much when he said: "I am sure we're not going to fight Uganda if she attacks Rwanda and, quote, 'oppresses her freedom.'"[52]

The imperialist logic of "civilization," however, reduced the Philippines from a country to a regressive lifestyle that had to be eradicated for the good of mankind and the Filipinos themselves. In the imperialist view, the periphery was characterized by a temporal and developmental lag that could only be corrected by a civilized power's tutelage and education.[53] This discourse conveniently overruled the "petty details" of the imperialism debate, the questions of whether there had been a wartime alliance with the Filipinos and of who had fired the first shot that started the war in early 1899. The "great world conditions," Josiah Strong maintained, simply determined that "these people cannot be permitted a lawless independence." Violence in the process might be deplored, Assistant Secretary Webster Davis conceded, but "the only way . . . to carry the blessings of civilization . . . to barbarous people is by force."[54] Despite all claims of "racial expertise" and corroboration from "authoritative voices" – mostly the soldiers engaged in the war against the Filipinos or those natives desirous of American annexation – the imperialist view remained conditioned by the convictions of the center instead of by concrete knowledge of the periphery. Imperialists felt they had only to look to their "first-hand experiences" with native Americans to know how to deal with the "savages" abroad. Perry Heath, secretary of the Republican National Committee, mused on this parallel, which actually had occurred to many:

It seems not to occur to many that the Tagalogs are in character like our North American Indians [*sic*], and throughout the Philippine Archipelago there are many tribes at war with one another and in more or less common war with our soldiers; but when we have them subdued they will be our friends and be happy. They are simply unable to learn because their leaders will not permit them, and that is why we want to master and protect them.[55]

---

52 McPherson, OH, LBJL.
53 On the juxtaposition between "past/periphery" and "present/center," see Anders Stephanson, "Commentary: Diplomatic History in the Expanded Field," *Diplomatic History* 22 (fall 1998): 600.
54 Strong, *Expansion*, 288–9; Webster Davis, Address at Washington Peace Jubilee, *Washington Post*, May 26, 1899.
55 Heath to Cortelyou, August 20, 1900, reel 11, series 1, McKinley papers (microfilm ed.), LC. On the "Indian policies" as model for the Philippines, see Richard Drinnon, *Facing West: The Metaphysics of Indian Hating & Empire Building* (Minneapolis, 1980; reprint, New York, 1990), 287–8; Walter L. Williams, "United States Indian Policy and the Debate over Philippine Annexation: Implications for the Origins of American Imperialism," *Journal of American History* 66 (Mar. 1980): 810–31. As Michael Adas has pointed out, however, Americans did undertake extensive studies of the Philippines after the initial period that is considered in this study. Comparisons with the experiences of other colonial powers then outweighed references to native Americans; Adas, "Improving on the Civilizing

Like Native Americans, the Filipinos were presumed to have a tribal rather than national organization and although, in the leitmotif of civilization, wars between organized national units no longer were justified except in self-defense, tribal and non-national rights did not have to be respected because they inhabited a lower developmental stage. Military action against the Filipinos thus was not even a war in the strict sense of the word. To speak of "tribes" also was very useful for rebutting charges that America faced a popular uprising in the Philippines. Instead, President McKinley could maintain that only an irresponsible fraction of one tribe opposed American sovereignty while the vast majority of the population supposedly welcomed it.[56]

Finally, the parallel with America's native inhabitants allowed for another disappropriating rationale, which Albert Weinberg has referred to as "destined use of the soil." This doctrine basically held that Native Americans had been wasting the resources of the continent because they did not culti-vate the land. Therefore, European settlers had not only been justified but even destined to take the land from them.[57] In the imperialism debate, this "continental" argument was globalized. When Mahan, for example, denied that the Filipinos possessed any "natural rights" to self-government, he made the latter not only dependent on political fitness but also on "developing [the land] in such manner as to insure the *natural right* of the world at large that resources should not be left idle but be utilized for the general good."[58] The common Western discourse on civilization was thus enriched by particularly American images, facilitating a view of the periphery that could comfortably rely on familiar memories instead of on first-hand studies or analyses of the periphery itself.

Although such overt racism no longer constituted a sanctioned discourse in the 1960s, quasi-racist or at least ethnocentric rhetoric crept back into the debate, more thoroughly recast in the language of development and culture.[59] In public, President Johnson steadfastly rejected racism and as-serted that "Asia is no longer sitting outside the door of the 20th century," but other administration members privately described South Vietnam as "medieval in its organization" and the American role as "trying . . . to pull

Mission?: Assumptions of United States Exceptionalism in the Colonization of the Philippines," paper presented at the Itinerario Conference, "The American Experience in Asia," Leiden University, Oct. 1998.

56 McKinley to Lodge, Letter of Acceptance of the Nomination for President, Sept. 8, 1900, box 16, General Correspondence, Lodge papers, MHS.

57 Weinberg, *Manifest Destiny*, chap. 3.

58 Mahan, "The Problem of Asia, Part III," *Harper's Monthly* 100 (May 1900): 929 (emphasis added).

59 Hunt, *Ideology and U.S. Foreign Policy*, 161–2; Darby, *Three Faces of Imperialism*, 217.

this undeveloped country into the 20th century as fast as we can."[60] Intending to compliment the South Vietnamese on their quick progress toward constitutional government, Johnson himself unwittingly affirmed the impression of a cultural and temporal lag: "It took us from 1776 to 1789 – not 13 months but 13 years – to get a Constitution *with our Anglo-Saxon background* and all the training we had had."[61] The non–Anglo-Saxon Vietnamese, one could interpret, were quick to learn, but they still had two centuries on which to catch up. These were the faint echoes of the temporal lag that the imperialists had claimed existed on the periphery.

Native American imagery re-emerged as well, particularly in the environment of the military effort. Territory occupied by the enemy was labeled "Indian country," whereas the American bases scattered throughout South Vietnam were compared with the isolated army forts of the nineteenth century. Hence, military operations frequently received names recalling the old frontier days, such as "Prairie," "Daniel Boone," or "Crazy Horse." The ambush narrative, usually reserved for novels and films about the historic conflict with Native Americans, was now transplanted to Vietnam, with the Vietcong taking the place of the "Indians" of old. Thus, in numerous presidential citations of bravery, the pattern was similar: A numerically inferior American force was surrounded by vicious enemy hordes and bravely managed to hold its position. A narrative of individual American heroism was paradoxically resurrected in the context of a modern technological war of enormous proportions.[62]

"Tribalism" also made a dubious although muted reappearance in administrative reasoning. Like his grandfather in relation to the Philippines, Henry Cabot Lodge, the ambassador to South Vietnam, explained that Vietnam's incoherence and turmoil was due to the tribal and ethnically diverse makeup of its population. Unable or unwilling to consider the possibility that North Vietnam and the Vietcong possessed more popular appeal than America's Southern client, Maxwell Taylor even asserted that the North was "more

---

60 LBJ, "Remarks to the American Alumni Council: United States Asian Policy," July 12, 1966, *PPP – 1966*, 2: 719. Lodge in "The Situation in Vietnam," Executive Hearing, July 27, 1965, Committee on Foreign Relations (hereafter CFR), *Executive Sessions of the Senate Foreign Relations Committee (Historical Series)*, vol. 17, 1965 (Washington, D.C., 1990), 1016. The other quote by Lodge in "Summary Record of a Meeting, Honolulu, June 1, 1964," *FRUS, 1964–1968*, 1:413.

61 LBJ, "The President's News Conference of November 17, 1967," *PPP – 1967*, 2: 1049 (emphasis added).

62 John Atherton, "The Vocabulary of the Vietnam War," in Jean-Robert Rougé, ed., *L'Opinion Américaine devant la Guerre du Vietnam* (Paris, 1992), 157–74; Drinnon, *Facing West*, 450–7. The ambush narrative has been recounted in Tom Engelhardt, *The End of Victory Culture: Cold War America and the Disillusioning of a Generation* (New York, 1995), 40. Such a typical citation for bravery can be found in LBJ, "Remarks upon Presenting the Medal of Honor to Maj. Howard V. Lee, USMC," Oct. 25, 1967, *PPP – 1967*, 2:943–5.

homogenous racially," whereas he attributed the South's weaknesses to its being a "federation, one might say – a confederacy of many races, of many religions, and they have not yet been welded into a single bloc."[63] Apparently, it was easier to resort to racial and cultural explanations than to seriously confront the possibility that the U.S. client state simply lacked popular support.

Asia thus remained *terra incognita* to imperialists and proponents of the Vietnam War, but it also was strangely familiar because they superimposed their own historical topography onto the region. To put it polemically, whatever Americans discovered in their encounters with the periphery they had already experienced at home. This displacement was completed by the interventionists' increasing perception that they were not only fighting external but also internal foes, namely, the critics of their foreign-policy endeavors. The determination and credibility that they wanted to project for friends and foes on the outside, they believed, was severely threatened by the domestic debates sparked by both wars. Critics were accused either of outright treason or at least of unwittingly prolonging the wars by encouraging the enemy. McKinley implied that his domestic opponents were cowardly when he admonished his audience that there was a choice only between "manly doing and base desertion" in the Philippines, whereas Johnson even predicted: "If we lose the war, it will be lost here – not in Vietnam."[64] Thus, in the final analysis, the wars themselves were internalized as tests of American strength and resolve. Maybe even more than to the outside world Americans had to prove to themselves their capability for world leadership.

V

American visions of the periphery always reverted back to the center. On one level, they reflected the tendency of imperial powers to view the periphery in the context of central power struggles, which Philip Darby has so eloquently described. Hence, Vietnam has to be understood against the background of Cold War bipolarity, whereas the desire to acquire the Philippines emerged at a time of intense jockeying for the last unoccupied colonial territories. Through positive or negative versions of the domino

---

63 Lodge in "The Situation in Southeast Asia," Executive Hearing, May 19, 1965, CFR, *Executive Sessions – 1965*, 548, 561. Taylor in "The Situation in South Vietnam," Executive Hearing, June 11, 1965, CFR, *Executive Sessions – 1965*, 708.

64 McKinley, "Speech at Banquet of the Ohio Society of New York," Mar. 3, 1900, in *Speeches and Addresses of William McKinley, from March 1, 1897 to May 30, 1900* (New York, 1900), 364. Notes of the President's Meeting with Jim Lucas of the Scripps-Howard Newspapers, Nov. 24, 1967, box 1, Tom Johnson's Notes of Meetings, LBJL.

theory and through the discourse of civilization, threats and opportunities were summarized and symbolized in order to relate to national well-being and security. These simplistic metaphors also encapsulated larger conceptions of world order to justify interventions in the otherwise nondescript periphery. Vietnam was portrayed as the symbolic battleground between the "free world" and "world communism," whereas the monumental struggle between civilization and barbarism took place out in the Philippines in a representative fashion. The comparison of both periods is instructive because it demonstrates that, in the United States, the tendency to view the periphery through the lens of larger power struggles existed prior to the achievement of a secure imperial status.

On a more abstract level, the comparison of the periods when America aspired to world power and when it realized this aspiration reveals that such symbolic sublimations can also be understood as congenial representations of American universalism and its exceptionalist mission. By definition, America's concern extended to the farthest reaches of the globe and, at least potentially, the remotest point on the periphery mattered as much as the center if America's cherished principles were at stake. The vision of global peace and democracy could be realized only if it encompassed the entire world.

Although the periphery acquired supreme importance as a symbolic battleground, it was virtually insignificant in its own right. The particularities of individual countries were subsumed in the broad discourses of civilization or of the domino theory. The logic of universalism assumed, moreover, that the periphery's wishes were virtually identical with those of the American center. At the same time, particularly American historical experiences, for example the conflict with the Native Americans, provided the guide to comprehending novel and difficult external challenges. Even the wars themselves, the interventionists occasionally intimated, depended on the outcome of inner-American debates. In short, we are confronted with a dialectical rhetorical strategy: While the periphery and the world were internalized within the American mental landscape, America's raison d'être, the universalism of its mission, was powerfully externalized. As long as such sweeping visions continue to inform the American worldview, a more nuanced representation of the periphery cannot be expected.

3

The Challenge of Revolutions and the Emergence of Nation-States

British Reactions to the Foundation of the United States and American Responses to the Socialist Republic of Vietnam, 1780–1980

T. CHRISTOPHER JESPERSEN

I

Revolutionary movements, like other major changes in the international system, affect the development of nations and directly or indirectly touch millions of people's lives. The responses they elicit from other nations provide further proof of the impact they have on a range of issues for international affairs. Of the revolutions that were also national independence movements over the past two-and-a-half centuries, the American Revolution stands out the most because of what it promised ideologically, for what it ostensibly championed subsequently, and for what it has ultimately meant to the nature of international relations once the United States assumed a greater role in the economic, political, and diplomatic conduct of those affairs. Its impact has been significant and enduring.

The case for comparing the American and Vietnamese revolutions is not an obvious one.[1] The United States fought for its independence against the nation and government whose policies had created the loose association of colonies in the first place. The familial and fraternal bonds across the Atlantic Ocean were strong. Both colonists and British spoke the same language. Economic ties were vigorous, and many well-to-do families in North America sent their children to England for schooling.

The relationship between Vietnam and the United States had none of the same qualities. In fact, Vietnam was not a significant part of American

---

1 Other historians have ventured the comparison, including John Shy and Don Higginbotham. See John Shy, *A People Numerous and Armed: Reflections on the Military Struggle for American Independence*, rev. ed. (Ann Arbor, Mich., 1990), and Don Higginbotham, *War and Society in Revolutionary America: The Wider Dimensions of Conflict* (Columbia, S.C., 1988).

history, culture, politics, or diplomacy prior to 1950. Vietnam did not rebel against American control; rather, the United States tried to interpose itself in the course of a determined Vietnamese independence movement, one that had its origins in opposition to French colonial rule in the nineteenth century. When the United States officially supplanted France in 1954 out of concern over how Vietnam fit into the global competition with the Soviet Union, it sought to contain the independence movement by setting up an indigenous government capable of competing for power. In most respects, therefore, Vietnam's fight was not akin to the American colonial effort to wrest control of North America from the British.

Despite the significant differences that separate the two revolutions in time, origin, and temperament, the responses to them deserve comparison because of how many things are so strikingly similar. In the 1770s, Great Britain possessed an empire that stretched from a budding presence in South Asia to a more fully established outpost in North America. Its size and extent were impressive, although it was to grow even larger in the coming decades. By the 1960s, the United States had troops stationed in countries from West Germany to Japan, and it had military and economic agreements with even more nations. The scope of American hegemony was daunting, even if it was on the decline. Both revolutions became enmeshed in larger conflicts between competing imperial powers. Both were fought with the goal of securing independence from foreign control. Both were civil wars and forced the dislocation of tens of thousands of people. And both were met with determined resistance during their struggle for victory and afterward.

It is through a comparison of the British reaction to the American Revolution in the late eighteenth century with the U.S. response to the Vietnamese revolution of the latter twentieth century that certain aspects of empire can be discerned. In the process of juxtaposing them, some things become clearer in terms of the general conclusions that can be drawn and the undeniable distinctions that must be made. Finally, in comparing these two responses to revolution, it is important to note that the common thread remains the United States. It is thus possible to examine the nature of American society over a two-hundred-year period and, from there, to draw conclusions about the nature of its politics, culture, and diplomacy.

II

The battle between the North American colonists and the Crown grew out of the British victory over the French in 1763. That conflict, alternately labeled the French and Indian War, the Seven Years' War, and the War for Greater Empire, pitted British forces against French troops in places as far away from each other (and from England) as India and the western frontier of the North American colonies. The burden of victory was heavy: Britain's national debt rose from £74.6 million to £132.6 million.[2] In addition, maintaining and protecting the North American holdings necessitated stationing troops there, which, in turn, led to a series of efforts to tax the colonies in order to offset the costs.[3] American colonists rebelled at the idea, challenging parliament's authority through various means for a decade before the onset of war. King George III, who "foresaw ruin ahead if the home country conceded American independence," was determined to put down the rebellion, and he had the backing of "significant sections of public opinion – probably by the majority of the political nation."[4] Bolstered by highly optimistic reports from the colonial governors about the ease with which the rebellion would be broken, reports that were further encouraged by the secretary of state for the colonies, Lord George Germain, the king committed Great Britain to putting down the revolution with force. He was unabashed about involving himself in the details of the matter. "The King was not one to sit back and allow his politicians and generals to conduct the war on their own – or at least not without liberally proffered advice."[5]

From April 1775 until the battle at Saratoga in October 1777, British military leaders focused their energies on New England and the mid-Atlantic states of New York and New Jersey. The demands of empire, however, meant that fewer British soldiers could be spared for the war in North America than were needed, putting a premium on foreign forces and necessitating alliances with Indian tribes in North America. The push for assistance began with an effort to recruit 20,000 Russian soldiers, the view being that "the mutinous Bostonians" were the "American version of the Cossacks." Russian troops, moreover, were "expected to have fewer scruples than British troops, who could be restrained by a belief they were fighting fellow subjects."[6] When Catherine II rejected the idea, Britain looked to the Dutch, who

2 Stephen Conway, "Britain and the Revolutionary Crisis, 1763–1781," in Peter J. Marshall, ed., *The Oxford History of the British Empire: The Eighteenth Century* (New York, 1998), 327.

3 Bruce P. Lehman, "Colonial Wars and Imperial Instability, 1688–1793," in ibid., 161. He indicates that the British Treasury spent "nearly £5.5 million on the army in America, nearly £1 million on the navy, and over £1 million to reimburse the colonies for their troops."

4 Conway, "Britain and the Revolutionary Crisis," 337. Stanley Ayling, *George the Third* (New York, 1972), 268.

5 Ayling, *George the Third*, 247, and 252 for the information on Germain.

6 Hamish M. Scott, *British Foreign Policy in the Age of the American Revolution* (New York, 1990), 218.

also refused. Ultimately, it was the Hessian states of Central Europe that supplied 18,000 troops at one time and 30,000 total for the duration of the war.[7]

General John Burgoyne's defeat in upstate New York markedly altered the military situation. The quick victory anticipated at the beginning of hostilities gave way to the realization that the fighting was going to require a greater cooperative effort with those subjects in North America still loyal to the king. After Saratoga, British strategy focused on securing the South, where it was believed a strong Loyalist base would assist in yielding decisive results. "It was at last admitted that, ultimately, restored British authority would have to depend on Americans themselves, and that even the strongest army and navy could do no more than create favorable conditions for the Americanization of the war."[8] Indeed, as John Shy has written, "during 1778, Loyalists moved from the periphery toward the center of the war."[9]

The British defeat at Saratoga bolstered Patriot spirits at a time when they were sagging badly. In writing to General George Washington, John Page extolled Saratoga as a vindication for the American side. "I have all along looked upon our Cause, as favored by Heaven; & I think I have seen many Instances of a divine Interposition in our Favour." He contrasted this with the arrogance of the other side: "Britain grown great & powerful & put into a Condition, by Heaven, to do infinite good to Mankind wickedly abused that Power – intoxicated with its success it ungratefully & impiously attributed them to its own Strength – For such abuse of power it seems consistent with the infinite Goodness & Justice to deprive them of it & for such Ingratitude & Pride they deserved to be humbled." Because the British "were therefore infatuated & permitted by Heaven to run head long into this War," Page and his countrymen had a mission. If they did not "forfeit the Favour of Heaven," they could "be the means of bringing back that haughty people to a sense of their Duty & of securing the Hapiness of millions yet unborn."[10]

---

7 Ayling, *George the Third*, 248. He indicates that there were only 48,000 British troops at the time, a quarter of whom were stationed in Ireland. John Shy, "The American Colonies in War and Revolution, 1748–1783," in Marshall, ed., *Oxford History of the British Empire*, 316. He puts the number of German troops hired to fight in North America at 18,000 at their peak. For the figure of 30,000, see Paul David Nelson, "British Conduct of the American Revolutionary War: A Review of Interpretations," *Journal of American History* 65 (Dec. 1978): 623–53.

8 John Shy, "The Loyalist Problem in the Lower Hudson Valley: The British Perspective," in Robert A. East and Jacob Judd, eds., *The Loyalist Americans: A Focus on Greater New York* (Tarrytown, N.Y., 1975), 4.

9 Ibid., 5–6.

10 Page to Weeden, Oct. 30, 1777, #8, George Weeden papers, American Philosophical Society Library, Philadelphia.

Despite the change in regional strategy, the British effort limped on, failing to gather anything but limited popular support in the southern states. However sympathetic to the Crown many individuals in the region may have been, "Readiness to die for King George was harder to enlist."[11] After partially subduing the Carolinas, General Lord Cornwallis headed north into Virginia, whereon American troops recaptured most of the areas he had occupied. Still, many in England were not ready to concede defeat. In 1780, John Adams reported on arguments being publicized in England in favor of continuing the war. According to the ardent Loyalist Joseph Galloway, should America achieve its independence, it would have profound consequences for all aspects of British economic life, which would jeopardize the nation's strategic position, even its sovereignty, vis-à-vis the other nations of Europe. He concluded, "It does not require the spirit of *divinatio* to perceive that Great Britain, robbed of her foreign dominions and commerce, her nurseries of seamen lost, her navy weakened, and the power of her ambitious neighbors thus strengthened and increased, will not be able to maintain her independence among nations."[12]

Continuation of the war, however, was becoming increasingly absurd, at least according to John Mathews, who wrote to George Washington just before the general's victory at Yorktown:

There appears a degree of arrogance, petulance, and Gasconade through the whole conduct of this corrupt, and infatuated nation, that is truely ridiculous. Beyond all doubt, the stake she is contending for, is of the last consequence to her. Therefore, she will leave nothing unessayed to carry her point. True, but when the seventh year of war, & every other expedient, has only served to exhibit a far greater degree of imbecility, than either of the preceding ones, it is presumable, their dear bought experience, would produce more moderation, and plyability.[13]

Cornwallis's surrender at Yorktown seemed to indicate that the game was up; certainly the king was forced to rethink his position. He conceded that independence for the colonies was unavoidable, a conclusion he reached with considerable remorse and anguish. Commenting on the state of Anglo-American relations and quoting British sources on the matter, Henry Laurens, the South Carolinian diplomat who had been imprisoned in London for part of the war after the British captured his vessel, wrote the president of Congress in 1784, "His Majesty was dragged into the late war

11 Ayling, *George the Third*, 252.
12 John Adams to President of Congress, June 16, 1780, in Francis Wharton, ed., *The Revolutionary Diplomatic Correspondence of the United States*, 6 vols. (Washington, D.C., 1889), 3:792–3.
13 John Mathews to George Washington, Oct. 1, 1781, in Paul H. Smith, ed., *Letters of Delegates to Congress: 1774–1789*, 26 vols. (Washington, D.C., 1991), 18:92.

as reluctantly as ever a bull was dragged to a baiting." The king confessed to Laurens his regret "at the shedding of so much blood." What, however, could he have done to prevent it? "They drew me in little by little," he said of his advisers; "I have been deceived."[14]

Preliminary articles for peace were not signed until a little over a year after Yorktown, on November 30, 1782; the actual signing ceremony took place in Paris on September 3, 1783; and the king's signature came the following year. There were three provisions that quickly became critical for subsequent relations. The first, and from the American standpoint the most important, was the British retention of forts along the western frontier. Coupled with the Crown's support for Indian tribes in lower Canada as well as the Ohio and Mississippi river valleys, the occupation of the forts was seen as part of a larger effort to restrain the new nation's territorial growth. Second was the American treatment of Loyalists. The treaty called for the states to recognize legitimate claims made by Loyalists to confiscated property. It also recommended that the states be advised to cease further confiscations and treat the Loyalists fairly and without recrimination. The third issue centered around the payment of American debts contracted to British merchants prior to the outbreak of war in 1775.

With respect to the confiscation of Loyalists' property, many Americans had other ideas. Certain states, upon getting wind of the final stipulations of the peace treaty, passed resolutions outlawing any compensation to Loyalists and denying any legal claims they might make on confiscated property. Some Virginians reasoned that, at the time of independence, individuals were forced to make a choice, and those who elected to remain loyal to the Crown lost their standing because they had opted not to become members of the new social compact. They could not subsequently appeal for legal protection under the laws of the new nation. As the Virginia House of Delegates put the matter, "if virtuous Citizens in defence of their natural & Constitutional rights, risque their life, liberty and property on their success, the vicious Citizens, who side with Tyranny & oppression, or who cloak themselves under the masque of neutrality, should at least hazard their property and not enjoy the benefits procured by the labours and dangers of those whose destruction they wished."[15] Lorrenzo Sabine, one of the foremost authorities

14 Henry Laurens to President of Congress, April 24, 1784, in Francis Wharton, ed., *The Revolutionary Diplomatic Correspondence of the United States*, 6 vols. (Washington, D.C., 1889), 6:796.
15 "Instructions to Virginia Delegates in re Confiscated Property," Virginia House of Delegates, Dec. 17, 1782, William T. Hutchinson and William M. E. Rachal, eds., *The Papers of James Madison*, 17 vols. (Chicago, 1962), 5:410.

on the issue, wrote that rather than introducing amnesty programs, "the state legislatures generally continued in a course of hostile action, and treated the conscientious and pure, and the unprincipled and corrupt, with the same indiscrimination as they had done during the struggle."[16]

This ran counter to the treaty, of course, but with no strong national government to ensure compliance, other states, along with Virginia, passed resolutions precluding Loyalist claims to lost property. The *Pennsylvania Packet* had expressed the idea during the war that Tory property "would become securities for the repairs" the states would have to make after the fighting ended.[17] And that, in many instances, is just what some of the states did after 1781.

The Loyalists were aware of what was coming, and the defeat of the British at Yorktown sealed their fates. William Franklin, former governor of New Jersey and son of the famous inventor, political operative, and diplomat, Benjamin Franklin, wrote Lord George Germain that had the British army only managed to extricate itself from Yorktown, and thus not suffer such a humiliating defeat at the hands of the combined French and Patriot forces, many in North America, "as well rebels as loyalists," were prepared to take up arms to compel Congress to end the resistance not so much because all were ready to join the British cause but because of their collective weariness over the continuation of hostilities. Yorktown dealt a fatal blow to their hopes. Not only that, but the provisions of the peace terms between the British and United States shocked Franklin. "It is scarcely possible to give your lordship an adequate idea of the surprise and distress which the perusal of the 10th article of the capitulation has occasioned in the mind of every American loyalist."[18]

The Yorktown debacle did not force the complete or immediate evacuation of the United States. Instead, British forces remained in New York, Charleston, and other sections of the South for the next two years, pending final negotiations between the two parties.

During this period, the battle for control over the United States continued as Loyalists held out hope that they would be rewarded. Additionally, some British officials wanted to take advantage of the overall weaknesses and divisions in and among the states. In February 1782, the Earl of Dunmore, writing from South Carolina, one of the strongest points for Loyalist activity,

16 Lorenzo Sabine, *The American Loyalists, or Biographical Sketches of Adherents to the British Crown in the War of the Revolution; Alphabetically Arranged; with a Preliminary Historical Essay* (Boston, 1847), 86.
17 American Crisis no. 11, *Pennsylvania Packet*, Feb. 18, 1777.
18 William Franklin to George Germain, Nov. 6, 1781, Kenneth G. Davies, ed., *Documents of the American Revolution, 1780–1783*, 21 vols. (Dublin, 1979), 20:255.

indicated to Lord Germain that there were still some who would take up the king's cause, "notwithstanding the many rebuffs they have met with," if they could act independently of the army regulars who had sneered at working with "men not bred of arms." Dunmore requested authorization for one of the provincial governors to be charged with raising an army to continue the fight. Should approval be granted, "the people of the country . . . would even now give such convincing proofs of their spirit and zeal for His Majesty's service as would give a favourable turn to affairs in the southern colonies at least."[19]

As the talks between the British and American negotiators proceeded in 1782, South Carolina delegates lamented the military weakness of the United States. Unable to follow up decisively after the victory at Yorktown, American forces could not expel the British from the states. And yet, as the delegates warned,

It is wished that this Consideration, & the Obstinate adherence of the British to their Plan of subjugating this Country (which I Evidenced by their answer to the Mediators) might rouse the U States to an early & animated Exertion. It is observed that the British are much embarras'd with respect to the measures they ought to pursue – That they still continue to represent America as a weak & divided people, hoping thereby to affect the Powers of Europe, & especially the Mediators – That it is not improbable G Britain will endeavour to make proposals to the States separately, & tho' it is not apprehended they would succeed in such an Attempt by detach[in]g any of them from the Alliance, yet it may be presumed whilst the Issue is unknown, they might avail themselves of it, to induce a Belief that They still have a considerable Interest in this country, & that the people at large still wish to be connected with them.[20]

A year after Yorktown, Loyalist hopes sagged. "The same anxiety and dejection of spirits," Sir Guy Carleton wrote, "seems to possess the minds of the loyalists and the same spirit of discontent appears still to pervade the eastern provinces."[21] As terms of the impending peace treaty became known, many Loyalists expressed their dismay. "Deserted as we are by our King, banished by our country, what resource is left us in the combination of calamities? I had hitherto during many distressing events supported a uniform cheerfulness (being determined never to despair) and hoped for the

---

19 Earl of Dunmore to Lord George Germain, Feb. 5, 1782, *Documents of the American Revolution, 1780–1783,* 21:36–7.

20 South Carolina Delegates to John Mathews, May 6, 1782, *Letters of Delegates to Congress: 1774–1789,* 26 vols. (Washington, D.C., 1991), 18:490–1.

21 Sir Guy Carleton to Secretary of State for Southern Department, Oct. 7, 1782, *Documents of the American Revolution,* 21:123. Speaking of the new political leaders, Carleton asserted, "Their danger is lest the people, detecting these views, should generally revolt, and to prevent this they employ every artifice to inflame the passions and mislead the understanding of the public."

best but alas! there is now not left the least glimmering of hope." Cataloging the exact manner in which he felt abandoned, the writer continued, "It's no small comfort, though, 'that it's not our crimes but our virtues that have distressed us.'" Specifically objecting to one of the articles of the peace agreement, he asserted, "but we who have borne arms, exposed our lives and sacrificed our properties, encountering innumerable hardships in the service of Britain, are particularly thrown out in a most severe and pointed manner instead of being the first provided for." He concluded, with no small amount of sarcasm, "I shall ever, though, remember with satisfaction that it was not I deserted my King but my King that deserted me."[22]

The number of Loyalists who left the United States during and immediately after the American Revolution is estimated at between sixty thousand and one hundred thousand. Considered as a percentage of the population, which in 1780 was a little under 2.8 million, the figure is higher than the number of emigres who left France during the French revolution.[23] Of those who fled, some relocated to the British islands in the Caribbean; others tried to establish lives in England, largely to discover how much higher the cost of living was there; some even tried returning to the United States with decidedly mixed results. But the vast majority settled in present-day Canada, specifically Nova Scotia and western Quebec, creating a British colonial diaspora that had a major impact on the demographics of the Western Hemisphere and the national evolution of Canada. According to Peter Marshall, "defeat in 1783 generated an influx of settlers on a scale that had long been unavailingly sought, even if the newcomers now came as refugees."[24] The Crown paid greater attention to Canada and played a more aggressive role in developing the remaining colonies in the hemisphere.

When the negotiations over the terms of the peace concluded, Americans were faced with the issue of how to carry out the provisions of the treaty. And in many respects, it was a collective decision, not one that simply resided with the national government, because no such entity really existed. There was a collection of states, each asserting its autonomy in terms of finance and diplomacy, which created divisions and numerous problems. Emotions ran the gamut from anger and revenge to prudence, caution, and even magnanimity. One of the soundest voices in the debate over how to handle the Loyalists was that of Alexander Hamilton.

22 M. Tattnall to John Street, May 30, 1783, *Documents of the American Revolution*, 21:174.
23 John Mack Faragher, ed., *The Encyclopedia of Colonial and Revolutionary America* (New York, 1990).
24 Peter J. Marshall, "British North America, 1760–1815," in Marshall, ed., *Oxford History of the British Empire*, 381.

During the revolution, Hamilton served as Washington's aide-de-camp, distinguishing himself by his excellent work. After the war, he returned to New York to practice law. From the beginning, Hamilton was a proponent of a moderate approach on dealing with the Loyalists because he understood the larger score: "Let the case be fairly stated: Great Britain and America two independent nations at war − The former in possession of considerable posts and districts of territory belonging to the latter − and also of the means of obstructing certain commercial advantages in which it is deeply interested."[25] The ramifications of not adhering to the agreement reached with Great Britain would be significant. The principal concern, as Hamilton expressed it, centered around how the trustworthiness of the United States would be questioned by other nations if it refused to carry out the provisions of the agreement reached with Britain. Treating Loyalists harshly would induce "a great number of useful citizens . . . to form settlements that will hereafter become our rivals animated with a hatred to us which will descend to their posterity." Specifically, Hamilton mentioned Nova Scotia, "a colony which by its position will become a competitor with us among other things in that branch of commerce in which our navigation and navy will essentially depend."[26] To do anything else would leave the new nation smarting from the loss of these citizens. "Our state," Hamilton wrote of New York, "will feel for twenty years at least the effects of the popular phrenzy."[27]

Robert Livingston agreed. Writing to Hamilton in August 1783, he stated: "I seriou[s]ly lament with you the violent spirit of persecution which prevails here and dread its consequences upon the wealth of commerce & future tranquility of the state. I am the more hurt at it because it appears to me almost unmixed with pure or patriotic motives. In some few it is a blind spirit of revenge & resentment but in more it is the most sordid interest."[28] John Jay said much the same. "Violence and associations against the Tories pay an ill compliment to Government and impeach our good Faith in the opinions of some, and our magnanimity in the opinion of many." Indeed, echoing Hamilton's sentiments, Jay insisted, "I would rather see the Sweat of their Brows fertilize our Fields, than those of our Neighbors which it would certainly water those Seeds of Hatred, in. Victory and Peace should in

25 Hamilton to George Clinton, June 1, 1783, Harold C. Syrett, ed., *The Papers of Alexander Hamilton*, 21 vols. (New York, 1962), 3:370.
26 Ibid., 371.
27 Richard B. Morris, ed., *Alexander Hamilton and the Founding of the Nation* (New York, 1957), 459–60.
28 Livingston to Hamilton, Aug. 30, 1783, in ibid.

my opinion be followed by Clemency, Moderation and Benevolence; & we should be careful not to sully the Glory of the Revolution by licenciousness and Cruelty."[29]

The signing of the Paris Peace Treaty in 1783 did not end the friction between the United States and Great Britain. As the principal architect of the peace, the Earl of Shelburne preferred a cooperative course with the Americans, one that included strong economic ties and possibly even a coordinated defense strategy. The economic fit certainly seemed clear enough: America could retain its status as a principal supplier of raw materials to Britain and, in return, the United States would serve as a customer for British goods. In this sense, Shelburne's plan was devious and ingenious. He proposed generosity toward the United States in return for resurrecting the colonial relationship in new guise.

Shelburne's plan did not prevail, however. First, "He greatly underestimated the enmity caused by seven years of fighting and civil war. It was impossible – on either side of the Atlantic – to wipe away the bitterness and bloodshed by one apparently magnanimous gesture."[30] Second, his plan withered under the fierce attack led by the diplomat William Eden (later Lord Auckland) and his friend Lord Sheffield, the two of whom, with the Order in Council of July 2, 1783, managed to restrict American trade with the British West Indies for the next decade. They played upon popular fears of economic decline as well as the frustration and anger focused at Americans for their ingratitude, insolence, and revolutionary success. Permitting the Americans to conduct trade freely, Sheffield demonstrated, "would be to invite the loss of the carrying trade and, inevitably, maritime decadence. The roar of approval which greeted his performance was the voice of the nation."[31]

The reaction was not surprising. The failed effort to put down the American Revolution cost Great Britain £115 million and nearly doubled the national debt. To Emperor Joseph II of Austria, the British position appeared to have declined so much that he declared in 1783, "England had fallen to the status of a second class power."[32] Or as it was put another way by one Loyalist, "O Englishmen, where is now your national honour? Nothing but bribery, corruption and treason prevails in your senate who promised protection and then basely betrayed."[33]

---

29 Jay to Hamilton, Sept. 28, 1783, in ibid., 459.
30 Scott, *British Foreign Policy*, 328.
31 Charles R. Ritcheson, *Aftermath of Revolution: British Policy Toward the United States, 1783–1795* (New York, 1969), 6.
32 Ayling, *George the Third*, 320.
33 Tattnall to Street, July 4, 1783, *Documents of the American Revolution*, 21:175.

As it turned out, predictions of Great Britain's imperial demise were greatly exaggerated. There was a period of governmental uncertainty, but it was followed by a resurgence that lasted more than a century and catapulted the nation to historic international preeminence.

III

The Vietnamese revolution differed from the American Revolution in almost every respect. Instead of involving one group of people in rebellion against the government that had greatly assisted in their historical development, the Vietnamese situation revolved around three major developments: two international, the other domestic. First was French colonialism. During the nineteenth century, it began with missionary assistance to Emperor Gia Long shortly after 1802 and culminated with French troops subduing Vietnamese forces in the early 1860s.

The second (domestic) issue was the development of a coherent nationalist ideology. Over the three-quarters of a century after France imposed its rule on Vietnam, indigenous nationalism evolved haphazardly, but it continued to grow just the same, eventually becoming a potent and cohesive force. Ultimately, it was the Vietnamese Communists under the leadership of Ho Chi Minh who came to the fore of the opposition against foreign domination. When Ho declared the creation of the Democratic Republic of Vietnam shortly after Japan's surrender in 1945, the Viet Minh's history of resistance, Ho's statements as well as his international travel and learning, and his actions during the war comprised a mélange of nationalism, communism, antiforeignism, and opportunism, all of which resonated with the majority of the Vietnamese people.

When France decided to oppose Vietnam's bid for independence, the United States sided with its European ally out of concern for what might happen to the French position in Europe should it not be able to re-establish its colonial empire. In making this choice, American foreign policy makers denied the nationalist character of Vietnam's push for independence and emphasized, exclusive of all other factors, its communist ideology. Thus, the Cold War competition between the Soviet Union and the United States constitutes the third element.

U.S. support for France began in a small and indirect fashion, but between 1950 and 1954 it became substantial – to the tune of $2 billion – and afterward, it became direct.[34] French forces were unable to stem the

---

34 George Herring, *America's Longest War*, 2d ed. (New York, 1986), 42.

tide; they surrendered ignominiously in May 1954. It was the subsequent determination – when the United States decided to back Ngo Dinh Diem as an alternative to Ho's claim on authority – that led to the decades-long involvement in Vietnam. Diem was propped up through a series of mechanisms, including military assistance in the training and supply of his South Vietnamese army (Army of the Republic of Viet Nam, or ARVN). It also included massive economic assistance.[35] In the process, the United States fostered a coterie of sorts, or more accurately, it expanded the existing group of Vietnamese whose livelihood had been dependent upon the French. This began with an effort to provide Diem with a base of support. Given that he was Catholic, American advisers enticed, cajoled, and even scared nearly 800,000 Vietnamese co-worshipers to relocate from the north to the south in the aftermath of the French withdrawal. From there, fidelity to Diem provided access to a system of economic rewards through a number of different avenues, including government or military service.[36] The result of all this activity was that the United States created its own group of loyalists.

American hopes that these faithful would stabilize the situation in Southeast Asia proved to be misguided. Aid begot more aid, and the South Vietnamese government became entirely dependent on the United States for its survival. Diem, not popular to start with, became increasingly isolated during his reign and finally fell victim to his own generals, who killed him in a coup in 1963. Subsequent South Vietnamese leaders were even more dependent on the United States.[37] Meanwhile, as the Viet Minh organized North Vietnamese society and pressed for elections to unify their country, a process opposed by the United States, an indigenous resistance movement developed in South Vietnam. When the National Liberation Front (NLF) began its armed struggle to topple Diem's rule in 1960, it was a small but rapidly growing force. Its success led policy makers and military personnel in the Kennedy and Johnson administrations to conclude that the only way to retain suzerainty was for American forces to assume a greater share of actual combat.

But why Vietnam? Unlike the North American colonies, which had been populated by so many British settlers with the assistance of the Crown

---

35 The principal mechanism through which this support came was the Commercial Import Program (CIP), which between 1955 and 1961 funneled nearly $1.5 billion in assistance to South Vietnam. For more, see George M. Kahin, *Intervention: How American Became Involved in Vietnam* (New York, 1986), 85–8.

36 Ibid., 76.

37 To state that Vietnamese leaders from Diem onward were dependent on the United States is not to suggest that they were powerless in the relationship. What it does indicate is the growing economic dependence that came to be.

over a century and a half and thus clearly represented a major investment and interest to England, Vietnam had received no such attention from the United States prior to 1950. In the end, the length or extent of the previous commitment mattered less than the perception of where North America and Vietnam fit into the larger imperial scheme of things and as pieces in the competition with archrivals France and the Soviet Union. A little over a decade before the American Revolution, for example, Britain had fought to deny France the opportunity to expand its holdings in North America. Having expended so much money, material, and men on ousting the French, the British were not about to allow the colonists their freedom in 1775. The Crown believed it could not permit the United States to act independently.

Similarly, the United States decided to make its stand in South Vietnam because of its importance for the larger empire in Asia. Japan was pivotal to American designs but it needed trading partners, and Southeast Asia, specifically a noncommunist South Vietnam, was critical. As Thomas McCormick has argued, "Empires were of a piece, and the loss of one member affected the organic health of the whole."[38] More commonly known as the domino theory, this idea posited that if Vietnam fell to communism, other nations would succumb, ultimately leaving the United States without a stake in the region. Equally unacceptable was the idea that a neutral South Vietnam could develop. When Diem made overtures to the NLF in 1963 with the intent of exploring just such an idea, his fate was sealed.[39] According to the Kennedy administration, Diem had to be removed. A neutral South Vietnam was almost as bad as a communist-controlled one.

It was necessary for the United States to organize the periphery and keep it from the clutches of its chief international competitor, just as it had been essential for Great Britain to prevent France from expanding in North America. As Don Higginbotham has summed up the comparison, "The Johnson government and to some extent the king and the North administration persisted in the face of dissent as long as they did because they believed in the domino theory – for Britain this meant the loss of the colonies would lead to secessionist movements in Ireland, the West Indies, and elsewhere; for the Johnson team, 'the best and the brightest,' it meant the fall to communism, one by one, of most Southeast Asian states." But in opposing Vietnamese unification and independence, American foreign policy

---

38 Thomas J. McCormick, *America's Half-Century: United States Foreign Policy in the Cold War and After*, 2d ed. (Baltimore, 1995), 149.
39 Kahin, *Intervention*, 153–8. See also Ellen J. Hammer, *A Death in December: America in Vietnam, 1963* (New York, 1987), 227–32.

makers pushed Vietnam into closer cooperation with the Soviet Union and China.[40]

Within five years, the Kennedy and Johnson administrations led the nation into a greater military commitment in South Vietnam. By the end of 1965, American ground troops totaled 180,000; a year later there were another 200,000, and the number came to just over 530,000 in 1968. Given its vast military commitments around the globe in the mid-1960s and considering the need for at least the appearance of an allied effort in Southeast Asia, the Johnson administration had to find its own Hessians to fight alongside American troops. In this respect, the American endeavor, which took shape in the form of the Many Flags Program, paralleled two aspects of the British struggle against the Americans. One was the recruitment of foreign mercenaries, be they Hessians or South Koreans, Thais, or Filipinos. The Many Flags Program had two principal attractions, according to George Kahin: "It had the potential of significantly reducing the U.S. military burden, and it also had the political advantage . . . of providing visible proof that the increased military intervention was sanctioned by, and enjoyed the tangible support of, some of Washington's allies."[41]

The other resemblance came in the economic benefits that accrued to areas in proximity of the fighting. During the American Revolution it was Canada and the British West Indies, especially the former, that received supplies, increased trade, and enjoyed the economic benefits from having troops and administrators stationed there. After Saratoga, for example, "British North America became an essential line of supply rather than a battleground. This brought about an increase of Imperial expenditures in Nova Scotia of 250 percent over the average for the previous decade."[42] Farther west, "The necessary deployment of troops in Quebec and the use of Halifax as the reception point of ships and supplies ensured that local economies received a powerful, if not a transforming, stimulus."[43]

During the Vietnamese revolution, it was Japan, followed by South Korea, Thailand, and the Philippines, that benefited the most from American military largesse. As Michael Schaller pointed out, between 1965 and 1972 "Japan earned at least $7 billion in 'extra' sales of goods and services related to Vietnam." From 1967 through 1969, South Korean soldiers in Vietnam sent home over $500 million, and the country earned about $1 billion from

---

40 Ronald Hoffman and Peter J. Albert, eds., *Arms and Independence: The Military Character of the American Revolution* (Charlottesville, 1984), 13. For a more detailed discussion of Soviet aid to North Vietnam, see Ilya V. Gaiduk, *The Soviet Union and the Vietnam War* (Chicago, 1996).

41 Kahin, *Intervention*, 332.   42 Marshall, "British North America," 381.

43 Ibid., 380.

1966 to 1970.[44] Proportionate to the number of troops they committed, Thailand and the Philippines did about as well.

By the end of 1967, the United States had just under five hundred thousand troops stationed in Vietnam. The war continued without signs of abating and despite the insistence of the American military leaders that the "cross-over point" had been reached – that is, the point at which North Vietnamese casualties exceeded their ability to replace them. Then again, American military personnel, like their British counterparts from the eighteenth century, had insisted from the start that the enemy would not be able to withstand a concerted military effort. In the eighteenth century, British assessments of the average American soldier ran from "a very effeminate thing, very unfit for and very impatient of war" to characterizations of the citizenry as "a worthless lot, a rabble, without discipline and without courage, running away from battle, deserting to the British ranks, leaving Mr. Washington with no army at all."[45]

In the summer of 1965, while discussing the consequences of escalating the conflict through the introduction of large numbers of American troops, the chairman of the Joint Chiefs of Staff, Earle Wheeler, spoke confidently of how the North Vietnamese would be placed in a bind. When Johnson asked about their matching the buildup, Wheeler asserted, "This means greater bodies of men from North Vietnam, which will allow us to cream them." And when Johnson followed up with an assessment of the likelihood of a greater North Vietnamese commitment, Wheeler stated, "The North would be foolhardy to put one-quarter of their forces in S[outh]V[iet]N[am]. It would expose them too greatly in the North."[46] But North Vietnamese regulars and Viet Cong guerrillas proved those predictions wrong and tenaciously battled American troops throughout South Vietnam. Nevertheless, according to many American military and civilian advisers in late 1967, the war was about to be brought to a conclusion.[47]

Although not a surprise, the Tet Offensive that came in January 1968 was a significant shock to the United States, and its impact was very similar to the effect Saratoga had had on Great Britain. Tet came a little less than three years after the onset of major hostilities. The period from Saratoga to the final peace treaty was five-and-a-half years; Tet to the Paris peace agreement

44 Quote is from Michael Schaller, *Altered States: The United States and Japan Since the Occupation* (New York, 1997), 198; also 199–201. For figures on South Korea, see Kahin, *Intervention*, 335.

45 Piers Mackesy, *The War for America, 1775–1783* (Cambridge, 1964), 30; and Marion Balderston and David Syrett, eds. *The Last War: Letters from British Officers During the American Revolution* (New York, 1975). Quotation is from the introduction by Henry Steele Commager, viii.

46 Kahin, *Intervention*, 373.

47 Marilyn Young, *The Vietnam Wars, 1945–1990* (New York, 1991), 214.

was almost exactly five years.[48] But far more important, and very much like Saratoga, Tet forced a fundamental reconsideration of strategy: The United States looked to rely more heavily on the indigenous forces, in this case ARVN, to shoulder a greater share of the fighting. According to George Herring, by March 1968, after the brunt of the Tet Offensive had been borne, the Johnson administration decided "the United States was willing to send limited reinforcements and substantial quantities of equipment but that continued American assistance would depend upon South Vietnam's ability to put its own affairs in order and assume a greater burden of the fighting."[49]

Tet signaled the beginning of the painful end of the American effort to control Southeast Asia. Upon his election in 1968, Richard Nixon embarked upon a twofold strategy to extricate the nation from the war: first was the withdrawal of American forces while maintaining military credibility by escalating the conflict through aerial bombardment, which included Cambodia; second was the buildup of South Vietnam through massive military and economic assistance. What John Shy has written about the impact of Saratoga holds true for Tet: "The new approach which emerged during 1778 emphasized the role of loyal Americans. It was at last admitted that, ultimately, restored British authority would have to depend on Americans themselves, and that even the strongest army and navy could do no more than create favorable conditions for the Americanization of the war."[50]

When the Paris Peace Accords were signed in January 1973, Nixon and his chief foreign policy adviser, Henry Kissinger, claimed that they had achieved an honorable peace and that South Vietnam was prepared to move forward as a viable political entity.

In truth, the situation looked a good deal different. South Vietnam was about as viable as the Loyalist governments set up in Georgia and South Carolina during the American Revolution. Once the supporting troops from abroad departed, the claims of the South Vietnamese government to legitimacy dissolved, less quickly than in the case of the Loyalists, but they vanished just the same. And with the disintegration of their state, South Vietnamese leaders lashed out at their American supporters who had deserted them. In writing to President Gerald R. Ford in March 1975,

---

48 Dating the major American military effort to March 1965 means that Tet occurred two years and ten months later; Saratoga, on October 17, 1777, came two years and six months after the start of major hostilities in April 1775. The fact that both battles, extremely significant as they were, occurred within the first three years of fighting is probably coincidental, but it is intriguing.
49 Herring, *America's Longest War*, 198.
50 Shy, "Loyalist Problem in the Lower Hudson Valley," 4.

General Nguyen Van Thieu sounded like William Franklin and so many other Loyalists two hundred years earlier. He asked for immediate and substantial American military support to stem the communist advance. He called "to the credibility of American foreign policy, and especially to the conscience of America."[51] When his solicitation proved futile, Thieu resigned and expressed his deep frustration at the lack of support from the United States. "The United States is proud of being an invincible defender of the just cause and the ideal of freedom in this world," he lamented. "I ask them: Are U.S. statements worthy? Are U.S. commitments still valid?"[52]

At the very bitter end it was the chief executives who remained defiant, impervious to the truth. For some time King George III had rejected "the arguments of his ministers that colonial independence was inevitable and refuse[d] to accept that the rebellion had succeeded."[53] In 1975, Ford and members of the Executive Branch seemed to be the only ones who failed to realize that the game was up, that the North Vietnamese had won. Beginning in January and continuing until just a few days before the actual collapse of the South Vietnamese government in late April, Ford tried repeatedly to secure congressional consent on a variety of military and economic assistance packages totaling anywhere from $300 million to $2 billion. In a cabinet meeting at the end of January, the president outlined a plan for supplemental assistance for South Vietnam and Cambodia and asked for support from everyone. He spoke of a "guilt complex" that afflicted the nation by withdrawing from Southeast Asia. Kissinger went further. Although the United States had "brought 550,000 troops home with honor," he worried about the impact that leaving South Vietnam to the communists would have on the nation's "international negotiating power" and "international negotiating ability," in addition to general credibility around the world.[54] Two years after the signing of the Paris Peace Accord, South Vietnam faced imminent destruction, Ford said, "and we apparently stand helpless, our fidelity in question, our word at stake." The American pledge to South Vietnam stood as a test for other commitments around the world. And Ford wondered whether America's allies would not suddenly doubt the advisability of working closely with the United States: "In this world of ours, it is not without hazard to be a friend of the U.S." Failure to provide

---

51 As quoted in Nguyen Tien Hung and Jerold L. Schecter, *The Palace File* (New York, 1986), 287.
52 Quoted in ibid., 331.   53 Scott, *British Foreign Policy*, 317.
54 Notes of the Cabinet Meeting, January 29, 1975, 1–2, 1975/01/29 Cabinet Meeting, box 4, James E. Connor papers, 1974–1977, Gerald R. Ford Library.

additional assistance to South Vietnam in its time of need would have serious and far-reaching complications. From negotiations in the Middle East to allies making "other accommodations to protect themselves," Ford foresaw a potentially catastrophic series of consequences emanating from the failure to provide supplemental assistance to South Vietnam and Cambodia. "The results would be an alien world in which the costs for our survival would dwarf anything we have ever known."[55] With the president and his advisers denying the reality of the situation while jockeying for political position, worried as they were about their positions in history, Congress made the hard decision and cut off the moribund Thieu regime from additional assistance.

In the war's aftermath, the United States placed severe restrictions on the Vietnamese economy through a number of punitive measures. The Ford administration froze $150 million in Vietnamese assets, expanded the embargo on North Vietnam – in place since the early 1960s – to include all of Vietnam and Cambodia, and denied Vietnam's entry into the United Nations. The embargo effectively undercut discussions between American oil companies and Vietnam about developing offshore reserves.[56]

The Nixon-Ford administrations, like the government of Lord North, failed to live long beyond the end of the fighting. And in their place came the American version of Lord Shelburne: Jimmy Carter. He wanted to heal the wounds of the war; he wanted to end the rancor. He wanted to put the war firmly into the past, and he tried to accomplish this by extending a diplomatic hand to Vietnam in 1977 through the normalization of relations without preconditions. But like Lord Shelburne, who had discovered that the "enmity caused by seven years of fighting and civil war" was impossible to expunge so quickly, Carter ran into strong emotions on both sides. Vietnamese negotiators were determined to get something for their long suffering. An equally resolute Congress was intent on providing nothing. In the end, the United States refused to give any consideration to the $4.75 billion in reconstruction assistance promised by Nixon in separate codicils to the 1973 peace agreement.[57] Moreover, Congress passed legislation in the spring preventing the payment of reparations and disallowing key international lending agencies from providing funds to Vietnam. For their part, the Vietnamese continued to press for something, almost anything, but the Americans remained firm and negotiations dragged into 1978,

---

55 Talking points for ibid.
56 Nayan Chanda, *Brother Enemy* (New York, 1986), 142.
57 Ibid., 148–50.

when they came up against the American desire to normalize diplomatic relations with the People's Republic of China.

The Vietnamese, who were initially as eager and expectant with regard to establishing diplomatic and economic relations with the United States as Americans had been with respect to Great Britain in the early 1780s, became frustrated at the impasse created by the American refusal to acknowledge its debt. Vietnam turned to the Soviet Union, signing a Treaty of Friendship and Cooperation in 1978 that, along with the Vietnamese invasion of Cambodia in December 1978, precluded a rapproachment with the United States for another decade and a half.[58]

The cost of the war to the United States was staggering. Between 1962 and 1975 South Vietnam was the largest recipient of USAID funds, a fact that bespeaks the distorting impact the war had on the nation's priorities. One estimate places the total cost of the war at $168 billion.[59] Approximately 150,000 Vietnamese escaped with the hastily departing Americans in 1975. Nearly one-and-a-half million left afterward, particularly during 1979 when Vietnamese "boat people" drifted in regional waters, searching for a place to land. Since 1975, approximately three-quarters of a million Vietnamese have settled in the United States. Others relocated to countries in Southeast Asia, creating a Vietnamese diaspora of growing economic importance.[60]

Of those Vietnamese who left, Hamilton's earlier warning held true: Many of the most productive citizens fled, along with their education, training, and skills. They departed just like the Loyalists did – out of fear of the reprisals against themselves and their families. The bloodbath predicted by American right-wing commentators never materialized, but the re-education camps were harsh and brutal environments.[61] Release meant a greater degree of freedom, but jobs were scarce for everyone, especially former loyalists to the American cause.

From a comparative perspective, if two million Vietnamese left after 1975, the figure represents less than 4 percent of the total population, which surpassed fifty million upon unification. If only sixty thousand Loyalists fled the United States during and after the revolution, the number comes to a little over 2 percent of the total population of roughly 2.8 million in 1780; if the higher figure of one hundred thousand is taken, it exceeds 3 percent. Some Loyalists who remained or tried to return after the end of the war

---

58 Ibid., 321–2.
59 Robert E. Wood, *From Marshall Plan to Debt Crisis: Foreign Aid and Development Choices in the World Economy* (Berkeley, Calif., 1986), 197.
60 Herring, *America's Longest War*, 267, 270. See also Arnold R. Isaacs, *Vietnam Shadows: The War, Its Ghosts, and Its Legacy* (Baltimore, 1997), 150–2.
61 For a resurrection of this thesis, see Henry Kissinger, *Diplomacy* (New York, 1994), 697–8.

found themselves imprisoned. The luckier ones were simply run out of town; the less fortunate ones were killed by mobs.

IV

What, then, are the major conclusions to be drawn from a comparison of the two revolutions and the principal responses they elicited from the powers that worked to thwart them? First, Great Britain and the United States sought a military solution once it became clear that the indigenous forces favorable to the imperial position were inadequate to stem the tide of revolution. By 1775, the British colonial authorities in North America had clearly lost control of the situation. With the Patriot attacks on British troops at Lexington and Concord in April, the Crown decided it was time to take stern action, to teach the colonists certain lessons. And from then until General Burgoyne's defeat in October 1777, those lessons would come from a contingent of British and foreign troops.

In Vietnam, it was the South Vietnamese government that was clearly losing the initiative by 1965, so much so that members of the Johnson administration concluded that the only way to bolster morale and instruct the North Vietnamese in the manner of American resolve was through a bombing campaign. That led to the introduction of regular ground troops to protect the airbases. When that strategy proved inadequate to the task, a major commitment of ground troops was deemed necessary, including foreign troops.

Second, both British and American military efforts failed in spectacular fashion to achieve their goals. Saratoga and Tet have come to represent turning points in both wars in similar ways. The former was clearly a British defeat, militarily speaking, and as such the plan to cleave New England from the other colonies gave way to the southern strategy and a greater reliance on Loyalists. Tet was not so much a military defeat for U.S. forces on a tactical level as it was a complete repudiation of the strategic assertions that the war was being won and that the Vietnamese were depleting their material and human resources to such levels that they no longer would be able to fight. The Vietnamese had to wait until 1972 to conduct another major military offensive, but comparatively speaking, colonial troops under General Washington never conducted a major offensive. Taking the offensive mattered less than outlasting the imperial power, something that both American and Vietnamese forces managed to do in the end and something that their opponents failed to comprehend at the time.

Third, faced with a longer and more costly conflict than they had anticipated, the British Crown and the U.S. government tried to rely on indigenous elements to assume a greater share of the fighting. In the case of the former it was the Loyalists; in the latter it was the ARVN troops in a process labeled Vietnamization, but in neither instance were these forces capable of stemming the tide of the revolutions they faced. With their defeat, the individuals who had fought for the empire looked for protection and assistance, sometimes during the hasty and mass exodus on the heels of the departing imperial troops, other times in the form of governmental aid for relocating somewhere else in the region.

Fourth, both Great Britain and the United States sought to curb the ambitions and activities of the victorious revolutionary nations immediately after they won independence. For Great Britain, this came through restricting Americans' access to the Caribbean trade they had previously enjoyed. It also meant maintaining and sometimes furthering alliances and relations with Indians along the western frontier of the new nation. And it included diverting resources to strengthen Canada. For the United States, this took shape in continuing a punitive economic embargo, freezing assets, and normalizing relations with Vietnam's principal nemesis in the region, China.

Fifth, the efforts to thwart the revolutions were costly both economically and politically. The British government saw a brief period of instability – from the North to the Shelburne administrations – before William Pitt the Younger became prime minister. In the United States, Nixon became the first president to resign from office. He was caught covering up an illegal break-in run by a group initially established to find and stop leaks concerning the administration's Vietnam policies. His hand-picked successor lasted a little over two years, and he was followed by the only Democratic president (other than John F. Kennedy, who was assassinated in his first term) not to be re-elected in the twentieth century. By the end of the Carter administration, commentators were writing about how the presidency had become an impossible job. Ronald Reagan changed all that.

Finally, despite assertions to the contrary, at the time of their defeat neither Great Britain nor the United States went into a dramatic decline as a result of having lost the fight. Instead, it was their global rivals who collapsed, leaving the international arena far less threatening for the immediate future. What is remarkable, then, is how many similarities exist between the American and Vietnamese revolutions and how strikingly alike are the responses they evoked from the principal imperial powers that sought to thwart them.

Ho Chi Minh appreciated enough of American history, both its eighteenth-century fight for independence and its more recent declarations about self-determination and anticolonialism during World War II, that he quoted portions of Thomas Jefferson's most famous work in proclaiming Vietnamese independence on September 2, 1945. And it is here that the comparison between the two revolutions and the decisions made in response to them becomes most poignant: The United States had the opportunity to act differently, especially given its own history, from the European powers that had colonized so much of the globe. Instead, Americans chose the path more heavily traveled and ended up becoming an imperial power very much like Great Britain, a fate the leaders of the revolution had anxiously sought to avoid.

4

Peripheral War: A Recipe for Disaster?

The United States in Vietnam and Japan in China

JOHN PRADOS

American national strategies, not to say many others, have long made a distinction between major wars and minor conflicts. Over the years the terminology has changed but the essential concepts remain. In the United States, for example, the Joint Chiefs of Staff, America's military high command, use the terms *general war* and *limited war*. A general war is an armed conflict in which the total resources of the belligerents are involved and their national survival is at stake. Limited war denotes a lesser conflict, one in which there is open fighting between military forces of two or more nations but basic existence is not at issue. The limited war falls short of the major war situation.[1] During the high Cold War, when the nuclear confrontation between the United States and the Soviet Union stood at the fore, different terms denoted these concepts. Military strategists then utilized the phrases "central war" and "peripheral war" in these same contexts. The central war would have been a direct conflict between Washington and Moscow. Peripheral war could be indirect and could take place anywhere around the world that forces, and not necessarily American or Soviet forces, were in contact.

This chapter aims to examine the impact of lesser conflicts upon the overarching security interests and key capabilities of major powers. For this purpose, I adopt the terminology of the earlier age, the age of the nuclear strategists, that is, "central" versus "peripheral" war. Note that no a priori judgments are being implied thereby: This examination of peripheral wars does not posit that the arenas of conflict lacked importance to the major powers, were geographically or economically unimportant, or in fact inferior in any respect. The use of the term "peripheral war" is intended instead

---

1 Department of Defense, Joint Chiefs of Staff Publication, no. 1: Dictionary of Military and Associated Terms (Sept. 3, 1974), Washington, D.C., Joint Chiefs of Staff, 1974.

89

to keep the focus on the fact that the major powers' primary enemies were countries other than those with whom they fought the limited wars under study.

Analyses of the impact of conflict can be given greater depth by according them a comparative aspect. To do so, I have selected two examples of peripheral war in the twentieth century. One is the Vietnam War and its impact on the United States; the second is Japan's war in China between 1937 and 1945. Comparison shows that the kinds of things that can happen to major powers embroiled in peripheral wars, and the dangers inherent in engagements of this type, are not so very different. Using the peripheral-war nomenclature permits us to view the specific conflicts, Vietnam and China, in their real relationship to the central security interests of the engaging major powers. Finally, adopting the terminology of peripheral war enables commentary on an emerging historical issue with respect to the Cold War as a whole: the place of Vietnam in accounts of the course of and eventual U.S. victory in the Cold War.

COMMONALITIES AND DIFFERENCES

There are a number of commonalities between the wars in China and Vietnam that suggest them as cases for a comparative examination. That China and Vietnam share a border and are both East Asian lands necessarily reveals similarities in climate, which in both nations ranges from tropical or semitropical to upland cold. North China, a frigid region, adds a difference, but Japan's war was fought in the central and southern parts of China most like Vietnam. In those parts of China, further, land-use patterns were similar to those in Vietnam: heavily populated coastal regions that emphasized agriculture, with much less population density in the interior. China's economy, featuring farming but including mining and manufacturing as well, was also similar to Vietnam's. A difference in the Vietnamese interior is its relative lack of urban areas; a number existed in the interior of China, particularly along major rivers.

But the most important commonalities have to do with the ways of warfare. Japan's war in China featured a mixture of conventional operations against Chiang Kai-shek's nationalist forces, plus counterguerrilla actions against Mao Zedong's Communists. The Imperial Japanese Army at all times retained the preponderance of force and could win any battle it chose to fight. The Japanese had a monopoly on naval power and could freely conduct amphibious operations along the China coast. Japanese warplanes held a substantial air superiority, although the

Chinese maintained a certain aerial capability and preserved it through the war.[2]

On the Chinese side, a painfully acquired and gradually formed pre-war elite military force was smashed by the Japanese in an initial battle (Shanghai, 1937). Following that was a lengthy period of resistance war in which Japanese forces expanded to control territory until they reached a point of rough equilibrium against Chinese defensive capability (in south-western China the location of the boundary is defined by the four battles that were fought for Changsha). The Chinese made an intrawar effort to create powerful new elite forces, first a mobile army and later a core of well-equipped infantry divisions.[3] Chinese efforts to form these forces and, indeed, to persist in the war effort were critically affected by outside aid: from Russia during the period from 1937 to 1939 and from the United States and Great Britain to a certain extent before 1939 but in a major way from then through the end of the war in 1945. The main effect of Chinese military efforts was to confront the Japanese with a situation in which they suffered a constant drain of resources plus casualties.

The United States' war in Vietnam also comprised a mixture of conventional and counterguerrilla operations. As with Japan's China war, moreover, the regular and counterinsurgency activity proceeded simultaneously. U.S. ground forces were at all times superior to those of the National Liberation Front (NLF) and the Democratic Republic of Vietnam (DRV). The Americans benefited from a local ally, South Vietnam; one Japanese action in the China war had been to create local puppet governments that then mobilized their own military forces to fight alongside the Japanese. As had Japan, the United States enjoyed a monopoly of naval power and complete impunity for amphibious, or indeed any other, operations on the Vietnam coast. The U.S. Air Force undertook a massive bombing campaign and at all times had undisputed aerial superiority in the war. The DRV air force, however, would never be eliminated and, as had the Chinese nationalists, always possessed a modicum of capability.[4]

During the war in Vietnam, the threads of commonality on the enemy side only deepened further. Just as in China, DRV regular troops were defeated in their first big battle (Ia Drang, 1965). And, of course, there is what everyone remembers about Vietnam, the lengthy resistance war.

---

2 In general, see Dick Wilson, *When Tigers Fight: The Story of the Sino-Japanese War, 1937–1945* (New York, 1982). See also Edgar Snow, *The Battle for Asia* (New York, 1941).

3 Edward O'Dowd, "General Chiang Pai-Li and Chinese Strategy in the Late 1930s," paper presented at the conference of the Society for Military History, 1990. See also Barbara Tuchman, *Stilwell and the American Experience in China, 1911–1945* (New York, 1970).

4 John Prados, *The Hidden History of the Vietnam War* (Chicago, 1995).

The Americans won any battle they chose to fight and controlled any territory they chose to occupy. Occupation here, as in China, did not necessarily deny the territory to the adversary, who remained free to infiltrate men and supplies to base areas scattered throughout the country. Even the patterns of occupation bore similarities – South Vietnamese and American troops held the towns and much of the densely populated lowlands, along with the routes and means of transportation, such as roads and railroads. The NLF and DRV forces freely circulated throughout the rest of the country. This had also been the case with Japan in China. As with Japan, once the sides had reached an equilibrium of force the battle lines largely stayed the same for many years. Meanwhile, as had been the case between Chinese nationalists and communists, there were delicate political, social, and ethnic divisions in the Vietnam War between the DRV and NLF. In certain critical military situations, such as during the Tet Offensive, this translated into failures in coordination between DRV and NLF troops in the field.[5] Even in terms of the strategy of guerrilla warfare followed in Vietnam and in China there were marked similarities, not least because the military theory propounded by the DRV's Vo Nguyen Giap had some of its intellectual roots in the writings of Mao Zedong.[6]

In sum, there are substantial enough similarities between Japan's war in China from 1937 through 1945 and America's war in Vietnam from 1965 to 1973 to warrant further comparative study. Turning the lens around to examine both of these cases in terms of the intervenor's strategy and actions in the specific conflict situation will considerably sharpen this point and substantially extend the analysis.

JAPAN IN CHINA

The key difference between political structures and government organization in the Japan of the 1930s, as compared with the United States in the 1960s, lay in two elements. First, in contrast to American democracy, the Japanese system was a constitutional monarchy created by the Meiji Restoration half a century earlier. Japan had the trappings of democracy in the form of political parties, elections, and a legislature, but power lay in the hands of an oligarchy. Industrialists had considerable influence, suffrage had yet to become universal, and the Diet, or legislature, held sway only in

5 Ngo Vinh Long, "The Tet Offensive and Its Aftermath," in Jayne Werner and David Hunt, eds., *The American War in Vietnam*, Southeast Asia Program Series no. 13 (Ithaca, N.Y., 1993).
6 Mao Zedong, *Problems of Strategy in China's Revolutionary War* (1936; reprint, Beijing, 1954); Vo Nguyen Giap, *People's War, People's Army* (New York, 1968).

some areas of policy. Defense and foreign affairs were strictly in the hands of the executive.[7]

At the same time, the cabinet government was skewed in favor of the military services, the Japanese army and Imperial navy, because of a provision that the cabinet minister for each must be an active-duty officer. This meant that the army minister, for example, could bring down the government simply by resigning. Informal understandings with fellow officers not to serve in place of a minister unless the cabinet adopted whatever policy the army favored could place a stranglehold on policy. Consequently, it is inaccurate to say that Japan in the 1930s had a national security policy; instead of a single policy there was a policy of the army and another of the navy, and ongoing debates were between proponents of various points of view within the armed services.[8]

This brings us to the question of Japanese national security writ large. Japan had fought Russia in a major war in 1904–5, and when national defense policy was revised in 1907 the army designated Russia as its hypothetical enemy, whereas the navy selected the United States. These choices reflected traditional army fixation on a continental strategy that focused on Korea and China. Following the Russo-Japanese War, when Japan formed what it called the Kwangtung Army to garrison concessions in Manchuria, preoccupation with Russia became even stronger. However, the Russian Revolution and Civil War temporarily seemed to weaken that country, and in a 1923 policy review the Japanese army followed the navy in viewing the United States as the main enemy. In 1928, Japanese fears revived as a result of observing an effective Russian military intervention in Manchouli. Annual Japanese war plans were assembled for approval by the Emperor, and these plans began to feature offensive operations against the Russian Far East.[9] Such trends would be further accentuated by activist officers in the army who, in 1929, effectively plotted to force Tokyo into a Japanese takeover of Manchuria. Suddenly Japan's interests in the area were huge, and it shared a border with the Russians. From 1929 on, it was an object of Japanese defense policy to be ready at all times for a war with Russia over Manchuria. Moreover, because the Japanese military doctrine remained an offensive one, strategic debate revolved around whether to "strike north," and a whole faction of army officers coalesced

7 Hugh Byas, *Government by Assassination* (New York, 1942).
8 Clark G. Reynolds, "The Continental Strategy of Imperial Japan," *United States Naval Institute Proceedings* 109, no. 8 (1983): 65–71.
9 Hayashi Saburo, with Alvin D. Coox, *Kogun: The Japanese Army in the Pacific War* (Westport, Conn., 1978), 2–4.

around the idea of an aggressive war against Russia. Obviously, the military preparedness of the Kwangtung Army became and remained a primary consideration.

China figured nowhere in all of this. China was a foreign policy interest, not a national security one, in a government where military interests dominated. Japan had pressured China repeatedly – during and after World War I, on extraterritoriality in the 1920s, and on trade arrangements. Japanese rhetoric frequently took the line that the Chinese did not appreciate Japan's efforts, a kind of arrogance that would mirror attitudes some Americans expressed during the Vietnam War. In 1932, these resentments boiled over into open fighting between Chinese and Japanese troops at Shanghai. Japanese labeled this clash the Shanghai Incident even though it had involved over 70,000 Japanese soldiers.

After Shanghai, the Japanese seemed to want China to acknowledge them in some way and kept encroaching on Chinese sovereignty. North Chinese provinces were taken over one by one until July 1937, when Japanese soldiers on maneuvers at the Marco Polo Bridge outside Beijing alleged they had been fired upon by Chinese troops. As with the Gulf of Tonkin in the Vietnam War in 1964, the truth of that episode would remain in dispute long afterward. In any case, this began the war, and the first big campaign started again at Shanghai and progressed into the Chinese interior and the "Rape of Nanking." The war then continued for eight long years. Between 1937 and 1941, when Japan's military quandary mushroomed with a global (central) war against the United States and Britain, the Japanese lost 190,000 men, with 520,000 wounded and another 430,000 sick. From Pearl Harbor to the end of the war, another 214,000 died.[10]

Costs come in many shapes and sizes. One cost is the impact of war on the military posture of the belligerent. In the Japanese case, at the outset of the conflict, research tells us, the army general staff planned for a maximum commitment of no more than eleven of the Imperial Army's thirty-four divisions. If reserves were to be mobilized, there could be up to fifteen. The plans failed the test of reality – by 1938 there were sixteen Japanese divisions in China, and at the end of 1939, twenty-three numbered divisions plus miscellaneous troops totaling the equivalent of fourteen more, 850,000 soldiers in all. That commitment remained constant through 1943, when the army began to draw on China for reinforcements to send to the Pacific war. Yet even in 1945 the number of Japanese troops in China still added

---

10 Alvin D. Coox, "Recourse to Arms: The Sino-Japanese Conflict, 1937–1945," in Alvin D. Coox and Hilary Conroy, eds., *China and Japan: The Search for Balance Since World War I* (Santa Barbara, Calif., 1978).

up to 19 percent of Imperial Army manpower, and the China area armies were Japan's largest coherent force.[11]

As with manpower, so too were there difficulties with supplies and equipment. War Ministry stockpiles in 1937 comprised sufficient ammunition for fifteen divisions to fight for eight months. Before that year ended, Japanese units at Shanghai found their munitions rationed, whereas units in North China had to transfer ammunition to the central front. A delicate, quasi-diplomatic process ensued wherein Japanese commanders in China had to beg the Kwangtung Army to give up some of its ammunition stocks and the latter determined to lie about how much it had in order to conserve. Then, in 1938 and again in 1939, the unimaginable happened and Japanese forces in Manchuria fought a series of sharp border battles against Soviet armies. The troops and ammunition in China were sorely missed. In the Pacific war, the large Japanese forces in China obliged the Japanese army to limit its commitments to the central war, the conflict against the Allies of World War II. As a result, when Japan stood at the height of its power the Imperial Army restricted its armies sent to the Pacific to just eleven divisions, leaving the Japanese without sufficient force to conduct military campaigns in Australia or India when those options were briefly possible in 1942.[12]

Another aspect of the peripheral war was the temptation to wage conflict on the side, as it were, as if the China imbroglio was not a war. Japan never did declare war during these hostilities and right through 1945 termed this conflict the "China Incident," as if it could be seen as a discrete crisis situation such as the Shanghai Incident of 1932. This Japanese omission had both political and diplomatic roots, political because the Meiji system accorded even greater powers to the military commands during wartime, and some Japanese wished to avoid giving that political power to the military. Diplomatic rationales flowed from international hostility toward Japan, which grew tremendously with the 1929–31 takeover of Manchuria and could be expected to mushroom if Japan went to war. However, the consequences of Japan's official stance of nonbelligerence were that it became much more difficult to mobilize national strength for the conflict, for example, to solve the ammunition shortage. In international law as well, without a state of war Japan lacked the rights of a belligerent and could not blockade China to seal that country off from outside supplies. That in turn had consequences for military strategy, forcing the Japanese into campaigns designed

---

11 Ibid.
12 John Prados, *Combined Fleet Decoded: The Secret History of American Intelligence and the Japanese Navy in World War II* (New York, 1995).

to seize all China's seaports. When the Chinese then shifted to a system of overland transport from Burma along what became known as the "Burma Road" and through French Indochina, it became clear the military strategy of isolation could not succeed within the existing limitations of the China Incident.[13]

The Japanese desire to cut off outside support to the adversary led Tokyo into a series of actions that greatly sharpened Japan's international difficulties and measurably increased the tensions that led to central war, which cannot have been Tokyo's original intent in conducting a peripheral war in China. First, Japan put diplomatic pressures on maritime nations to reduce Chinese imports. Additional pressures were then applied to Britain in an effort to reduce the use of the Burma Road and against France to preclude use of Indochina as an avenue of entry for Chinese supplies. In 1940–1, the Japanese forced additional sanctions on French Indochina and ultimately emplaced garrisons there. Many analyses of the central war that began at Pearl Harbor hold that Japan's occupation of French Indochina was the final move that made the larger conflict inevitable. Once war did begin, Japan promptly invaded Burma as well in an attempt to choke off the Burma Road. Ultimately Japan failed to completely cut off outside help to China.

Finally, over the course of the war years there were a series of abortive efforts at negotiation. These ranged from a German mediation in 1937–8, to direct diplomatic feelers, to Japan's creation of puppet regimes with which it then reached settlements that proved pyrrhic. In each case, its peripheral war put Tokyo in a false position because, with a clear perception of itself as the stronger power, the Japanese saw no need to negotiate the issues that were truly important to their adversaries. Thus, settlement was never possible and the conflict raged on, sapping Japanese strength along the way.[14]

In summary, Japan conducted a peripheral war in China that contributed to its entrapment in a bigger conflict, a central war with its own existence at stake. The purposes of the peripheral war were not clear, the desire to conduct it on the side led to an inability to wage the conflict effectively, the Japanese power position deluded Tokyo that it did not have to settle, and all along the way Japan lost strength. Meanwhile, military strategy did not succeed and measures taken to isolate the adversary also proved ineffective. The China Incident became a recipe for disaster.

13 Masatake Okumiya, "The Lessons of an Undeclared War," *United States Naval Institute Proceedings* 98, no. 12 (1972): 27–32.
14 Akashi Yoji, "A Botched Peace Effort: The Miao Pin Kosaku, 1944–1945," in Coox and Conroy, eds., *China and Japan*. See also Gerald E. Bunker, *The Peace Conspiracy: Wang Ching Wei and the China War, 1937–1941* (Cambridge, Mass., 1972); and John H. Boyle, *China and Japan at War, 1937–1945: The Politics of Collaboration* (Stanford, Calif., 1972).

THE UNITED STATES IN VIETNAM

American national security strategy never envisaged fighting a war in Vietnam, Indochina, or Southeast Asia as a whole. Rather, American strategy from the end of World War II onward aimed at containing communism. Observers can argue over the degree to which Washington misperceived communism as monolithic and directed only by Moscow, and thereby failed to appreciate the importance of the developing Sino-Soviet split. Nevertheless, Russian communism was and remained the main enemy. Western Europe, epitomized by Berlin, was the key place at which the adversaries were in contact and thus the focal point for national security planning. When the question of American military intervention in Vietnam and Indochina first arose, in the context of the 1954 crisis over the battle of Dien Bien Phu, the Joint Chiefs of Staff, confronted with near-term demands to actually send U.S. forces to Vietnam, replied that: "With reference to the Far East as a whole, Indochina is devoid of decisive military objectives and the allocation of more than token U.S. armed forces in Indochina would be a serious diversion of limited U.S. capabilities."[15] In contrast, preparations for a war with the Soviet Union stayed at the top of the list of U.S. priorities.

Unlike the Japanese case, this was not just the national security policy of one segment of the U.S. government. In its National Security Council system, the United States had a regularized procedure for elaborating a consensus policy. National security goals should therefore be considered those of the U.S. government as a whole.[16]

On the European front, the United States and its Western allies created the North Atlantic Treaty Organization (NATO) to put a broad umbrella over the defense preparations of each of the separate nations. Without such joint planning the nations would have had little defensive capability against a Soviet force nominally put at about 225 divisions during the 1950s and 175 in the 1960s. Regular U.S. combat strength through that period fluctuated between eleven and sixteen divisions, with a peak strength of twenty-two. There also were three divisions of U.S. Marines, but addition of those forces did not match Soviet strength. Defense analysts in Robert McNamara's Pentagon in the 1960s reevaluated the nominal value of Soviet forces; even afterward NATO's chances in a European ground war depended overwhelmingly on such equalizers as troop quality and tactical

15 Memorandum, Admiral Arthur Radford to Charles E. Wilson (chairman, Joint Chiefs of Staff to secretary of defense), May 26, 1954. Reprinted in United States-Vietnam Relations 1945–1967 (*Pentagon Papers*, government editions), 12 vols. (Washington, D.C., 1971), 9:487.

16 John Prados, *Keepers of the Keys: The National Security Council from Truman to Bush* (New York, 1991).

nuclear weapons.[17] It is hardly surprising that American planners devoted so much of their thinking to Europe.

To the extent that Americans thought about the security of Asia, the focus remained on Japan, the economic engine of the Far East, and South Korea, where the United States had fought a war from 1950 to 1953 and retained a forward-deployed infantry corps of two divisions. The key adversary was China, which had fought on the other side in the Korean war, and the more real (but less capable) threat of North Korea. Vietnam was never a serious national security issue.

As with the Japanese in China, the opening wedge in U.S. involvement in Vietnam stemmed from general foreign policy concerns. Washington had assumed the role of great-power ally as a result of the 1954 Geneva Agreement, which followed the French defeat at Dien Bien Phu and the political machinations thereafter. The great-power hubris that had bedeviled the Japanese in China also affected Americans in Vietnam. When a given panacea did not work, which was often, Americans frequently asserted that the failures were due to Vietnamese implementation and that had Americans done the same things they would have succeeded.[18] In the early 1960s, the desire for American, as opposed to Vietnamese, action became an important driving factor in demands for the commitment of U.S. troops to South Vietnam.

By 1964, Washington had laid plans for an aggressive war in Vietnam that hinged on use of U.S. forces, the deployment of which nevertheless seemed unjustified. As Tokyo had done with the Marco Polo Bridge incident, Washington seized on the Tonkin Gulf incident, an attack by North Vietnamese torpedo boats on U.S. warships in August 1964. An alleged second attack in the Gulf of Tonkin, which never occurred, became the direct reason for the first U.S. combat action in the Vietnam War. Subsequently, Vietnamese guerrillas retaliated with bombings of American facilities, and U.S. warplanes returned the insult in a cycle of escalation that led to the dispatch of U.S. ground troops in March 1965 and to President Lyndon B. Johnson's July 1965 decision to commit major land, naval, and air forces to Vietnam.[19]

The arrival of the U.S. Army in South Vietnam coincided in a big way with North Vietnam's commitment of its army in support of the Viet Cong

---

17 Alain C. Enthoven and K. Wayne Smith, *How Much Is Enough? Shaping the Defense Program, 1961–1969* (New York, 1971), 117–64.

18 David Halberstam, *The Best and the Brightest* (New York, 1972).

19 Brian VanDeMark, *Into the Quagmire: Lyndon Johnson and the Escalation of the War in Vietnam* (New York, 1991).

guerrillas. The Americans and North Vietnamese collided in Vietnam's central highlands, where the U.S. First Cavalry Division (Airmobile) defeated the North Vietnamese at Ia Drang. Thereafter Americans waged one campaign after another, always seemingly successful but never actually winning anything. From 1965 to 1973, a rough equilibrium prevailed in the war situation. Some observers now argue that the Americans were winning in the latter part of the war, but this does not concord with significant defeats suffered in Laos in 1971 or in the countrywide Easter Offensive of 1972. In any case, in 1972 internal political problems forced the United States to negotiate its way out of the Vietnam War, and withdrawal was accomplished in 1973. By then, America had suffered 59,000 dead, over 300,000 wounded, and more than 2,000 missing in action.[20]

The peripheral war in Vietnam had important effects on the U.S. military posture in the central-war situation, that is, in the military balance on the NATO front between the West and the Soviet Union. By 1968, ten of Washington's already depleted combat divisions were deployed in Vietnam. The standard planning factor at the Pentagon in those days was to prepare for "2 1/2 wars," that is, a NATO contingency, a Korean contingency, and one other possible hostile situation. For planning purposes, a major contingency involved the commitment of ten divisions, a minor one, of five. By that measure, in 1968, when eight of the army's sixteen divisions were in Vietnam (plus two of three Marine divisions), the U.S. military could scarcely have met a major contingency in Europe, and had there been an outbreak on the Korean peninsula (as briefly seemed possible in the wake of the Pueblo Incident of January 1968), Washington would have found itself completely swamped. Peripheral war in Vietnam robbed the United States of the ability to deal confidently with its central-war contingency.

These basic data put Washington in a poor enough light, but the truth is that the U.S. military posture was even worse than the surface facts reveal. Munitions were a problem, as had been true for Japan in the 1930s. The Navy and Air Force, for example, could not get enough 500- and 750-lb. bombs to fully supply their air campaigns, and the United States was obliged to buy back from Germany bombs that had previously been declared surplus and given to the Germans at minimal cost. Had there been a European war, NATO capability would have been further reduced. The army had problems with helicopters, some kinds of artillery and, above all, experienced

---

20 Prados, *Hidden History*. See also Phillip B. Davidson, *Vietnam at War: The History, 1946–1975* (New York, 1991).

officers and noncommissioned officers. Problems of the Vietnam deployment were solved by reassigning the best men from other Army units all over the world. The result was predictable: As early as June 1966, the majority of the army's major combat units outside Vietnam – the ones that would have had to fight in Europe or Korea – were rated as only marginally or not at all prepared for combat by the army's own rating system. In a biography of Army Chief of Staff General Harold K. Johnson, the author notes, "meeting the ever-increasing requirements in Vietnam had ripped hell out of the army's readiness, cohesion, and morale in every other part of the world."[21]

North Vietnamese Military Commander General Vo Nguyen Giap was exactly right in noting, in a study published in Hanoi in the autumn of 1967, that "the present United States mobilization level has far exceeded initial U.S. forecasts and is at sharp variance with U.S. global strategy."[22]

President Johnson had made this entire problem more complicated by refusing to seek a declaration of war, to mobilize U.S. reserve and National Guard forces, and to expand war production. This is typically seen as Johnson choosing between "guns or butter" and coming down on the side of his domestic programs. Despite the particular rationale for Johnson's decision, however, the fact that in its peripheral war in China, Japan chose to do exactly the same thing under very different circumstances suggests a process at work and not necessarily a unique sequence of events. In the American political system, however, the dragging on of the peripheral war without a political consensus ever having been built brought steadily increasing dissatisfaction with the war, culminating in widespread opposition, even open confrontation. This growth of political opposition forced Washington to end its direct participation in the Vietnam War.

Before that happened, Washington tried, as Tokyo had before it, to cut off outside support for the adversary, which came from China and the Soviet Union and was funneled through North Vietnam into Laos and Cambodia, and then to the forces fighting in South Vietnam. The Americans resorted to a variety of actions that ranged from establishing border posts on the Vietnamese border, to covert operations against the North Vietnamese supply lines, to massive bombing of those routes, which became known as the "Ho Chi Minh Trail." The military efforts devoted to this increased until 1970 brought an actual invasion of Cambodia, and 1971 brought one

---

21 The Army readiness ratings were C-3 and C-4. Lewis Sorley, *Honorable Warrior: General Harold K. Johnson and the Ethics of Command* (Lawrence, Kans., 1998), 252.
22 Vo Nguyen Giap, *Big Victory, Great Task* (New York, 1968), 90.

of Laos. Antiwar opposition in the United States greatly intensified with the perception that the United States had now expanded the Vietnam War into Indochina in its search for victory.[23]

Finally, again as had been the case in the China Incident, for years there were abortive attempts at negotiation over Vietnam. These proved fruitless until 1972 because American negotiators were never authorized to advance proposals that were realistic. One can argue over how realistic Hanoi's proposals were as well, but North Vietnam understood that the U.S. political position weakened daily and therefore saw no reason to settle on American terms. Negotiations did not begin to move forward until Washington abandoned its insistence that all North Vietnamese forces withdraw from the war as a condition of settlement; this would have meant a negotiated defeat for the Viet Cong and would always remain unacceptable to Hanoi. Settlement only became possible when American politics made Washington's continuation of the war impossible.[24]

In summary, the United States conducted a peripheral war in Vietnam that greatly hampered its capabilities against the Soviet Union in Europe and China in Korea, the areas of its central-war interest. It proved extremely fortunate for Washington that no conflict evolved in the arenas of main confrontation, but the fact that no central war occurred does not mean that engaging in the peripheral war had not been an error. In terms of process, it is striking that so many features of America's peripheral war in Vietnam find more-or-less precise analogs in Japan's war in China. The similarities include the hubris with which engagement began; the use of "incidents," real or otherwise, to excuse acts of force carried out for concealed purposes; the mistaken notion that the peripheral war can be carried out without impact on the great power's central interests; the notion that the peripheral war can be waged on the side, without formal declaration or national mobilization; the corollary effects on military strategy of waging war without benefit of full resources; the campaigns to isolate the adversary from its supply sources and the corollary effects these campaigns had on the great powers' political or international problems; and the illusion that the great powers' apparent capability ensured that any negotiated settlement could only be on its own terms. As in the case of Japan's war in China, Washington's war in Vietnam became a recipe for disaster.

23 John Prados, *The Blood Road: The Ho Chi Minh Trail and the Vietnam War* (New York, 1998).

24 For the Johnson administration period, see George Herring, ed., *The Secret Diplomacy of the Vietnam War: The Negotiating Volumes of the Pentagon Papers* (Austin, Tex., 1983). For the later period, see Allen E. Goodman, *America's Search for a Negotiated Settlement of the Vietnam War* (Stanford, Calif., 1978).

AFTER THE BATTLE

Today some prefer to argue that the Vietnam War forms merely one episode in a larger tapestry, a lost battle, perhaps, in a Cold War that America won. This is not a correct view. First, to refer back to the distinction between peripheral and central wars, Vietnam clearly meets the definition of a peripheral war but does not meet that of a central conflict. Moreover, to take the argument head-on, were Vietnam a battle in the larger Cold War, it would relate in some way to the conflict of which it formed a part. Instead, we find that the military tactics used in the Vietnam War do not match those planned for central war, that the forces sent to Vietnam impeded planning for central war, and that the political and social processes set in motion by Vietnam undercut the unity required for central war.

The American economic juggernaut that the pundits tell us was the driver in Cold War victory turns out to have been significantly retarded in its development by the Vietnam War. In fact as well as in logic, the Vietnam War remained a diversion from Washington's real interests in its central conflict.

On a second level, although this argument cannot be made in detail here, to see Vietnam as a Cold War episode denies its place in the scheme of Vietnamese history. The Vietnam War to Vietnamese was about national independence and reunification. Had there been no Cold War, the Vietnam War would still have happened. Had the United States not intervened, the Vietnam conflict would have been shorter but would still have occurred. For Vietnam to have been a simple Cold War battle requires that the war took place *because* of the Cold War, and this clearly is not the case.

It is true that American administrations in various contexts used Cold War rhetoric to justify the Vietnam intervention or in efforts to build support for the war, but rhetoric is a construct and is employed to convince. The assertion of something does not make it true. On the other side, although it is also true that North Vietnam benefited from the assistance of nations who were America's Cold War enemies, this also does not make Vietnam simply a Cold War battle. The degree of Chinese and Soviet involvement in, and support of, the war did not rise to a level sufficient to make Vietnam a peripheral war for them as well as for the United States. Only if the United States had forced Soviet and/or Chinese counterintervention, which it did not do, could Vietnam be categorized as a true Cold War battle. In the absence of such action, Vietnam itself always was and remained the key conflict partner in this war, which brings us back to Washington, which failed to understand the Vietnamese conflict and so conducted a peripheral war that diverted its strength and resources.

Finally, a few words on peripheral war as a phenomenon. In the post–Cold War world, with no overarching global conflict, no "Cold War" on the horizon, most wars for the United States will be peripheral wars. The campaign in Afghanistan following the September 11, 2001, attacks on New York and Washington, D.C., for example, could be seen as a peripheral war. This may prove highly problematic if what we have seen here is true. That is, the comparative study in these two cases suggests that great powers tend to enter peripheral wars without thinking through their policies; are tempted to conduct them on the side, without national consensus; maneuver to attempt to isolate the enemy without regard for the international consequences of their actions; construct their military strategies without regard for their central security interests; and negotiate from the premise that the only possible settlement is one on their own terms. In the global world of the post–Cold War era, national power is highly interdependent and will tend to be fleeting. A mistaken peripheral war can indeed be a recipe for disaster.

5

The Panmunjom and Paris Armistices

Patterns of War Termination

JEFFREY KIMBALL

I

War termination research emerged as a recognizable field of historical and social scientific inquiry during the decade of the 1960s – a time of intensifying nuclear confrontation between the United States and the Soviet Union, expanding Third World rebellion against First World dominance, and escalating Americanization of the war in Vietnam.[1] Historians, political scientists, social psychologists, and sociologists identified three major types of war endings: (1) the decisive victory of one side and the conditional or unconditional surrender of the other, as in the 1918 and 1945 closings of World War I and World War II; (2) the imposition of a peace upon the belligerents by one or more external powers, as with the Dayton Agreement that terminated the Bosnian War of 1992–5; and (3) armistices negotiated by belligerents, such as those that led to the cessation of fighting and limited compromises on political and military issues in the Korean War (1950–3) and the U.S.-Vietnam War (ca. 1959–73). Although appearing simplistically reductionist to some other scholars of diplomacy, peace, and war, these commonsensical generalizations nonetheless prove quite useful in clarifying the complexities of war termination by focusing attention on its essential elements.

War endings of the third kind raise an important question: Why do belligerents turn to negotiations in the midst of wars they have not yet lost?

---

1 For purposes of analysis, the word "termination" can be taken to mean simply the cessation of violence and not necessarily the final solving of a war's causes or the abandonment by the belligerents of the political and strategic goals for which they fought. The first scholarly panels organized by the Conference on Peace Research in History in the mid and late 1960s centered on the question of how some historic wars had ended and, implicitly, how current ones could be brought to an end. The war in Vietnam was much on the minds of panelists and was the main stimulus for the founding of CPRH (now the Peace History Society). See the *Journal of Peace Research*, no. 4 (1969), for papers from these panels.

Theorists suggest that the most important determinant is the appreciation by decision makers on both sides that a condition of military stalemate has been reached, coupled with their judgment that the chances of favorably altering the military balance of power on the field of battle are slight or nonexistent, or that the effort will be too costly in relation to some standard of cost-effectiveness. In this instance, decision makers have decided that a compromise armistice will better serve their reduced aims, offer more hope of achieving their goals in the long run, or at least lessen the heavy human, material, and political costs of continued war. The costs of war include not only military and civilian casualties but economic burdens, physical and environmental damage, territorial loss, and political repercussions on the home front that undermine the leadership's hold on power. Constraints include public war weariness and active antiwar opposition, pressure from allies, and sanctions imposed by the international community.

War leaders may nevertheless continue to prosecute a war in spite of its burdensome costs and constraints. Their persistence may be the product of such "irrational" factors as nationalism, political ideology, ethnic prejudice, religious intolerance, and bellicose, power-seeking personality traits, as well as such "rational" factors as their not having palpably felt the pressure of internal dissent or international disapprobation. Much depends on structural factors such as the nature of a belligerent nation's political system and the ability or inability of dissidents among the elite and the general public to countervail those who support the war. War leaders may also miscalculate, believing that military options are still available, that the stalemate can be broken through will and skill, and that they, their armies, and their nations can bear the costs of continued war. Moreover, their ethical standards may be such that they are more willing than others to tolerate the human suffering caused by war and to risk greater destruction to their country and its material and human resources.

One obvious and generally recognized axiom concerns the negotiations: Once begun, they will fail if the two sides do not compromise their differences on key issues. The nature of war – the most violent relationship between two states or factions within a state – is such that its causes are rooted in the breakdown or rejection of diplomatic means of compromising issues to the satisfaction of each antagonistic group of decision makers. Both sides are likely to begin negotiations and subsequently agree to compromise, however, if they recognize – even to different degrees – the reality of military stalemate and the cost-ineffectiveness of continued fighting. There is perhaps less consensus about the following point: In negotiations that are taking place during a war of indecisive fighting, the losing side – that is, the side least able or willing to bear the prospective costs of a continuing war – makes the most important concessions and therefore more greatly influences the timing of an armistice agreement.[2]

II

The armistice concluded at Panmunjom in 1953, which brought the Korean War to a close, well illustrates war termination generalizations of the third kind. Truce talks had begun at Kaesong on July 10, 1951, after a year of rapid but bloody and destructive advances and retreats along the length and breadth of the Korean peninsula. The offensive launched on June 25, 1950, by Kim Il Sung of North Korea (Democratic People's Republic of Korea or DPRK). In a dramatic turnabout after weeks of desperate flight and then defensive fighting around the Pusan Perimeter, the American-led United Nations Command (UNC) opened a strong counteroffensive in mid-September, which was greatly aided by a risky but successful amphibious landing behind North Korean lines at Inchon on the northwestern coast of South Korea. By the end of the month, UNC forces had driven the DPRK army back to the thirty-eighth parallel – the original boundary separating the north and south. Having decided to seek victory through the reunification of the two Koreas, the UNC had sent its forces across the parallel. By the end of November, one spearhead had reached the Yalu River, which separated North Korea from the People's Republic of China (PRC). Then, in another major turnaround, Chinese forces (Chinese People's Volunteers or CPV) had intervened with powerful thrusts south of the Yalu, surprising the UNC commander American General Douglas MacArthur. Driven into a precipitous retreat, the UNC had fallen back as far south as the thirty-seventh parallel by mid-January. Between late January and late June 1951, UNC counteroffensives had pushed the CPV and DPRK armies back to a line intersecting the thirty-eighth parallel – roughly to where the war had begun. Except for attacks by both sides aimed at consolidating positions or influencing negotiations, the front more or less remained stationary for the

---

2 I am indebted to Helena Meyer-Knapp, who in 1993 shared in correspondence with me her insightful thoughts about cease-fires and whose ideas caused me to begin thinking about historical patterns of war termination. For relatively recent summary accounts of war termination theories as well as additional source citations, see Gordon A. Craig and Alexander L. George, *Force and Statecraft: Diplomatic Problems of Our Times*, 3d ed. (New York, 1995), 229–44; Allan E. Goodman and Sandra Clemens Bogart, eds., *Making Peace: The United States and Conflict Resolution* (Boulder, Colo., 1992); Paul R. Pillar, *Negotiating Peace: War Termination as a Bargaining Process* (Princeton, N.J., 1983); and Jeffrey Kimball, "How Wars End: The Vietnam War," *Peace and Change: A Journal of Peace Research* 20 (Apr. 1995): 183–202.

remainder of the war, leaving surviving troops and civilians to wonder what the fighting had been about.[3]

By June 1951, a month before negotiations opened at Kaesong, armies on both sides had suffered heavy battle casualties; millions of Korean civilians were dead, wounded, or refugees; hundreds of Korean cities and villages were in ruins; the economies of South and North Korea were in tatters, and those of the major powers, the United States, the USSR (which backed the DPRK/PRC side in the war), and China were, in different ways and degrees, strained. Leaders on both sides recognized that military victory in the war was beyond reach without incurring enormously greater costs and risks.[4]

High casualties, declining troop morale, financial concerns, supply and equipment shortages, and fears of further military setbacks had led Mao Zedong and Kim Il Sung in early June 1951 to seek Joseph Stalin's support for the opening of negotiations with the UNC.[5] After meeting in Moscow with Kim and Gao Gang, Mao's representative, Stalin telegrammed Mao that he "recognized . . . an armistice is now advantageous."[6] If nothing else, communist leaders hoped the negotiations might serve to prevent continuing UNC attacks and allow Chinese–North Korean forces to strengthen their defensive line, regroup, and counterattack in order to influence the terms of the negotiations.

Among civilians in the American government, coincidently, there was little will to push farther north in the face of the growing costs and developing constraints. American and allied casualties, for example, were mounting. During the previous year, moreover, there had been a precipitous decline in American public support for the war. In addition, European allies insisted on an armistice, and Washington policy makers had come to recognize that the war could not be won short of turning the conflict into a world war.

3 Useful and relatively recent accounts of the war include: Bruce Cumings and Jon Halliday, *Korea: The Unknown War* (London, 1988); Burton I. Kaufman, *The Korean War: Challenges in Crisis, Credibility, and Command* (New York, 1986); William Stueck, *The Korean War: An International History* (Princeton, N.J., 1995); and Shu Guang Zhang, *Mao's Military Romanticism: China and the Korean War, 1950–1953* (Lawrence, Kans., 1995).

4 Stueck, *Korean War*, 225; memorandum of conversation with Zhou Enlai, July 24, 1951, diary of N. V. Roshchin, doc. 9 in David Wolff, "One Finger's Worth of Historical Events': New Russian and Chinese Evidence on the Sino-Soviet Alliance and Split, 1948–1959," Working Paper no. 30, Cold War International History Project, Washington, D.C., 2000, 41–2.

5 Ciphered telegrams, Stalin to Razuvaev, with message for Kim Il Sung, May 29, 1951; Stalin to Mao, June 5, 1951; Mao to Stalin, June 5, 1951; Mao to Stalin via Roshchin, June 13, 1951; docs. 64, 65, 66, and 70 in "New Evidence on the Korean War: New Russian Documents on the Korean War," introd. and trans. by Kathryn Weathersby, *Cold War International History Project Bulletin*, nos. 6–7 (winter 1995–6): 59–61.

6 Ciphered telegram, Stalin to Mao, June 13, 1951, subj. Meeting in Moscow with Gao Gang and Kim Il Sung, ibid., 60.

President Harry S. Truman, finally fed up with MacArthur's insubordinate lobbying for an expanded war, and receiving complaints from allies about the general's irresponsible bellicosity, had removed this archly hawkish, anticommunist crusader from his command of UNC forces in mid-April. Yet, there was continuing pressure from the military to retain limited military options in order to influence the negotiations, and there was also vocal pressure from South Korean President Syngman Rhee and the McCarthyite Right wing in the United States to press on northward to liberate North Korea and roll back communism regardless of the risks.[7]

The composition of the two delegations that came together at Kaesong on July 10, 1951, to negotiate an armistice mirrored the international and political complexities of this costly struggle on the divided Korean peninsula. On the communist side, General Nam Il of the PRC headed a delegation consisting of one other Chinese general and three North Korean generals. Admiral C. Turner Joy of the United States headed the UNC delegation, consisting of three other American military commanders and one South Korean general. (General William Harrison replaced Joy on May 22, 1952.) During the next few weeks, the negotiators were able to approve an agenda calling for discussion on the cessation of hostilities, a demarcation line separating the two sides, an armistice for the peninsula, the creation of a supervisory organization for carrying out the terms of the cease-fire and armistice, and arrangements for the release of prisoners of war (POWs). They failed, however, to reach agreement on any of these agenda items. Amid posturing, ill-will, and cultural misunderstanding, the communist side suspended negotiations on August 23, 1951, although subdelegations continued to meet. The domestic, international, and military pressures on the belligerents were such, however, that the two sides resumed plenary talks on October 25 at Panmunjom, a more neutral site in relation to the battle line dividing the opposing armies. Soon negotiators came to terms on a thirty-day cease-fire and an armistice line that followed the battle line, even though there was considerable haggling about precisely where to draw the line.

Agreement on this point amounted to a concession by the PRC-DPRK side, insofar as it had originally proposed the thirty-eighth parallel as the dividing line, but the thirty-day cease-fire and the new demarcation line was also a concession by the UNC side, inasmuch as it permitted the Chinese and North Koreans to strengthen their defenses and prevented UNC forces

7 Stueck, *Korean War*, chap. 6; John E. Mueller, *War, Presidents, and Public Opinion* (New York, 1973), chap. 3.

from exerting substantial military pressure at a time when they seemed to enjoy a military advantage. Civilians in the Truman administration believed, however, that such an effort would have been matched by Beijing and Moscow, would be excessively costly in lives and treasure, and risked the loss of allied support. After the military debacles of the previous year, moreover, they distrusted those in the military who predicted the possibility of victory.[8]

Although negotiations continued, progress was impeded by differences between the two sides regarding post-armistice military reinforcement and airfield reconstruction rights, membership on the international supervisory commission, and, especially, the repatriation of prisoners of war. Truman's feisty personality, his sense of principle, and his perception of political necessity – all matched by Mao's "military romanticism" – compounded the problem of arriving at an agreement. Standing on what he considered high principle, Truman, in violation of the Geneva Convention, decided to insist on the voluntary repatriation of POWs; Mao decided he could not yield on this issue of principle and honor, and he also believed he was preventing a third world war by holding the United States at bay in Korea. But whatever the motives of the two belligerents – an issue that historians still debate – the repatriation question stalled the talks for another year and a half.[9]

After considerable bickering and a great deal of bloody fighting on the ground and bombing from the air, the diplomatic ice was broken on February 21, 1953, when General Mark Clark advanced a proposal passed in December by the League of Red Cross Societies calling for a gesture of goodwill through the repatriation of sick and wounded POWs. On March 28, the Chinese and North Koreans accepted Clark's offer for such an exchange, but they also proposed that those prisoners who did not "insist upon repatriation" be turned over to a neutral state in order to discover their true wishes.[10] Additional progress was made in the negotiations in late April and early May at the time of "Little Switch" – the exchange of sick and wounded POWs. On May 7, General Nam Il of the DPRK-PRC delegation took a step in the direction of the UNC position in proposing that nonrepatriated POWs remain in Korea to be processed by a multination repatriation commission as opposed to being removed to a neutral

---

8 Stueck, *Korean War*, 238–43; Kaufman, *Korean War*, 209–14; Pingchao Zhu, "The Road to an Armistice: An Examination of Chinese and American Diplomacy During the Korean War Cease-Fire Negotiations, 1950–1953," Ph.D. diss., Miami University, 1998, chap. 3.

9 Stueck, *Korean War*, 245; Shu, *Mao's Military Romanticism*, chap. 9; Pingchao, "Road to an Armistice," chap. 4.

10 Stueck, *Korean War*, 313.

country. On May 13, the recently elected U.S. administration of Dwight D. Eisenhower countered with proposals on repatriation procedures that met some of Rhee's objections, but which the communist side branded as unacceptable and which threatened to wreck the talks and split the Western alliance. On May 25, American negotiators retreated from several of the May 13 provisions; the communists accepted the new U.S. proposal on June 4, even though it did not fully meet their previous requirements on repatriation; and on June 14, final agreement was reached on the demarcation line. The armistice was signed by both parties on July 27, 1953, after the Eisenhower administration had with carrots and sticks won Rhee's grudging acceptance of the treaty.[11]

In the decades following the Panmunjom armistice, conventional wisdom in the United States held that communist concessions had been made in response to Eisenhower's nuclear threats against China in May 1953. Admiral C. Turner Joy had offered up this version of Cold War history in 1955. In the next several years, President Eisenhower and his secretary of state, John Foster Dulles, repeated the claim, causing it eventually to enter popular political culture, with no little help from professional and lay historians.[12]

It is true that Eisenhower had entered office intending to use expanded conventional bombing and the threat or reality of nuclear attack to force concessions from the other side. It is also true that the July armistice agreement followed Eisenhower's accelerated bombing campaign and his nuclear threats, giving the appearance that conventional bombing and nuclear threats had caused the armistice to come about. Beyond the testimony of Joy, Eisenhower, and Dulles and the apparent logic of the principle of *post hoc, ergo propter hoc*, however, there was and is little or no documentary evidence to support the claim that the Chinese caved in to these pressures; indeed, the contextual and primary evidence suggests that if nuclear attack entered their calculations, it was only one of many considerations.

Eisenhower's nuclear threats in any event were not clearly or forcefully delivered and were not substantively different from those implied threats made by the Truman administration in the fall of 1951, when B-29 bombers actually carried out A-bombing test runs over North Korea with large conventional bombs. Eisenhower's threats, as well as the bombing of the DPRK's dam-irrigation system in May, moreover, took place after communist

11 Ibid., 313–42; Kaufman, *Korean War*, 306–21; Pingchao Zhu, "Road to an Armistice," 231–55.
12 C. Turner Joy, *How Communists Negotiate* (New York, 1955), 161–2; James Shepley, "How Dulles Averted War," *Life*, Jan. 16, 1956, 70–80; Dwight D. Eisenhower, *Mandate for Change, 1953–1956* (Garden City, N.Y., 1963), 181.

negotiators had several weeks previously indicated a change in policy by accepting General Clark's proposal for Little Switch, coupled with their proposal to turn nonrepatriates over to a neutral state. Further, Chinese forces in late May and early June – after the bombing of dams and nuclear threats – carried out strong, punishing attacks against positions held by Turkish and South Korean units along the front line. These attacks signaled their continuing resolve and had the specific purposes of imposing additional costs on their enemies, influencing the negotiations, obviating the possibility of U.S. amphibious landings, and teaching Rhee a punitive lesson for having obstructed progress on the POW issue.[13]

The full chronology of events and the evidence itself suggests a more complicated causal process leading to the armistice; namely, that it came about after hawks on both sides had been silenced, replaced, or had experienced a change of mind. Those whose minds were changed had responded to economic burdens, military losses, political and military constraints, risks of expanded war, the recognition of de facto stalemate, and the pressure of allies and the international community. There is evidence that Mao and Kim were ready at least as early as February 1952 to end the war because of food shortages in North Korea, budgetary strain in China, their estimate that the UNC was also ready to settle, and their assessment that military conditions were unlikely to change.[14] There is some evidence that Stalin, the most hard-line of major communist leaders, was moving in the direction of accepting a compromise settlement before his death on March 5, 1953. Whether this assessment is correct or not, his demise meant the ascension to power in Moscow of a new leadership that had long been concerned about economic difficulties in Eastern bloc countries and calculated that a less confrontational policy toward the West not only entailed less risk of general war but was also more likely to split the Western alliance in the event that Eisenhower pursued hard-line policies in Korea.[15]

Although Eisenhower had entered office determined against making concessions at Panmunjom, he had also pledged to the public to end the war sooner rather than later and was personally committed to doing so.

---

13 On Chinese resolve regarding U.S. bombing a year earlier, see Mao to Stalin, July 18, 1952, document 108 in "New Evidence on the Korean War," 78. On atomic threats, see Mark A. Ryan, *Chinese Attitudes Toward Nuclear Weapons: China and the United States During the Korean War* (Armonk, N.Y., 1989), 64, 156; Roger Dingman, "Atomic Diplomacy During the Korean War," *International Security* 13 (winter 1988–9): 50–1; Edward Keefer, "Eisenhower and the End of the Korean War," *Diplomatic History* 10 (summer 1986): 267–8; Daniel Calingaert, "Nuclear Weapons and the Korean War," *Journal of Strategic Studies* 11 (June 1988): 177–202; and Stueck, *Korean War*, 329. Cf. Kaufman, *Korean War*, 319.

14 See, e.g., ciphered telegrams, Mao to Stalin, Jan. 31 and Feb. 8, 1952, docs. 100 and 102 in "New Evidence on the Korean War," 74–6.

15 Stueck, *Korean War*, 326–8.

Notwithstanding his own hawkish-leaning strategic instincts and the political pressure he felt from Rhee and the Republican Right, he prudently yielded to stronger pressures: declining public support for war; budgetary demands; allied entreaties; his recognition of the high risk of general war and the doubtful efficacy of nuclear bombing; and the knowledge that renewed ground offensives could not be launched until 1954 – a timetable beyond the endurance of allies, the war-weary public, and dissenting elites. In the end, both sides conceded points on the POW repatriation issue, which, while having served to prolong the war, had never been as fundamental as those issues that had already been agreed to in November 1951: a cease-fire and an armistice line, both of which acknowledged the failure of the war and the acceptance of a divided Korea. Neither side, therefore, can be said to have alone been the "losing side"; both were losers, and both had come more or less simultaneously to the conclusion that it was time to end this costly, deadlocked war.

III

Besides having served as a "consciousness-raising" stimulus for war termination research in the West, the Vietnam War[16] provides examples of all three types of war endings: the Geneva Agreements of 1954, which resulted from military deadlock on the battlefield, internal costs, and international pressures upon the belligerents (type 2); the armistice of 1973, which was the product of negotiations between the main belligerents under conditions of military stalemate (type 3); and the decisive communist victory of 1975, in which there were clear winners and losers (type 1).

The 1973 ending, which occurred during the "Richard Nixon phase" of the Vietnam War but began at the end of the "Lyndon Johnson phase," has been the most frequently cited case of this long conflict's three endings. After the Tet Offensive of 1968 had driven home the point that the Johnson phase of the long war was militarily deadlocked, the White House in Washington and the Politburo in Hanoi began to take meaningful steps toward negotiations. Neither side had chosen to open talks because of a peace-loving, goodwilled desire to compromise with its enemy. The decision of each was based instead on hardheaded calculations of cost and opportunity.[17]

---

16 Technically, "the Vietnam War" was at least two wars: the First Indochina War, or Anti-French War, of 1945 to 1954, and the Second Indochina War, or Anti-American War, from approximately 1959 to 1973, which had a civil war sequel from 1973 to 1975.

17 Kissinger, as well as some historians, have claimed that "our [American] mode of settling conflicts was to seek a solution somewhere between the contending positions. . . . To them [the North Vietnamese and southern guerrillas] the Paris talks were not a device for settlement but an instrument of political warfare" (Henry A. Kissinger, *White House Years* [Boston, 1979], 259–60). In *Nixon's Vietnam War*

As demonstrated by the deliberations of President Johnson's Senior Advisor Group of "Wise Men" in March[18] and by internal surveys of bureaucratic opinion ordered by president-elect Nixon in November,[19] a significant portion of U.S. policymakers not only believed that the war was militarily stalemated but that the economic and political costs of the conflict in the domestic and international arenas were becoming intolerable. Besides the opposition of the antiwar movement, which included individuals and groups within both elite and grassroots segments of the society, American policymakers now had to deal with a large, war-weary portion of the electorate that was not actively opposed to the war but wanted it to end sooner than later and was opposed to escalatory military steps in the ground war in Vietnam.[20] Nixon's election had been made possible in part because he was able to convince enough swing voters to think of him as a peace candidate, or at least as one who advocated an end to the war. His opponent, Hubert Humphrey, had not been able to win the support of a critical mass of Democratic and independent antiwar doves who would normally have voted for him over Nixon but were then disenchanted with his past support of Johnson's policies.[21]

Although President Nguyen Van Thieu of the Republic of Vietnam (RVN), America's South Vietnamese client, attempted to slow the momentum toward negotiations – as had Syngman Rhee during the Korean War – he had no choice but to acquiesce when president-elect Nixon finally threw his support behind the process. On the other side, the casualties, physical

---

(Lawrence, Kans., 1998), however, I argue that Washington's view of a middle position was that it would win its fundamental objective while the other side won minor, less fundamental, points. The fact was, until the very end, both sides saw negotiations as "political warfare."

18 Relevant sources include Walter Isaacson and Evan Thomas, *The Wise Men: Six Friends and the World They Made: Acheson, Bohlen, Harriman, Kennan, Lovett, McCloy* (New York, 1986); Clark Clifford, with Richard Holbrooke, *Counsel to the President: A Memoir* (New York, 1991); memoranda, Mar. 27, 29, 1968, box 571, special files: Public Service, Kennedy-Johnson administrations, 1958–71, W. Averell Harriman papers, Manuscript Division, Library of Congress; and proposal by H. C. Lodge for Johnson, Mar. 26, 1968, papers of Henry Cabot Lodge II, general correspondence, microfilm, reel 8, Massachusetts Historical Society.

19 Vietnam – RAND, box 3, National Security Council (hereafter NSC): Henry A. Kissinger Office Files (hereafter HAKOF), Administrative and Staff Files (hereafter HAKASF), Nixon Presidential Materials (hereafter NPM), National Archives.

20 Many if not most military and diplomatic historians either ignore, discount, or misconstrue the impact of the antiwar movement on the American prosecution of the war; see, e.g., Robert J. McMahon, "Commentary: Nixon, Kissinger, and the Costs of Empire," *Peace and Change: A Journal of Peace Research* 20 (Apr. 1995): 217–25. Citing histories of the movement and documents of the Nixon administration, I argued in *Nixon's Vietnam War* that although the movement was not the decisive contributory cause of Nixon's withdrawal from Vietnam, it was an important contributory cause, at least as early as 1969 and even as late as 1972, when its influence was manifested in electoral politics and in Congress. Although a vague term, the fact or degree of "war weariness" can be inferred from opinion polls, voting patterns, and politicians' perceptions of the public mood.

21 On Nixon's presidential campaign, see Kimball, *Nixon's Vietnam War*, chap. 3.

damage, and erosion of morale suffered by the Democratic Republic of Vietnam (DRV) and its guerrilla allies in the National Liberation Front of South Vietnam (NLF) after the Tet Offensive were probably not quite as critical in the decision of Politburo members to negotiate as was their appreciation of the current state of military equilibrium, which they believed now made it possible for them, the weaker power, to negotiate on equal terms with the United States, the stronger power.[22]

By the time Nixon had been inaugurated as president on January 20, 1969, talks had already begun in Paris between the United States, RVN, DRV, and NLF. Soon frustrated in this public venue, Washington and Hanoi opened a parallel but secret bilateral negotiating channel in August 1969. Another three years would pass, however, before they would be ready to make the compromises necessary to bring about a cease-fire. Hawks, who held the reins of power on both sides, continued to believe that different military and diplomatic strategies would, despite the current stalemate, turn the tide at some propitious moment in the future, enabling them to achieve their essential political goals. Neither internal nor external pressures were yet sufficient to force an end to the war. Neither Washington nor Hanoi viewed negotiations primarily as good-faith, give-and-take discussions between reasonable parties in search of an evenhanded, compromise settlement. Negotiations, when backed by military power and diplomatic maneuvering in the international arena, were seen as but one other means of winning a favorable peace. Leaders on both sides, not just on the Vietnamese side, were, as the phrase went, "negotiating while fighting."[23]

Hoping to win a "negotiated victory" within the first nine months of his presidency, Nixon initially put his faith in a strategy consisting of several diplomatic, military, and political elements: separating political

---

22 See, e.g., Speech, General Nguyen Van Vinh, doc. 8, and "Some Characteristics of the Development of the Situation," Apr. 1971, doc. 92, both in *Vietnam Documents and Research Notes Series: Translation and Analysis of Significant Viet Cong/North Vietnamese Documents* (microfilm) (Bethesda, Md., 1991); and Luu Van Loi and Nguyen Anh Vu, *Le Duc Tho–Kissinger Negotiations in Paris* (Hanoi, 1996), chap. 2, and 65–7.

23 Contrary to conventional wisdom, Nixon and Kissinger were committed to *winning* a "peace"; that is, to coercing or coaxing the other side into consenting to a settlement that preserved the Saigon government and ensured its supremacy over the NLF, thereby, they assumed, serving U.S. global interests. For a description and analysis of the goals of Washington and Hanoi, see Kimball, *Nixon's Vietnam War*, chaps. 4, 5; Loi and Vu, *Le Duc Tho–Kissinger Negotiations*, 74–6; and Zhou Enlai and Pham Van Dong, Apr. 19, 1968, and Mao Zedong and Pham Van Dong, Nov. 17, 1968, both in "77 Conversations Between Chinese and Foreign Leaders on the Wars in Indochina, 1964–1977," ed. Odd Arne Westad, Chen Jian, Stein Tønnesson, Nguyen Vu Tung, and James G. Hershberg, Working Paper no. 22, Cold War International History Project (Washington, D.C., 1998), 128, 146, 153. For Hanoi, an added bonus of negotiations was the cessation of American bombing in the North.

and military issues in negotiations with Hanoi; levering the Soviet Union with carrots and sticks into pressuring the DRV to make concessions in its negotiations with the United States; making "mad" threats to escalate the war in Indochina dramatically and also to destroy North Vietnam through air bombardment; expanding U.S. bombing into Cambodia; assuaging American public opinion by withdrawing U.S. troops; and building up the Saigon army in order to compensate for U.S. withdrawals while also preparing it for the anticipated struggle with the NLF in a post-armistice environment.[24]

Nixon's negotiating stance and his faith in the madman theory were partially based on his experience as vice president under Eisenhower, and particularly his belief that Eisenhower's alleged nuclear threats in 1953 had been the "biggest factor" in causing the communists to agree to an armistice at Panmunjom. The Korean War analogy appealed to Nixon because the predicament in which he found himself was similar to the one Eisenhower had inherited from Truman: a deadlocked civil war that included great-power involvement; a war-weary electorate; the negotiations at a standstill; and a hard-line client government in the South. Even though both Nixon and Thieu would have liked to bring about a Korean-like solution to the Vietnam war, there were differences between the two conflicts that would prove significant; for example, revolutionary-guerrilla forces in South Vietnam were stronger than they had been in South Korea; the determined Politburo in Hanoi, by choice and circumstance, was in control of the direction of the war, not China or the Soviet Union; Soviet nuclear parity with the United States undermined the credibility of Nixon's madman threats; and the antiwar movement was a force with which Korean War American presidents had not had to contend. Committed to victory in South Vietnam, wanting to avoid defeat, and believing in his new stratagems, Nixon miscalculated.[25]

Having failed to achieve his goals by the end of 1969, Nixon revised his strategy, putting more emphasis now on maintaining political support on the home front and shoring up the Saigon government through "Vietnamization," while he sought "mad" opportunities on the military front to make what he called "big plays." In 1970, these included the intensified bombing of Laos and North Vietnam and the invasion of Cambodia. In early 1971, Nixon's big military play was to initiate and support the South Vietnamese army's invasion of southern Laos.

---

24 "Negotiated victory" is from Vietnam – RAND, box 3, NSC: HAKOF, HAKASF, NPM; see also, Kimball, *Nixon's Vietnam War*, chap. 5.
25 Kimball, *Nixon's Vietnam War*, 82–6.

During the same period (January 1969 through May 1971), the Politburo remained committed to its long-standing goals of replacing Thieu's government and bringing about the complete withdrawal of U.S. forces from Indochina. Simultaneously, it resisted U.S. demands for the withdrawal of DRV forces and rejected U.S. insistence on aiding the Saigon government after the signing of an armistice agreement. Acknowledging the existing military equilibrium and understanding Nixon's intentions, the Politburo revised its own military strategy from one that projected progressively higher stages of offensive violence to one that was defensive, de-escalatory, and flexibly responsive to altered conditions and new challenges. Politburo members believed, however, as Nixon did, that in the end everything would depend on the battlefield situation, and so, while they turned to a strategy of flexible retrenchment, they prepared for a future military showdown with the United States.[26]

Meanwhile, there was noteworthy movement in the negotiations in Paris. At the September 7, 1970, meeting between U.S. and DRV negotiators, Kissinger for the first time indicated his government's willingness to abandon the mutual withdrawal formula that the Johnson and Nixon administrations had long insisted on, and he also communicated his willingness to discuss political as well as military issues. During talks on May 31, 1971, Kissinger formally dropped the long-standing American demand for the mutual withdrawal of forces and offered for the first time to set a terminal date for the withdrawal of U.S. forces, but he attached conditions that led the DRV to interpret the proposal as one that was cunningly but obviously designed to preserve Thieu while winning the release of POWs. Nonetheless, in the intervening period before the next meeting in Paris, the Politburo prepared a counterproposal. On June 26, the DRV's chief delegate, Le Duc Tho, offered to accept a cease-fire if the United States shortened its withdrawal timetable, stopped its air attacks against the North, agreed to the payment of war reparations, and withdrew its support of Thieu in the forthcoming fall presidential elections in South Vietnam. (This last proposal revised previous demands from the DRV and NLF calling for the removal of Thieu and other top officials of the Saigon government.[27])

---

26 Ibid., chaps. 6–10; Loi and Vu, *Le Duc Tho–Kissinger Negotiations*, chaps. 3–5; Conversation, Zhou Enlai and Pham Van Dong, Sept. 1970, in "77 Conversations," 174–5.

27 Pertinent documents include Loi and Vu, *Le Duc Tho–Kissinger Negotiations*, 150–1, 165–80; the May 31 and June 26, 1971, entries in "Chronology of U.S.–DRV Negotiations, 1969–1973 (Private Meetings)," published in *The Foreign Ministry Internal Circulation Chronology on Diplomatic Struggle and International Mobilization in the Anti-American War, 1954–1975* (Hanoi, 1987), translated from Vietnamese by anonymous (held by Jeffrey Kimball); and the following memos from White House/NSC: POW/MIA, NPM: Memorandum, Kissinger to Nixon, May 28, 1971, folder: Camp

Positive and negative incentives had encouraged each side to offer new proposals. Progress in talks with Beijing and Moscow led Nixon and Kissinger, despite the setback they suffered in the Laotian invasion, to become optimistic about their prospects in using détente with the Soviets and rapprochement with the Chinese to extract concessions from Hanoi in the Paris talks. If an armistice could be negotiated before the end of the year, they hoped, it would prevent the North Vietnamese from launching what they expected would be a major offensive during the spring 1972 dry season. If this diplomatic effort failed, they calculated that they would at least have established a record of attempting to negotiate seriously, which would later serve them well politically on the home front, where public approval for Nixon's handling of the war was gradually declining. On the negative side, there was growing impatience among congressional conservatives with the administration's inability to conclude the war and pressure from congressional liberals to withdraw.[28]

For its part, Hanoi had been encouraged by the success of its army in turning back the South Vietnamese invasion of southern Laos. The poor showing of Thieu's forces in Laos implied that Vietnamization was failing, while American troops were steadily withdrawing from Indochina. On the other hand, North Vietnam's major suppliers of military aid, the Soviet Union and China, were advising in favor of diplomatic compromise and against military escalation, and it faced the prospect of a major American air offensive in 1972 in the Red River Delta. The Politburo calculated that if the United States agreed to remove its support from Thieu, then it was willing to settle for less than total victory in the South.[29]

Nonetheless, the talks begun in late May collapsed in early November 1971. Washington had spurned the opportunity to withdraw its support of Thieu and had in fact actively assisted in his reelection. Hanoi had refused to accept a cease-fire absent a political solution. Furthermore, the American cease-fire plan would have prevented Hanoi from using its primary military option: a ground offensive in the spring. At the same time, the plan would have permitted the United States to threaten the North with air strikes,

David – Sensitive – vol. 7, box 4 (3); memorandum, Kissinger to Nixon, June 27, 1971, subj. My June 26 meeting with the North Vietnamese; and memorandum of conversation, June 26, 1971, folder: Camp David – Sensitive – vol. 8, box 4 (4). See also Henry A. Kissinger, *White House Years* (Boston, 1979), 1022–3, 1488–9n11; and Luu Van Loi, *Le Duc Tho–Kissinger Negotiations*, 165–80.

28 Concerning the shift in conservative opinion, see, e.g., Kissinger, *White House Years*, 979, 969; and cable, Nixon to Kissinger, 10:55 A.M., Nov. 24, 1972, folder: HAK Paris Trip 18–25 Nov. 1972 TOHAK [2 of 2], box 26, NSC: HAKOF, HAK Trip Files, NPM.

29 See Loi and Vu, *Le Duc Tho–Kissinger Negotiations*, 166–8; and Le Duc Tho and Ieng Sary, Sept. 7, 1971, in "77 Conversations," 180–1.

to retain "residual" forces in the South, and to continue supplying Thieu's government.[30]

Hanoi now decided to proceed with its offensive. The Politburo believed that the military and political balance could be altered by means of a spring 1972 offensive, whose maximum goal was to rout the South Vietnamese army and drive Thieu from power, and whose minimum goal was to regain territory, rejuvenate the NLF, and undermine Saigon's morale, thus preparing the ground for a post–cease-fire civil struggle. Washington put its faith in great-power diplomatic moves, the defensive and offensive values of air bombardment, and accelerated Vietnamization.[31]

The spring offensive that began on March 30 achieved Hanoi's minimum goals. It did not decisively alter the military balance, but it did accelerate the diplomatic momentum, serving as a catalyst in speeding up the interaction of all the other causes that pointed toward an armistice agreement. By August 1972, each side at last began practicing the diplomacy of military and political stalemate. Both considered their overall prospects with an armistice to be comparatively better than without one. The heavy, manifold costs of the war, the psychological exhaustion of the Indochinese and American peoples, and complex international pressures and constraints now persuaded both groups of leaders to settle. Neither the United States nor the DRV/NLF governments had relinquished their fundamental goals, but both now turned to practical, minimal solutions. On balance, however, Hanoi and the NLF possessed more military and political flexibility. Although pressed by Moscow and Beijing to settle, Hanoi did not seem to have been influenced as much by this pressure as they were by a readiness to formalize American withdrawal from Vietnam in order to continue their struggle with a government in Saigon that would lack air and ground support from the United States. On the other hand, in the face of political realities and budgetary constraints and the loss of military leverage on the ground, the Nixon administration was ready to settle, even eager to settle, before the beginning of Nixon's next term.

An agreement was reached in late October, just before the American presidential election, only to be rejected by Thieu. More negotiations and more bombing took place as Nixon sought revisions that would please Thieu and protect Nixon's credibility as a president who had stood by his client and

---

30 For a fuller discussion of the Paris negotiations in 1971 and the documentary citations, see Kimball, *Nixon's Vietnam War*, chaps. 10–11; and Luu Van Loi, *Le Duc Tho–Kissinger Negotiations*, 168–212.

31 Kimball, *Nixon's Vietnam War*, chap. 12; Loi and Vu, *Le Duc Tho–Kissinger Negotiations*, 193, 212.

achieved peace with honor. The agreement reached on January 13, 1973, however, was barely distinguishable from the October draft. It was the U.S. government, on balance the "losing side" in the stalemate, that made the key political and military concessions and determined the timing of a cease-fire. Washington had agreed to withdraw all of its forces from Indochina and to recognize the NLF's legal authority as a government in the territory it controlled.[32]

War termination generalizations, at least as summarized here, are clearly applicable to Korea and Vietnam. Although seemingly simplistic, they are useful to anyone attempting to understand why and how these wars ended – a search that always involves finding one's way out of a maze of conflicting and contradictory explanations offered by partisans for or against the wars and on both sides of conflicts. War termination principles serve as guidelines for the asking of proper questions, which is half the battle of finding answers, and they suggest that policymakers on both sides of a conflict made their decisions for war or peace on the basis of the military balance and the costs and constraints of battle. This is not to say that in any particular war both sides are equally guilty, equally immoral or moral, or that goodwill and good intentions play no part in war termination.

IV

Are war termination theories generally applicable? This question is now and forever unanswerable in any definitive sense, of course; there have been too many wars in too many places during the course of too many centuries and with too little reliable information about the motives and actions of the principals. There are also too many variables in the calculus of war termination. Intuitively and anecdotally, however, these theories resonate with what we think we know about wars through history. Based on Thucydides' account of the Peloponnesian War, for example, the Peace of Nicias of 421 B.C.E., which brought an end to the Archidamian phase of the long war between Athens, Sparta, and their allies, was the result of war termination causes of the third kind. Donald Kagan summarized Thucydides' explanation of why the Archidamian war ended: "Weariness, the desire for peace, the desire of the Athenians to restore their financial resources, the Spartans' wish to recover their men taken prisoner ... and to restore order and security in the Peloponnesus, the removal by death in battle of the leading

---

32 Kimball, *Nixon's Vietnam War*, chap. 13; Loi and Vu, *Le Duc Tho–Kissinger Negotiations*, chap. 7.

advocate of war in each city, [and] the central role played in it by Nicias."[33] Within five years, however, the Peloponnesian conflict resumed, until Athens met with decisive defeat in 404 B.C.E., an ending of the first kind.[34]

33 Donald Kagan, *The Peace of Nicias and the Sicilian Expedition* (Ithaca, N.Y., 1981), 17. The relevant passages in Thucydides' *The History of the Peloponnesian War* are in bk. 5, chap. 15, para. 11–25.

34 For a general account that synthesizes the latest research, see Sarah B. Pomeroy, Stanley M. Burstein, Walter Donlan, and Jennifer Tolbert Roberts, *Ancient Greece: A Political, Social, and Cultural History* (New York, 1999), 289–321.

6

Versailles and Vietnam

Coming to Terms with War

SABINE BEHRENBECK

World War I began in August 1914 with the German declaration of war against Russia and France. It ended four-and-a-half years later with the military defeat of the German army. The first modern war, World War I witnessed the use of new weapons that caused horrible injuries and mass destruction. Nearly two million German soldiers were killed, and two-and-one-half million returned from the front as "war cripples." The so-called Great War was the first total war that involved countries' entire populations in the production and execution of war. This involvement also meant hardship, sometimes extreme, for noncombatants and demoralization on the home front.

The Vietnam War was never declared. It began as a conflict between France and the Vietnamese nationalist movement during World War II, when the Japanese temporarily displaced the French as colonial rulers and thus created an opening for the communist Viet Minh. The United States first sent military advisers to Vietnam in 1950 as part of its strategy to contain communism; troops followed later. The conflict in Southeast Asia took place thousands of miles from the United States, whose territory was never threatened. American civilians were not directly involved, whereas three million Vietnamese were killed. Approximately three million Americans served in the armed forces during the United States' direct involvement in Vietnam; fifty-eight thousand of them were killed. The longest war of the twentieth century ended in 1975 with the fall of Saigon, two years after the armistice of Paris had allowed the United States to withdraw its troops.

In the aftermath of World War I, Germany experienced economic crisis, political instability, and, eventually, a drift toward dictatorship. Although the United States experienced some political and economic problems in the 1970s after the end of the Vietnam War, the most important issues were social and cultural. From 1965 onward the brutal images of the war – transmitted via television – shocked an increasing number of Americans. The antiwar movement saw the Vietnam conflict as a civil war in a foreign country where the United States did not belong, not as a justified battle against communism.

This chapter compares two attempts to come to terms with war: Germany after World War I and the United States after the Vietnam War. Although there are many differences between the German and American cases, comparing these two histories may help us make sense of the larger question of how societies handle traumatic postwar experiences.

I

The experience of defeat undermined the national myths and self-images that Germany and the United States had brought with them, respectively, to World War I and the Vietnam War. Both countries had histories of impressive military successes behind them when the wars began. The humiliation of defeat shook their sense of invincibility and influenced political life for decades afterwards. The wars were reduced to catchphrases: Versailles and Verdun in the case of Germany, 'Nam in the United States.[1]

Both societies had to integrate military defeat and traumatic war experiences into their collective memories. They had to come to terms with wars that had produced more conflict than solidarity.[2] The divisions these wars provoked stand in sharp contrast to the seeming social harmony that prevailed when they began. In Germany the events of August 1914 appeared to herald the advent of a new internal unity: The concept of nation had seemingly become all-embracing. But by 1917–18, this unity had crumbled. In America the era of Eisenhower and Kennedy seemed a period of ideological consensus and agreement on the ideals of the American creed – an era that, after the violent debates that followed later in the 1960s, seemed a golden age to many.[3] That was before television coverage

---

1 In Germany, the use of "Versailles" reduced the war to its unsuccessful outcome. In the United States, "Vietnam" signaled a new kind of warfare as well as that country's first military defeat. In both postwar eras, each nation was obsessed with the trauma and the injuries suffered, and ignored the aggression that had preceded defeat. On this point, see Rick Berg and John Carlos Rowe, "The Vietnam War and American Memory," in Rick Berg and John Carlos Rowe, eds., *The Vietnam War and American Culture* (New York, 1991), 1–17.

2 Berg and Rowe, "Vietnam War and American Memory," 3.

3 This consensus was already fixed in the 1950s, fed by attempts to fend off the twin menaces of the Soviet threat from without and communist subversion from within. Because the spectrum of political dissent was limited, the division of society during and after the era of the Vietnam War was particularly painful. See Manfred Berg, "Die innere Entwicklung der USA seit dem Zweiten Weltkrieg," in Willi Paul Adams et al., eds., *Länderbericht USA*, 2 vols. (Bonn, 1992), 1, 2:195.

of the war in Southeast Asia raised public doubts about its legitimacy and outcome.

Public commemoration of the fallen soldiers in both nations changed fundamentally after the wars in question. Earlier traditions and narratives of heroic warriors defending their fatherland or fighting for honor and glory no longer were convincing. The deaths of millions of soldiers in World War I and the incredible destruction of Vietnam seemed to be without meaning.

How could death in war be legitimized in a postwar society? Without meaningful structuring narratives, the millions of deaths caused by World War I and the Vietnam War became the focus of heated debates and long-lasting public division.[4] Collective memory became a social and cultural "combat zone." In this process of social self-assessment, the vehicles and media of collective memory came to use a different code of commemoration and new artistic means.

Because of their traumatic impact, modern wars are remembered not by "monuments" but by "memorials." The difference is reflected in the German distinction between *Denkmal* (monument) and *Mahnmal* (memorial). "We erect monuments so that we shall always remember, and build memorials so that we shall never forget."[5] Memorials force public commemoration to deal with the past. Whereas "monuments (and victories) are usually anonymous, the irony of lives lost for an unattained goal...in a memorial seems to demand the naming of the individual."[6]

It was not, however, the experience of defeat that established memorials as the main form for commemorating the war dead during the twentieth century. After 1918, victorious and defeated belligerents alike built memorials, not monuments, to their dead. One reason was the new scale of death in war. The sheer number of fallen soldiers in World War I led to a new practice: Soldiers were buried where they fell, and their graves were marked by crosses bearing their names. The locations of these informal graves were recorded, and after the end of the war the corpses were transferred to war

---

4 Studies on the dissent and struggle over the past include Peter Reichel, *Politik mit der Erinnerung: Gedächtnisorte im Streit um die nationalsozialistische Vergangenheit* (Munich, 1995); Klaus Naumann, *Der Krieg als Test: Das Jahr 1945 im kulturellen Gedächtnis der Presse* (Hamburg, 1998); Henry Rousso, *The Vichy Syndrome: History and Memory in France Since 1944* (Cambridge, 1991); and John Bodnar, *Remaking America: Public Memory, Commemoration, and Patriotism in the Twentieth Century* (Princeton, N.J., 1992). Considering the multiplicity of memories and the different politics of commemoration competing with each other in many societies, it is very interesting to observe how various groups come to believe they share a unique national memory. On this point, see Alon Confino, "Collective Memory and Cultural History: Problems of Method," *American Historical Review* 102 (1997): 1398.

5 Arthur C. Danto, "The Vietnam Veterans Memorial," *The Nation*, Aug. 31, 1985, 152.

6 Marita Sturken, "The Wall, the Screen, and the Image: the Vietnam Veterans Memorial," *Representations* 35 (1991): 118.

cemeteries. The stones on all graves were uniform and could be distinguished only by the names. Often a central stone of remembrance bore the inscription, "Their name liveth forevermore."[7] Many cemeteries included a wall or other structure where the names of all the buried soldiers were engraved. The typical memorial and site of mourning – both in war cemeteries and in village squares across Europe – became a place for the display of names.[8]

Names were all that remained of many of the soldiers killed during World War I. The unknown war dead – the men who disappeared, the unidentified corpses – provided a second focus of memory in the aftermath of World War I.[9] It found expression in the ceremonial burial of the unknown soldier. This ceremony took place in most European capitals and created a symbolic figure: the body that represented all bodies. "The unknown warrior became the opposite pole in the formation of memory to the graves. . . . While the names . . . cry out their specificity . . . the unknown warrior becomes in his universality the cipher that can mean anything," Thomas Laqueur has written. "A common denominator body . . . is the opposite end of the same discursive strategy that is evident in the enumeration of names."[10] This discursive strategy influenced public commemoration in both of the cases under examination.

II

The landscape of remembrance that developed in the aftermath of World War I shows a great variety of memorials for the fallen. Immediately after the end of the war nearly every local community wanted its own memorial that would express the gratitude of the *Heimat* (homeland).[11] These early memorials were rather small – due mainly to the precarious economic situation – and they were traditional and simple in design. Most were abstract pieces without comment on the meaning of war and death in war.[12] The

---

7 Thomas W. Laqueur, "Memory and Naming in the Great War," in John R. Gillis, ed., *Commemorations: The Politics of National Identity* (Princeton, N.J., 1994), 150–67.

8 Whereas 70 percent of the fallen American soldiers were repatriated, in Europe relatives were prohibited from bringing the bodies home. The only one allowed to return home was the unknown warrior.

9 Reinhart Koselleck, "Einleitung," in Reinhart Koselleck and Michael Jeismann, eds., *Der politische Totenkult: Kriegerdenkmaler in der Moderne* (Munich, 1994), 9–20.

10 Laqueur, "Memory and Naming," 158.

11 Sabine Behrenbeck, "Heldenkult oder Friedensmahnung? Kriegerdenkmale nach beiden Weltkriegen," in Gottfried Niedhart and Dieter Riesenberger, eds., *Lernen aus dem Krieg? Deutsche Nachkriegszeiten 1918–1945* (Munich, 1992), 347–8.

12 Reinhart Koselleck, "Der Einfluss der beiden Weltkriege auf das soziale Bewusstsein," in Wolfram Wette, ed., *Der Krieg des kleinen Mannes: Eine Militärgeschichte von unten* (Munich, 1992), 339.

inscriptions commonly dedicated the monuments "To the Fallen Warriors of 1914–1918."[13] Death in war was no longer legitimized by political explanations. Many local communities did not hold competitions, but rather made their choices from catalogs offering ready-made monuments.[14] Public discussion of the design and meaning of memorials became prevalent only in the second half of the 1920s. After 1918, recording the names of the fallen soldiers in a "book of remembrance" also became a popular custom, and panels with the names of the fallen were a common feature of war memorials in small towns.

Another type of memorial was a symbol of mourning that represented the painful loss of a loved one. These were erected in large numbers in the first years after the war, while the sense of loss was still fresh, but were still commissioned into the early 1930s. Those who ordered memorials of this sort primarily hoped to receive religious consolation. They therefore turned to Christian symbols, such as the pietà or the cross, and they often placed these memorials in churches or graveyards.[15] For example, the relief by Emil Cauer titled "Sacrifice" was placed in two churchyards in Berlin in 1930 (Figure 1). Frequent reference to religion did not necessarily indicate deeply felt devotion, but rather was a response to a disorientation that had no traditional pattern of meaning.[16]

The Christian hope of resurrection was often given a secular meaning. Soldiers, commonly portrayed as slayers of evil, became martyrs for the fatherland and warriors for the faith.[17] Death in war was interpreted as an analogy to the death of Jesus Christ. The soldier's death was seen as a voluntary self-sacrifice leading to national redemption. Nonfigurative Christian symbols such as temples, chapels, crypts, and "altars of the fatherland" were meant to express the consecration of the fallen. For example, Bernhard Bleeker's "Sleeping Warrior" (1925) at a secular crypt in Munich was laid out in the manner of a king or saint. This young man seems to sleep peacefully, and no wounds mar his perfect body. He symbolizes the youth and innocence of the *ver sacrum*, the nation sacrificed for freedom (Figure 2).

---

13 Gerhard Armanski, *". . . und wenn wir sterben müssen": Die politische Ästhetik von Kriegerdenkmälern* (Hamburg, 1988), 125, 131.

14 "Arbeit fürs Ganze," *Die Plastik* 5 (1922): 17–18; and Bernd Ulrich and Benjamin Ziemann, eds., *Krieg im Frieden: Die umkämpfte Erinnerung an den Ersten Weltkrieg* (Frankfurt am Main, 1997), 131–2 (doc. 18-j).

15 Martina Weinland, *Kriegerdenkmäler in Berlin 1870–1930* (Frankfurt am Main, 1990), 96.

16 See, by contrast, the numerous secessions from the churches at this time: Clemens Vollnhals, "Der deutsche Protestantismus: Spiegelbild der bürgerlichen Gesellschaft," in Niedhart and Riesenberger, eds., *Lernen aus dem Krieg*, 163.

17 Weinland, *Kriegerdenkmäler in Berlin*, 98.

Figure 1. Emil Cauer, "Das Opfer" ("Sacrifice"). This sculpture was installed at the Kaiser Friedrich Memorial Cemetery (Berlin-Wedding) and the Luisenstadt Parish Cemetery (Berlin-Neukölln). Photo: Zentralinstitut für Kunstgeschichte, Munich.

During the second half of the 1920s, heroic warriors increasingly became the main focus of monuments ordered, in most instances, by military organizations or veterans' associations. One example is the memorial at Bad Neuenahr designed by Heinrich Faltermeier (Figure 3). The soldier wears a complete uniform, and beneath the steel helmet we see a pugnacious face. The man is about to throw a hand grenade at the enemy. Monuments like this depict not a fallen soldier but a standing, fighting warrior – if not a victor – and support a glorious and heroic idea of death in war. After the Nazi seizure of power in 1933, this became the one and only way to remember the war.[18]

While Germany began building memorials to its dead shortly after the war, few memorials to the soldiers killed in the Vietnam War were built in the United States before 1982. These early Vietnam War memorials show a great variety in design, but, with few exceptions, they commonly drew upon traditional symbols of remembrance. In 1974, for example, nine aircrew

18 For more on this subject, see Sabine Behrenbeck, *Der Kult um die toten Helden: Nationalsozialistische Mythen, Riten und Symbole 1923–1945* (Vierow, 1996).

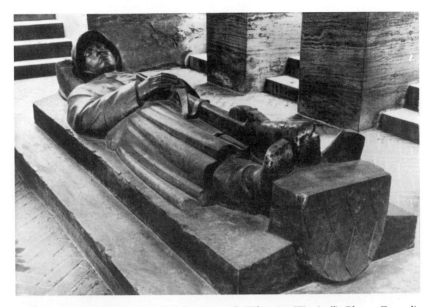

Figure 2. Bernhard Bleeker, "Ruhender Krieger" ("Sleeping Warrior"). Photo: Zentralinstitut für Kunstgeschichte, Munich.

members were honored with a stone monument erected in their memory at Blytheville Air Force Base in Arkansas. Sometimes the names of the war dead from Vietnam were added to existing war memorials. In memory of his son David, Dr. Victor Westphal built a sanctuary near Angel Fire, New Mexico, in 1971. Two mothers of Gold Star recipients conceived of the idea for a veterans' park in Johnstown, Pennsylvania, and commissioned a statue showing a soldier with a child in his arms to remind viewers "of the kindness of so many American soldiers to the children of war." The memorial was dedicated in 1974.[19]

The symbolism of these early monuments is neither religious nor heroic.[20] None of the memorials offers a political interpretation of death in this particular war. They honor, rather, the soldiers' service to their country. These memorials had their origins in the initiatives of private persons or military bases, not local political authorities.

19 Jerry L. Strait and Sandra S. Strait, *Vietnam War Memorials: An Illustrated Reference to Veterans Tributes Throughout the United States* (Jefferson, N.C., 1988), 11, 67, 144, 169–70. On the monument at the Blytheville Air Force Base, see also *USA Today*, Nov. 11, 1987, sec. A6.
20 For a contrasting example – the Green Beret Monument at Fort Bragg, North Carolina – see James M. Mayo, *War Memorials as Political Landscapes: The American Experience and Beyond* (New York, 1988), 199.

Figure 3. Heinrich Faltermeier, memorial for Bad Neuenahr. Photo: Zentralinstitut für Kunstgeschichte, Munich.

Many more Vietnam War memorials were erected after the national monument was built on the National Mall in Washington, D.C. in 1982.[21] The memorial in the capital was obviously the model for numerous state, city, and local monuments. In Germany the story developed the other way around.

III

In 1924, after many local communities and parishes had erected their memorials, the German government discussed erecting a national monument in the capital. The minister of the interior proposed that a simple column be placed in front of the Brandenburg Gate.[22] On August 3, 1924, the tenth anniversary of the beginning of World War I, President Friedrich Ebert appealed to the nation to collect money to build a *Reichsehrenmal*. He identified the "freedom and safety of the fatherland" as the legacy of the fallen; as their highest principle, survivors should remain united and devoted to Germany.[23]

But there was no unity or agreement about the meaning of death in war. The mostly conservative veterans' associations had reservations about allowing a democratic government to decide how those who died fighting for the Kaiserreich were to be honored. The veterans claimed they had not been appropriately involved in the project.[24]

The Prussian state government, run by the Social Democrats, was opposed to launching a public donation drive while the German people were still suffering the war's consequences and an economic crisis. Money would be better given to the 2.5 million disabled veterans and war widows. As a result of the Prussian government's dissent, a subcommittee was established that, in turn, postponed the decision indefinitely.

In the meantime, the public showed great interest in the issue of erecting a national memorial to the war dead. More than two hundred design proposals were submitted. Many of the proposals envisioned projects of enormous dimensions – a gigantic dome in Berlin, for example, or a subterranean hall of fame, or a commemorative site in the countryside at the base of a mountain and surrounded by a sacred wood. National Curator of Art Edwin Redslob suggested burying an unknown soldier in the Rhine.[25]

The Stahlhelm, a right-wing veterans' organization, rejected Redslob's proposal because the burial of an unknown soldier was an idea "of our

21 Ibid.
22 Annegret Heffen, *Der Reichskunstwart – Kunstpolitik in den Jahren 1920–1933: Zu den Bemühungen um eine offizielle Reichskunstpolitik in der Weimarer Republik* (Essen, 1986), 231ff.
23 *Berliner Tageblatt*, Aug. 3, 1924, quoted in Heffen, *Der Reichskunstwart*, 236–7; see Ulrich and Ziemann, eds., *Krieg im Frieden*, 134 (doc. 18-l).
24 Heffen, *Der Reichskunstwart*, 238.   25 Ibid., 240ff.

former enemies." Germany, the Stahlhelm insisted, needed its own answer to the question of what death in war meant. The soldiers had fallen to keep the *Heimat* untouched by the terror of war. Therefore, in the view of the Stahlhelm, the only acceptable solution for the *Reichsehrenmal* would be a design that could demonstrate the beauty of the undamaged *Heimat* that the dead heroes had protected. The memorial was to be surrounded by a nature reserve that every German would enter with a feeling of veneration.[26] The soldiers found their graves in God's own nature; therefore, nature was the only place to contemplate the meaning of their death. The spirit of nature would express the union of all members of the community in a cosmic sense.[27] Planting trees and creating sacred groves (*Heldenhaine*) for war cemeteries was seen as a new and appropriate way of honoring the dead.[28] And because all German states and regions had sacrificed their beloved sons in war, the memorial should be placed at the very heart of the Reich, far away from the cities and yet within everyone's reach.[29]

Even the location of the *Reichsehrenmal* remained a matter of disagreement. The capital had to contend with the provinces, the north with the south, and the west with the east. After years of discussion, two concrete plans emerged: the island Lorch in the Rhine and a forest near Bad Berka in Thuringia. In 1926, the veterans split into two groups, one preferring the Rhine, the other Bad Berka.[30] The *Reichsehrenmal* – meant to be the memorial of a united people – had become a cause of disunity.

In 1927, after three years of discussion, a compromise was reached. Instead of one monument, three would be erected: the *Reichsehrenmal* in Thuringia; a monument on the Ehrenbreitstein near Koblenz remembering the liberation of the Rheinland; and a remodeling of Berlin's Neue Wache as a remembrance hall.[31] The third was realized in 1930–1 with the collaboration of the Reich and Prussia.

---

26 "Vorschlag für ein Reichehrenmal vom Juli 1925," *Der Stahlhelm*, quoted in Heffen, *Der Reichskunstwart*, 244.
27 Heffen, *Der Reichskunstwart*, 247.
28 This was the title of a picture book of several war memorials, which together represented a symbolic sacred grove (*Heldenhain*): Friedrich Ilgen, *Deutscher Ehrenhain für die Helden von 1914/18* (Leipzig, 1931).
29 See Ulrich and Ziemann, eds., *Krieg im Frieden*, 137ff (doc. 18-o).
30 Heffen, *Der Reichskunstwart*, 252–3, 256.
31 Ibid., 258. But Reich President Paul von Hindenburg did not agree and insisted on the Reichsehrenmal project. A countrywide competition was announced, and 1,828 proposals were received (ibid., 236). The committee never came to a final decision. None of the artists had presented an idea that would express the feelings of the entire population. However, as Bruno Taut, a famous modernist architect mentioned in 1922, as long as the German people had no general agreement about the war, no artist could solve this problem. See Bruno Taut, "Gefallenendenkmal für Magdeburg," in Ulrich Conrads, ed., *Frühlicht: Eine Folge für die Verwirklichung des neuen Baugedankens* (1921–2; reprint, Frankfurt am Main, 1963), 109–13.

Figure 4. Unter den Linden, Berlin, 1936. The Neue Wache (left) and the Zeughaus (right). Photo: German Information Center, New York.

IV

The Neue Wache was built in 1817–18 by one of the most famous German architects of the time, Karl Friedrich Schinkel. Designed as a royal guardhouse, it was situated on Unter den Linden between the palace and the Brandenburg Gate and next to the arsenal (*Zeughaus*) (Figure 4). The statues of four Prussian generals were set up in front of it. The Neue Wache thus served as both a victory monument for the wars of liberation fought against Napoleon and a guardhouse until World War I.

After 1918, the Neue Wache was used for several temporary purposes. Because the Prussian government decided in 1930 that constructing a new building for a war memorial would be too expensive, only the interior of the Neue Wache's existing structure was remodeled. The exterior remained unchanged and there was no outward indication that it was a war memorial. Thus, the remodeled Neue Wache did not affect the traditional prewar interpretation of German history. Quite modest in comparison to the ambitious plans for the *Reichsehrenmal*, the Neue Wache project only implicitly acknowledged the defeat of 1918.

The 1930–1 redesign of the Neue Wache's interior by Heinrich Tessenow was minimalist, elegant, and noble. A simple black rock was placed at the center of the rectangular room. The rock was topped by a gilded garland of oak leaves.[32] An open skylight above this assemblage let in natural light and rain, often giving the room an atmosphere of twilight. Two iron lanterns on the back wall opposite the entrance gently lit the space. The windowless walls were covered with unadorned slabs of limestone; a plaque on the floor in front of the rock was inscribed "1914–1918."

By using these artistic devices, this memorial was not at first sight explicitly connected to a national or political context. It was tied, rather, to the private memories of the individual visitors entering the quiet chamber. The design competition jury described Tessenow's proposal as "touchingly unpretentious" and praised its "hallowed solemnity, demanding devotion," and its balanced proportions.[33]

But not all observers were impressed. Some wanted a more heroic representation of death in war. The leftist journal *Weltbühne*, on the other hand, mocked the architect as a "lyrical spirit" and said the memorial served as "a patch on the horrible face of our patriotic crimes."[34] Whereas one group criticized the lack of heroism, the other group accused the memorial of being *verharmlosend*, of trivializing the horrors of the war.

Careful examination of the memorial reveals a second level of meaning. The two lanterns remind the visitor of the traditional symbols of sacrifice and devotion, but they also function – like the wreath – as a universal sign of eternal remembrance of the dead. In combination with the black rock and the inscription, this assemblage may well be seen as an "altar to the fatherland." With the combination of rock and wreath (earth), lanterns (fire), and skylight (sky and rain), Tessenow drew upon the nature symbolism that the conservative veterans had wanted for the *Reichsehrenmal*.[35] The temple-like atmosphere reinforced this symbolism. The implicit message it offered was that death in war is a holy duty, a sacrifice for the nation. Tessenow's design expressed the minimal national consensus in 1931, but it hardly did justice to the new dimensions of death in war.

32 Sabine Behrenbeck, "Denkmale einer Niederlage: Architekturdenkmale zwischen 1926 und 1936 und ihre Symbolsprache," in Behrenbeck et al., *Historische Denkmäler: Vergangenheit im Dienste der Gegenwart?* (Bergisch Gladbach, 1994), 77.
33 Quoted in Daniela Büchte und Anja Frey, eds., *Im Irrgarten deutscher Geschichte: Die Neue Wache 1818–1933* (Berlin, 1994), 24–5.
34 Quoted in ibid., 24–5.
35 Hans-Ernst Mittig talks about "nature remembrance" (*Naturandacht*) and elemental symbolism (*Elementarsymbolik*) by the political right. See Akademie der Künste, ed., *Streit um die Neue Wache: Zur Gestaltung einer zentralen Gedenkstätte* (Berlin, 1993), 79–81.

V

The American case is surprisingly similar. Official recognition of the soldiers who died in Vietnam did not take place until 1978, when, without public ceremony, a small plaque with a vaguely formulated inscription was affixed at the Tomb of the Unknown Soldier in Arlington National Cemetery.[36] The absence of public ceremony on this occasion reflected the uncertainty in dealing with this undeclared war.[37] It therefore does not come as a surprise that this solution satisfied neither the veterans of the Vietnam War nor the general public.

In 1979, Jan Scruggs, a Vietnam veteran, established the Vietnam Veterans Memorial Fund with the aim of erecting a national monument honoring those who had served and died in the war. Having studied the problems of demobilized troops, his goal was "to replace the veterans' nightmare with the American Dream."[38] Toward that end, the memorial was to be placed on the National Mall in Washington, D.C., surrounded by the country's most prominent historical monuments. The design would be selected through a competition open to all American citizens. The final decision was placed in the hands of eight experts. As Catherine M. Howett later wrote, "The program stipulated that the memorial must include a list of names of the war dead, that it must relate sensitively to the Washington Monument, the Lincoln Memorial . . . and that it should be 'reflective and contemplative in nature,' refraining from making any 'political statement regarding the war or its conduct.'"[39] The task thus was to combine a traditional monument with the new idea of avoiding any symbol of national glory in order to distinguish between the honor of the soldiers and the war they fought.[40]

In May 1981, the jury chose the proposal submitted by Maya Ying Lin, a twenty-one-year-old Yale undergraduate, from a pool of 1,421 entries.

---

36 Robin Wagner-Pacifi and Barry Schwartz, "Die Vietnam-Veteranen-Gedenkstätte: Das Gedenken einer problematischen Vergangenheit," in Koselleck and Jeismann, eds., *Der politische Totenkult*, 398–9 (first published in the *American Journal of Sociology*, 1991). In 1984, an unidentified Vietnam-era serviceman was buried at Arlington National Cemetery, giving Vietnam veterans a sense of being equal to those who died in the two world wars and in Korea. See Mayo, *War Memorials as Political Landscapes*, 205.

37 That same year, Congress planned to organize a Vietnam veterans week instead of constructing a monument. The promoters wanted to unite the nation and honor the veterans as patriots deserving of material compensation. See Wagner-Pacifi and Schwartz, "Die Vietnam-Veteranen-Gedenkstätte," 399–400.

38 Elizabeth Hess, "A Tale of Two Memorials," *Art in America* 71, no. 4 (Apr. 1985), 121; Wagner-Pacifi and Schwartz, "Die Vietnam-Veteranen-Gedenkstätte," 401ff.

39 Catherine M. Howett, "The Vietnam Veterans Memorial: Public Art and Politics," *Landscape* 28, no. 2 (1985): 4.

40 Wagner-Pacifi and Schwartz, "Die Vietnam-Veteranen-Gedenkstätte," 401–2; Fred Turner, *Echoes of Combat: The Vietnam War in American Memory* (New York, 1996), 167–84.

Lin's design was a combination of minimalist sculpture and earthwork: "It consisted of two walls – each 250 feet long and made of 140 panels – which met at a 125-degree angle; beginning at ground level . . . both walls gradually rose to a height of 10 feet at the . . . apex of the angle."[41] The walls were to be constructed from black granite – all other monuments on the Mall are white – and inscribed with the names of the fallen soldiers. The polished surface reflects, like a mirror, the surroundings and the visitors themselves (Figure 5). Descending into the earth and ascending again, the visitor can read the names of the dead. The names are listed chronologically by date of death rather than alphabetically. The names of the first and the last men killed in the war meet where the two walls form the angle: "They thus form a narrative circle, in which one can read from the last name to the first. This refusal of linearity is . . . appropriate to a conflict that has had no superficial closure. The hinge between the two walls thus becomes a pivotal space."[42] The inscription reads: "In honor of all men and women of the Armed Forces of the United States who served in the Vietnam War. The names of those who gave their lives and of those who remain missing are inscribed in the order they were taken from us."

The jury was struck by this design's simplicity, the quiet power of its sculpted form, its unobtrusive character, as well as by the fact that it avoided conventional symbolism.[43] It shares several features with Tessenow's design of the Neue Wache: the plain walls, the black stone, the minimalist form, the incorporation of natural elements in place of traditional symbols, and a location amid other memorials and historical buildings.[44]

Placing the Vietnam Veterans Memorial on the Mall alongside well-known historical monuments expressing the nation's self-image meant giving this recent conflict a place in American history.[45] Until the dedication of the Korean War Memorial in 1995, the Vietnam Veterans Memorial was the only monument on the Mall commemorating a particular war.[46] One wall points to the Washington Monument, a symbol of independence, the other to the Lincoln Memorial, a symbol of a reunited nation.[47] "It is as though

41 Hess, "A Tale of Two Memorials," 122.
42 Sturken, "Wall, the Screen, and the Image," 128.
43 Howett, "Vietnam Veterans Memorial," 4.
44 It is worth noting that the memorial was built in the 1980s on the site where antiwar protest marches took place in the 1960s. Thus, by remembering the war, the dissent about it could be forgotten.
45 Cf. Charles L. Griswold Jr., *Warriors & Statesmen: Symbolism in the Vietnam Veterans Memorial and Nearby Monuments* (Bethesda, Md., 1990).
46 Robert Maxwell Euwer, *No Longer Forgotten: The Korean War and Its Memorial* (Baltimore, 1995). All other war memorials are located at Arlington National Cemetery; see Shirley Neilsen Blum, "The National Vietnam Memorial," *Arts Magazine* 59 (Dec. 4, 1984), 125.
47 Mayo, *War Memorials as Political Landscapes*, 201.

Figure 5. Maya Lin, Vietnam Veterans Memorial, Washington, D.C. Photo: Sabine Behrenbeck.

the Vietnam Veterans Memorial asks whether America's involvement in Vietnam was true to Lincoln's justice and healing as well as to Washington's founding intentions, struggles against foreign tyrants, and military genius."[48]

To Scruggs, who published a history of the memorial titled *To Heal a Nation*, the memorial seemed to have a therapeutic effect, rendering "the loss of these individuals a matter of national concern."[49] How does this therapeutic effect work? The walls appear to sink into the ground or to be just half-excavated, and thereby function as a symbol of the subconscious burden of war's meaning. The conflict over the war is seen as a psychic problem, and therefore – in contrast to the German case – it is therapeutic catharsis rather than religion that offers consolation.[50] Walking into the embrace of the walls, following the path down into the earth and joining the dead, then ascending into the space of life, the visitor can find relief.

The walls do not dominate the surroundings; they do not reflect a specific point of view, but offer the individual a space for contemplation. The design is focused on the individual, "for death is in the end a personal and private matter," as Maya Lin has explained.[51] "One cannot help seeing him- or herself looking at the names. . . . The dead and the living thus meet, and the living are forced to ask whether those names should be on that wall."[52] Fundamentally interrogative, the memorial challenges each visitor individually to give death in war a meaning.

The memorial does not rise into the sky but descends into the ground as a symbol of the only place where the problem can be solved: at the bottom of the heart, with sorrow for the dead and gratitude toward the spiritually wounded veterans. A second inscription reads: "Our Nation honors the courage, sacrifice, and devotion to duty and country of its Vietnam Veterans." The memorial thus functions as a source of pride to the veterans; for them the therapeutic effect is the reaffirmation of the values for which the nation stands.[53]

Maya Lin herself said about her work: "I had the impulse to cut open the earth . . . an initial violence that in time would heal. The grass would grow back, but the cut would remain."[54] The scar created by Lin's cut would from now on symbolize the dividing line between the living and the dead, the

---

48 Griswold, *Warriors & Statesmen,* 14.   49 Ibid., 22.
50 The artist intended "to bring out in people the realization of loss and a cathartic process," interview from Nov. 21, 1983, quoted in Griswold, *Warriors & Statesmen,* 29.
51 Maya Lin in her statement after having won the competition, quoted in Griswold, *Warriors & Statesmen,* 29.
52 Ibid., 24.   53 Ibid., 25.
54 Quoted in Adrienne Gans, "The War and Peace of the Vietnam Memorials," *American Imago* 44 (winter 1987): 317.

soldiers and the civilians, the opponents and the proponents of the war. This scar could be seen as an open wound that remained painful, as the public reaction to the memorial demonstrated.

A violent debate ensued soon after the jury's choice of Lin's proposal was announced. Many conservative politicians and veterans were unhappy about the design. One characterized it as "the most insulting and demeaning memorial to our experience that was possible."[55] The design refused to evoke heroism and victory, and it opposed the codes of vertical monuments symbolizing power and honor. The color black was attacked as a "universal color of shame, sorrow, and degradation." To H. Ross Perot, a prominent Texas businessman, the memorial was "a slap in the face" because it looked like a tombstone. He organized a poll of 587 one-time POWs, 70 percent of whom disliked the design. The V-shape of the memorial was seen by some in 1981 as a subversive sign of the antiwar movement, a "tribute to Jane Fonda."[56] To some, it even represented the Vietcong since it did not incorporate an American flag.[57] The monument sinking into the earth was interpreted as "an admission of guilt – an acknowledgement that we committed crimes in Vietnam."[58] "The American public had held a negative image of soldiers who fought in the Vietnam War. Once again, many veterans felt that the winning design further perpetuated negative images of them. This time, however, they resisted."[59]

Although the opponents of Maya Lin's design exerted enormous pressure on the Memorial Fund, they could not block its realization. They did, however, force a compromise. In January 1982, both sides agreed that an American flag and a figurative sculpture should be added.[60] Frederic Hart was commissioned to design a maquette. Three young men – one white, one black, one Hispanic – stand on a small base (Figure 6). They look to their right (and, as they have been placed, toward the walls). Only by their uniforms can they be identified as soldiers of the Vietnam War. Although portrayed in realistic style, the three men are not supposed to be individuals but rather timeless, ideal soldiers: "alive, healthy, strong, alert, and cast immortally."[61] The statue is eight feet high and is located one hundred twenty feet from Lin's walls. It stands informally on a low base within a cluster of trees. There is no heroic expression in the work itself or in its presentation.

55 Tom Cahart, quoted in Hess, "A Tale of Two Memorials," 122.
56 Hess, "Tale of Two Memorials," 123ff.
57 Mayo, *War Memorials as Political Landscapes*, 202.
58 Hess, "Tale of Two Memorials," 125.
59 Mayo, *War Memorials as Political Landscapes*, 202.
60 Hess, "Tale of Two Memorials," 125.
61 Gans, "The War and Peace of the Vietnam Memorials," 327.

Figure 6. Frederic Hart, "Fighting Men." Photo: Sabine Behrenbeck.

The inscription on the nearby flagpole reads: "This flag represents the service rendered to our country by the veterans of the Vietnam War. The flag affirms the principles of freedom for which they fought and their pride in having served under difficult circumstances."

"Fighting Men" is a rather misleading title for the sculpture because these men do not look very combative or belligerent. They seem, instead, bewildered. The conservative veterans were eager to have a representation of their war experience and of the camaraderie they had shared.[62] Unlike the aesthetic of Maya Lin, which diverges sharply from the traditional design and message of prior war memorials, Hart's statue employs the traditional iconography and the commemorative codes of earlier war memorials, such as the Iwo Jima Marine Corps War Memorial.[63] "Fighting Men" sends the message that the debate over the war has come to a close: Vietnam should finally be seen as a "normal" war.

For the veterans, the period following demobilization was a painful part of their lives.[64] They needed symbolic recognition of their service "under difficult circumstances" and thereby moral re-integration into society. For this symbolic politics, the veterans wanted a work that employed a traditional sign that could not be misunderstood. Maya Lin's abstract design was criticized for being nihilistic and elitist, whereas Hart's sculpture would be populist.[65] This sculpture was meant to show the "youth and innocence" of the combatants, whose average age had been nineteen. It would "give a little dignity to the people who fought the war," and the artist's position was claimed to be humanist, not militarist.[66]

On Veterans Day 1984, the statue and flagpole were added to the memorial that had been dedicated two years earlier. Since then, the two very different memorials challenge each other with contrasting points of view and aesthetics.[67] Together they form an ensemble that visualizes the different interpretations of war. The visitors interact with them in very different ways. Today it is evident that the abstract walls are anything but elitist.

We do not know what people thought of Tessenow's design in 1931. We only have the reviews of art historians and journalists, which discuss style in general terms and offer personal impressions. It is not known how the memorial was used by the population, whether people used the chamber for contemplation and private mourning. The Vietnam Veterans Memorial in Washington is, as we know, a living monument. It is the most visited

---

62 Ibid., 325.
63 Sturken, "Wall, the Screen, and the Image," 126.
64 Mayo, *War Memorials as Political Landscapes*, 201.
65 Interview with Frederic Hart, quoted in Hess, "Tale of Two Memorials," 124.
66 Interview with Frederic Hart, quoted in ibid.
67 But as Griswold, *Warriors & Statesmen*, 23, stated: "Yet the physical and aesthetic distance between these two additions and the Vietnam Veterans Memorial is so great that there exists no tension between them."

site on the Mall, a public space used for private rituals of mourning and remembrance. Visitors touch the wall and look for specific names, take rubbings of them. And they leave behind mementos – flowers, letters, personal items, and little flags. Often veterans and the family members of those who served kneel and weep in front of the wall of names.[68] Most visitors pause to look at Hart's statue, many take photos of it, but it does not attract the attention or provoke the strong emotional response that Lin's abstract sculpture does. Lin's wall "has tapped into a reservoir of need to express in public the pain of this war, a desire to transfer private memories into a collective experience."[69] The National Park Service is compiling an archive of the materials that have been left at the Vietnam Veterans Memorial, and a selection is displayed at the National Museum of American History. The wall has become a place where private tokens of remembrance are converted into artifacts of cultural memory.

It would overtax any memorial "to heal a nation" as Scruggs and the Memorial Fund set out to do.[70] But with the Vietnam Veterans Memorial the conflict over the war in Southeast Asia has found a site of memory. The design is open to diverging interpretations: "The memorial is seen as representing a wound in the process of healing.... This wound in turn represents the process of memory; healing is the process of remembering and commemorating the war. To dismember is to fragment a body and its memory; to remember is to make a body complete."[71] The therapeutic capacity of the memorial thus depends on the position of the viewer. For the veterans, healing comes as society remembers their service and thereby ends their social marginalization. For society, the process of healing means forgetting the mistreatment of the veterans, forgetting the losses the war caused – particularly the losses of the Vietnamese people – and overcoming the disruption of the national self-image. By lending themselves to multiple interpretations, the design of the memorial and its inscription transcend these contradictions. This may explain why the Vietnam Veterans Memorial has so often been imitated.[72]

---

68 Gans, "War and Peace of the Vietnam Memorials," 321, compares the Wall of the VVM to the Western Wall in Jerusalem.

69 Sturken, "Wall, the Screen, and the Image," 135.

70 This was the intention of the Memorial fund. See Jan C. Scruggs and Joel L. Swerdlow, *To Heal a Nation: The Vietnam Memorial* (New York, 1985).

71 Sturken, "Wall, the Screen, and the Image," 132.

72 Another reason can be seen in the narrative of the memorial constructing an identity for the veterans after their return from war: "The central theme of this narrative is the way the veterans had been invisible and without voice before the memorial's construction" (Sturken, "Wall, the Screen, and the Image," 129).

VI

To summarize this comparison of two postwar periods and war memorials, it is useful to look more closely at some differences. It is remarkable that the German memorials after World War I were without exception dedicated to the fallen soldiers (*Gefallenendenkmäle*), whereas most of the American monuments after the Vietnam War are dedicated to the veterans and are called "veterans' memorials." This is a consequence of numbers. Germany lost 1.8 million men in battle, someone from nearly every family. Two-and-one-half million men returned from combat with serious injuries. German society after 1918 was a community of survivors. As a consequence, German memorials focused on the relation of the living to the dead. The most important questions were: Who was responsible? What purpose could legitimize the war victims? The answers were publicly displayed in the design of the war memorials: The fallen were presented as idealistic men who offered their lives in sacrifice for the fatherland. Notwithstanding their failure, their service remained a noble gesture of devotion and patriotism, and the victims of war thus were always seen as having made a great sacrifice as well. It is noteworthy that the German language has only one word for both victim and sacrifice: *Opfer*.[73]

Over three million American troops served in Vietnam, and 58,000 died there. Many of those who returned belonged to minority groups and – after the demobilization – were treated as a social problem, not as honorable patriots.[74] They had to deal with severe social and psychological problems, and many tried to overcome these problems with drugs and alcohol. Their main concern was not to get monetary compensation but rather public recognition for what they had done and suffered for the nation. "The primary narrative of the veterans in the discourse around the memorial is not their war experience but their mistreatment since the war."[75] The memorials are therefore focused on the veterans and their need for social and moral reintegration.

---

73 Sabine Behrenbeck, "Heldenkult und Opfermythos: Mechanismen der Kriegsbegeisterung 1918–1945," in Marcel van der Linden and Gottfried Mergner, eds., *Kriegsbegeisterung und mentale Kriegsvorbereitung: Interdisziplinäre Studien* (Berlin, 1991), 143–59. Reinhart Koselleck has already noticed that since 1945 this ambivalent meaning has changed: "Opfer" today is used in the sense of a passive victim, not of an active sacrifice. By this interpretation, the dead of World War II – whether innocent or guilty – can all be seen as victims of the war or the NS regime. Their deaths can be separated from their lives. Reinhart Koselleck, "Stellen uns die Toten einen Termin?" *Frankfurter Allgemeine Zeitung*, Aug. 23, 1993.

74 Wagner-Pacifi and Schwartz, "Die Vietnam-Veteranen-Gedenkstätte," 399–400.

75 Sturken, "Wall, the Screen, and the Image," 131.

One of the most important differences between the two cases stems from the political self-image of each nation. Germany was unable to tolerate conflict about the war and the memorial, and thus it could only fail in its search for one symbol that could express the feelings of the people as a whole. That symbol did not exist, and no artist would have been able to design a memorial blending all the different opinions. The German government was able to resolve neither the partisan struggle between conservative veterans' groups and politicians on the left nor the disagreement among the states on the location of the proposed memorials. In the end, the Prussian memorial on Unter den Linden was used as the sole national memorial, but it could not mask the fact that the debate over the meaning of death in war could not be brought to a close. Tessenow's minimalist design for the Neue Wache was open to so many different interpretations – as the later usurpations for the heroic rituals of the Nazis and the postwar communists demonstrated – that it was incapable of reuniting the German people.[76]

Maya Lin's design for the memorial in Washington was realized with the backing of both one-time opponents of the war and many veterans. There also was enough tolerance to accept a "counter memorial" nearby that offered a more traditional message about death in war. This compromise indicates how the American people came to a new interpretation of the Vietnam War: After losing the war, the United States won the peace.

In 1985, ten years after the fall of Saigon, the Vietnam War veterans finally were welcomed home with a ticker-tape parade in New York City.[77] The division of the nation and the self-destructive, exhausting debate seemed to be over: The United States made its peace with the Vietnam War.[78] The conservative Reagan administration repeatedly declared an end to the country's shame and feelings of guilt. And with the end of the Cold War – a U.S. victory in the eyes of many Americans – the meaning of the Vietnam War has been devalued. President George Bush tried to interpret the Gulf War in 1991 as evidence that America's triumphal march continued: The doubts about America's mission caused by the failure in Vietnam were eradicated by the success against Iraq.[79]

---

76 Finally, in 1935 the new Reich Chancellor Adolf Hitler declared the existing war monument in Tannenberg, East Prussia, built in 1927, to be the official *Reichsehrenmal*. After the Nazis came to power, the only legitimate way to remember the war and its dead was the myth of tragic heroes betrayed by domestic politics. Hitler promised them: "Your fight was not in vain!" meaning the Third Reich was the aim for which they had fought and died.

77 See articles in the *New York Times*, May 7, 8, 1985.

78 Bernd Hey, "Zeitgeschichte im Kino: Der Kriegsfilm vom Zweiten Weltkrieg bis Vietnam," *Geschichte in Wissenschaft und Unterricht* 47, no. 10 (1996): 587–8.

79 Berg, "Die innere Entwicklung der USA," 247.

The American example of a monument that does not gloss over but represents the conflicts of public memory has been taken as an important point of reference in similar debates in Germany. In the 1993 discussion of the remodeling of the Neue Wache as a "memorial for the victims of wars and terror," historian Reinhart Koselleck pointed out that by following the American example of the Vietnam Veterans Memorial in Washington, German society would be encouraged to engage in a needed debate. Consensus, Koselleck noted, can never be decreed.[80]

The addition of the statue of the three "Fighting Men" robbed the abstract architecture of the original memorial of its universality. No longer a symbol that included all veterans, it needed another supplement so that female veterans would feel included.[81] In 1993, the Vietnam Veterans Memorial was supplemented by another statue dedicated to the women who served as nurses, secretaries, and interpreters in Vietnam. Sculpted by Glenna Goodacre, the statue shows three female figures in fatigues (Figure 7). The Caucasian figure is arranged somewhat like a pietà holding a wounded soldier on her lap, the African American figure looks to the sky, and the third figure, an Asian, has a helmet in her hands. The statue is placed the same distance from the wall as Frederic Hart's "Fighting Men," but the three women form a circle without any relation to the wall.

In Germany, a similar phenomenon can be observed in the ten-year debate over a national Holocaust memorial in Berlin. Such a memorial was missed particularly after the national memorial for the victims of World War II was installed in the Neue Wache. The new national memorial employed a representational statue, based on a pietà by Käthe Kollwitz, and a much-discussed inscription. The use of Christian iconography has been read by many observers within Germany and abroad as a sign that the memorial did not embrace Jewish victims. The construction of the Holocaust memorial in Berlin will probably lead other groups of victims to ask for a memorial of their own.

A comparative perspective suggests that codes of commemoration remain fluid in the first decade after a war. It takes time for a people to make sense of the experience and to work out and communicate a new narrative. The Vietnam Veterans Memorial was part of this process. It does not directly address the war or explain why the soldiers had to die. Rather, the inscription

80 Reinhart Koselleck, "Stellen uns die Toten einen Termin?" *Frankfurter Allgemeine Zeitung*, Aug. 23, 1993.
81 It was Hart's depiction of three men who make the absence of women so visible. See Sturken, "Wall, the Screen, and the Image," 130–1. There are other groups, such as Air Force pilots, Navy seamen, and Native Americans, who are demanding their own memorial. See *The Nation*, June 4, 1988, 780.

Figure 7. Glenna Goodacre, Vietnam Women's Memorial. Photo: Sabine Behrenbeck.

honors the service of the veterans and records the names of "those who gave their lives . . . in the order they were taken from us."

After having separated the war from the warriors, it was possible to honor the Vietnam veterans without commenting on America's Vietnam policy.[82] The memorial on the Mall serves as a metaphor and is used for the social "ritual of passage" the nation needed to heal the divisive wound of war. As a result of this healing process the Vietnam War "can now be safely woven into the traditional stories Americans have told about themselves. . . . Once young and innocent, like its soldiers, America went to Southeast Asia to rescue a democracy, to fight for 'principles of freedom'; the rescue failed and America became a victim of the conflict, but the sacrifices it made, like those of its soldiers, were noble."[83]

It has become clear that there is a relationship between the history of memory in the twentieth century and the experience of total war and mass death. Since World War I the public rituals and narratives commemorating

82 Scrugg and Swerdlow, *To Heal a Nation,* 17.   83 Turner, *Echoes of Combat,* 183–4.

national pasts have fundamentally changed.[84] One result of this process is the development of a new, transnational narrative among the democratic states: Instead of victories and the heroic virtues of patriotic warriors, the victims of military, political, and moral catastrophe are the focus of public memory.[85] The new national narratives in which war and death in war are located present ruptures with the past as new beginnings and give discontinuity higher value than tradition.

Professional historians no longer ignore the impact of traumatic events on group identity and commemoration. They have noticed that remembering a catastrophe serves as a formal acknowledgment of the specific significance of a particular event for redefining and highlighting a society's moral and political values. The aftermath of catastrophic events has become of more interest than their origins, memory of more interest than genesis. There may thus be a connection between the experience of war and memory, as professional historians have adopted the term: Memory has become a name for the ways people construct meaning from the past.

---

84 Paul Fussell, *The Great War and Modern Memory* (New York, 1975); Eric J. Leed, *No Man's Land: Combat and Identity in World War I* (Cambridge, 1979); Jay M. Winter, *The Great War and the British People* (Cambridge, 1986); George L. Mosse, *Fallen Soldiers: Reshaping the Memory of the World Wars* (New York, 1990); Guenther Kurt Piehler, "Remembering War the American Way, 1783 to the Present," Ph.D. diss., Rutgers University, 1990.

85 A tendency that can be observed in many countries indicates that the national past no longer can serve as a vehicle for positive identification. But this tendency stands in sharp contrast to current values and politics. See Helmut Dubiel, *Niemand ist frei von der Geschichte: Die nationalsozialistische Herrschaft in den Debatten des Deutschen Bundestages* (Munich, 1999), 292.

PART TWO

International Relations and the Dynamics of Alliance Politics

7

Who Paid for America's War?

Vietnam and the International Monetary System, 1960–1975

HUBERT ZIMMERMANN

The slow dissolution of America's postwar hegemony probably is the most popular analytic device for explaining the history of European-American relations from the 1950s through the 1970s. Bestsellers such as Paul M. Kennedy's *The Rise and Fall of the Great Powers* popularized the image of superpower USA, which, due to its supreme economic, military, and moral resources, reigned after World War II with hegemonic benevolence over a large system of economic and military alliances until, in the 1960s and 1970s, it succumbed to the imperial burden and went into decline.[1] The two events cited most frequently to support this idea of hegemonic decline are the Vietnam War and the breakdown of the U.S.-dominated postwar monetary system in the early 1970s. The question of whether those two processes were linked, and if so how, has not yet been tackled by researchers in any systematic way. What role did the war play in the collapse of the monetary system, and how did the monetary crisis influence the United States' Vietnam policy?

This question leads me directly into the story of mutual disenchantment between the United States and Europe during the 1960s and 1970s. The Europeans suspected that Vietnam was diverting America's interest from Europe. This feeling was intensified by economic conflicts, particularly on international monetary issues. Vietnam became a central argument for European critics of American monetary policy in the 1960s and 1970s. The "exorbitant privilege" (a term coined by Charles de Gaulle) of the dollar's reserve currency role is said to have allowed the United States to finance the war by printing money: "The United States had used its exorbitant

---

1 Paul Kennedy, *The Rise and Fall of the Great Powers* (New York, 1987). This interpretation is not confined only to historical writings. See for example the highly influential works by political scientists such as Robert Gilpin, *The Political Economy of International Relations* (Princeton, N.J., 1987) or Mancur Olson, *The Rise and Decline of Nations* (New Haven, Conn., 1982).

privilege as the center country of a gold-exchange system to run a perpetual balance-of-payments deficit and to finance a distant and expensive war in Vietnam by inflationary credit creation rather than by a transfer of resources from the civilians to the military by means of taxation."[2] Did America's partners in fact ultimately shield the American domestic economy from the inflationary shocks that the war produced by absorbing the dollar glut that resulted from American balance-of-payments deficits? American policy makers vehemently denied this. To them the Vietnam War added to a burden the United States was already carrying: the preservation of a monetary system that was beneficial to all participants. By refusing significant support in the economic field, the Europeans threatened to bring down the monetary system at a time when the American economy no longer was able to carry the double burden of economically and militarily defending the free world. This interpretation, brought forward forcefully by Secretary of Defense Robert S. McNamara and others, was increasingly shared by Congress. Consequently, they argued that if the Europeans were not willing to support the war effort directly and throw their full weight behind preserving the international monetary system, the United States no longer was obliged to carry most of the defense burden in Europe.

The transatlantic security system that had developed after World War II and that provided the framework of the European-American alliance would not have been feasible in the form we know it without its monetary foundation (and vice-versa). This fact is often ignored by researchers. To truly understand the impact of Vietnam on both transatlantic economic and political relations, it is essential to keep in mind how this link developed. After 1945, the dollar rapidly became the most important global currency. This development had not been planned during the international conference at Bretton Woods in 1944 when American and British experts formulated the guidelines for postwar monetary relations. However, it was inevitable given the preeminent U.S. economic position after the war vis-à-vis its former competitors. The United States became the bank to a large part of the world. Countries that chose to hold their reserves in dollars, to link the value of their currencies to the American currency, and to use dollars to settle their international balances accorded to the United States a huge influence over their monetary policy. In practice, by holding and using dollars they

---

2 Susan Strange, "Interpretations of a Decade," in Lucas Tsoukalis, ed., *The Political Economy of International Money* (London, 1985), 11. For a similar interpretation, see David P. Calleo, "De Gaulle and the Monetary System," in Robert O. Paxton and Nicholas Wahl, eds., *De Gaulle and the United States: A Centennial Reappraisal* (Oxford, 1994), 239–55.

extended credit to the United States.[3] The American side of this implicit bargain was to guarantee that its currency, as the principal reserve asset of the Western world, retained its value and credibility. This was done first by linking the dollar to gold at a fixed value ($35 an ounce). In order to establish confidence in the stability of its currency, the U.S. government committed itself at the Bretton Woods conference to defend this price and to exchange every dollar foreigners presented to the U.S. Treasury for gold at this rate.[4]

The second commitment, and the essential condition for keeping the dollar-gold pledge intact, was that the United States manage its domestic economic policy in a way that preserved the strength of its currency, particularly by keeping inflation low and by seeing that the costs of its external commitments did not become exorbitant. There was another extremely important side to this bargain. The postwar years not only saw economic reconstruction but also an unprecedented expansion of U.S. political and military commitments related to the containment of communism – which also was a primary political objective of almost all European states. This expansion of American commitments was made possible by the reserve role of the dollar. The American economy, in terms of financial impact, sustained a ceaseless war effort during the Cold War, but the construction of the international monetary system buffered the inflationary impact and thus prevented an erosion of fragile domestic support. For most Europeans, the expansion of U.S. commitments was very welcome. Thus, Europe willingly accorded to the United States the privilege of creating international credit, and in exchange it was granted military security, economic aid, and protection for its weak trade position against overwhelming American competition. European-American relations were founded on a virtual, never formulated but extremely important bargain.[5] The postwar security and monetary systems were two sides of the same coin.

At first the bargain worked well. European governments were eager to accumulate dollars that, unlike gold, even paid interest. The Americans set

3 Harold van B. Cleveland, *The Atlantic Idea and Its European Rivals* (New York, 1966), 77.

4 In a seminal article on the working of monetary systems, Ronald McKinnon showed that the famous dollar-gold link was not a necessary condition for the working of the postwar monetary system. It was essential, however, that the United States managed its external account according to the necessities of the system. See Ronald I. McKinnon, "The Rules of the Game: International Money in Historical Perspective," *Journal of Economic Literature* 31 (Mar. 1993): 1–44.

5 This formula has already been employed by Benjamin J. Cohen, although in a more limited sense. In his version, the American part of the bargain was to accept trade discrimination by Europe in the interest of political objectives. See Cohen, "The Revolution in Atlantic Economic Relations: A Bargain Comes Unstuck," in Wolfram Hanrieder, ed., *The United States and Western Europe* (Cambridge, 1974), 106–33.

the economic and political guidelines of the alliance. The enormous cost of the American military commitment in Europe seemed to have no negative impact on the value of the dollar. However, there was a major snag in the system: The international monetary structure was *not* based on economic rationality. The best-known expression of the system's irrationality is the so-called Triffin Dilemma, named after the Belgian-American economist Robert Triffin. He claimed that a system that relied on continuing U.S. deficits (in order to provide liquidity for the expanding world trade) would undermine itself because these deficits impaired confidence in the dollar.[6] Every dollar abroad represented a claim on the gold in Fort Knox, and every year of deficit added to the overall sum of claims. When the American gold stock no longer was large enough to cover them all, confidence would wane. If, however, the outflow of dollars was restricted, the international economy would face a liquidity gap. The Triffin Dilemma signified that the postwar monetary system worked not because it was economically sound, but rather because of its political rationality. Europe and America saw eye-to-eye on basic political and economic issues, and thus both were interested in preserving the implicit bargain. American commitments abroad, which were responsible for the deficit, were seen as beneficial and necessary by Europeans – until Vietnam. The real danger to the monetary system therefore was not so much its economic flaws; it was the erosion of its political base.

The first cracks in the system appeared in the late 1950s. From 1958 on, American balance-of-payments deficits swelled to unprecedented proportions.[7] International financial markets reacted with surprise. European central banks presented portions of their dollar holdings at Fort Knox, and the American gold stock shrank considerably. Of $21.8 billion in 1954, $17.8 billion remained in 1960. The fall continued to $10.2 billion in 1971.[8] In 1960, Secretary of the Treasury Robert B. Anderson warned, "Continuing on this course would bring us the greatest Holocaust we had ever seen."[9] He argued for a reduction of the expensive military commitment in Europe. The State Department, which placed much more emphasis on the "security" part of the transatlantic bargain, naturally judged the

6 Robert Triffin, *Gold and the Dollar Crisis* (New Haven, Conn., 1960).
7 In 1954, the United States recorded a deficit of about $1.5 billion. In 1959–60, the deficit surpassed $3.5 billion each year. Until the mid-1960s, it stayed close to $2.5 billion despite increasing efforts by successive administrations to bring it down. For the precise figures, see *Survey of Current Business*, Oct. 1972, 26, and June 1975, 26–7.
8 *Economic Report of the President* 1975, 356.
9 Memorandum of discussion at the 465th meeting of the National Security Council (hereafter NSC), Oct. 29, 1960, in U.S. Department of State, ed., *Foreign Relations of the United States* (hereafter *FRUS*) *1958–1960*, IV, 529.

situation differently: "There seems . . . to be no greater problem facing this government than whether or not to warp our military doctrine and stunt our military establishment to meet temporary economic pressures. We face the alternative whether to run an uncertain risk of some loss of confidence in the dollar or the certain risk of a loss of confidence in America's determination to make common cause with its allies and maintain a rational and credible deterrent to communist aggression. If this happens, the standing of the American dollar and a great deal more besides will inevitably be prejudiced."[10]

The possibility that the United States would cancel its part of the bargain if the Europeans refused to cooperate in solving the monetary problem became a persistent element of the European-American debate. However, despite those signs of crisis, the general feeling was that, with some imagination and increased transatlantic cooperation, the situation still could be managed. John F. Kennedy made the balance-of-payments problem one of his political priorities: "If confidence in the dollar is not maintained, those holding dollar and gold obligations against us could easily create difficulties for us. Any bank in which confidence is weakened faces great dangers."[11] The defense of the dollar became – simultaneously with the defense of Southeast Asia – an issue of American prestige and international leadership. The new president and his team developed a series of initiatives in the field of international monetary cooperation. New monetary mechanisms such as the gold pool[12] were created to deal with speculative movements. The Europeans (including the French) by and large went along with most of the American proposals. For all the imagination that went into the measures taken by the Kennedy administration, no fundamental reform of the system was envisaged despite the vast transformation in the economic balance of power in the West since World War II. The central role of the dollar was not put into question. Kennedy probably was the last president whose prestige and freedom of maneuver were sufficient to undertake the Herculean task of reforming the system without wrecking it.

---

10 Memorandum from the Acting Secretary of State, Smith, to Christian Herter, Oct. 29, 1959, in *FRUS 1958–1960*, VII/1, 496.

11 Summary of Kennedy's Remarks at the 496th Meeting of the NSC, Jan. 18, 1962, in *FRUS 1961–1963*, VIII, 239.

12 A pool of $270 million worth of gold, established by the United States, the United Kingdom, West Germany, Italy, Belgium, the Netherlands, and Switzerland, to undertake interventions in the gold market and buffer the impact of speculation on the American gold stock. The history of the gold pool and of the many other devices to shore up the monetary system in the 1960s is described in detail by what probably still is the best monetary history of this period: Susan Strange, *International Monetary Relations of the Western World, 1959–71* (London, 1976).

When Lyndon B. Johnson became president, the balance-of-payments problem still was not solved. New ideas were necessary. In July 1965, Secretary of the Treasury Henry H. Fowler announced that the American government was ready to talk with its allies about the creation of a new reserve medium that would supplement the dollar as reserve currency and free the United States from some of the constraints its balance-of-payments situation had created.[13] The core issue of the talks was clear: Who was to control the creation of this new form of credit? Was America ready to guarantee that it would not abuse the new instrument as a device to liberate itself from the limits imposed on its dollar policy by the dollar–gold link? The European Economic Community (EEC) countries, together with Britain, were to be the main interlocutors, and they were determined this time to have a voice in the process of reserve creation. At the time, however, it was not clearly realized that not only a broad consensus on the economic intricacies of reforming the international monetary system was necessary but that broad agreement on the political foundations of the system also was needed. The United States no longer was in a position to impose its will unilaterally as it had been at Bretton Woods. Therefore, the antagonism between France and the United States was to become a major problem, although their principal objective was similar: relieving the dollar of the burden of its reserve role.

The negotiations on the creation of new reserve assets proved extremely difficult because the overall political situation was rapidly changing. In 1964–5, a new element entered the scene that decisively increased the pressure on the United States: escalation of the war in Southeast Asia. Important events in Vietnam and with the monetary system coincided: In February 1965, the Vietcong attacked the Marine barracks at Pleiku, and the Americans decided to respond by bombing North Vietnam. In the same month, de Gaulle issued an open call for the end of "dollar hegemony." Concomitantly, Fowler developed his new initiative, which was meant to dilute the pressure on the dollar. In July, as Johnson announced he would send 50,000 additional men to Vietnam,[14] Fowler went on a tour of Europe to propose the creation of a new reserve medium. Given the relative calm on monetary markets, it seemed possible to bring the process quickly to a mutually acceptable conclusion. Nobody thought that what had happened in Southeast Asia would render this optimism illusory. Stable economic and political conditions for monetary reform became increasingly difficult to achieve. The more hostilities intensified, the more it became clear that

---

13 For the genesis of the proposal, see John S. Odell, *U.S. International Monetary Relations: Markets, Power, and Ideas as Forces of Change* (New York, 1982).
14 George C. Herring, *LBJ and Vietnam: A Different Kind of War* (Austin, 1994), 1–24.

Vietnam would have a major impact on America's international position in the political and financial fields. The cool reception Fowler's proposal received was partly due to this factor.

When Johnson made the decision in 1965 to escalate the conflict in Vietnam, the likely effects of this step on the external balances played no role. However, the expansion of the war soon had direct and indirect monetary consequences. The direct impact was obvious: With increasing activities in Southeast Asia, U.S. military expenditure abroad was bound to rise. When McNamara assumed the post of secretary of defense, he began a concerted effort to limit the monetary consequences of American military commitments abroad. In January 1968, the Pentagon produced a twenty-seven-page report on military expenditures abroad, listing the multitude of savings measures that had been introduced during the previous years.[15] The sobering conclusion was that Vietnam had ruined those efforts. Only in 1966 did the U.S. government begin to realize what a tremendous impact the war would have on its external balances. McNamara had to admit that his cost estimates had been much too low.[16] The dollars that had been saved in Europe disappeared in the jungles of Southeast Asia. Between 1960 and 1965, military expenditures abroad had been stabilized at about $3 billion, despite general increases in prices. In Europe, they even fell from $1.652 billion to $1.468 billion. After 1965, the dollar outflow began to rise steeply due to the Vietnam conflict. In 1968, the military deficit increased to $4.5 billion, and outlays in Asia rose from $825 million in 1960 to $2.491 billion in 1968.[17] Of course, this expenditure was an easy target for those in Congress who were critical of military involvement in Southeast Asia. Curiously, however, Johnson's Vietnam policy was not directly challenged: instead, a strong congressional movement for reducing the long-term commitment in Europe developed. The troops in Europe became an indirect and popular target used to attack the administration.[18] In a way, this attack had its uses for the administration. In countless conversations with European politicians, the Americans were able to point to congressional pressure for troop reductions in Europe that would mount if the Europeans took no measures to correct the monetary imbalance. However, these threats also

15 Statement summarizing actions by Department of Defense to reduce the net foreign-exchange costs of defense activities, Jan. 4, 1968, box 1, Fowler papers, Lyndon B. Johnson Library, Austin (hereafter LBJL).
16 Minutes of Meeting of Cabinet Committee on Balance of Payments, Mar. 25, 1966, in *FRUS 1965–1968*, VIII, 245.
17 Figures from Cora E. Shepler and Leonard G. Campbell, "United States Defense Expenditure Abroad," *Survey of Current Business* (Dec. 1969): 44.
18 Phil Williams, *The Senate and U.S. Troops in Europe* (London, 1985), 129–48.

were problematic because they undermined a core element of the transatlantic bargain: the confidence in the American security guarantee, which
was a central factor in the European willingness to support an American-led
economic system. Congressional grumbling and the situation on the currency markets made it imperative that the American government intensify
its efforts to keep direct Vietnam expenditures under control. After the first
huge wave of investments, the Pentagon introduced programs similar to the
ones in Europe to keep the Vietnam-related foreign-exchange cost down.
In fact, after 1968 the rise in direct expenditures leveled off. All in all, despite its precipitous rise, the direct foreign-exchange cost of the war turned
out to be manageable. It therefore was not an important element in the
monetary crisis of the 1960s; however, it constituted a convenient target for
those critical of U.S. military engagement in general.

Much more dangerous was the indirect economic impact of the war.
The construction of the international monetary system with the dollar at
its center signified that changes in the domestic economic policy of the
United States and the way the government would deal with the economic
impact of the war would resonate all over the world. In the first two decades
after World War II, the United States had achieved an impressive record of
price stability, if only because the monetary system had helped to absorb
the inflationary impact of the Cold War. The precipitous rise of military
spending prompted by the expansion of the war in Southeast Asia, at a
time of a booming domestic economy and rising government expenditures
for the "Great Society" programs, introduced a new, dangerous element.
In mid-1966, these indirect effects became only too visible for the government.[19] Inflation became the greatest danger. What to do about this
situation? Clearly, "the most powerful medicine would be a large general
tax increase," Johnson's economic adviser Francis Bator noted.[20] Precisely
that also was demanded by the Council of Economic Advisers and, incidentally, by the financial authorities of America's European friends. However,
hardly any government action is less popular than a tax increase. In 1965–6,
it would inevitably have been termed a war tax, providing Johnson's
adversaries with an ideal opportunity to attack his foreign and domestic
policies.[21] Thus, it took a long time before the administration managed
to make a decision and tried to get some half-hearted measures through

19 It is impossible to give an exact figure for the adverse impact of Vietnam activities on the U.S.
   balance of payments. One estimate for the period 1964–7 produced the substantial figure of $3.5–
   4 billion for calendar year 1967. See Leonard Dudley and Peter Passell, "The War in Vietnam and
   the U.S. Balance of Payments," *Review of Economics and Statistics* 50, no. 2 (Apr. 1968): 437–42.
20 Memorandum for the president: Balance of Payments, May 11, 1966, LBJ Collection, National
   Security Archive, Washington, D.C.
21 Anthony S. Campagna, *The Economic Consequences of the Vietnam War* (New York, 1991), 33–5.

Congress. David Halberstam asserted that Johnson, in order to get both "guns and butter" – the means to fight the Vietnam War and to fund his Great Society programs – chose to hide the real cost of the war. Therefore, the president resisted his adviser's call for a tax increase until it was too late and a "virulent inflationary spiral" had been unleashed.[22] Closer to reality than this picture of deceitful manipulation is the image of the president caught in a dilemma.[23] He knew the first victim of a tax hike would not be the war but the Great Society programs.

For the U.S. economy, the consequences of this policy were grave, and they turned out to be even more serious for the international monetary system. Paul Volcker, President Richard M. Nixon's undersecretary for monetary affairs, stated that Vietnam "was the period when inflation really gained momentum in the United States and threatened to spread to Europe, too, and if we weren't willing to finance the war properly, then maybe we shouldn't have fought it at all."[24] The Johnson administration gave up the long-held objective of bringing the balance into equilibrium.[25] Vietnam was presented as the major cause, which implied that as soon as the war came to an end the situation would correct itself. "Had it not been for the direct and indirect impact of the expanding scale of our efforts in Southeast Asia to resist aggression and preserve freedom and self-determination, the United States would have had balance or surplus in 1965 and 1966," Fowler informed Johnson at the end of 1967.[26] This was probably true, but the problem of the international monetary system lay much deeper, as has already been illustrated. Fowler's claims did not fool the experts, and the American government knew that it had to continue – Vietnam notwithstanding – its efforts to hold down the deficit. Numerous bookkeeping exercises and statistical gimmicks were invented to keep the year-end figures artificially low.[27] This alone was not enough. Fowler presented another idea:

I propose that we give serious consideration to asking the key dollar-holding nations . . . to pledge not to convert dollars they presently hold and *not* to convert

---

22 David Halberstam, *The Best and the Brightest* (New York, 1993), 603–10.
23 Donald F. Kettl, "The Economic Education of Lyndon Johnson: Guns, Butter, and Taxes," in Robert A. Divine, ed., *The Johnson Years*, 3 vols., vol. 2: *Vietnam, the Environment, and Science* (Kansas City, 1987), 54–77.
24 Paul Volcker and Toyoo Gyoohten, *Changing Fortunes* (New York, 1992), 62.
25 "There was tacit recognition during 1966 that the efforts to achieve equilibrium in our balance of payments would not be successful as long as the hostilities in Vietnam continued on such a large scale"; see Administrative History of the Department of the Treasury, vol. I, pt. 2, chap. 9: "Balance of Payments," LBJL.
26 Fowler to President: Action Program for Maintaining the Strength of the Dollar, Dec. 18, 1967, box 54, NSC Histories: The 1968 Balance-of-payments Program, National Security Files (hereafter NSF), LBJL.
27 Martin Gilbert, *Quest for World Monetary Order* (New York, 1980), 140.

any additional dollars [original emphasis] that may accrue to them as long as the Vietnam struggle continues. To accomplish this, we will have to state in the strongest possible terms that: 1. We most emphatically do intend to bring our balance of payments into equilibrium. 2. The Vietnam War, with its attendant direct and indirect balance of payments costs, has made it difficult for us to do this as soon as we hoped. But we will do it. 3. We are bearing virtually the entire burden of the Vietnam conflict. We view this as commitment on behalf of all free nations. We do not ask others to see it this way, but we do ask that they not act in a manner that will prevent us from meeting our commitments and/or destroy the international financial institutions that are such a vital part of the world we are attempting to defend.[28]

This meant that Europe would have to forgo its principal element of control over America's management of its reserve currency and instead trust in an unbinding promise that the United States would do its best to behave responsibly in the future. This strategy would work only if there was a large basis of confidence in American economic policies and, moreover, agreement with its foreign policies. However, it was confidence in the wisdom and continuity of American policies that suffered most in the Vietnam fallout. The war sowed serious doubts among those who believed in the soundness of U.S. policies, and it provoked grave apprehensions as to whether the United States would honor its side of the bargain and keep the dollar stable while preserving its security commitments in Europe.

Johnson was at a dead end. Anything he could possibly do would wreck the primary objectives of American policy after World War II or the basic goals of his administration's policy, which he could not give up without admitting complete failure. The inflation caused by spending for the war in Vietnam precluded any possibility of further delays in monetary reform. The only recourse was a policy that had been tried, with varying success, since the end of Dwight D. Eisenhower's presidency: to get the allies to help on presumed moral grounds. They had refused to answer even strong calls for direct military and economic aid in Vietnam.[29] Now they were called upon on a much larger scale in the international monetary field. The bargain was put to a hard test: How would the Europeans react? Particularly unforeseeable was the reaction of de Gaulle.

No other country recognized as clearly as did France the fundamentally political background of the international monetary questions at issue during

---

28 Memorandum by Fowler to Johnson, May 10, 1966, in *FRUS 1964–1968*, VIII, 276–7.
29 For an aide-mémoire to the Federal Republic requesting a list of possible German aid projects for South Vietnam, see McGhee papers, July 6, 1964, box 1, 1988 add., Georgetown University. On the European reaction to the Vietnam War, see also the chapter by Fred Logevall in this book.

the 1960s. Thus, it became the most outspoken of all European countries regarding reforms in the international monetary system and, by disagreeing with the United States, its principal opponent. On February 4, 1965, during one of his famous press conferences, de Gaulle launched a full-scale attack against the dollar. He asserted that the present monetary system allowed the American government to finance its external commitments, including Vietnam, by simply printing dollars and that it enabled American firms to buy up foreign industries with this overvalued currency. De Gaulle demanded a return to the gold standard, and he announced that France would from now on immediately present all dollars it earned to the U.S. Treasury for conversion to gold.[30] France, although it profited probably most of all countries from American aid after World War II, had become the country most disenchanted with the transatlantic system, and it was only logical that the French challenge to the U.S. in the security field would be accompanied by one in the monetary field as well. French politicians had never been entirely content with the fact that their proposals at the Bretton Woods conference attracted polite attention but little response. A high-placed collaborator of de Gaulle's called Bretton Woods a "*Yalta monétaire fait à deux*" in retrospect.[31]

However, it would be too simplistic to see France's monetary policy as just an extension of Franco-American conflicts in the political field.[32] In its less confrontational form, as postulated by Finance Minister Valéry Giscard d'Estaing some weeks after de Gaulle's press conference, it was an expression of traditional French monetary policies that in the 1920s and 1930s had already advocated a close link of all currencies to gold.[33] The high degree of ambiguity in French policy is evident in the fact that France by and large cooperated in the monetary initiatives that had been proposed by the Kennedy administration. Thus, France joined the gold pool, participating in it until July 1967. It also supported multilateral rescue operations for the British pound. Regarding the necessity for a reform of the international monetary system, Paris and Washington saw eye to eye. However, they disagreed both on the extent and the method. In September 1964, France presented a plan for a new reserve asset, called the Composite Reserve Unit,

30 Charles de Gaulle, *Discours et Messages*, vol. 4: *1962–1965* (Paris, 1969), 332.
31 Jean-Yves Haberer testimony, in Institut Charles de Gaulle, ed., *De Gaulle en son Siècle III* (Paris, 1992), 155–6.
32 E.g., see Frank Costigliola, *France and the United States: The Cold War Alliance Since World War II* (New York, 1992), 149–53.
33 Michael D. Bordo, Dominique Simard, and Eugene N. White, "France and the Bretton Woods International Monetary System 1960–68," in Jaime Reis, ed., *International Monetary Systems in Historical Perspective* (London, 1995), 153–80.

that in effect prefigured the American Strategic Dollar Reserve (SDR) proposal. In January 1965, André de Lattre, the director of the Department of External Finances at the French Finance Ministry, had, with the consent of Giscard d'Estaing, called for a common European currency.[34] These proposals were designed to provide escape routes for the Europeans in case the American deficits got completely out of control. Unfortunately, the constructive elements of French policy soon were swept away by the grandeur of its leader. De Gaulle's press conference incited open confrontation rather than serious negotiation. Johnson publicly reaffirmed his administration's determination to defend the $35-per-ounce ratio, and from then on every move in the international monetary field became deeply entangled with notions of national prestige. Thus, de Gaulle's strategy alienated both the Americans and other possible allies who were not willing to take up the challenge.

As a result of this politicization of the issue, it proved extremely difficult to find a common position among the Europeans toward Fowler's reform proposals although they agreed on the necessity to procure a stronger voice for Europe. Due to their disunity, and despite their monetary power, they did not have enough political leverage to decisively change American financial policies. Ironically, the resulting failure to achieve monetary reform in the mid-1960s came at great expense to France. The civil and social unrest of May 1968 sparked a huge flight of capital, and, within a short time, France lost a third of its reserves. De Gaulle had overplayed his hand, and in August 1969 the French currency was devalued. By then de Gaulle had retired, clearing the way for France's more cooperative attitude toward monetary collaboration with its allies: too late for the Europeans, as it turned out. Europe's limited bargaining power had to do not only with the consequences of French obstructionism but also with the absence of another major monetary player from the European ranks: Britain.

In the emerging conflict between the United States and its Western European partners over the global monetary structure, Britain found itself in a strange and uneasy position, torn between the continuing obligations of its special relationship and the necessity to finally find its role in Europe after World War II. Vietnam clearly exposed this dilemma. One core issue in this conflict was the role of sterling.

Successive British governments were determined to hold on to the reserve-currency role of the pound, which since the nineteenth century

---

34 Paris Embassy to Auswärtiges Amt, Jan. 23, 1965, Dept. III A 1, vol. 176, Politisches Archiv des Auswärtigen Amts, Berlin (hereafter PA-AA).

had been among the most important expressions of Britain's worldwide influence. This objective became increasingly hard to achieve, particularly after the economic and political disaster of the Suez Crisis in 1956.[35] From Suez on, the most important elements of London's worldwide role, its military commitments and its reserve currency, were increasingly beleaguered. Britain incessantly aimed at freeing itself from the constraints imposed by this situation, as the chief secretary of the treasury, John Diamond, told German ministers: "In order that Britain should never again need to seek emergency assistance from its Allies, the British government needed to reorganise its affairs, and, in particular, its expenditure across the exchanges. In many respects British policies were directed and redirected by the balance-of-payments problem; it lay behind every Cabinet decision concerning economic affairs and defence, and the Government would never feel free to carry out its policies . . . until it had solved its foreign exchange difficulties."[36] In this endeavor, Britain needed allies.

Having a reserve currency was, apart from its remaining military commitments, the major difference that separated Britain from its European neighbors. Due to the lasting weakness of the pound, the Europeans acquired an important means of pressure: Their support was indispensable to enabling the pound to weather the successive waves of speculation. At the same time, the Americans, under the shadow of Vietnam, began to demand a higher price for Britain's special relationship. The burden of accommodating these conflicting demands fell on Prime Minister Harold Wilson. Soon after the inauguration of his Labour government in autumn 1964, and partly provoked by speculation about the economic policies of the new government, a violent currency crisis rocked the country. Wilson made what was probably the most important economic decision of his term: He decided to defend the parity of sterling. This was achieved only by a multilateral rescue package, consisting of the then enormous sum of $3 billion.[37] The Americans had taken the lead in getting the other rich nations to help Britain.

In summer 1965, Wilson was scheduled to visit Washington. The position of the pound had deteriorated rapidly during the weeks prior to the trip, and monetary help was an important issue on the agenda. The Johnson administration was heading toward an extended military commitment in Southeast Asia and was much less accommodating to British requests than

---

35 See Lewis Johnman, "Defending the Pound: The Economics of the Suez Crisis, 1956," in Anthony Gorst, Lewis Johnman, and W. Scott Lucas, eds., *Postwar Britain, 1945–64* (London, 1989), 166–81; and Diane B. Kunz, *The Economic Diplomacy of the Suez Crisis* (Chapel Hill, N.C., 1991).

36 Record of meeting between Finance Minister Rolf Dahlgrün and John Diamond, June 28, 1965, FO 371/183101, Public Record Office, London (hereafter PRO).

37 Charles Coombs, *The Arena of International Finance* (New York, 1977), 107–30.

it had been in 1964. An intensive debate was under way on the question of
what the British should pay for future monetary help. The "shopping list"
the Johnson administration finally drew up included British agreement to
maintain their troops both East of Suez and in Germany, defend the current
value of sterling, support American trade and nuclear nonproliferation policies, as well as support American policy in Vietnam.[38] Prior to Wilson's visit,
the idea of exacting a British military commitment in Vietnam as a price for
rescuing the pound had been ventured.[39] However, the State Department
vigorously counseled against such a request: "Any suggestion of this in the
context of the bal[ance] of payments would give the British the reaction we
are asking them to be Hessions [sic]. [George] Ball thought any suggestion
of this type would kill any cooperation we could get. Ball said he was sure
the British would say their troops are not for sale – not Hessions [sic] or mercenaries."[40] This judgment was quite accurate. Some months earlier Wilson
had advised his foreign secretary that if Johnson tried to link Vietnam "with
support for the pound I would regard this as most unfortunate. . . . If the
financial weakness we inherited and are in the process of putting right is to
be used as a means of forcing us to accept unpalatable policies or developments regardless of our thoughts, this will raise very wide questions indeed
about Anglo-American relationships."[41] However, Wilson told his cabinet,
it was true that although there was no formal link between the British
presence in Asia and support for the pound, a certain connection between
these issues was undeniable. Put in its crudest form by Wilson himself, the
consequence was: "We can't kick our creditors in the balls."[42] Preserving
the reserve role of sterling became a major reason for Britain to support
American policies, whether on Vietnam or on international monetary
matters.

Britain's weakness prevented the Americans from putting through all the
claims they would have liked. The Treasury Department feared a devaluation of the pound if Britain were pressed too much; the State Department
worried about Britain's troops in Europe (a conspicuous negative factor in
Britain's external balance); and the Pentagon feared for the British presence

38 Bator memorandum for McGeorge Bundy: The UK Problem, July 29, 1965, Declassified Documents
    Reference System 1978, No. 211A.
39 Memoranda to the president: McGeorge Bundy, July 28, 1965, box 4, NSF, LBJL. See also John
    Dumbrell, "The Johnson Administration and the British Labour Government: Vietnam, the Pound
    and East of Suez," *Journal of American Studies* 30 (1996): 211–31.
40 Telephone conversation McBundy–Ball, July 29, 1965, box 1, George Ball papers, LBJL.
41 Harold Wilson to Michael Stewart, Mar. 23, 1965, PREM 13/693, PRO.
42 Philip Ziegler, *Wilson: The Authorised Life* (London, 1993), 228–9; see also Richard Crossman,
    The Diaries of a Cabinet Minister, 1964–68, 2 vols. (London, 1975), 1:456.

East of Suez. Thus, the Americans had a strong interest in repeatedly helping the British out of their currency troubles, albeit at a high cost to the United States and to the stability of the international monetary system.[43] In the wake of Wilson's visit to Washington in the summer of 1966, Ball sketched an alternative option in a lengthy memorandum. He advised Johnson to urge Britain to take a decisive step toward Europe by ending support for sterling and by not insisting on a British flag East of Suez.[44] However, Ball was on his way out of the government, and his position was shared neither by his colleagues nor by the British public.

Thus, both countries followed monetary policies that were ultimately doomed to failure, and both reacted with thinly veiled contempt for the recriminations of the Europeans, who were increasingly unwilling to go along with them. In July 1966, Wilson told Johnson that the "one problem the British have, as well as the United States, is that of the balance of payments; we must correct this. Otherwise, the two great reserve currencies of the world will be driven into a corner by the self-righteous members of the Group of Ten who do not have any responsibilities for world development, banking or military assistance." Fowler replied in the same vein: "The other seven countries – Germany, Italy, Holland, Belgium, Japan, Canada and Sweden – must share in the multilateral defense of sterling. They cannot go their own way since their whole position would be threatened if sterling were endangered."[45] Washington and London thus teamed up against a European bloc. The defense of the British currency became an element linking their policies and at the same time blocking possibilities for more imaginative efforts by both. Two other results were less need for America to accommodate European wishes and increasing antagonism toward Europe, particularly on the British side.

The special relationship and domestic agricultural interests had been the prime reasons for de Gaulle to veto the British application for EEC membership in 1963. Nevertheless, the issue remained on the European agenda. However, following one sterling crisis after the other, it became clear that the state of the British currency would be a huge obstacle. In September 1965, de Gaulle upbraided the British: "I think we have to abstain from participating [in future rescue operations for the pound]. It would indeed be very bad if we would extend our help for an action of which we know

43 Diane B. Kunz, "Cold War Dollar Diplomacy," in Diane B. Kunz, ed., *The Diplomacy of the Crucial Decade* (New York, 1994), 105.
44 Memorandum for the president, July 22, 1966, box 72–73, Fowler papers, LBJL.
45 Conversation between American and British officials, July 29, 1966, in *FRUS 1964–1968*, VIII, 299, 301.

that nothing will come out of it and which even risks prolonging Britain's sluggish negligence."[46] When the British made their second official application in 1967, the French insisted that the British give up the reserve role of sterling.[47] Even those who desired British entry into the EEC saw sterling as a major problem. In a report on the perspectives for future British membership, the European Commission listed the reserve currency role of sterling as the major liability.[48]

At the end of 1967, the futility of the British position became apparent. In November, market pressures became too great, and the British were forced to devalue the pound. The shock of the devaluation initiated a slow change in British policies. No longer absolutely dependent on American support to keep the exchange value, one of the first reactions was to end their presence East of Suez. In January 1968, the British government announced a series of cost-saving measures, which included an end to the British military presence in Southeast Asia and in the Persian Gulf.[49] It also grudgingly initiated a policy destined to relinquish the reserve currency role of sterling, a major concession to the Europeans for extending further monetary and economic support.[50] In November 1969, at the Hague Summit of EEC countries, the process of Britain's admission was set in motion. At the same meeting, the EEC declared for the first time its intention to create a common European currency that might constitute an alternative to the dollar and to increasingly unpredictable American monetary policies. However, drawing up a common currency turned out to be an immensely complicated process. The absence of Britain from this process during the 1960s cost both it and Europe valuable time and exacted a high financial price.

Apart from the United States, the key player in the international monetary game of the 1960s was the Federal Republic of Germany. The emerging transatlantic conflict on monetary issues inevitably became a vital issue for the Federal Republic, which was the country most fervently committed to the transatlantic bargain, owing to its exposed position at the Cold War frontier, its reunification policy, which pitted it against the Soviet Union, and the strong export orientation of its economy, which created a particular interest in the smooth operation of the world economy. At the same time,

---

46 Charles De Gaulle, *Lettres, notes et carnets 1964–66* (Paris, 1987), 187.
47 Ambassador Hans-Georg Sachs (EEC) to Foreign Minister Willy Brandt on Brandt's conversation with Maurice Couve de Murville, Dec. 15, 1967, in Instutut fur Zeitgeschichte, ed. *Akten zur Auswärtigen Politik der Bundesrepublik Deutschland* (hereafter *AAPD*) 1967, III, doc. 437, 1627–8.
48 Report of the EEC Commission, Sept. 29, 1967, in *Europa-Archiv* 1967, D 499.
49 Her Majesty's Stationery Office, *Statement on Defence Estimates 1968* (London, 1968), command paper no. 3540.
50 Eric Hoffmeyer, *The International Monetary System* (Amsterdam, 1992), 49–50.

Germany's relationship with France was crucial and was symbolized by the Franco-German Friendship Treaty of January 1963. This double allegiance formed the core of Bonn's foreign policy. In the 1950s, this twin orientation had been in equilibrium, and Germany's integration into the West coincided with an impressive economic performance.[51] With the emergence of transatlantic political and economic conflicts, equilibrium in Bonn's foreign policy became increasingly difficult to achieve. Particularly in the monetary field, pressure by the United States, Britain, and France to support their ideas of international monetary policy became stronger from year to year, reflecting the fact that the German currency, the deutschmark, was the preferred safe haven for speculative money. Germany became crucial to France in the creation of an alternative to the dollar-gold system, crucial to Britain in the defense of the pound, and crucial even to the United States in its efforts to preserve the value of the dollar despite the pressures of Vietnam.

It came as no surprise, then, that Washington turned first to Bonn when it looked for help in alleviating the strains in the monetary system that had become visible at the end of Eisenhower's presidency. Three weeks after taking office, the Kennedy administration addressed a memorandum to the Federal Republic in which it stated that the payments difficulties of the United States originated from the burden of its defense commitments and that Germany, as the world's principal surplus country that benefited from a huge American military commitment, had a particular responsibility to rectify this situation.[52] Although it disagreed with the methods proposed by the memorandum, the German government expressed its general willingness to cooperate. In the series of multilateral operations in the international monetary field that were initiated by the Kennedy administration, the Germans were always on the forefront. Probably the most effective part of this commitment to the transatlantic bargain, namely, the offset agreements, was kept secret. Starting in 1961, the Federal Republic began to offset the foreign-exchange cost of American troops in Germany by buying weapons from the United States.[53] These complex agreements incorporated the transatlantic bargain in a nutshell: The Federal Republic undertook to neutralize the monetary

---

51 From DM 800 million in 1950, German reserves had risen to more than DM 30,000 million by 1966, more than half of it in gold. Much of this success was due to strong export performance, but a very important part was also directly related to the Cold War: the foreign exchange expenditure of about 300,000 American GIs stationed in Germany. See Impact of foreign exchange expenditure by foreign troops for the German payments balance, Dec. 4, 1959, B 330/10161, Bundesbank Archives.

52 Rusk to Kennedy, Feb. 15, 1961, box 117, President's Office File, Countries: Germany, John F. Kennedy Library, Boston, Mass.

53 See Hubert Zimmermann, *Money and Security: Troops, Monetary Policy, and West Germany's Relations with the United States and Britain, 1950–1971* (New York, 2002).

cost of the American commitment for the defense of Europe. Secretary of the Treasury Douglas Dillon referred to the offset agreements as "our top priority financial objectives."[54] They were essential to alleviate the monetary pressure on the United States, and they bought time for necessary reforms. This time was not used because of increasing Franco-American antagonism and the effects of Vietnam in the mid-1960s. However, as long as the basic rationale behind the offset agreements – security in exchange for economic support – was intact, it was out of the question that the Federal Republic would follow de Gaulle's call to topple the dollar–gold standard. Political Director Günther Harkort at the German Foreign Office (Auswärtiges Amt) noted that although Germany saw some value in the French approach to monetary problems because of its anti-inflationary bias, it was its underlying political motivation against the dollar-gold system that wrecked it.[55]

When in 1965 Secretary Fowler traveled to Europe to gather support for his proposal on the creation of new reserve assets, the German reaction was hesitant. In unison with other EEC countries, they asserted that at that moment there seemed to be no need for new liquidity. In the background loomed the suspicion that the situation in Vietnam might have prompted the American move.[56] When the negotiations about reserve creation became increasingly overshadowed by transatlantic political conflict, a tug-of-war started between America and France over the monetary soul of the Federal Republic. In April 1967, Vice President Hubert H. Humphrey told Chancellor Kurt Georg Kiesinger that the liquidity negotiations were closely linked to the maintenance of U.S. troops in Europe, to the effort in Southeast Asia, and to American foreign-aid levels. He added that, in case the French position in the EEC prevailed, his government would be forced to take "drastic measures."[57] Later in the month, Johnson met Kiesinger in Bonn on the occasion of former chancellor Konrad Adenauer's funeral and again emphasized in no uncertain terms the importance he placed on the liquidity negotiations.[58] De Gaulle, for his part, took the very same opportunity to lecture Kiesinger about the necessity of a common European position in monetary policy, which he termed "an issue of the utmost symbolic value."[59] Caught between these two positions, the Germans usually leaned toward

54 Dillon to Ball, May 31, 1963, box 3455, FN 12 WGER, Record Group 59, National Archives, College Park, Md.
55 Memorandum on Fowler proposal for international monetary conference, July 28, 1965, handwritten note, Dept. III A 1, vol. 176, PA-AA.
56 Ibid.
57 Conversation Kurt Georg Kiesinger–Hubert Humphrey, April. 5, 1967, B 150/1967, PA-AA.
58 Kiesinger–LBJ conversation, Apr. 24, 1967, B 150/1967, PA-AA.
59 Kiesinger-De Gaulle conversation, Apr. 25, 1967, *AAPD* 1967, II, 644–6.

that of the Americans. A major reason for this was the security relationship that linked both countries, as the events in 1966–7 demonstrated.

During these years the consequences of Vietnam began to put a strain on the mutual bargain. The offset system entered a deep crisis: Germany simply needed no more weapons, and its government was in serious budgetary trouble. Chancellor Ludwig Erhard asked for a moratorium on German payments required under the offset agreement. The Americans showed no sign of compromise. Fowler, confronted by now with the full impact of Vietnam, stated categorically that he would not "take a nickel's loss in the balance of payments this year."[60] Johnson turned down the German request.[61] The way the Americans treated Erhard during the meeting in Washington created deep resentment in Germany. His failure contributed to his fall from power soon afterward. The new government was determined to avoid Erhard's mistakes and stake out a more independent monetary policy. In January 1967, the possibility of joining de Gaulle's call for a hike in the price of gold was seriously considered by the German government.[62] It was clear that such a move would have precipitated a deep political crisis with the United States. In early 1967, trilateral negotiations (which included the British) began; the core issue was whether the Germans and Americans could find a structure that would permit the United States both to retain the dollar–gold standard and to live up to its security commitments in Europe. The solution was an idea that had been considered earlier by the American government: a formal pledge by the most important central bank of Europe to refrain from exchanging dollar reserves into gold. Bator described the basic idea:

There is no hope for any sort of new 100 percent military offset deal with the Germans. However, we may be able to get them to agree to financial steps which would be far more valuable. Specifically: that they will not use their dollars, old or new, to buy gold; that they will join us in pushing the other Europeans, ex-France, to agree to the same sort of rules; to support us against France in negotiations on longer-range monetary reform; to neutralize the military imbalance by buying and holding securities which would count against our balance-of-payments deficit. If we can also get the Italians, Dutch and the Belgians, as well as the U.K., Canada, Japan, to play by such rules we will have negotiated the world onto a dollar standard. It will mean recognition of the fact that, for the time being, the U.S. must necessarily play banker of the world.[63]

60 Telephone conversation Rostow–Ball, Sept. 26, 1966, box 1, Ball papers, LBJL.
61 Conversation Ludwig Erhard–LBJ, Sept. 26, 1966, in *FRUS 1964–1968*, XIII, 471–7.
62 Memorandum on rise in the gold price, Jan. 12, 1967, B 136/3322, Bundesarchiv, Koblenz.
63 Bator to president: U.S. Position in the Trilateral Negotiations, Feb. 23, 1967, box 4, Bator papers, LBJL.

The consequence of such a step was that "we will no longer need to worry about reasonable balance-of-payments deficits. This arrangement will not give us an unlimited printing press. But as long as we run our economy as responsibly as in the past few years, it will permit us to live with moderate deficits indefinitely. It will be the ideal transition arrangement until Joe Fowler's major liquidity reform goes into effect."[64] The hitch in this arrangement is easy to see in retrospect: The government's economic policy had not been this responsible since 1965, and chances that it might improve were slim. However, at least the Johnson administration demonstrated that it would fight for the continuation of the dollar-gold standard, even under the pressure of Vietnam. The Germans, of course, knew that what was requested of them would have extremely important political and economic consequences.[65] Agreeing to such a proposal signified agreement with American monetary and security policies. The Bundesbank requested a political policy decision by the German cabinet before signing such a commitment.[66] In the interest of reaffirming once more the transatlantic bargain, the German government agreed to a public pledge by its Central Bank that West Germany would refrain from presenting dollars for gold at the American treasury.

German monetary aid thus was essential all through the 1960s in maintaining the value of the dollar, especially when the pressure due to Vietnam rose. The political and economic importance of this support must not be underestimated: An early breakdown of the monetary system, with Vietnam as the likely culprit, would have been a powerful symbol of the economic consequences of the war. In a 1971 interview, Bundesbank President Karl Blessing regretted the pledge: "I should have been more firm with the Americans. We simply should have systematically converted the dollars we were accumulating to gold until they were driven to despair."[67] His bitterness is understandable, considering what happened to the American promise to manage its balance of payments in a responsible way. In late 1968, Richard Nixon was elected president, and it soon turned out that his administration did not feel bound by the commitments of his predecessor. Blessing's lament raises the question whether the Federal Republic should have deserted the dollar-gold system earlier. This was a political impossibility, as even Blessing recognized. The Cold War still was in full swing, and the Europeans were far from having a monetary fallback position. In part, this was Germany's

---

64 Bator to president, Mar. 8, 1967, box 50, NSF, NSC Histories: Trilaterals, LBJL.
65 Memorandum by Günther Harkort, Jan. 16, 1967, B 150/1967, PA-AA.
66 Ibid., Mar. 6, 1967.
67 Author's translation from Leo Brawand, *Wohin steuert die deutsche Wirtschaft?* (Munich, 1971), 61.

own fault. Unlike the French, the Germans had no clear monetary policy and reacted only defensively to the turmoil on the currency markets. Trying to steer a delicate course between France and the United States, and convinced of the soundness of their economy, they undertook enormous efforts to preserve the transatlantic bargain; yet, although they were the strongest monetary power, they presented no coherent solution for a reform of the system, even when the situation got out of control. When Nixon canceled part of the bargain and decided to go it alone, it became clear that Germany and the rest of Europe had waited too long. The weight of the entire system's imbalanced structure fell on European and Japanese shoulders.

It was an interesting coincidence that in early 1965, at about the same time that the U.S. government decided to escalate the war in Vietnam, the Treasury Department started a major monetary initiative. This undertaking, in the end, produced few results. Directly and indirectly, Vietnam contributed much to the failure by rendering almost impossible a smooth transformation of the international monetary system. In late 1967, after the sterling devaluation, the system entered a new crisis. A huge wave of gold speculation in February and March of 1968 forced the members of the gold pool to stop the supply of private markets with gold. The monetary disorder now was to have an impact on Vietnam policy. At the same time that markets forced the partial closing of the U.S. gold window, the Tet Offensive in early 1968 marked the turning point of the war. When the Johnson administration considered the military's request for more troops in the wake of Tet, McNamara opposed this, citing the cost, the danger of inflation, and the necessity of new taxes.[68] The monetary crisis was a powerful reminder of the havoc Vietnam had wreaked on the domestic economy and on the postwar system of international cooperation. It became an important element in the decision to stop military escalation.[69] The United States began a long process of pulling out of the disastrous situation in Vietnam and out of the international monetary field, and it did so with little regard for those countries primarily affected.

Nixon's attitude toward international monetary matters was pointedly summarized in a remark made by his secretary of the treasury, John B. Connally, to a flabbergasted group of European finance ministers: "The Dollar is our currency, but your problem."[70] The pursuit of international monetary cooperation had a very low priority on Nixon's list of foreign

---

68 Lloyd C. Gardner, *Pay Any Price: Lyndon Johnson and the Wars for Vietnam* (Chicago, 1995), 436–7.
69 Robert M. Collins, "The Economic Crisis of 1968 and the Waning of the 'American Century,'" *American Historical Review* 101 (Apr. 1996): 413–6.
70 Volcker and Gyoohten, *Changing Fortunes*, 81.

policy issues. No new initiatives to reform the monetary system were developed by the new administration. This policy, termed "benign neglect,"
was certain to produce the next monetary crisis as soon as the United States
reversed the anti-inflationary course pursued in 1969–70 to get inflation
prompted by military spending under control. Between 1968 and 1972,
American liabilities abroad rose from $21 billion to $80 billion.[71] Between
January 1970 and March 1973, Germany alone took in foreign exchange to
the tune of DM 71 billion, most of it from American sources.[72] Those were
unheard-of sums. The Europeans, particularly the Germans, feeling morally
bound by Blessing's letter, were helpless against the currency flood. In August
1971, faced with requests by worried Europeans for guarantees of the value
of their mounting dollar reserves, Nixon officially closed the gold window
and imposed a 10 percent surtax on all imports into the United States.[73] In
the ensuing turmoil on the currency markets, the dollar lost approximately
40 percent of its value through 1973, and the reserves of America's partners
shrank, insofar as they consisted of dollars, by the same percentage. This
devaluation of the world's dollar reserves was an indirect "Vietnam tax" on
America's allies partly because it can be attributed to the Vietnam War.

These events made overtly clear who really held the strings in international monetary affairs. Europe had grown stronger and more assertive
during the 1960s but not strong enough to develop an alternative to the
dollar. The dollar-gold link had been a symbol of European-American
partnership, a guarantee for the economically weaker Europeans that the
Americans would not abuse the privilege they had in printing the world's
money. This guarantee was cancelled. The policies of Nixon and Connally
demonstrated that the traditional Cold War bargain had seen its time. The
United States would still preserve its military commitments, largely because
the containment of the Soviet Union remained a central goal; however, it no
longer would necessarily cooperate in the economic sphere but rather play
out its full economic strength if it considered that in the national interest.

Slowly and painfully the Europeans began to develop an alternative.
Germany's aim was to find a strategy "to unwind the dependence on the dollar, and this attitude was the foundation of the policy that set out the path to
confrontation. The genuine European support for international cooperation

---

71 Hoffmeyer, *International Monetary System*, 89.
72 Otmar Emminger, "Deutsche Geld- und Währungspolitik im Spannungsfeld zwischen innerem
    und äußerem Gleichgewicht, 1948–75," in Deutsche Bundesbank, ed., *Währung und Wirtschaft in
    Deutschland 1876–1975* (Frankfurt, 1976), 532.
73 Charles Coombs, who had been responsible for the foreign-exchange operations of the Federal
    Reserve from 1961 to 1975, termed this a "flagrant breach in the code of international behavior
    [the U.S.] had spent a quarter-century in promoting." See Coombs, Arena, 211.

in the early 1960s changed in the latter part of the 1960s to animosity or even hostility toward what was conceived as dollar hegemony – in parallel with reservations toward the U.S. engagement in Vietnam. The German idea of creating a zone of monetary stability independent of the dollar – even though unprofessional – was an economic expression of this political attitude."[74] Serious attempts at European monetary unification derive from this time.

Who really paid for Vietnam? The simple answers suggested by some of the literature cannot be verified before the winners and losers of the economic turmoil in the early 1970s are clearly identified. It must be emphasized that the major recipients of the dollars leaving the United States were not holding paper money but IOUs that paid interest. Even if the dollars could not be exchanged for gold, they could be used for investment in American goods or in raw materials, mainly oil. The Gaullist claim that Europeans paid for a great part of the Vietnam War is therefore untrue. They did, however, contribute toward financing the war by assuming more of the costs of preserving the transatlantic bargain and by holding inflated dollars, which after 1971 rapidly declined in value.

The monetary system itself fell victim to a drastic turn in American foreign economic policies, which was provoked to a great degree by Vietnam. The war alone did not destroy the Bretton Woods system, but it put grave strains on an international monetary structure that already was in serious trouble. The most serious impact of Vietnam in the context of European-American relations was that it progressively undermined confidence in America's ability to hold to its part of the transatlantic bargain and deal with the currency problem. The growing political conflict with the Europeans about Vietnam spilled over into the monetary sphere. Thus, reform proposals had only very limited chances of success. The sequence of events from 1968 to 1971, particularly the failure of the American guarantee to value Germany's dollar holdings, played a central role in a long-lasting effort by the Federal Republic to escape the grasp of the United States. This process was so long and complicated because Germany was neither willing nor able because of historical factors to exercise its monetary power on a full scale or to become a reserve currency country itself. The only way out of this dilemma was the creation of a European currency, and the euro should be seen as the culminating point of a development that began when Vietnam unraveled the postwar transatlantic economic and monetary bargain.

74 Hoffmeyer, *International Monetary System*, 194.

8

America Isolated

The Western Powers and the Escalation of the War

FREDRIK LOGEVALL

At the height of the Second Indochina War, Washington officials typically explained U.S. involvement in international terms.[1] The demands of American "credibility" necessitated standing firm in Vietnam, they said, even if that meant committing U.S. ground troops to fight and die there. U.S. prestige was on the line in Southeast Asia as a result of many years of steadily expanding involvement in the struggle and constant public assertions of South Vietnam's importance to American security. An early withdrawal from the war, so the argument went, would cause allies elsewhere in Asia and around the world to lose faith in the reliability of America's commitments and would embolden adversaries in Moscow and Beijing to pursue aggressive designs all over the globe.

In fact, however, neither friends nor foes around the world tended to see American credibility as being at stake in Vietnam. The newly opened archives in Western Europe and Canada, as well as those in the United States, show that key allied governments believed at the end of 1964 that U.S. credibility would suffer more from a deepened commitment to what they saw as an incompetent and corrupt (and increasingly anti-American) Saigon government than from some kind of fig-leaf withdrawal. What these powers questioned was not America's will but its judgment. Canada, France, Great Britain, Japan – all these nations registered private opposition to Americanization in the key months of mid-1964 to 1965. Other governments were more ambivalent, sympathetic to Washington's aims but doubtful

---

1 On American policymaking in the 1961–73 period, see Robert D. Schulzinger, *A Time for War: The United States and Vietnam, 1941–1975* (New York, 1997), 124–304; and George C. Herring, *America's Longest War: The United States and Vietnam, 1950–1975*, 3d ed. (New York, 1996), 120–283. The early part of the period is covered in detail in Lloyd C. Gardner, *Pay Any Price: Lyndon Johnson and the Wars for Vietnam* (Chicago, 1995); George M. Kahin, *Intervention: How America Became Involved in Vietnam* (New York, 1986); and Fredrik Logevall, *Choosing War: The Lost Chance for Peace and the Escalation of War in Vietnam* (Berkeley, Calif., 1999). Portions of this chapter are drawn from *Choosing War.*

175

that even the introduction of major American fighting forces would bring long-term success. Hence the miserable failure of the Johnson administration's "More Flags" campaign, which was designed to increase allied military involvement in the fight against the National Liberation Front but which yielded very little.[2]

The primary concern for most foreign governments was the deep and worsening politico-military problems faced by the Saigon government. Far from gaining increased stability and popular legitimacy with the passage of time, the regime seemed to grow steadily weaker. An expanded American military effort could probably help stabilize the situation on the battlefield, these observers acknowledged, but would not make the mass of the South Vietnamese population any more inclined to support the government, much less fight for it. If anything, a larger American presence in the South would deepen the problem by making the regime seem more like a puppet than ever before. Those already resentful of American involvement would become more so; those apathetic about the struggle would become more apathetic because they could now rely on Americans to do the job. Among Asians generally, sympathy for the Vietcong and North Vietnam would increase as they took on a very big, very white, Western power in the same way that the Vietminh before them had taken on the French.

Nor was it merely pessimism about the outcome of the war effort that animated these foreign analysts; many also possessed deep doubts that the outcome in South Vietnam really mattered to Western security. None questioned the need to contain possible Chinese communist expansion in Asia, only whether it was necessary or wise to fight in Vietnam to do so. Most opponents of American escalation also rejected the standard assertion by the administration that the outcome in Vietnam would have a direct bearing on developments elsewhere in the region, that a defeat would start the dominoes falling. What mattered, they were convinced, was the constellation of forces within each individual country, not what occurred in a civil war in Vietnam.

Policymakers in Washington were well aware of these widespread and fundamental doubts about the direction of U.S. policy. Indeed, the best proof for the absence of international support for a larger war is the phenomenal amount of energy American officials expended fretting about it. It is sometimes argued with respect to French President Charles de Gaulle that the Johnson administration disregarded his criticisms of American intervention and his calls for a unified Vietnam free of external influences.

2 I examine this issue in more detail in *Choosing War*.

This is false, or at least misleading. Senior U.S. officials may have refused to consider seriously exploring the French president's proposals for a political solution to the conflict, but they were concerned about his potential for influencing others and worried that other Western leaders would come to share his position on the war as well as his willingness to articulate that position publicly. They knew that some 17,000 French citizens lived in South Vietnam in 1964, that French cultural and economic influence remained significant, and that any announcement out of the Elysée Palace was sure to get widespread notice on the streets of Saigon. Hence the concerted effort they made trying to convince the French leader to come around to the administration's point of view, or at least keep his objections quiet. They also made efforts to keep other governments, especially the British, from joining Paris in opposition to U.S. policy.

This American isolation on Vietnam in the prelude to major war has received little attention from students of the war. One reason for this gap in the literature is that the archival documentation needed to explore international thinking on the war has become available only recently. Another is that students of the war have tended overwhelmingly to be America-centric in their focus, focusing virtually all their attention on the thinking in Washington and, to a much lesser extent, Saigon and Hanoi.[3] Finally, American isolation on Vietnam has been underexamined in the literature because most Western governments, in the key years of 1964 and 1965, voiced their concerns only in muted tones. Averse as they were to an expansion of the fighting, most were reluctant to publicly challenge U.S. policy. Canada, Great Britain, and Japan, for example, put maintaining American support on several other bilateral issues before trying to head off large-scale war in Indochina. As a result, even though officials in these countries privately held much the same opinion as the French, they offered tepid public support for U.S. efforts, much to the administration's relief.

The historical implications are important. In the same way that prominent domestic American critics on Capitol Hill and in the press foresaw a great calamity ahead should escalation occur, so did the governments in London, Ottawa, and Tokyo. They failed, that is, to truly confront the administration with the choice it was making. In so doing, they performed an essential function in allowing Lyndon Johnson in late 1964 and the first half of 1965 to escalate the Vietnam War by stealth.

The British government's posture was especially important in this regard. As America's leading ally in international affairs and a major world power

3 Logevall, *Choosing War*, xiii; Herring, *America's Longest War*, 335.

Fredrik Logevall

in its own right, Britain's position mattered to Washington in a way that no other government's mattered. Even Japan's importance paled in comparison. American officials could live with de Gaulle's carping, but they were petri-fied that the same noises might start emanating from across the Channel. A British government publicly opposed to American policy could spell major trouble, they knew, and they worked very hard in the months leading up to Americanization to keep British Prime Minister Harold Wilson in their court, with general success.

Even in later years, when the fighting raged with no end in sight and when public revulsion to the war had grown dramatically in the NATO countries and Japan, Wilson and many other Western leaders proved unwilling to break openly with Washington over the war. From the American perspective, then, the ultimate outcome of the pressure campaign was mixed. The Johnson administration may have failed spectacularly in its bid to generate enthusiasm among key allies for the Southeast Asian war, but it had considerable success in the more limited objective of damage control, of keeping allied grumbling largely private.

As with so many aspects of the Vietnam War, 1964 was the crucial year in cementing international opposition to a large-scale war on behalf of South Vietnam. To be sure, the warning signs were there well before. Franco-American friction over Indochina, for example, went back to the Franco-Vietminh War, when the two nations disagreed frequently over the best approach to the war. The squabbles continued during and after the Geneva Conference.[4] Meanwhile, ever since the Korean War British leaders had consistently seen Asian communism as less of a threat to world peace than had their American counterparts. London officials did not see communism as monolithic and were deeply dubious about notions of falling dominoes. As a result, from the time of the Geneva Conference of 1954, important differences separated London's and Washington's thinking on the nature of the struggle in Indochina.[5]

---

4 See Mark A. Lawrence, "Selling Vietnam: The European Colonial Powers and the Origins of the American Commitment to Vietnam, 1944–1950," Ph.D. diss., Yale University, 1998; Kathryn C. Statler, "From the French to the Americans: Intra-Alliance Politics, Cold War Concerns, and Cultural Conflict in Vietnam, 1950–1960," Ph.D. diss., University of California at Santa Barbara, 1999; Frédéric Turpin, "Le Gaullisme et l'Indochine, 1940–1956," University of Paris IV, Sorbonne, 2000; and Alfred Georges, *Charles de Gaulle et la guerre d'Indochine* (Paris, 1974).

5 On the earlier period of Anglo-American disagreement in Indochina, see Arthur Combs, "The Path Not Taken: The British Alternative to U.S. Policy in Vietnam, 1954–1956," *Diplomatic History* 19, no. 1 (winter 1995): 33–57. On Geneva, see James E. Cable, *The Geneva Conference of 1954 on Indochina* (New York, 1986).

Nevertheless, developments in 1964 were essential in shaping the per-spectives of leaders in the key allied capitals – Paris, London, Ottawa, and Tokyo. This was due in large measure to developments in South Vietnam. The year 1964 in South Vietnam is a story of almost unrelieved decline in the Government of Vietnam's (GVN) fortunes and the Army of the Republic of Vietnam's (ARVN) will to fight, a story of growing war weari-ness and attachment to "neutralism" (meaning, in this context, a swift end to the war on whatever terms) among the peasantry and many in the urban areas of the South. Already in the first weeks of the year, one finds evi-dence of what became starkly apparent by year's end: that decision makers in Washington were more committed to the war effort than to the mass of the South Vietnamese people they were ostensibly working to help. Even Nguyen Khanh, who assumed leadership in Saigon after a bloodless coup d'état at the end of January, would in time fall out of favor with American officials for failing in their eyes to be vigorous enough in prosecuting the war. Like the Ngo Dinh Diem regime and Duong Van Minh junta before, Khanh would learn that his ability to win broad-based domestic support would be directly linked to his ability to preserve a degree of independence from the Americans.

Changes outside South Vietnam also influenced allied thinking about Indochina and what ought to happen there. The Sino-Soviet split had grown wider and deeper in 1963, and in the minds of many observers this develop-ment created opportunities for facilitating a political solution to the conflict in Vietnam. The reduced tensions in the Soviet-American relationship also suggested to some, including United Nations Secretary General U Thant, that conflicts in Third World nations need no longer loom as important in superpower politics as they once did. Hence the equanimity with which most Western leaders reacted to the French government's decision to extend recognition in January 1964 to the People's Republic of China. Washington officials tried to dissuade Paris from following through with the plan while Canadian and British officials quietly assured the French that they had no objection to the move – Canadian Prime Minister Lester Pearson indeed told de Gaulle that he hoped Ottawa too could soon extend recognition to Beijing.[6]

On January 31, 1964, during a much-publicized news conference, de Gaulle drew a direct link between his government's recognition of China and the war in Vietnam. "There is no political reality in Asia," he said,

---

6 Entretien entre Couve and Martin, 30 Jan. 1964, Secreteriat General, dossier 20, Ministère des Affaires Entrangères, Paris (hereafter MAE); Paris to Foreign Office (hereafter FO), Jan. 17, 1964, FO 371/175923, Public Record Office, Kew, England (hereafter PRO).

"which does not interest or touch China. Neither war nor peace is imaginable on that continent without China's becoming implicated. Thus it is absolutely inconceivable that without her participation there can be any accord on the eventual neutrality of Southeast Asia." With Beijing on board, however, the prospects for such a successful neutralization were excellent, de Gaulle insisted, provided that the agreement was guaranteed on the international level, that it outlawed "armed agitations" by the states involved, and that it excluded "the various forms of external intervention." Such a neutrality, the general concluded, "seems, at the present time, to be the only situation compatible with the peaceful existence and progress of the peoples concerned."[7]

The French leader knew that the Johnson team would not be receptive to this line of thinking, but, he asked aides, what choice did the administration really have? The reports from Vietnam and from Vietnamese émigré groups in Paris showed that the peace movement in the South was growing stronger each day and that no U.S.-backed government could ever win broad popular support. Americanizing the war thus offered no hope for success. "If the Americans are not too stupid they will put an end to this absurd Vietnam War," de Gaulle told Information Minister Alain Peyrefitte after a cabinet meeting on January 22. "The only way to get out is through an agreement of neutrality." The ultimate result of such an agreement would likely be a communist-controlled Vietnam, de Gaulle allowed, but he saw little to fear in such an outcome, in view of the historic Sino-Vietnamese friction and the deepening Sino-Soviet split. Ultimately, Hanoi might gain control of all of Vietnam, but it would take time and would in any event not be a big blow to the West. In the long run, de Gaulle was certain, Vietnam would be more Vietnamese than communist.[8]

Notwithstanding the strength of his convictions on these points, de Gaulle was not prepared to call explicitly for negotiations leading to a neutralization agreement. Vagueness suited his purposes, just as it had suited him on August 29, 1963, when he had first publicly called for a unified Vietnam

---

7 The de Gaulle quotation is in French Embassy, Press and Information Division, *Chronology of Charles de Gaulle's Press Conferences, 1958–1966* (New York, 1968), 89. A State Department statement issued the day of the announcement described the French action as an "unfortunate step, particularly at a time when the Chinese communists are actively promoting aggression and subversion in Southeast Asia and elsewhere." *New York Times*, Jan. 31, 1964.

8 Alain Peyrefitte, *C'était de Gaulle: La France reprend sa place dans le monde* (Paris, 1997), 494; Paris to Washington, Feb. 2, Cambodia-Laos-Vietnam, dossier 71, MAE; CIA Report: Indications of French Policy, Feb. 5, 1964, box 169, National Security File, Country File, Lyndon Baines Johnson Library, Austin, Tex. (hereafter NSF CF, LBJL); Paris to FO, Feb. 12, 1964, FO 371/175488, PRO; Paris to FO, Feb. 13, 1964, FO 371/175488, PRO; Saigon to FO, Mar. 4, 1964, FO 371/175488, PRO; Hanoi to FO, Nov. 13, 1963, FO 371/170107, PRO.

free of outside interference. Well aware that France's continuing cultural and social presence in Vietnam gave his pronouncements outsized attention, he could afford to be ambiguous – his comments would reverberate throughout Vietnam whatever their level of specificity. Thus, he saw no reason to provide either side specifics with which to attack him and torpedo the prospects for talks. A certain blurring of categories was essential to get negotiations started. In addition, de Gaulle felt no particular sense of urgency about the situation. Not altogether displeased to see the United States floundering in its efforts to achieve what he had long said it could never accomplish (and in a place where France too had been defeated), he was content to play a waiting game, meanwhile giving tacit support to neutralist forces in the South and issuing periodic calls for a diplomatic solution.

Significantly, de Gaulle's take on the war corresponded closely with the analysis in London. It is striking to observe how differently from the Johnson administration the British interpreted the situation in early 1964. At the conclusion of Anglo-American talks in Washington in February, the two sides issued a communiqué that affirmed both nations' commitment to thwarting aggression in South Vietnam and Malaysia (the confrontation between the newly formed Malaysian federation and Indonesia had in the preceding months pinned down large numbers of British forces in and around Singapore), and Johnson got Prime Minister Alec Douglas-Home to agree that neutralization was no solution in Vietnam at present. Behind closed doors, however, the two countries differed markedly in their assessments of what ought to happen in Southeast Asia. In the talks, the British continued to disagree with the administration's determination to prevent a reconvened Geneva conference on Cambodia, for which Cambodian leader Prince Norodom Sihanouk had been urging for several months and which London had agreed to forestall. Moreover, Douglas-Home, while declaring staunch British support for South Vietnam in its defense against the Vietcong, expressly ruled out any significant increase in British military assistance.[9]

In the ensuing weeks, as British officials learned that the Johnson administration contemplated attacking North Vietnam by air, they grew more and more alarmed. Like the French, they doubted such action would yield success. A study by the British government's Joint Intelligence Committee (JIC) in late February concluded that even a complete severing of all links between North Vietnam and the Vietcong in the South – which the report

9 Meeting notes, Feb. 12, 1964, Prime Minister's Papers (hereafter PREM) 11/4789, PRO.

called virtually impossible to bring about – would not significantly reduce the problem of defeating the insurgents, given their basic self-sufficiency. In addition, an attack on the North would strengthen relations between Hanoi and Beijing, would bring increased Chinese and Soviet assistance to the Democratic Republic of Vietnam (DRV), and would generate widespread condemnation in the international community. J. Kenneth Blackwell, head of the small staff at the British consulate in Hanoi and a longtime skeptic regarding Saigon's chances in the war, told London that dropping bombs on North Vietnam would do little to stop the transport of men and materials from North to South and would not induce the Hanoi leaders to "throw in the sponge"; on the contrary, it would make them more determined to resist and less willing to reach a compromise. A major war might well result. Even if one could inflict serious pain on Hanoi, Blackwell added, it would not really matter, since the Vietcong could and would carry on very effectively even without Northern assistance. Therefore, "the appalling risks which an American attack on North Vietnam would run would have been incurred to little purpose. I sincerely hope the American Government will think many times before committing themselves to such a disastrous policy."[10]

Blackwell was unusual among British officials in the depth of his pessimism regarding the prospects of the war effort, but his superiors fully shared his belief that expanded U.S. military action would be a mistake. On February 29, Foreign Secretary R. A. Butler informed Secretary of State Dean Rusk that British support for the administration's policy in South Vietnam, as affirmed in the Washington communiqué, was based on the assumption that this policy would remain defensive in character and not involve any kind of expansion of the fighting – it would be the same kind of defensive posture, Butler said, that Britain maintained in Malaysia. Should the administration opt for escalation, he emphasized, London would have to re-evaluate its position. Part of Butler's concern stemmed from fears of growing popular opposition in Britain to the government's public backing of U.S. policy – rumors of possible impending action against the DRV received widespread play in the British press – but there can be no doubt that Butler and his colleagues endorsed the basic findings of the JIC study. That is, they believed that the Southern insurgency was largely self-sustaining, that the Khanh government lacked the requisite ability and popular support to meet the challenge, that Hanoi leaders would not buckle in the face of

10 "The United States Government and South Viet-Nam," Feb. 27, 1964, FO 371/175494, PRO; Hanoi to FO, Feb. 25, 1964, FO 371/175495, PRO; Hanoi to FO, Feb. 29, 1964, FO 371/175493, PRO. See also FO to Saigon, Mar. 10, 1964, FO 371/175494, PRO.

military pressure, and that escalation across the seventeenth parallel therefore made little sense.[11]

Did Butler's intervention have an impact in Washington? It appears that it did. Johnson had been annoyed by Douglas-Home's refusal during the Washington talks to increase British aid to the GVN,[12] but London's clear opposition to bombing the North probably reinforced his determination to avoid any immediate escalation of the fighting if at all possible. Butler's warning added to long-standing administration concerns about the impact of an expanded war on world opinion. Bombing North Vietnam would cause considerable international outcry, some officials feared, with both foes and friends around the world seeing it as disproportionate to what the North was doing in the South. The result was sure to be increased sympathy for some kind of political settlement along the lines proposed by de Gaulle. "What is worse," Assistant Secretary of State for Far Eastern Affairs Roger Hilsman warned in a widely circulated memorandum penned shortly before he left the administration, "I think that premature action will so alarm our friends and allies and a significant segment of domestic opinion that the pressure for neutralization will become formidable."[13]

With an expansion of the war off the table, at least for the near future, Washington officials looked for other ways to bolster the Saigon government and demonstrate determination to leaders in Hanoi. One way they did so was through the "More Flags" campaign, an effort launched by the State Department in April 1964 to increase allied contributions to the war effort.

From the start the campaign floundered. At a NATO meeting at The Hague in May 1964, Secretary Rusk asked alliance members for at least token material and manpower participation in the conflict; the response was underwhelming, to say the least. Some members agreed to provide very modest amounts of nonmilitary support to the South Vietnamese regime, but all refused to send troops. In the wake of the meeting, Rusk ordered embassy staff in key capitals to press the host governments for greater participation in the struggle. A cable to the Bonn embassy, for example, instructed staffers to inform West German officials that their country's contribution to the war effort was insufficient, that a German embassy in Saigon needed

---

11 "Our principal concern," the Foreign Office cabled the embassy in Saigon, "is that our support for U.S. policy in Viet-Nam is really understood by the U.S. government to apply to the original defensive policy and not to constitute any implied commitment to support a new offensive strategy" (FO to Saigon, Mar. 10, 1964, FO 371/175494, PRO).

12 See Johnson's comments in LBJ–Allen Ellender telephone conversation, Feb. 16, 1964, Johnson tapes, LBJL.

13 Roger Hilsman to Dean Rusk, Mar. 14, 1964, box 3, NSF VN, LBJL.

to be constructed immediately and "with suitable publicity and fanfare," and that Bonn needed to make a "public commitment of additional aid to GVN."[14]

It proved a hard sell, as Secretary of Defense Robert S. McNamara found out when he visited Bonn in May and tried to impress on his hosts the need for all Western allies to act in concert and to combat communism not merely in Europe but outside it. McNamara said he understood that Bonn could not contribute military assistance to South Vietnam, but he asked for the dispatch of a German medical unit. The Germans were noncommittal. Chancellor Ludwig Erhard said he was supportive of American policy, but officials in the Ministry of Foreign Affairs were skeptical that allied help of any sort would do much good in view of the situation on the ground – only a massive, Korean-type American commitment could have any hope of turning the tide, most appear to have believed. A few weeks after the defense secretary's visit, a State Department cable to the U.S. embassy in Bonn summarized well the tepid nature of German support. German officials, it said, "have on several occasions agreed in principle to increased support for Southeast Asia but have not repeat not fulfilled these increases." The generally pro-American Hamburg daily *Die Welt* defended Bonn's policy, noting that Germany could not be expected to "take upon itself the burdens of a policy [about which] it has never been consulted in the slightest." On May 26, the Foreign Ministry in Bonn made known that it had resisted heavy U.S. pressure for stepped-up West German aid to the Saigon regime.[15]

This ambivalent German attitude would not change in the months that followed. Erhard periodically voiced steadfast support for American policy in Vietnam but made little effort to boost West German assistance to Saigon. In the Foreign Ministry, meanwhile, general sympathy for Washington's aims mixed with growing pessimism about the chances of turning the war around and a general desire for a negotiated solution as proposed by de Gaulle.

In London, policymakers continued in the spring and summer of 1964 to rule out any significant increase in the British presence in South Vietnam. But they faced a dilemma, one that would bedevil them in the months to come: how to reconcile firm opposition to increased British involvement in the war and preference for a negotiated settlement, on the one hand, with the desire to preserve good relations with Washington, on the other. Had

---

14 *Newsweek*, May 18, 1964; memorandum for the Record, Apr. 27, 1964, box 3, NSF VN, LBJL; State to Bonn, June 8, 1964, box 5, NSF VN, LBJL.

15 Bonn to FO, May 14, 1964, FO 371/175496, PRO; Bonn to FO, May 25, 1964, FO 371/175091, PRO; State to Bonn, June 8, 1964, box 5, NSF VN, LBJL. *Die Welt* quote is from *Newsweek*, May 25, 1964. See also *New York Times*, May 27, 1964.

the time come, some in the government wondered, to mount a vigorous effort to dissuade Johnson from escalating the war and to make clear to him that Britain would not support such an escalation? Or, in view of the fact that Johnson would be irritated by any such effort, should London continue to bide its time, hoping that the American administration would reach this conclusion on its own?

British officials would ask themselves these questions again and again in the weeks to come, which meant, in effect, that they had decided on the latter course: to avoid a confrontation with Washington. Increasingly, convinced of Johnson's obsession with the November election and his desire to avoid any major decision on Vietnam until after that event, British leaders chose to keep a low profile until the fall. Said James Cable in a memorandum in May, summarizing the British position: "The possibility of negotiations on Viet-Nam is not a subject that we can broach with the Americans at present, with their entire effort devoted to the survival of South Viet-Nam. However, when the presidential elections are over, the next administration (assuming it is a Democratic one) will no doubt consider very carefully the long term implications of continuing the military struggle and may give some thought to the possibilities of a diplomatic solution as an alternative." Administration officials might not even then seek a face-saving exit, Cable conceded, "but they must be as conscious as we are of one uncomfortable possibility: that the growing war-weariness of the South Viet-Namese people will find expression in a third coup d'état and the emergence of a government in Saigon eager to attempt a negotiated solution. If this happened, the existence of the Geneva Agreement, and the basis for contact with the Russians it provides, might be very useful in enabling the West to salvage something – above all United States prestige – from the wreck."[16]

Or, as another member of the Foreign Office put it: "We should probably be thinking of a continuing stalemate until the U.S. elections ... [anticipating] that thereafter all sides might in fact welcome a negotiated 'Geneva' solution in which the co-Chairmen could play their traditional roles. But it would be unwise to breathe a word of this to the Americans at present." Until the November election, London officials could agree, Britain should voice rhetorical support for current American policy, work behind the scenes to prevent an escalation of the war, and resist pressure from Washington for significantly increased British participation in the war effort.[17]

16 FO to Saigon, May 1, 1964, FO 371/175496, PRO.
17 Minute by E. H. Peck, Apr. 17, 1964, FO 371/175506, PRO.

Canadian leaders, too, worried about the possibility of an American escalation of the fighting. When U.S. and Canadian officials met in Ottawa in late May to go over the message that Canadian diplomat J. Blair Seaborn would convey to the North Vietnamese during a visit to Hanoi a few weeks later, External Affairs Minister Paul Martin registered concerns. Canadians would not look kindly on the prospect of an enlarged war, he told the State Department's William Sullivan, and he insisted that Seaborn not be compelled to "agree with or associate his Government with the substance of some of the messages" he would be transmitting, so long as he transmitted them faithfully. Martin further said he agreed with American columnist Walter Lippmann's most recent column in which he said that even an imperfect political settlement via a conference was preferable to pursuing a costly and unwinnable war. How could Johnson avoid a conference, Martin asked Sullivan, particularly when the only alternative seemed to be direct military intervention? Sullivan's response was telling: These were "extreme alternatives," he said, and the administration hoped to find a middle ground. But he acknowledged that intervention seemed a more likely course than a conference at the present time. Martin was unmoved. He repeated Canadian objections to direct intervention and repeated his view that a conference, perhaps including the whole of Indochina, seemed the best bet.[18]

There was one notable exception to this unwillingness of allied governments to become meaningfully involved in backing the Saigon regime: Australia. The conservative government under Robert Menzies had long sought close military relations with the United States, particularly following Britain's gradual withdrawal from the region; that desire grew stronger as instability increased in Southeast Asia in 1963–5. From Canberra's perspective, an increased U.S. presence in the region was essential as a check on Chinese ambitions. When rumors emerged in early 1964 of a possible American escalation of the fighting in Vietnam, Australian officials were pleased and moved quickly to boost Canberra's commitment to the war effort. Their concern was not so much saving South Vietnam per se as drawing the United States deeper into the region. As Alan Renouf, a minister at the Australian embassy in Washington, put it in a secret cable in May 1964, an increased Australian contribution to the GVN would allow Australia "to achieve such an habitual closeness of relations with the United States and a sense of mutual alliance that in our time of need . . . the United States would

---

18 Summary Record of Conversation, William Sullivan and Paul Martin, May 29, 1964, Record Group 25, vol. 3092, #29-39-1-2-A, North Vietnam–USA Relations–Special Project (BACON), National Archives of Canada, Ottawa; State to Saigon, 30 May 1964, *FRUS* 1964–1968, I, 395.

have little option to respond as we would want."[19] In June, the Menzies government significantly boosted its financial and manpower commitment to South Vietnam and urged Washington in the strongest terms to continue steadfast in the war.

But the important point here is that Australia was exceptional. Other governments declined altogether to provide assistance or made vague pledges of limited future support, almost invariably of a token character and often not kept.[20] Americans understood only too well that these attitudes represented further proof of fundamental international doubts about the importance of Indochina to the West's security, as well as concerns about the dangers of an escalated war, and that any U.S. expansion of the war therefore was a perilous proposition – as Hilsman had already warned back in March, premature action would surely increase international pressure for precisely that which Washington did not want: a conference-table solution to the conflict.[21]

In July, the administration tried to give the "More Flags" campaign more teeth by circulating a message from President Johnson himself that sought to underline the importance of increased allied involvement. "I am gravely disappointed," the president wrote, "by the inadequacy of the actions by our friends and allies in response to our request that they share the burden of Free World responsibility in Vietnam." Johnson professed to be puzzled by this allied attitude and ordered his ambassadors to work even harder to change it. "I am charging you personally with the responsibility of seeing to it that

---

19 Quoted in Carl Bridge, "Australia and the Vietnam War," in Peter Lowe, ed., *The Vietnam War* (New York, 1998), 185–6. On Australia's position in this period, see Peter G. Edwards, *Crises and Commitments: The Politics and Diplomacy of Australia's Involvement in Southeast Asian Conflicts, 1948–1965* (North Sydney, 1992), chap. 15.

20 A study by the State Department's Intelligence and Research desk indicated that a number of Asian countries, among them India, Pakistan, Burma, and Cambodia, would welcome neutralization, either for South Vietnam alone or for a unified Vietnam.

21 Robert McNamara, John McCone, and William Bundy put the matter bluntly in a draft memo to the president on May 18: "[T]he NATO nations as a whole are only passively in sympathy with our position, and the French drumfire of gloom and doom is having a serious effect principally in Europe but to some extent in other areas. Even the British, although they recognize the direct link to their own struggle in Malaysia, would probably have to buck a very weak public opinion to stick with us, and would exert major pressures from the outset toward a negotiated solution. The above attitudes simply highlight the great difficulty we would have, once we initiated action, in resisting pressures for premature and unsatisfactory negotiations that would leave us short of our goal of an independent and secure South Viet-Nam. While we can in theory stick to our guns and refuse to negotiate until Hanoi agrees to our essential terms, the damage to our worldwide relationships will be substantial." McNamara-McCone–William Bundy to LBJ, draft memo, May 18, 1964, box 4, NSF VN, LBJL. Charles Bohlen had heard more of de Gaulle's "drumfire" earlier that month. In a meeting on May 5, the French leader had told him that the United States was in the wrong war in the wrong way, and that a U.S. defeat was inevitable. David Klein to McGeorge Bundy, May 5, 1964, box 171, NSF CF, LBJL.

the Government to which you are accredited understands how seriously we view the challenge to freedom in Viet Nam and how heavily the burden of responsibility for defending that freedom falls on those Governments who possess freedom in their own right," he wrote. "They must, if necessary, be reminded that their share of this burden is increased proportionately where they owe their own freedom to assistance they have received from others."

How much did Johnson think these governments should contribute? He said merely that it should be "adequate" and should involve manpower. "Our interest," he said, " is that this contribution should be as large and visible as possible in terms of *men on the scene*, in each case" (emphasis added). Given that more than 16,000 American military personnel were on the scene, the allies, especially the larger ones, should have been thinking in terms of hundreds of men each, not mere dozens. Johnson hammered home the importance of the effort: "I know of no other task imposed upon you in your current assignment which ... precedes this one in its urgency and its significance. I therefore ask you personally to undertake this task in working with the highest levels of the Government to which you are accredited." To underscore the gravity of the situation, the president concluded with a none-too-subtle warning: "I will review reports of the progress being made responsive to this cable at regular intervals ... [and] hope to see evidence of your success in the very near future."[22]

The evidence would not be forthcoming. Not one of the eleven countries targeted in the Johnson cable was prepared to contribute manpower.[23] Sympathetic to Washington's problem in Vietnam and not opposed per se to what the United States sought to accomplish, these governments nevertheless doubted that it could be done, for the same reasons as de Gaulle. ("Most people," one British official wrote Prime Minister Douglas-Home, "feel that if the South-Vietnamese cannot cope [even] with American help, it is because they are war-weary, apathetic, and fed-up."[24]) Like the French leader, they also downplayed Vietnam's importance to Western security. They remained unwilling to openly challenge Washington over the war and on occasion even made tepid public professions of support, but they ruled out even a token military contribution to the war. Their pledges to provide a few million dollars in economic aid to Saigon meant little

22 LBJ circular cable, July 2, 1964, box 6, NSF VN, LBJL.
23 The eleven were Tokyo, Bonn, London, Rome, Brussels, Ottawa, Copenhagen, Bangkok, Taipei, Karachi, and Athens. For obvious reasons Paris was not on the list, although the embassy did receive a copy of the cable.
24 Wright to the Prime Minister, June 18, 1964, PREM 11/4759, PRO.

to a Johnson administration already spending over $1.5 million a day in Vietnam.[25]

Even Asian allies were lukewarm in their support for the war effort. Several of the countries that Johnson railed against in his cable were in Asia. The two most important, from Washington's perspective, were Pakistan and Japan. Karachi's position, which mattered to U.S. officials primarily because Pakistan was a member of SEATO, had become increasingly anti-American in the first half of 1964, and increasingly supportive of reconvening the Geneva conference.[26] In Japan, the government of Ikeda Hayato prized close relations with Washington and worked hard to maintain them. But it also sought a measure of independence from American tutelage, and the result was Japanese-American friction over several issues: the status of Okinawa, which the United States occupied but which Tokyo wanted returned to Japanese control; the presence of U.S.-controlled nuclear weapons on Japan's territory; and Japan's desire to increase trade with Beijing despite Washington's objections. The Ikeda government did agree in August to send a small medical team to Saigon and to provide the Khanh regime with $1.5 million in aid, in the form of medicines, prefabricated buildings, twenty-five ambulances, and 20,000 radios. Although U.S. officials certainly welcomed this aid, it was not what they had in mind – it was not the "large and visible" contribution Johnson had wanted, with "men on the scene."[27]

Senior officials in Tokyo viewed the deepening U.S. involvement in Vietnam with considerable concern. Few Japanese had a taste for communism or wanted a North Vietnamese victory in the conflict, but many on all parts of the political spectrum were haunted by memories of Japan's own misadventure in China a quarter century earlier;[28] much as Japanese forces had bogged down then, they predicted, Americans would now if they chose to fight. The imbalance of forces in Vietnam, with a shockingly weak GVN aligned against a strong, determined adversary in the NLF and Hanoi, also impressed the Japanese and pointed to the futility of what

25 On July 29, British Prime Minister Alec Douglas-Home wrote Khanh with the following happy news: Britain would provide $50,000 for road-making machinery and $6,000 for marine diesel engines. PREM 11/4760, PRO.

26 Hughes to Rusk, July 25, 1964, box 170, NSF CF, LBJL; *New York Times*, Aug. 7, 1964; Robert J. McMahon, "Disillusionment and Disengagement in South Asia," in Warren I. Cohen and Nancy Bernkopf Tucker, eds., *Lyndon Johnson Confronts the World: American Foreign Policy, 1963–1968* (New York, 1994), 138–9; Yaacov Vertzberger, *The Enduring Entente: Sino-Pakistani Relations, 1960–1980* (New York, 1983), 7–14.

27 Thomas R. Havens, *Fire Across the Sea: The Vietnam War and Japan, 1965–1975* (Princeton, N.J., 1987), 19–22; Michael Schaller, *Altered States: The United States and Japan Since the Occupation* (New York, 1997), 184–7; Walter LaFeber, *The Clash: A History of U.S.-Japan Relations* (New York, 1997), 339–41.

28 See also the chapter by John Prados in this book.

Washington sought to achieve. Much as France had failed earlier, the United States would fail now. Finally, an escalated war ran the risk of growing to include China. Officials in Tokyo thus ruled out both a vigorous rhetorical defense of the American effort and a meaningful material contribution to the war effort. When U.S. Ambassador Edwin O. Reischauer pressed Tokyo officials for more substantial involvement, they steadfastly refused. Before long, Reischauer later recalled, Vietnam would "cast a dark shadow over all Japanese-American relations."[29]

All of this added up to a More Flags effort in deep trouble. When Johnson in mid-July asked aides to update him on the state of the campaign, they could only mumble that no real progress had been made. The Australians had come through with a manpower contribution but no one else had. Many American policymakers, never expecting the campaign to be easy, nevertheless were taken aback by the difficulties they had encountered. It did not seem to them that they were asking a lot of their allies – notwithstanding Johnson's talk of a "large and visible" presence, Washington would have been satisfied if the other governments had merely matched Canberra's modest commitment, which points to an important truth in the More Flags campaign: The flags were needed in South Vietnam not for material, military reasons but for symbolic, psychological ones. Even a small allied presence, U.S. officials reasoned, would demonstrate to the nervous South Vietnamese, to an ambivalent American public, and to the enemy the commitment of the anticommunist world to the struggle. And still, ally after ally said no. Perhaps, American strategists hoped, the pressure tactics Johnson called for in his cable just needed more time to work – only a couple of weeks had passed, after all, since the message had gone out. But they knew there was little reason to be optimistic.[30]

American officials could take comfort in one thing: that these failures in the drive to get global support for U.S. policy were slow to manifest themselves. The reluctance of most allied governments to openly confront Washington with their doubts and fears, and the willingness of several to offer rhetorical support for the American position and to make vague pledges of economic assistance to Saigon, allowed Washington in 1964 to maintain the facade of noncommunist unity on the war. The administration could publicly claim, disingenuously but with little fear of protest, that the free

---

29 Edwin O. Reischauer, *The Japanese* (Cambridge, Mass., 1977), 347, and Edwin O. Reischauer, *My Life Between Japan and America* (New York, 1986), 257, as cited in Nancy Bernkopf Tucker, "Threats, Opportunities, and Frustrations in East Asia," in Cohen and Tucker, eds., *Lyndon Johnson Confronts the World*, 116.
30 Ball–McGeorge Bundy telephone conversation, July 9, 1964, box 1, Ball papers, LBJL.

world backed its policy. Still, U.S. policymakers were correct to attach great importance to the "More Flags" campaign and to worry about the consequences of its failure. Skeptics in Congress, the press, and the general population could rightly ask how the administration could wax eloquent about defending the Western world in Vietnam and yet find almost total unwillingness among fellow Western nations to join the team. Likewise, they might ask, why did the U.S. government seem more keen on fighting the war than those in Southeast Asia itself, those in the vicinity of Vietnam who presumably had the most to lose? That few Americans were actually asking these questions yet was of scant comfort to officials; they knew that this could change, especially if more countries joined France's lead and made a public break with the administration.

The most striking aspect of what one might call the "Few Flags" problem is not that it complicated the effort to win support for the war among Americans, important as that was; rather, what really stands out is that it threatened to do the same thing in South Vietnam itself. Indeed, boosting the morale of the South Vietnamese had from the start been a key rationale behind the effort to get allies to commit manpower to the conflict. The argument went roughly as follows: The allies will make a commitment; the Saigon regime will see that the free world is behind it; and the government, army, and people of the South will become more committed to the struggle. That Americans should need to worry about the commitment of the very people they were fighting for pointed, as we have suggested, to the fatal flaw that existed at the epicenter of the war effort. War-weariness and apathy among the South Vietnamese were a constant source of concern to U.S. officials in both Washington and Saigon in June and July, more so even than they had been earlier in the year. As always, concern about neutralist sentiment followed closely behind.

The administration did not give up on gaining increased allied participation in the war effort. In late August, after the military clash in the Gulf of Tonkin, Johnson dispatched former Saigon ambassador and prominent Republican Henry Cabot Lodge on a tour of European capitals. In early September, Lodge returned to Washington and proclaimed that only France, among the countries he had visited, opposed American involvement in the region. "Broadly speaking," Lodge said, "the governments which I visited expressed appreciation for the Unites States efforts in Vietnam, hoped for the success of these efforts, and gave assurances of help."[31]

---

31 *New York Times*, Sept. 11, 1964.

This statement was misleading. Lodge actually found little encouragement on the trip. Some governments – notably those in Belgium and
Denmark – openly expressed their opposition to the direction of American
policy and their fear of a larger war. Others were perfectly prepared, à la
London, to express vague appreciation for the U.S. effort – so long as it
remained limited and defensive in nature – and to *hope* for its success. At the
same time, however, they were more pessimistic than ever that it actually
would succeed, and more doubtful than ever that it was necessary to try.

In Rome, for example, officials did not reveal to Lodge their deep doubts
about the war (stemming partly from a stream of pessimistic telegrams
from the Italian ambassador in Saigon) but urged that every avenue for
a political solution be explored. In Bonn, Chancellor Erhard voiced strong
support for American policy, but Foreign Ministry officials asked him why
the administration viewed the convening of an international conference so
negatively. According to the U.S. embassy, the Germans, "left to their own
devices . . . would probably have chosen a course closer to that favored by
the French." The reason: Bonn did not consider Vietnam a vital concern to
the West.[32]

As for the question of material or manpower assistance to South Vietnam,
Lodge found no reason to be encouraged during his trip. Many European
leaders were happy to give Lodge "assurances of help," but all continued to
resist making meaningful contributions to the war effort.

This was yet another sign of the failure of the administration's More
Flags campaign. Several weeks earlier, thirty-four countries, including some
in Latin America and Africa, had been approached and asked to provide
aid. Virtually nothing materialized. "Most countries have been reluctant to
provide military assistance," a State Department report on the effort noted,
"and where it has been given it has been of a largely token character."[33]

That would be the pattern in the crucial months of late 1964 and early
1965: Most friendly governments would continue to offer tepid rhetorical support for America's mission in Vietnam but rule out meaningful

---

32 Bonn to FO, Aug. 27, 1964, FO 371/175501, PRO; Hughes to Rusk, Aug. 28, 1964, box 7, NSF
    VN, LBJL; Rome to FO, Sept. 10, 1964, FO 371/175502, PRO; Bonn to State, Aug. 20, 1964,
    box 7, NSF VN, LBJL; Bonn to FO, Sept. 3, 1964, FO 371/175501, PRO. Shortly before Henry
    Cabot Lodge's arrival in Rome, the Vatican issued an appeal from Pope Paul IV for peace through
    diplomacy in Vietnam and in the other contemporaneous hot spots, Cyprus and the Congo.
33 Hughes to Rusk, Aug. 28, 1964, box 7, NSF VN, LBJL; Bonn to FO, Aug. 27, 1964, FO 371/
    175501, PRO; Rusk to LBJ, Aug. 14, 1964, box 7, NSF VN, LBJL. At year's end, the NSC's James
    C. Thomson Jr. and Chester Cooper succinctly summarized the situation: Despite a "whirlwind of
    activity and a mass of cable traffic" on "third country assistance," they informed Bundy on New
    Year's Eve that "very little has yet come out of the funnel." Thomson/Cooper to McGeorge Bundy,
    Dec. 31, 1964, box 13, Papers of James C. Thomson Jr., JFKL.

assistance to the cause. When Wilson, the new British prime minister, visited Washington in December 1964, he affirmed Britain's support for current U.S. policy but warned against any expansion of the war and resisted strong pressure from Johnson to commit manpower to the struggle. In advance of Japanese leader Eisaku Sato's visit the following month, a National Security Council memo warned that even in conservative circles in Japan "there are serious misgivings about the prospects for success of U.S. Southeast Asia policies and the long-term risk to Japan in over-commitment to the U.S. position." During his talks with American officials, Sato pledged support for current levels of U.S. assistance to South Vietnam but voiced opposition to American bombing attacks on the DRV on the grounds that such attacks would fail to achieve their objectives and would send the wrong message to the peoples of Asia. The same basic sentiments were voiced privately by the Canadian government in December 1964 and January 1965.[34]

Did these allied misgivings impact U.S. decision making in this period? Yes, although not as much as they might have. It is clear from the massive internal record that American planners ruled out a more rapid and far-reaching escalation of the war in early 1965 in large part because of concerns over how key friendly governments would react. In the interagency working group deliberations in November 1964, the Joint Chiefs of Staff representative pressed hard for the adoption of "Option B," involving early, heavy military pressure against North Vietnam. The actions would continue at a rapid pace and without interruption until the United States achieved its present objective – that is, an end to the insurgency. Option B never had much of a chance, however, because of deep fears among civilian officials about the likely response from audiences at home and abroad. There would be worldwide condemnation of the United States, they feared, if the administration went in with guns blazing. The all-important British backing would evaporate, and momentum would build rapidly for early negotiations.

Herein lies one important reason (among several) why the strategy of graduated pressure, for all its flaws, was the only possible escalatory strategy in 1965. Military-affiliated authors continue to this day to blast the strategy and the people responsible for it, but the civilians in charge had a better sense of the realities, of the possibilities, than their military counterparts. Graduated pressure ("Option C"), the strategy ultimately adopted, offered the hope of staving off a collapse in Saigon while also keeping the major allied governments, all of whom favored early negotiations but who were

---

34 Thomson to Bundy, Jan. 11, 1965, box 12, Thomson papers, JFKL; "Background Paper, Sato Visit," Jan. 7, 1965, box 253, NSF CF, LBJL; *Washington Post*, Jan. 13, 1965.

anxious to preserve good relations with Washington if at all possible, from joining the French in open opposition to the war.

And so it would be. London, Ottawa, and Tokyo were unhappy about the initiation of Rolling Thunder in late winter 1965 and about the dispatch of U.S. fighting forces that followed, but they continued to offer half-hearted rhetorical support for the administration's policy throughout these all-important weeks (while attempting through diplomatic channels to get Washington to come around to the need for negotiations). American planners breathed a big sigh of relief particularly because of Prime Minister Wilson's continued support. On February 11, William Bundy told Australian and New Zealand officials that British opinion was crucial. If the British government stood firm in public in support of American action, Bundy said, the pressure for early talks would be lessened.[35] Wilson obliged not merely in February but in the months that followed as well.

If Bundy and other senior presidential advisers were relieved by this state of affairs, Johnson was less so. The president continued in the first half of 1965 to rail against Wilson and other Western leaders for their failure to contribute meaningfully – by which he meant primarily manpower on the ground – to the war effort. As American fighting forces arrived in Vietnam in ever greater numbers, he knew it was more vital than ever to get increased "third country" help in order to show lawmakers and the American public that the defense of South Vietnam was indeed a Free World effort. In the spring of 1965, on Johnson's orders, the administration undertook its last great effort to convince the few governments supportive of the war effort to make significant manpower contributions. Little materialized, much as presidential advisers had expected.[36] By June 15, Australia had committed one infantry battalion, a 73-man air force unit, and 100 combat advisers, whereas South Korea had agreed to send a 2,200-man task force that included one infantry battalion. New Zealand had committed an artillery battalion. All three told the administration to expect little more.[37]

35 Washington to Office of the High Commissioner for Australia, London, Feb. 11, 1965, FO 371/180594, PRO.

36 LBJ letter to Keith Holyoke, Apr. 8, 1965, box 12, Thomson papers, JFKL; Taylor (Washington) to Saigon, Mar. 30, 1965, box 45, NSF VN, LBJL; Ball–Bundy telephone conversation, Apr. 6, 1965, box 7, Ball papers, LBJL; William P. Bundy unpublished manuscript, chap. 23, p. 21, and chap. 24, p. 16; Bundy to LBJ, Apr. 1, 1965, in U.S. Department of State, ed., *Foreign Relations of the United States*, 1964–1968, II (Washington, D.C., 1996). In the memo, Bundy noted that help was likely to come only from Australia, New Zealand, and South Korea, and that the Canberra and Wellington commitments would be small. Even the Korean situation, he said, was "touchy." See also White House Meeting Notes, July 21, 1965, ibid., III, 189–97.

37 "Free World Assistance to Vietnam," June 15, 1965, FO 371/180578, PRO; Wellington to Commonwealth Relations Office, Aug. 6, 1965, PREM 13/697, PRO; Canberra to Commonwealth Relations Office, July 2, 1965, PREM 13/696, PRO.

Small though these contributions were, the White House could have been content with them had Great Britain come through with even a token troop commitment. Johnson was outraged by Wilson's steadfast refusal to bend on this issue, telling aides that he thought he had made it clear to the prime minister in their December 1964 meeting that the only effective contribution Britain could make to the war effort was ground troops. Johnson said he wanted a few British soldiers to get killed in Vietnam alongside Americans so that their pictures could appear in the U.S. press to demonstrate to the public that America's principal ally was contributing to a joint effort. In June and July, top American officials, including the big three – McNamara, Rusk, and McGeorge Bundy – leaned hard on the Wilson government to commit a brigade or a couple of battalions. Their hope was that London's dependence on American assistance in propping up the beleaguered pound would cause Wilson to yield on the issue. Dollars were dangled. On the evening of July 25, Bundy told Sir Patrick Dean, the new British ambassador to Washington, that what Johnson really wanted was a British military contribution in the form of ground troops. Such a contribution, he added, would be worth "several hundred million dollars." Dean said he would relay the request to his government. McNamara, meanwhile, told colleagues he was prepared to give London a billion dollars in exchange for a brigade. Whether he actually made that offer to the British is not clear, but in any event Wilson refused to go along. There would be no British fighting forces sent to Vietnam.[38]

In the months and years following the 1965 escalation, public opinion in Britain and other allied countries became much more outspoken in opposition to American policy. By the latter part of 1967, Wilson recalled wearily, yelling mobs of demonstrators "became a familiar routine."[39] Large public demonstrations against the war were by then a regular feature in cities the world over – in London and Tokyo, in Stockholm and Vancouver, in Brussels and Johannesburg. This growing popular revulsion in the Western democracies against the war did not, however, bring major changes in the ways leaders in these countries approached the war. Most continued to try

---

38 Canberra to Commonwealth Relations Office, July 2, 1965, PREM 13/696, PRO; Washington to FO, July 26, 1965, FO 371/180542, PRO; Washington to FO, July 29, 1965, FO 371/180543, PRO; A. M. Palliser minutes, July 28, 1965, FO 371/180543, PRO; Ball–Fowler telephone conversation, July 29, 1965, box 7, Ball papers, LBJL; Ball–Bundy telephone conversation, July 29, 1965, box 7, Ball papers, LBJL.

39 Harold Wilson, *A Personal Record: The Labour Government, 1964–1970* (Boston, 1971), 445. See also Richard J. Barnet, *The Alliance: America, Europe, Japan: Makers of the Postwar World* (New York, 1983), 266–70.

to have it both ways – to refuse all American pleas for manpower contributions to the war effort while at the same time offering lukewarm rhetorical
backing of U.S. intervention.

Several Western leaders did make half-hearted efforts to promote a political settlement to the conflict – usually with little encouragement from
Washington – and many of them lamented that Washington's preoccupation
with Indochina resulted in the neglect of other vital international issues,
including Middle East tensions, relations with Moscow, and the growing
frictions in North-South relations. The Western alliance seemed increasingly to be what de Gaulle had so frequently said it was: a one-way street.
Nevertheless, for most leaders the time-honored policy of not challenging Washington directly over the war remained sacrosanct even into 1967
and 1968.

Thus, for all of Johnson's ire at friendly governments for failing to commit
manpower to the war, he could be thankful that the picture was not worse
than it was. As early as the beginning of 1964, well before the decisions
that made Vietnam an American war, key Western governments registered
opposition to an enlarged war and resisted strong American pressure to
participate. Even then, most possessed deep doubts that the GVN could
emerge victorious in the struggle, even with large-scale American support;
most thought the outcome in Indochina was not crucial to Western security
in any event. Far from American "credibility" being enhanced or preserved
by a decision to wage large-scale war in Vietnam, these observers predicted
that it would more likely suffer as a result. Leaders in London, Paris, Tokyo,
Ottawa, and numerous other capitals therefore concluded that negotiations
even from an inferior bargaining position were preferable to an expansion of
the war. Yet only the French were explicit and public about that belief, and
even they cannot be considered *agitators* for negotiations in the key months
of 1964 and 1965. Unwilling to participate in the "absurd war" in Vietnam,
key allied leaders also showed themselves unwilling to work to prevent or
end it.

9

Bamboo in the Shadows

Relations Between the United States and Thailand During the Vietnam War

ARNE KISLENKO

With the Union Army bogged down in the Potomac Valley during the winter of 1862, Abraham Lincoln could have used all the help he could get to bring the American Civil War to a successful conclusion. Among the more curious propositions he received was an offer of war elephants from King Mongkut (Phra Chom Klao, or Rama IV, 1851–68) of Siam. Although the beleaguered president may have happily contemplated the specter of bull elephants in full armor crashing through Confederate lines, he graciously declined the king's gift. It would be a problem, Lincoln said, because "our political jurisdiction does not reach a latitude so low as to favor the multiplication of the elephant."[1]

One hundred years later, the Thais again offered to assist in an American war, this time much closer to home and far more important to their nation and society. The Vietnam War era was without question the most significant period in the history of diplomatic relations between the United States and Thailand. During the 1950s and 1960s, the two countries developed an extremely close relationship premised on the need to contain the perceived spread of communism in Southeast Asia. For the United States, Thailand represented a bastion of anticommunism in a region plagued by political uncertainty. It also represented a valuable Asian ally in the Cold War and a strategic base from which to prosecute both overt and covert military operations in Indochina. For Thailand, the United States represented protection from both the external threat of communist neighbors and the risk that an indigenous communist insurgency posed. Moreover, close association with the United States served to legitimize military authoritarianism in Thailand and advance the personal interests of an elite few running the country. In this, the Vietnam War also represents a crucial watershed in Thai history that

---

1 Russell H. Fifield, *America in Southeast Asia: The Roots of Commitment* (New York, 1973), 14.

greatly affected not only Thailand's external relations but also its economy, domestic politics, and even its culture and society.

An ancient proverb likens Thai foreign policy to the bamboo in the wind: always solidly rooted but flexible enough to bend whichever way it has to in order to survive. This reflects not simply pragmatism but rather a long-cherished, philosophical approach to international relations, whose precepts are very much enshrined in Thai culture.[2] The Thais guarded their independence jealously and were rightfully proud of being the only country in Southeast Asia to have avoided being absorbed into the much more powerful European colonial empires during the nineteenth century. Although historically the Thais occasionally entered into diplomatic pacts with foreign powers, they were extremely careful to avoid anything more than temporary arrangements. Formal alliances of any kind were infrequent in Thai history, and Thais considered the stationing of even friendly foreign troops on their soil a serious threat to their independence.[3] However, after World War II the Thais were faced with an ever more challenging world order. Like the rest of Southeast Asia, Thailand found itself part of the struggle for dominance between the Cold War superpowers. Its own stake in this rivalry was high. Communism threatened not only the country itself but also the Thai way of life. In their advocacy of violence, revolution, and atheism, communists represented the antithesis of Thai cultural traditions. And although the internal communist threat was often exaggerated in Bangkok for political reasons, this incompatibility was undeniably a crucial factor leading to the informal Thai-American alliance that developed during the late 1950s and early 1960s.

However, it was not just communism per se that concerned Thais. More than anything, Thailand's perceptions were shaped by the fact that communist insurgency there was sponsored by a familiar and formidable adversary. Like the rest of Southeast Asia, Thailand lived in the shadow of China. Ancient Siam had been a vassal to the Chinese emperor up until the nineteenth century, and the threat of Chinese domination was a very real part of Thai history. From the early nineteenth century until 1949, China was a sleeping dragon weakened by the domination of foreign powers and civil strife. Communism had awakened the dragon, and from the Thai point of

---

2 William J. Klausner, *Reflections of Thai Culture* (Bangkok, 1981), 79–80.
3 Aside from periodic invasions by neighbors throughout the centuries, the most notable example of foreign military presence in Thailand was from 1941 to 1945, when Japanese troops occupied positions throughout much of the country. Thailand's role in World War II, and particularly its association with Japan, remains the subject of considerable historical controversy. For an excellent account of this topic, see Edward Bruce Reynolds, *Thailand and Japan's Southern Advance, 1940–1945* (New York, 1994).

view it appeared that China was bent on expansion. Intervention in Korea seemed only the most glaring illustration of Chinese aggression. Most Thais believed it was the Chinese and not so much the Soviets who were behind supposedly indigenous communist movements throughout Southeast Asia. A large, closely knit, and affluent ethnic Chinese community in Thailand only added to the fear that Beijing was acting out an ancient impulse to dominate the region.[4] In this view, although communism was a dangerous commodity on its own, it was also considered a "banner" behind which the old Chinese dragon spread its wings.

To counter this threat, closer relations with the United States was a logical alternative for the Thais. Although there is no doubt that Thailand's association with the United States during the Vietnam War era was the longest and most intense external relationship the country has ever had, it was entirely consistent with traditional Thai "bamboo" foreign-policy flexibility in light of the danger Communist China posed. American hostility toward the Chinese Communists after 1949 brought Asia sharply into focus for Washington, and almost immediately the United States sought to extend the Military Defense Assistance Program (MDAP, and later MAP) to its Asian clientele. In this process, U.S.-Thai relations came to the forefront. In the fall of 1950, the Truman administration concluded a series of economic and military agreements with Bangkok, bringing Thailand fully into the MAP program. During the Korean War, Thailand contributed several hundred troops and provided much-needed rice shipments to the U.S.-led multinational United Nations force. Washington reciprocated by helping to secure for Thailand the first ever World Bank loan to a Southeast Asian nation and by delivering unilateral assistance recommended by a number of fact-finding missions.[5] Shortly thereafter, the Truman administration demonstrated its own commitment by dispatching a Military Advisory Assistance Group (MAAG) to Thailand. Between 1951 and 1953, military aid to Thailand rose from $4.5 million to $56 million, and eventually reached a high of $130 million by 1968, making it a major recipient in the region during much of the Vietnam War era.[6]

---

4 William F. Skinner, *Chinese Society in Thailand: An Analytical History* (Ithaca, N.Y., 1957), passim. See also Sukhumbhand Paribata, *From Enmity to Alignment: Thailand's Changing Relations with China* (Bangkok, 1987).
5 R. Sean Randolph, *The United States and Thailand: Alliance Dynamics, 1950–85* (Berkeley, Calif., 1985), 14–15.
6 Background briefings, "Visit of Prime Minister of Thailand," with Marshall Wright, White House, May 7, 1968, file BB #32 – Background Briefings etc. May 7, 1968–June 28, 1968, #1437, Background Briefings, box 83, White House Press Office Files, Lyndon Baines Johnson Presidential Library (hereafter LBJL).

The intimate relationship between Washington's struggle to contain communism in Southeast Asia and the entrenchment of a military government in Bangkok is key to understanding U.S.-Thai relations during the Vietnam War. The Thais believed that the Americans had successfully fought the spread of communism in Korea and that they were dedicated to the rejuvenation of Japan as an industrial and democratic power. Throughout the 1950s, Washington made clear that the United States would protect Taiwan, and when the French withdrew in humiliation from Indochina, the Americans seemed willing and able to take over. Moreover, the American dedication to freedom and liberty was greatly admired by most Thais, who considered themselves "democratic" despite their military government.[7] In a much less idealistic vein, the Thais also saw the United States as a land of inexhaustible wealth and opportunity. Many realized that their economic situation would likely improve substantially in any closer relationship with such a prosperous and generous country. They believed that national security would facilitate prosperity, which in turn would allow for the development of a more pluralistic polity. In contrast, Thai military leaders were unconcerned with fostering greater democracy. Rather, they saw an association with Washington as a source of personal financial gain and as a means of legitimizing their rule.

With the support of successive American presidential administrations, the Thai military came to dominate the government in Bangkok after World War II. Whereas military authoritarianism most definitely had its roots in Thai political culture irrespective of American influence, the fact remains that U.S. economic and military aid after World War II had solidified the position of the Thai armed forces in politics. Thus, American policies aimed at containing the spread of communism in Asia and military authoritarianism in Thailand were inextricably linked and, as the 1950s and 1960s unfolded, mutually reinforcing. Although communism never enjoyed more than a marginal following in Thailand, the Thai military was particularly adept at using this threat to its own advantage. Successful government propaganda convinced many Thais that communism elsewhere in Asia posed a real and imminent threat to them. With conflict in Laos, Vietnam, Burma, Indonesia, and Malaya, it seemed to many Thais that their country was next on the "timetable" for a communist takeover. Consequently, most

---

7 John S. Girling, *Thailand: Society and Politics* (Ithaca, N.Y., 1981), 11–12. Girling contends that Thai society is based on a consensus of traditional values and behaviors, and not necessarily on cooperation or tolerance. He does not believe that Thai society is inherently democratic by Western standards. However, most Thais view their country as democratic in its essence by Asian and self-defined standards, primarily because it has not experienced the brutal dictatorships or civil wars of some of its neighbors.

Thais accepted military rule as necessary to protect the country from communist aggression.[8] This unquestionably undermined the development of Western-style democracy in the near term, but it also provided the stability that promoted the economic development on which the motivation for democratic reforms was contingent that surfaced by the mid-1970s.

The augmentation of military rule in Thailand and the development of a closer relationship with the United States was initially predicated on the conflict in Laos. Although remote, landlocked, and undeveloped, Laos nonetheless emerged as a national security concern to the United States in the late 1950s. For the Eisenhower administration, Laos and Vietnam represented a "proving ground" for U.S. foreign policy in Asia. Washington's resolve to prevent the spread of communism was on the line, and following the tenets of the "domino theory," President Dwight D. Eisenhower could not allow even tiny Laos to "fall." It was in Laos, Eisenhower told his successor, John F. Kennedy, that the United States should stand against Asian communism, and he feared American military involvement was inevitable, "with others if possible, alone if necessary."[9]

For Thailand, Laos was not a pawn in the international struggle between superpowers or a remote battleground of the Cold War. Laos, and the specter of communism, were right on Thailand's doorstep. Linguistically and culturally, Thais and Lao are close, and prior to the era of European colonialism Laos was effectively a Thai suzerainty. In many ways Thailand regarded Laos as its "little brother." Ethnic Lao had long been the majority in several regions of Northeastern Thailand, and elsewhere they were closely integrated into the Thai mainstream. Historically the buffer against China and Vietnam, Laos was of extreme importance to any Thai regime.[10] By the late 1950s, this was an even more acute concern, given the establishment of a seemingly aggressive Communist China and the insurgency unfolding in Vietnam. Thus, in many ways Laos was the "dagger" pointing at the heart of Thailand.

From Laos, Indochinese communists could easily make their way across the Mekong River into Thailand. Playing on the regional tensions between

---

8 For a very solid and recent analysis of this evolution during the Truman and Eisenhower administrations, see Daniel Mark Fireman, *A Special Relationship: The United States and Military Government in Thailand, 1947–1958* (Honolulu, 1997).

9 Dean Rusk, *As I Saw It* (New York, 1990), 429. See also Charles A. Stevenson, *The End of Nowhere: American Policy Towards Laos Since 1954* (Boston, 1972), 1–4.

10 Geoffrey C. Gunn, *Political Struggles in Laos, 1930–1954* (Bangkok, 1988), passim. Thailand is geographically exposed to external assault from Laos. The Thai border with Laos is essentially the Mekong River, which at crucial points along the frontier narrows to only a few hundred feet. Much of Laos also is a valley, with little in the way to impede an invasion launched from China or Vietnam.

the northeast and Bangkok, communists could potentially stir up trouble. Bangkok's physical and political distance from the region left the people there isolated from the rest of the nation, something the Central Intelligence Agency (CIA) worried promoted "serious factional infighting" among Thai parties and politicians. The northeast lagged behind the rest of the country economically, and it suffered the additional burden of acutely corrupt local government and police. Officials in Bangkok also regularly skimmed off large amounts of aid money earmarked for the northeast for their personal use, taking to heart the old Thai edict *kin muang,* or "eat the country."[11] Moreover, most people in the area were considered passive and apolitical, qualities the CIA believed were conducive to the expansion of communist ideals and support. The northeast also was considered the "wild frontier" of Thailand, rife with gangs, gamblers, smugglers, and drug addicts. For these and other reasons the northeast was a difficult place in which to instill a strong sense of nationalism.[12] The vulnerability of the region was compounded by the presence of almost 50,000 ethnic Vietnamese, many with allegiances to Ho Chi Minh. In the mid-1960s, American intelligence analysts confirmed North Vietnamese and Chinese sponsorship of communists in northeastern Thailand, estimating that some 3,200 guerillas operated in the northeast in four battalions made up of mostly ethnic Chinese and Vietnamese Thai.[13]

Therefore, by the mid-1950s, the fragility of the northeast and its proximity to the crisis in Laos became a major concern for both Bangkok and Washington. The communist Pathet Lao posed a considerable threat to the already shaky government in Laos, and after the French defeat at Dien Bien Phu in May it seemed that communism in Indochina was unstoppable. The Pathet Lao were clearly linked to the North Vietnamese, who in turn received support and direction from Moscow and Beijing. From the Thai point of view, this situation was worsened by Beijing's creation of the "Thai Nationality Autonomous Area" in Yunnan province in January 1953, where ethnic Thais still resided. Some Thais interpreted the move as a paternalistic reminder of their ancestral connection with China. Others saw it as an attempt to get Southeast Asians to accept Chinese influence in the region.

---

11 State Department Report, "Counterinsurgency in Thailand," no date, Thailand file 2, #41–42, National Security Files, Country Files Thailand (hereafter NSF, CFT), box 286, LBJL.

12 CIA memorandum 1595/66, "Communist Insurgency in Thailand: Strengths and Weaknesses," Aug. 11, 1966, file Thailand vol. 4, 1/66 to 10/66, #105, NSF, CFT, box 283, LBJL. See also Charles F. Keyes, "Ethnic Identity and Loyalty of Villagers in Northeastern Thailand," *Asian Survey* 6 (July 1966): 85–90.

13 U.S. Army chief of staff, memorandum of conversation, General William Westmoreland and General Praphas Charusthian, Oct. 16, 1968, file Thailand Memos vol. 8, 7/68 to 12/68, #96, NSF, CFT, box 284, LBJL.

But most Thais took the message as a thinly veiled warning that Thailand was next on the agenda for communist expansion, especially if it continued its friendship with the United States.[14]

Washington responded with dramatically increased aid channeled to areas deemed most important to Thai national security. A primary example is the construction of all-weather roads, railways, and regional airports to greatly improve Bangkok's access to the geographically and politically remote Northeast.[15] This development also facilitated Thailand's role as a conduit for covert CIA operations in Indochina. As early as 1951, the CIA and National Security Council (NSC) were covertly building an anticommunist paramilitary force in Laos with close cooperation from Thailand. The Thai national police and Police Aerial Reconnaissance Units (PARU) were indispensable liaisons between the Americans and Lao. American agents also trained Thai police units in guerilla warfare for top secret deployment in Laos.[16] By 1953, there were some two hundred CIA operatives in Thailand, training Thais in everything from sabotage to parachuting. From secret bases in northern Thailand, the CIA even planned a coordinated attack by Kuomindang renegades against Chinese military positions in Yunnan province.[17]

Thailand also played a critical role in American efforts to reach a negotiated settlement to the crisis in Laos. The Thai prime minister from 1958 to 1963, Sarit Thanarat, gave the United States an invaluable personal link to the convoluted world of Laotian politics. He was himself part Lao in

14 Adulyasak Soonthornrojana, "The Rise of United States–Thai Relations, 1945–1975," Ph.D. dissertation, University of Akron, 1986, 87–9.

15 Randolph, *The United States and Thailand*, 22–4. Between 1954 and 1960, almost 47 percent of total U.S. economic assistance went to transportation, with 33 percent alone devoted to road construction. $350 million was spent on highways from 1951 to 1965, creating a network of roads from the Bangkok region all the way up to near the border with Laos. By February 1960, American money had helped build large- and medium-scale airports at Korat, Takli, Udon Thani, Ubon, Chiangmai, and Bangkok, all with facilities specifically geared for military use.

16 Timothy Neil Castle, "At War in the Shadow of Vietnam: U.S. Military Aid to the Royal Lao Government, 1955–73," Ph.D. dissertation, University of Hawaii, 1991, 96–8. See also Official Meeting Minutes (hereafter OMM), National Security Council (hereafter NSC), 144th meeting, May 13, 1953, OMM box 5, 130–45, records of the NSC, Record Group (hereafter RG) 273, U.S. National Archives (hereafter USNA); OMM, NSC 159th meeting, Aug. 17, 1953, OMM box 8, 158–9; and OMM, NSC 189th Meeting, Mar. 11, 1954, OMM box 10, 170–99, RG 273, USNA.

17 Daniel Mark Fineman, "United States Foreign Policy and Military Government in Thailand, 1947–1958," Ph.D. dissertation, Yale University, 1993, 238–48. "Operation Paper" was approved by the Truman administration in January 1951, no doubt influenced by events in Korea. General Li Mi headed Kuomingtang forces, which received crucial logistical and intelligence support from the Thai police and U.S. advisers. In June 1951, Li managed to take an airfield in Yunnan, but his troops were twice pushed back. Despite Thai efforts to cover for the Americans, virtually everyone knew that Washington was somehow involved in what Fineman characterizes as a "comic opera."

ancestry and was related to one of the most forceful leaders in Laos, Phoumi Nosavan, who effectively took over the rightwing in late 1959. Kenneth Young, a State Department official and later ambassador to Thailand under President John F. Kennedy, once remarked that political culture in Laos was not understood by more than "one or two people," and Sarit was clearly one. He offered important leverage on Phoumi and the Lao rightists. The problem for Washington was getting Sarit to cooperate with a policy that placed little confidence in Phoumi. By the early 1960s, American policy supported the creation of a coalition government in Laos led by Souvanna Phouma, whom the Thais considered a naive neutralist and even a "crypto-communist."[18] Sarit was determined to aid rightists in Laos, and when U.S. officials balked at the idea of escalating American military aid to them, he became very uncertain of Washington's anticommunist resolve. As the 1960s unfolded, Thai support became critical to the success of any American policy with respect to Laos, and Sarit did not hesitate to remind the United States how important Thailand was to its overall regional policy. Never fully convinced that the Americans could or would oppose communism in Southeast Asia by force, Sarit was frequently aloof and expected considerable economic and military aid in return for his help. In this way, Thailand exerted considerable influence on U.S. policy, perhaps disproportionately to the intrinsic value of Laos, as historian Arthur Dommen pointed out.[19]

Kennedy inherited the United States' Southeast Asia policy from Eisenhower, but he did not share his predecessor's conviction that Laos was crucial to U.S. national security. Even with a more concerted response from the United States, the situation in Laos seemed intractable to Kennedy. Many in the administration believed that U.S. policy in Laos under Eisenhower was guided by an obsessive anticommunism blind to the political realities of that country and too fixated on the developing crisis in South Vietnam. They believed communism was not the only issue. Journalist Bernard Fall once commented that Laos was a country by virtue of "geographical convenience" only, and Kennedy fully endorsed this view.[20] The Laotian crisis seemed to Kennedy to be more the by-product of regional disintegration and ethnic conflict than the precursor to an invasion of Southeast Asia masterminded by Moscow or Beijing. Countering the extension of the Pathet Lao could not be reasonably done without a dramatic military commitment, and this could only come from the Americans. Chester Cooper, an NSC

---

18 Oral history interview, Kenneth T. Young with Dennis O'Brien, February 25, 1969, file HUG(FP) 26.3, folder one, 51–6, Kenneth Todd Young Jr. papers, Pusey Library, Harvard University Archives.
19 As quoted in Randolph, *The United States and Thailand*, 39.
20 Stevenson, *The End of Nowhere*, 1.

staff member from 1961 to 1967, later observed that in the opinion of the Kennedy administration, "Laos was not all that god-damned important."[21]

Although he had no desire to look weak by surrendering Laos to communism, Kennedy also had no intention of being drawn into a war, especially over such an indefensible country. He was optimistic that Laos, together with Cambodia, could form a *cordon sanitaire* protecting Thailand and the rest of the region.[22] Consequently, Kennedy developed a more conciliatory approach to the Laotian crisis and sought out avenues of international negotiation along the lines of the 1954 Geneva Accords. However, this policy toward Laos was anything but reassuring to Bangkok. The Thais saw a negotiated settlement as a sellout to the communists, convinced that even if one were achieved in talks, it would be untenable in the field. U.S.-Thai relations were dramatically and adversely affected by Kennedy's decision to pursue a negotiated settlement in Laos, and Thai dissatisfaction was a real problem for Washington. After so many years of vacillation with regard to American policy on Laos, the Thais were disillusioned by what appeared to be an admission of defeat. Restoring Thailand's faith and regaining its support would undoubtedly involve considerable effort and expense on Washington's part.

Only after months of often difficult discussions and promises did the Thai government finally agree to endorse the American position on Laos in January 1962, but not without grave reservations. Always with a flare for the dramatic, Sarit warned American Ambassador Kenneth T. Young, "[I]f the U.S. is wrong in Laos, Thailand is finished. We cannot afford mistake or regret."[23] But whereas American representatives pursued international negotiations on Laos, the Kennedy administration pursued a "second track" policy with Bangkok toward the crisis, clearly designed to demonstrate the U.S. commitment to Thailand. In the spring of 1961, the American ambassador to Thailand, U. A. Johnson, had approached Sarit about the possibility of introducing U.S. troops to protect Thailand and possibly to serve in Indochina. The Kennedy administration also continued, and in some cases extended, covert operations throughout the region, many based in Thailand.[24]

---

21 Ibid., 5.

22 Leonard Unger, "The United States and Laos, 1962–1965," in Joseph J. Zasloff and Leonard Unger, eds., *Laos: Beyond the Revolution* (London, 1991), 274–8.

23 Cable, Bangkok 1047 to State, Jan. 21, 1962, 751.J00/1–2162, Central Decimal File Laos 1960–63, box 1769, RG 59, USNA.

24 Castle, "At War in the Shadow of Vietnam," 96, 277–80. For example, in April 1961 the CIA began "Project Ekarad," which involved the training of a whole battalion of Royal Lao troops at bases in Northeastern Thailand. "Volunteers" from the Thai Army and Air Force were trained to serve in Lao special operations units, complete with Lao identification tags, all on the CIA payroll. PARU and Thai border police patrols were frequently engaged in surveillance operations with more

In light of the situation in Laos, the Thais wanted a unilateral security guarantee from Washington, something that no American president was prepared to offer for fear of overextending U.S. military and economic obligations in Southeast Asia. Thailand was considered an invaluable component in the emerging struggle in Indochina, but throughout the Vietnam War era, Washington continued to champion the Southeast Asian Treaty Organization (SEATO) as the vehicle for U.S. commitment to Thailand's security. From the Thai point of view, SEATO was little more than a paper tiger: Almost from its inception in 1954 it was considered an ineffective deterrent to communist expansion in Southeast Asia. Neither Britain nor France seemed to favor using SEATO as a military alliance, and both consistently distanced themselves from any suggestion that the organization should plan for the deployment of troops in Indochina. The Thais wanted and expected a show of resolve from the West in Indochina, particularly in Laos, which SEATO clearly was not going to provide. Consequently, differences over the effectiveness of SEATO and Bangkok's quest for a bilateral alliance were major stumbling blocks in U.S.-Thai relations.

To prevent a deterioration in relations with the Thais, the Kennedy administration therefore considered an alternative arrangement to SEATO. In March 1962, the State Department, after much deliberation, publicly issued a joint communiqué on the occasion of a visit to Washington by Thai Foreign Minister Thanat Khoman. Dubbed the "Rusk-Thanat Agreement," the communiqué reaffirmed American determination to maintain "the preservation of the independence and integrity of Thailand as vital to the national interest of the United States and to world peace." It also spoke about Washington's "firm intention" to aid Thailand in resisting communism. In what was clearly a major concession by Thanat, SEATO was recognized as "an effective deterrent to direct Communist aggression." In return, Rusk assured that the United States would give "full effect to its obligations under the [SEATO] Treaty to act to meet the common danger in accordance with its constitutional processes."[25] The United States would not, he said,

than the occasional rumor surfacing that they had even partaken in combat against the Pathet Lao. In the summer of 1961, the CIA enlisted Thai special operations squads to help "convert" Hmong tribesmen in the central highlands of Laos and Vietnam. They were taken to Thailand for military training. Joint U.S.-Thai covert operations were in fact formalized with the establishment of the "Joint Liaison Detachment" in late 1962. The CIA orchestrated through this body much of the training and logistics required for clandestine activities in Laos with full support and knowledge of Thai military authorities.

25 U.S. State Department Circular, "Proposed Joint Statement to be Issued By His Excellency the Foreign Minister of Thailand and the Secretary of State," file Thailand General 3/1/62 to 3/8/62, National Security File Thailand, box 163, John F. Kennedy Presidential Library (hereafter JFKL). For an excellent overview of U.S. policy toward SEATO after the agreement, see report PD/FE–1,

depend on the prior agreement of other signatories because the obligation was individual as well as collective.

In Thailand, the Rusk-Thanat Agreement was received with great public enthusiasm. It was the next best thing to a bilateral alliance, and in fact the Thais quickly came to see it as the equivalent of such an alliance. Far from being a question of semantics, this difference of opinion between Washington and Bangkok on the Rusk-Thanat Agreement would prove to be fundamental to U.S.-Thai relations in the years to come.[26] Within just a few days of its signing, it was apparent that the Thai military establishment had misunderstood the purport of the agreement. U.S. military advisers reported that the Thais were asking for additional funding, believing that the communiqué was in effect a formal treaty.

The Rusk-Thanat Agreement faced its first challenge very quickly, in May 1962. Early in the month Pathet Lao forces had scored a huge tactical victory by taking the town of Nam Tha in northwestern Laos. Fearing this was the precursor to a communist invasion of Thailand, Sarit ordered the deployment of several thousand troops along the Mekong River. The resulting standoff was very tense, especially given Sarit's earlier threat to occupy the Lao side of the river if Thailand was threatened. In Washington, Kennedy responded quickly and decisively to the dangerous possibility of collision between Thai and Pathet Lao forces. He ordered the U.S. military command in Asia to prepare for possible intervention along the Thailand-Laos frontier, ostensibly to prevent a communist incursion into Thailand. Within hours a battle group was assembled. After considering a number of options, including shoring up Phoumi's men with U.S. forces and bombing Pathet Lao strongholds, Kennedy decided to send troops into Thailand.

The Kennedy administration wanted troops in Thailand as a warning to the Pathet Lao and their backers in Beijing and Hanoi, and the president knew the deployment could also prove to be a valuable bargaining

---

"Future of SEATO," no author, Apr. 5, 1962, file Policy Directives, Bureau of Far Eastern Affairs, Assistant Secretary of State for Far East Asia, Subject, Personal Name and Country files 1960–63, box 15, RG 59, USNA.

26 The U.S. Historical Studies Division of the State Department later characterized the Rusk-Thanat Agreement as the culmination of Thailand's "persistent campaign of several years to pry out of the United States a firm, unilateral, and public pledge." See report, "The United States Commitment to Thailand: Background, Formulation, and Differing Initial U.S. and Thai Interpretations of the Rusk-Thanat Communique 1962," research project 986, Sept. 1970, folder: Research Project 986, The U.S. Commitment to Thailand, Historical Studies Division, Historical Office, Bureau of Public Affairs, Department of State, Executive Secretariat, Historical Office Research Projects, 1969–1974, box 7, RG 59, USNA.

chip during negotiations in Geneva.[27] Sending the troops also was a clear demonstration of how important Thailand was to the United States and of how resolved Kennedy was to intervene militarily against perceived communist expansion in the region. On May 18, 1962, just over 6,500 U.S. Marines from the aircraft carrier USS *Valley Forge* landed in Thailand. It was the first overt deployment of American combat soldiers in Southeast Asia since World War II, and it marked the first time foreign combat troops entered Thailand for a purpose other than invasion or occupation.[28]

The U.S. troops were welcomed by most Thais, but there were many questions as to how long they would stay and what exactly Washington planned. The U.S. Joint Chiefs of Staff feared that the presence of American soldiers might prompt the Thai military to try and occupy Sayabouri Province in southern Laos, directly across the Mekong River from Thailand. This would dangerously escalate tensions and diminish American control of the situation. Intelligence reports suggested that communist strength in the region totaled twenty active battalions, much more than the Thais alone could take on. If they conducted military operations there without coordinating with the United States, Washington would face a serious quandary. It was not so much that the Americans ruled out expanded action in the theater; in fact, Washington planned for possible offensive operations in Laos, mostly with SEATO in mind. Kennedy even ordered that plans to occupy the Lao side of the Mekong River be "undertaken unilaterally by the United States without discussion at this time with the Thais or the Lao."[29] Washington was not anxious for such involvement and could hardly afford to go into Laos with guns blazing, but Kennedy could not afford to let the Thais be beaten if they did.

---

27 National Security Action Memorandum (hereafter NSAM), #157, "Presidential Meeting on Laos, May 24, 1962" (National Security Adviser McGeorge Bundy), May 29, 1962, as quoted in Senator Mike Gravel, ed., *The Pentagon Papers*, vol. 3 (Boston, 1971), doc. #114, 672–3. See also Roger Hilsman, *To Move a Nation: The Politics of Foreign Policy in the Administration of John F. Kennedy* (New York, 1967), 163–5.

28 See top secret report 18–62, "Southeast Asia Situation Report," Director of Operations, Joint Chiefs of Staff, May 16, 1962, file Top Secrets, FE 5000–5599, Bureau of Far Eastern Affairs, Assistant Secretary of State for Far East Asia, Top Secret Files of the Regional Planning Adviser 1955–1963, box 1, RG 59, USNA.

29 NSAM 157, "Presidential Meeting on Laos, May 24, 1962," May 29, 1962, NNSDD INDEX Record Number 241: Presidential Directives on National Security from Truman to Clinton, the National Security Archive, the George Washington University Library. See also top secret message, "Coordinated Military Planning Southeast Asia," chairman of the Joint Chiefs of Staff 4790 Washington to Commander in Chief, Pacific (CINCPAC) and Commander in Chief, U.S. MAAG Thailand, May 25, 1962, file Top Secrets, FE-5600–5699, Top Secret files of the Regional Planning Adviser 1955–1963, box 1, Bureau of Far Eastern Affairs, Assistant Secretary of State for Far East Asia, RG 59, USNA.

Most observers in Washington and Bangkok expected the American troops in Thailand to remain for quite some time, maybe even indefinitely. The notion to maintain U.S. forces in Thailand on a permanent basis received serious consideration in Washington.[30] However, after signing a final declaration on Laos in Geneva on July 28, 1962, Kennedy made the decision to withdraw U.S. forces from Thailand. Wary of extended military commitments, and no doubt relieved by the settlement at Geneva, Kennedy quickly set about removing the task force. The Thai government was very upset. After meetings with Sarit and his closest staff, U.S. Ambassador Kenneth Young reported that the "tone, attitude, and expression" of the Thais "was one of concern, reproachfulness, disappointment, defiance, and what I can only describe as peevishness personally taken out on me sarcastically and bitterly." Nonetheless, the withdrawal began immediately, and by the end of September 1962 most troops had been shipped out of Thailand. Kennedy apologized personally to the Thais, reassuring them that congressional pressure in the United States was the main reason for the quick departure. But both Sarit and Thanat Khoman remained highly critical of the decision and increased their criticisms of American foreign policy in Asia. Young reported that Sarit's bitterness reflected "some of that psychological defeatism affecting many Southeast Asians which stems from fear of Chinese take-over and American disengagement."[31]

Thai confidence in Washington reached a low ebb in the aftermath of the Geneva settlement and the abrupt withdrawal of U.S. troops. The situation in Laos looked bleak, with communist advances against not only Phoumi's men but also neutralists. In late September, State Department intelligence estimated that between 7,000 and 9,000 Vietminh combat forces remained in Laos, notwithstanding denials from Hanoi. The Kennedy administration anticipated that Hanoi's strategy was to gradually and secretly consolidate its control of Laotian provinces adjacent to the Vietnamese border. Washington also knew that Laos was being used as a conduit by North Vietnam in infiltrating the South along the infamous "Ho Chi Minh Trail." The Kennedy administration thus continued to reevaluate its position on U.S. troops in Thailand. A strong U.S. military presence in Thailand would

---

30 See messages, Department of the Army 915036 DTG 02190Z, Commander in Chief, U.S. MAAG Thailand to Secretary of Defense, June 2, 1962, folder 2, Roger Hilsman papers, box 2, JFKL; and Navy Department P032205Z, Admiral Harry Felt at CINCPAC to Secretary of Defense, June 5, 1962, in ibid. See also top secret National Intelligence Estimate 58-5-62, Director of Central Intelligence, May 23, 1962, file Laos General 6/1/62 to 6/5/62, #5d, National Security Country File Laos, box 131, JFKL.
31 Cable, Bangkok 167 to State, July 28, 1962, file 792.00/7–162, Central Decimal File Thailand 1960–63, box 2137, RG 59, USNA.

reassure Bangkok of Kennedy's resolve to oppose communist expansion in the region and send a strong message to Hanoi and Beijing. So, just as the troops sent during the crisis in May left Thailand, the Kennedy administration began to explore avenues to send them back in. Kennedy saw this as a necessary step not so much to save Laos or even to protect Thailand, but rather to prepare for an expanded military involvement in South Vietnam.[32]

U.S. military operations in Thailand during the 1962 deployment laid much of the groundwork for American and Thai involvement in Vietnam. The Marine task force in Thailand was directed by Operations Plan (OPLAN) 32–59, which stipulated that the primary purpose was defensive: to hold the border, maintain a cease-fire, and integrate Thai and American forces. Nevertheless, it was clear that Washington had other objectives: Developing better counterinsurgency operations in Northeast Thailand was a priority of OPLAN 32–59, but not only for defensive purposes. Along with the American Marines came additional special forces trainers who quickly went to work developing Thai units capable of extended guerilla action in Laos. American technicians and engineers also arrived, tasked with bringing Thai air bases to full military capacity in the event that large-scale offensive operations were required against either Laos or North Vietnam.[33] The upgrading of air bases and landing strips throughout Thailand was in fact the real success of the deployment. Korat quickly became an important nerve center and "rumble seat" for secret air strikes against Laos and North Vietnam. Although the Thais were very sensitive about having such missions originate there, they did not object to the base's use for logistical support. Nor did they refuse to participate in not-so-secret joint training programs in South Vietnam. Thai-based aircraft regularly flew reconnaissance missions over Laos, and air strikes against Pathet Lao and North Vietnamese positions near the Cambodian border were also orchestrated in Thailand. Thai units even engaged the Pathet Lao near Muong Soui, Laos, in what the U.S. Embassy in Bangkok referred to as "covert harassment."[34]

32 Memorandum, "Laos: The Troop Withdrawal Question," Roger Hilsman to Averell Harriman, Sept. 24, 1962, folder 9, Roger Hilsman papers, box 2, JFKL. See also memo, "U.S. Troops in Thailand," Hilsman to Harriman, July 26, 1962, folder 14 in ibid.

33 Top secret message, CINCPAC P310001Z to Joint Chiefs of Staff Washington, May 26, 1962, file Top Secrets FE 5600–5699, Bureau of Far Eastern Affairs, Assistant Secretary of State for Far East Asia, Top Secret Files of the Regional Planning Adviser, box 1, RG 59, USNA.

34 Report, "Southeast Asia Situation Report," Joint Chiefs of Staff Director of Operations 23–63, June 6, 1962, file Top Secrets, FE 5600–5699, Bureau of Far Eastern Affairs, Assistant Secretary of State for Far East Asia, Top Secret Files of the Regional Planning Adviser, box 1, RG 59, USNA.

Early in 1964, the new U.S. ambassador to Thailand, Graham Martin, was directed to approach the Thais about expanding the U.S. Air Force F-100 detachment near Korat and to gauge their reaction to a permanent stationing of American ground troops near the Laotian border. Contingency plans attached to so-called Project 22 were drawn up in 1965, anticipating joint U.S.-Thai occupation of key spots along the Mekong River and the seizure of cities, airfields, and bridgeheads in Laos. Thai army units were assigned to "Operation Triangle," a top secret plan involving Thai participation in American covert activities,[35] and it was revealed during 1969 Senate hearings on U.S. military activities in Indochina that Thais, dressed as Lao and Meo tribesmen, made up a good portion of *l'armee clandestine* operating throughout Laos.[36]

In March 1964, the new Thai prime minister, Thanom Kitakachorn, permitted the United States to bomb Vietcong sanctuaries and supply routes in Laos from Thai bases, and even discussed the possibility of supporting systematic American air strikes against North Vietnam.[37] Thanom worked carefully to secure political support for an expanded American military presence in Thailand, which he assumed would follow from the air strikes. Most significantly, shortly after the Gulf of Tonkin incident in August, Thanom lifted all restrictions on U.S. combat sorties originating in Thailand. This crucial decision reversed Bangkok's long-standing insistence that it be informed of every mission, and it reflected Thanom's commitment to the United States and gave Washington exactly the sort of leeway it needed to expand both covert and overt operations against North Vietnam and in Laos.

Both the official and popular reactions in Thailand to Washington's "retaliatory" bombing of North Vietnam after the Gulf of Tonkin incident were overwhelmingly favorable. In fact, most Thais felt that the United States had finally seen the light about communism in Southeast Asia and was going to take forceful action. Although there was some concern about Beijing's

35 Cable, Bangkok 157 to State/Joint Chiefs of Staff/Defense, Aug. 7, 1964, file Thailand vol. 2, 8/64 to 3/65, NSF, CFT, #13, box 282, LBJL.

36 "United States Security Agreements Abroad: Kingdom of Thailand," Hearings before the Subcommittee on United States Security Agreements and Commitments Abroad of the Committee on Foreign Relations, United States Senate, 91st Congress, 1st sess., pt. 3, Nov. 10–14, 17, 1969, microform 1970–9912, cards 1–2, 620–2, Robarts Library, University of Toronto. In February 1968, the U.S. Embassy reported on intelligence leaks in the Northeast that confirmed Thai Special Forces had massacred seventy-two Meo villagers at Chong Pai village on October 16, 1967. No formal investigation was ever made, and Bangkok dismissed the episode as communist propaganda.

37 Memorandum, McGeorge Bundy to LBJ, "Basic Recommendation and Projected Course of Action on Southeast Asia," May 25, 1964, file Luncheons with the President vol. 1, McGeorge Bundy Files, boxes 18–19, LBJL.

response and the chance of a wider war in the region, most Thai news-papers welcomed the demonstration of American military power. Many Thais welcomed an expanded American military role in Vietnam and were relieved that Washington was finally acting in earnest against the spread of communism. Their belief was that sooner or later military action was nec-essary, and they were glad it was on Vietnamese soil rather than Thai.[38] However, in solidly tying itself to the United States and to the anticommu-nist struggle in Vietnam, Thailand risked a great deal. Unless the Americans were totally successful in defending South Vietnam, Thailand could find itself in a very delicate position. The Thais believed that an American with-drawal, or even a neutralist settlement in South Vietnam, would likely re-sult in an eventual victory for the communists. Such an outcome would inevitably result in the fall of Laos and Cambodia to communism, and per-haps Burma as well, leaving Thailand completely isolated. Despite all the money and aid the United States could lavish on Thailand, the Americans might one day go home, leaving it surrounded by potentially hostile neigh-bors.[39] Consequently, being inconspicuous in its support of the United States became an obsession in Bangkok that frequently took on comic proportions.

Despite vigorous denials by Martin and the Thai government, it was common knowledge that U.S. planes based in Thailand were being used against North Vietnam. Martin characterized Thailand's and his own ef-forts to conceal the fact as "a useful facade, but an absolutely necessary concession to Thai sovereignty."[40] The American public affairs officer in Bangkok, John R. O'Brien, described Thai efforts to limit press coverage of events surrounding the air bases to be "as elaborate as the Japanese tea ceremony."[41] Thailand's connection to the war in Vietnam definitely hinged on the American air campaign. At the beginning of 1966, there were over 200 American combat aircraft based on Thai soil, with a complement of over 9,000 U.S. Air Force personnel. By the end of the year, there were over 400 planes and nearly 25,000 men. The capstone of this rapid buildup was the construction of the supposedly secret B-52 air base at Utapao, near Sattahip, south of Bangkok. Completed in the spring of 1966, it was the sixth base built by the U.S. military in Thailand since 1960 and it was easily

38 CIA Special National Intelligence Estimate, "Communist Reactions to U.S. Actions Taken with Regard to Laos," June 18, 1963, file Laos General 6/16/63 to 6/30/63, National Security Files, Country Files Laos, box 132, JFKL.
39 Thanat Khoman, "Which Road for Southeast Asia?" *Foreign Affairs* 42, no. 4 (July 1964): 663.
40 Randolph, *United States and Thailand*, 77.
41 Oral history interview, John R. O'Brien with Hans Tuch, February 1988, diskette 9, Georgetown University Association of Diplomatic Studies Oral History Program.

the most important and expensive. Construction of the base cost nearly $40 million and required the labor of 25,000 American servicemen and 2,000 Thais. Utapao boasted its own self-sustaining community, complete with nightclubs staffed by local Thais. A cluster of shantytowns sprouted up around the base as it was being built, offering servicemen everything from souvenirs to prostitutes.[42] For Washington, the deployment of B-52s to Thailand meant a savings of $8,000 per round trip for each plane as compared to the costs for a round trip from Guam, nearly 2,000 miles away. Utapao quickly became the workhorse of U.S. air bases in Thailand, responsible for the majority of the 1,500 weekly bombing runs flown between December 1965 and November 1968. Considering that Thai-based U.S. aircraft accounted for nearly 80 percent of all ordnance dropped on North Vietnam and Laos during this period, Utapao's military importance is very clear.[43]

The lack of secrecy surrounding Utapao's role in the American war in Vietnam marked a decisive turning point for Thanom's government. Bangkok did little to deny the existence of the base, effectively making Utapao an open symbol of Thailand's commitment. This was well received by the Johnson administration, which wanted to avoid the perception that this was an exclusively American war by engaging as "many flags" in Vietnam as possible. Thanom continued his strong show of support for the United States when in early 1966 he made clear that Thailand would be willing to send its own ground troops into South Vietnam. Following a visit to Thailand by President Lyndon Johnson in October 1966, the Thanom government announced it would contribute 1,000 "volunteer" troops for service in Vietnam. So popular was the idea with the Thai public that by the end of January 1967 nearly 5,000 men in Bangkok alone volunteered for the contingent.[44]

In October 1967, after months of negotiations with American representatives, the Thai government pledged an additional 10,000 men. Washington agreed to cover all of the contingent's training, supply all the military equipment, issue overseas salary allowances, and provide training for troops on rotation. Thailand also received its long-desired Hawk missile antiaircraft battery and training for military personnel to man it. More importantly, Washington agreed to increase MAP funding for 1968 from $60 million to $75 million and to maintain it for 1969. The first Thai troops, nicknamed the "Queen's Cobras," arrived in South Vietnam in September 1967 and

42 Surachart Bamrungsuk, *United States and Thai Military Rule, 1947–1977* (Bangkok, 1986), 153.
43 Randolph, *The United States and Thailand*, 59.
44 Adulyasak, "The Rise of United States–Thai Relations," 201.

were assigned to the "Bearcat" region east of Saigon, between U.S. units at Bien Hoa and Long Binh.[45] Thailand had become a full participant in the Vietnam War.

Although the exact motivation behind Thailand's decision to send troops is unclear, it is likely that Bangkok saw the move at least in part as a political necessity. Denying involvement with the United States was becoming more and more unrealistic given the burgeoning American military presence. Moreover, the Thai military and in fact the entire Thai economy was dependent on the American connection. Consequently, the legitimacy and stability of Thanom's regime was directly connected to Thailand's relationship with the United States and the war in Vietnam. To maintain and possibly expand its aid programs and investment, Thailand needed to show its resolve in terms of being an American ally, especially when congressional and public attention was focused on the nature of U.S. commitments in the region. However, these were not the only considerations. The vast majority of Thais, particularly those serving in the Thanom regime, were devoted anticommunists, and not just for economically advantageous reasons. Their perception of the communist threat in Vietnam, Laos, and Cambodia unquestionably affected their readiness to expand the Thai contribution to the American war effort. They wanted to curb this threat before their own territory became a main battlefield.[46]

In this light, the contention that Thais were motivated purely by the prospect of more money is simplistic. This conclusion assumes that the Thais had no legitimate political, strategic, or ideological concerns with respect to the conflict in Vietnam, and that the Thanom regime was devoid of any thought beyond the money it could exact from Washington. This explanation ignores the artful complexity of Thai diplomacy, which for centuries had helped to secure the country's independence and which since the late 1940s had dealt effectively with the Americans to the country's benefit. Unquestionably, economic factors were part of the Thai decision-making process, just as they always were. The Thanom regime clearly anticipated that the deployment of Thai troops would produce even more military and economic largesse from Washington. But money alone was not the only factor concerning Thailand: Security and survival greatly outweighed any mercenary tendencies the Thais may have had.

---

45 Memorandum, Walt Rostow to LBJ, Oct. 6, 1967, file Vietnam 5D(3) Allies: Troop Commitments; Other Aid, 1967–69, #124, NSF, Country Files Vietnam, box 91, LBJL. For a detailed account of U.S. concessions, see Robert M. Blackburn, *Mercenaries and Lyndon Johnson's "More Flags": The Hiring of Korean, Filipino, and Thai Soldiers in the Vietnam War* (Jefferson, N.C., 1994), 110–11.
46 Randolph, *United States and Thailand*, 78–80.

Despite their closer relationship with the United States and their open involvement in the Vietnam War, many Thais had serious reservations about the expansive American presence in their country. Bowing to the pressure of conservatives, early in 1967 Thanom began a campaign to combat the ill effects of the large American presence. Efforts were made to toughen public morality laws, and Thanom publicly urged young Thais to preserve their heritage by avoiding contact with foreigners. However, little came of the campaign. Attempts at restricting contact between U.S. servicemen and Thai bar girls failed dismally, in part because Americans spent an estimated $22 million a year on "rest and relaxation" (R&R) facilities.[47] The powerful minister of the interior, Praphas Charusthian, successfully opposed Thanom's move with this in mind, noting that "if people come here to help wash the dishes and drop and break a dish, it would not be proper to ask them to pay for it."[48] Thais simply had no experience hosting foreign troops, and the inevitable clash of cultures and attitudes proved very challenging to bilateral diplomatic relations. The editor of the influential newspaper *Siam Rath* (and later Thai prime minister) Kukrit Pramoj suggested that Americans were "too base" to understand Thai reverence for their king and that they "threw money around, destroying Thai culture." The impact of American money and culture was hard to ignore, giving rise to hotels, nightclubs, massage parlors, and neon signs.[49] Bangkok was particularly changed in this regard, and in the shadow of its ancient temples emerged a "sin district" that one U.S. Embassy staffer characterized as a "pig heaven" for a young, single American with a few dollars.[50] Even the Thai military voiced its concerns about the American presence, claiming that U.S. bases with better jobs and pay drew already scarce skilled workers away from the mainstream economy. The diversion of American goods into Thai markets was another worrying aspect of the American presence, as were the inadequate housing and services available to people who flocked to the bases for jobs.

U.S.-Thai relations were also affected by considerable scrutiny by Congress. In early 1966, the relationship became a political volleyball in Washington, a means of addressing the larger issue of American policy in Vietnam. Opposition in Congress to the expansion of U.S. military operations in Southeast Asia was well known to the Johnson administration,

---

47 Adulyasak, "Rise of United States–Thai Relations," 187–91. For an interesting discussion on the "Americanization" of Thai culture, see Nitaya Kanchanawan, "Elvis, Thailand, and I," *Southern Quarterly* 18, no. 1 (fall 1979): 18–24.

48 As quoted in Adulyasak, "Rise of United States–Thai Relations," 172.

49 *New York Times*, July 9, 1966.

50 Oral history interview, Frederick Z. Brown with Charles Stuart Kennedy, Feb. 2, 1990, diskette 16, Georgetown University Association of Diplomatic Studies Oral History Program.

and much of it came from within the Democratic Party. Senator William J. Fulbright called for open hearings on American assistance to Thailand, arguing that the insurgency in the Northeast was "trumped up" by Thais as an excuse to get more money from the United States. Fulbright also questioned whether Thailand could be considered a trustworthy ally and if supporting an undemocratic military regime was consistent with American political objectives. Suggesting that Thailand was already a "U.S. colony," Fulbright accused the Johnson administration of trying to conceal the exact nature of a suspiciously close relationship.[51] Thanat Khoman blasted back to reporters that the Thais "would rather go down fighting Communism by ourselves than be a pawn for Senator Fulbright. We are not the 51st state."[52] In defense of Thailand, Dean Rusk stated emphatically that "no country has been stronger in its support for the concept of collective security, and no country has been quicker to recognize that collective security carries obligations as well as benefits."[53] Graham Martin countered Fulbright by pointing out that Thailand was the only Asian nation that acted to prevent Chinese hegemony in Southeast Asia. He also warned that "glib, over-simplified" characterizations of Thailand had the "same perverse tendency" of views that the *Vietcong* constituted "merely a genuine, indigenous revolt."[54]

Johnson's decision not to run in the 1968 election sent major shock waves through the Thai government and marked a significant turning point in the history of U.S.-Thai relations. The Thais were worried that a new administration might not keep promises made by Johnson for economic and military assistance. In fact, Prime Minister Thanom worried that Robert Kennedy would win the White House and that he would withdraw from Southeast Asia altogether.[55]

Disillusioned by Johnson's decision, the bombing halts, and talks with North Vietnam, many senior officials in the Thai government began openly to question Bangkok's ties with Washington. The key spokesperson for Thai foreign policy, Thanat, warned that an American withdrawal from Southeast

---

51 Report, Senate Foreign Relations Committee Executive Session on Thailand, Sept. 20, 1966, file Thailand vol. 4, Memos and Misc, 1/66 to 10/66, #100, NSF, CFT, box 283, LBJL.

52 *New York Times*, Sept. 24, 1966.

53 Rusk statement to press, Mar. 22, 1967, *Department of State Bulletin* 56, no. 1450 (Apr. 10, 1967): 597.

54 Cable, Bangkok 3051 to State, Sept. 8, 1966, folder: Def 15 Thai-U.S., Central Foreign Policy Files 1964–66 (Political and Defense), Thailand, box 1686, RG 59, USNA.

55 Cable, Bangkok 6308 to State, Apr. 1, 1968, file Thailand vol. 7, 8/67 to 7/68, #32, NSF, CFT, box 284, LBJL. Thai leaders followed the 1968 party nominations and the election carefully. Most favored Richard M. Nixon. He had been to Thailand and had always spoken of the Thais as being important allies. Hearing the election results in November, Thanom was pleased, and he predicted that Nixon would not abandon Asia.

Asia was analogous to the Western powers' abandonment of Czechoslovakia during the Munich crisis in 1938. As early as 1966 he anticipated U.S. disengagement from the region and tested the winds with Hanoi and Beijing by arguing that Thailand was "not necessarily anticommunist, nor for that matter anti-Chinese, anti-Russian, anti–North Korean or anti–North Vietnamese."[56] Shortly after Johnson's announcement in 1968, Thanat said that "Thailand should not be blamed if we were to seek an accommodation with Communist China." And at a Tokyo press conference in February 1969, the foreign minister stunned the audience when he announced, "[T]o show that Thailand is not anticommunist and anti-Chinese we are prepared to sit down and talk – and have meaningful discussion – with Peking to establish peaceful coexistence." Just a few days later Thanat suggested that he was willing to meet Chinese representatives at any place and time to "help draw China out of her isolation so that she could become a member of the Asian family."[57]

From statements like this it is clear that by the end of 1968 Thailand was reevaluating its relationship both with Washington and with Beijing; and it is no coincidence that this process occurred simultaneously with fundamental changes in the American prosecution of the war in Vietnam. Some observers in Washington no doubt considered the change in Thailand to be amoral, as if the Thais were classic fair-weather friends abandoning the United States during a difficult time. Many in Washington took changes in Thai attitudes to be typical "Siamese talk," appearing disillusioned only to elicit more aid.[58] Although the latter had definitely not been uncommon in U.S.-Thai relations, by the end of 1968 it was a thing of the past. Many Thais were beginning to realize that the United States was going to pull out of Southeast Asia, no matter what Americans said to the contrary. A negotiated settlement in Vietnam would only delay the inevitable, and in this respect, the Thais seemed to anticipate the end well before the Americans. Seni Pramoj, the old sage of Thai politics (and twice prime minister of Thailand), warned Thais that "we have let the U.S. forces use our country to bomb Hanoi. When the Americans go away, they won't take that little bit of history with them."[59] Accepting this fact, Thailand reverted to its ancient ways. Surviving in the post–Vietnam War era became the priority, and this meant accommodating communism.

---

56 As quoted in Likhit Dhiravegin, *Thai Politics: Selected Aspects of Development and Change* (Bangkok, 1985), 419, 546.

57 As quoted in R. K. Jain, ed., *China and Thailand, 1949–1983* (New Delhi, 1983), 155.

58 Kenneth T. Young, "Thailand's Role in Southeast Asia," *Current History* 56/330 (Feb. 1969): 90–4.

59 W. Scott Thompson, *Unequal Partners: Philippine and Thai Relations with the United States, 1965–75* (Lexington, Ky., 1975), 161.

   Although Thailand continued to play an important role in assisting U.S. policy in Indochina, by 1969 the end was definitely clear. In August of that year, President Richard M. Nixon went to Thailand to discuss the war in Vietnam. Nixon did not consider Thailand nearly as important as any of his predecessors, but he still needed Thai support for American military operations in the region. Much to Washington's surprise, the Thai government seized the occasion of Nixon's visit to launch a diplomatic first-strike. Thanom announced that Thailand would be ending its participation in clandestine operations with the United States, and he asked the president to look for ways to disengage American troops from Thailand. The communist insurgency in the Northeast was, Thanom pointed out, under control, and he warned that the large American military presence did more harm than good by encouraging Hanoi and Beijing to continue their support of local insurgents. The *Washington Post* hailed the Thai decision as a "stroke of genius," noting that Thanom's surprise announcement was a "blow to American diplomatic aplomb."[60]

   Nixon managed to negotiate an honorable and gradual withdrawal of troops from Thailand beginning in September 1969, but in early 1971 developments in Thai politics again drew attention to relations with the United States. Anti-Americanism reached a fever pitch in Thailand, particularly among increasingly aware and active youth. Public disclosure by Thanat that the Thai Foreign Ministry was conducting secret talks with Hanoi through the International Red Cross stimulated divisions within the bureaucracy and military over what course the country should take in its external relations. After a bloodless internal coup in November, the invaluable Thanat was fired and an even more authoritarian government was reconstituted by Thanom. However, the success of the Nixon administration's rapprochement with Beijing starting in 1972 and official peace talks with Hanoi the following year effectively undermined Thanom's credibility. Unwilling or unable to accommodate either development, Thanom by 1973 was in the unusual position of being more committed to a military solution in Indochina than the U.S. president. A groundswell of public support for domestic reform and foreign-policy change in Thailand culminated in the fall of 1973, when over 500,000 Thais took to the streets in protest against the Thanom regime. Clashes with police turned violent, and only after intervention by the revered King Bhumipol was a major conflict averted. The Thai military supported the king, and fearing for their personal safety, many top government officials, including Thanom

60 *Washington Post*, Aug. 17, 1969.

himself, fled the country.[61] Although military rule in Thailand was by no means ended, the events of 1973 demonstrated the desire for greater democratic reform and changes to the long relationship with the United States.[62]

Despite communist victories in Indochina, Thailand was no domino. Even with the withdrawal of U.S. military power from the region, and although surrounded by hostile neighbors, Thailand emerged as a relatively stable economic and political power in Southeast Asia by the 1980s. Without question this development owed much to the American security umbrella, but the presence of U.S. forces in Thailand throughout the 1960s and early 1970s does not provide the only explanation. Although there was an indigenous communist insurgency in the Northeast, it was never a serious threat to Thailand's stability. Thais did not experience the emotional, divisive, and convulsive nationalism of their neighbors but instead enjoyed a comparative unity, reinforced by their ancient reverence for the monarchy and the Buddhist faith. With the departure of the American military from Southeast Asia by the mid-1970s, traditional flexibility in Thai foreign policy managed to help accommodate the external communist threat while at the same time maintaining fairly solid relations with the United States.

Although they were certainly not without problems, and ultimately faded in their intensity, U.S.-Thai relations during the Vietnam War era were successful and mutually beneficial. Thailand insulated itself with American help from the turmoil that consumed Indochina, achieving considerable economic progress in the process. The United States gained an invaluable ally in Southeast Asia, without whose help the prosecution of overt and covert wars in Indochina would have been much more difficult. Although American foreign policy with respect to the latter ultimately failed, in terms of preventing the collapse of Thailand and the rest of the region under the weight of communism's expansion it was in fact a considerable success. For this, Thailand is indebted in part to its long association with the United States in the shadow of the Vietnam War. Long held to be the next domino, Thailand did not fall. The bamboo bent, but it never did break.

---

61 Thompson, *Unequal Partners*, 129–30.
62 In fact, in elections following the communist victories in Laos, Vietnam, and Cambodia, rightwing parties with close connections to the military dominated the Thai government. Thanom returned to the country in October 1976, welcomed by thousands of Thais and very much a symbol of the right's resurgence. Demonstrations by students opposing his return quickly turned bloody and led to a massive clampdown by the Thai military and police. Thousands of Thais were killed in what is easily one of Thailand's darkest moments in history. See David K. Wyatt, *Thailand: A Short History* (New Haven, Conn., 1982), 300–3. For an interesting account of the dynamics surrounding both the 1973 and 1976 crises, see Ross Prizia, *Thailand in Transition: The Role of Oppositional Forces* (Honolulu, 1985).

10

The Strategic Concerns of a Regional Power

Australia's Involvement in the Vietnam War

PETER EDWARDS

The overwhelming proportion of what has been written and recorded about the Vietnam War has been about America's war in Vietnam. Given the size, the significance, and the cost of America's commitment, this is understandable enough, but it has two unfortunate outcomes concerning the way in which Australia's involvement in the war is remembered. First, it means that it is all too easy for Americans and other non–Australians to read any number of books about the war and, unless one's eye is caught by a minor footnote, to remain quite unaware that Australia was even involved in the war. The commitment is remembered in diplomatic and defense circles in Washington – not an unimportant point, given Australia's motives for participation – but otherwise probably few Americans are conscious that Australians fought alongside Americans in this as in every other major war this century. And few from other countries are aware that the United States had a willing ally in Australia during this most controversial of conflicts.

The second misperception concerns Australians themselves. Most Australians are generally aware that their country was involved in the war, but they are in danger of losing sight of the distinctiveness of that experience, for many Australians now receive most of their images of the war from American sources. In this, perhaps the only war of which the history has been written predominantly by the losers, there has been a flood of material relating and interpreting the American experience, ranging from works of meticulous scholarship to Rambo movies. Amid the plethora of history books, memoirs, novels, television series, documentaries, Hollywood movies, and comics, Australians are coming to assume that Australia's Vietnam story was essentially identical to that of the United States, albeit a little less severe and more slowly paced.

This chapter seeks to confront these two misperceptions.[1] First, Australia was there. Australia's commitment was more limited and less costly than the United States', even in proportion to population, but it was not insignificant. From a total population of about 12 million, a little over 50,000 Australians served in the war, with a maximum commitment of about 8,000 at the peak and with a death toll of just over 500. This made it Australia's third largest overseas military commitment, bigger than the Korean War and smaller only than the two world wars. Australia was the only "third country" – that is, the only ally of the Republic of Vietnam other than the United States – to have elements of its army, navy, and air force committed to Vietnam. Australia and New Zealand paid for their military commitments from their own resources, unlike the Asian allies – the Republic of Korea, the Philippines, and Thailand – which were effectively subsidized by the United States. The political controversies, the social dissent and division, and the diplomatic and defense ramifications of Australia's involvement were all pronounced.

And, contrary to the second false impression, Australia's Vietnam story was not the same as that of the United States. In the broader picture, there were certainly many parallels: the initial beliefs about the "domino theory" and the threat from international communism; the widespread confidence that victory, although not quick, was inevitable; the increasing frustration as the hopes of clear victory proved illusory; the political and moral criticism of both the aims of the war and the way in which it was fought; the rise of two distinct streams of dissent, the moderates who wanted to end the war and the radicals who wanted fundamental changes to Western society; the impact of the communist victory in 1975; the postwar prominence given to the disaffected veterans who complained of the alleged effects of Agent Orange. Nevertheless, there were important, if often subtle, differences between the Australian and American experiences. This chapter is concerned only with the differences in strategic policies and attitudes. It considers how Australia's strategic concerns – before, during, and after the war – differed from those of

---

1 This chapter is a distillation of some of the major themes in two volumes of *The Official History of Australia's Involvement in Southeast Asian Conflicts, 1948–75*, an eight-volume series of which I am the general editor. The two volumes are Peter Edwards, with Gregory Pemberton, *Crises and Commitments: The Strategy and Diplomacy of Australia's Involvement in Southeast Asian Conflicts, 1948–65* (Sydney, 1992); and Peter Edwards, *A Nation at War: Australian Politics, Society and Diplomacy During the Vietnam War, 1965–75* (Sydney, 1997). Both these volumes, in the tradition of Australian official war histories, were written with unrestricted access to Australian government records and with freedom from official or political censorship. For a series of essays on Australian involvement aimed at an American readership, see Jeff Doyle and Jeffrey Grey, eds., *Australia R&R: Representations and Reinterpretations of Australia's War in Vietnam*, a special issue of *Vietnam Generation* 3, no. 2 (1991), including the present writer's "The Australian Government and Involvement in the Vietnam War," 16–25.

the United States. While respecting the reluctance of most New Zealanders to have an Australian act as their spokesman, this chapter will, at the editors' request, make some comments on how New Zealand's strategic approach differed from both Australia's and that of the United States.

The differences in strategic perspectives reflected the differences between a superpower with global interests and responsibilities and a small to medium power with mainly regional interests. The American commitment to Indochina in the 1950s and 1960s was based on three fundamental concerns: the desire to see France restored as a strong democratic and capitalist country in a noncommunist Western Europe; a similar concern to ensure that Japan became an economically and politically strong Asian ally, rather than a Cold War associate of China; and a determination to maintain the faith of American allies around the world in the assurances of Washington's support. These were understandable goals for a global superpower, but the concerns of a middle power, situated uncomfortably close to turmoil-ridden Southeast Asia, were necessarily different. Australian policy was always focused on two elements: the fate of the band of countries to its immediate north, from the Malayan peninsula through the Indonesian archipelago to the island of New Guinea; and the state of Australia's own relations with its principal allies, the United Kingdom and the United States, which its longest-serving prime minister, Robert Menzies, liked to call Australia's "great and powerful friends."

Australia's commitments in Southeast Asia were based on two arguments. First, Canberra, like Washington, believed that international communism, thwarted in Europe by the creation and operations of the North Atlantic Treaty Organization, was concentrating its efforts in Asia, especially Southeast Asia. Policymakers in both capitals accepted, in varying degrees, the validity of the domino theory, which postulated that a communist victory in any part of postcolonial Southeast Asia would imperil the noncommunist or anticommunist governments, mostly newly established and often fragile, in the rest of the region. Second, Australians also accepted that they had to pay a premium for their insurance policy. In other words, if the United States was the ultimate guarantor of Australian security, as was implied by the terms of the Australia–New Zealand–United States (ANZUS) Treaty of 1951, then Australia would have to show that it was willing to bear its fair share of the political and military cost of the defense burden of the Western alliance.

Against this background, Australia in the 1950s and 1960s responded to the perceived threat of communism in Asia and the need to ensure the security of a large and sparsely populated continent by developing a policy known as "forward defense." Essentially, this meant organizing Australian forces and Australian diplomacy to work in Southeast Asia in close collaboration with great-power allies – principally Britain and the United States, but also France in the mid-1950s. Australia's contribution, apart from unreserved support in public diplomacy for Western policies in the region, was confined to small forces, of more political than military significance. Despite the inevitable criticism of being an accomplice to neocolonialism, Australia was quite happy to work in a subordinate position to a powerful ally that was external to the region and that was carrying the greater burden. In 1959, the government's defense advisers, including the service chiefs, recommended that Australian forces should be designed "to act independently of Allies." The Cabinet explicitly overruled this goal, even as a long-term aim, insisting that Australian forces should be designed to work closely with allies in limited wars in Southeast Asia.[2] Australia's overriding concern was to ensure that Britain and America remained committed and militarily involved in the defense of Southeast Asia.

For about two decades after 1945, the forward defense policy worked remarkably well. Its value was amply demonstrated, in Australian eyes, by the outcome of two conflicts whose importance as precursors to the Vietnam War is often overlooked.[3] In the first of these, generally known as the Malayan Emergency, Australia sent small forces to support British and other Commonwealth forces to defeat a communist-led insurgency. Although the cost of Australia's involvement was fairly small, the Emergency lasted twelve years, from 1948 to 1960, and the commitment of troops in 1955 became a major issue at a time of upheaval in Australian domestic politics. Consequently, it was prominent in the thinking of Australian policymakers. Only two years after the end of the Emergency, Australia responded to pressure from U.S. Secretary of State Dean Rusk and sent a small team of army advisers to Vietnam, Australia's first military commitment to that country. The Cabinet minutes explicitly compared the position there to that in Malaya, where Australian troops had helped to defeat the "Communist bandits."[4] It

---

2 Cabinet submission 59, "Strategic Basis of Australian Defence Policy" (enclosing report by the Defence Committee, Jan. 1959), A. Townley (Minister for Defence), Feb. 1959, Commonwealth Record Series (hereafter CRS), A5818/2, Australian Archives (hereafter AA); Cabinet decision 113, Mar. 23, 1959, CRS A4943, AA; Cabinet decision 522, Nov. 9, 1959, CRS A4943, AA; see Edwards, *Crises and Commitments*, 205–6.

3 The diplomatic background to Australian involvement in these two conflicts is related in Edwards, *Crises and Commitments*. Australia's military involvement is recorded in Peter Dennis and Jeffrey Grey, *Emergency and Confrontation: Australian Military Operations in Malaya and Borneo, 1950–1966* (Sydney, 1996).

4 Cabinet decision 241, May 15, 1962, Cabinet Secretariat (hereafter CS) file C4643 part 1, CRS A4940/1, AA.

seems highly likely that when Australian Prime Minister Robert Menzies heard critics from academia, journalism, and the churches warn him against intervention in Vietnam, he disregarded their views because the same circles, often the same individuals, had made similar warnings against intervention in Malaya in the 1950s. This is not to say that the many differences between Vietnam and Malaya – ethnic, religious, political, economic, geographic, even topographical – were ignored; but there was an understandable inclination to believe that Western intervention in a former European colony in Southeast Asia, in order to ensure the victory of an anticommunist government over a communist insurgency, was not necessarily doomed to failure.

Moreover, the "forward defense" policy had achieved its goals at low cost. After the climax of the Korean War, Australia had placed a low ceiling on defense expenditure. Between the early 1950s and the early 1960s, defense spending was almost halved as a proportion of gross domestic product. Australia in this time was able to concentrate on (to use the political catchphrase of the day) "national development," building the infrastructure of a prosperous Western economy. But this low expenditure made Australia vulnerable to pressure in the 1960s, when American leaders like Rusk and President Lyndon Johnson pressed their allies for "more flags" in Vietnam, in order to show that the American commitment was part of an international crusade against communism, not an exercise in American imperialism. The premium on Australia's insurance policy was being raised.

In the 1960s, there was another factor affecting the strategic outlook of many countries in Southeast Asia, one usually overlooked in American accounts of the origins of the Vietnam War. This was another regional conflict, Indonesia's "Confrontation" of the newly formed federation of Malaysia. When the prime minister of Malaya, Tunku Abdul Rahman, first announced the aim of joining the states of Malaya with Singapore and two British territories on the island of Borneo to form a new federation of Malaysia, President Sukarno of Indonesia seemed unconcerned, but in January 1963 his government adopted a policy of *Konfrontasi* or Confrontation. The meaning of this term was left ambiguous, but it amounted to a repetition of the mixture of economic, political, diplomatic, and low-level military measures, including large quantities of bluff, by which Sukarno had recently gained control of West New Guinea (now the Indonesian province of Irian Jaya). Sukarno's opposition to Malaysia was a blend of ideology and opportunism. A radical nationalist who aspired to lead the world's "newly emerging forces" against the "neo-colonialists and imperialists," Sukarno saw the Malaysian leader as the tool of the British. His own position depended on retaining a balance between the anticommunist Indonesian army and the growing power of the Indonesian Communist Party. Opposition to Malaysia was one policy on which they agreed.[5]

Indonesia's confrontation with Malaysia, although a small-scale conflict, posed major dilemmas for Australian policy. As we have noted, Australian policy was based on close cooperation with both the United States and the United Kingdom and on persuading both to remain committed to involvement in Southeast Asia. The two major powers, however, had markedly different priorities. For Britain, Indonesian ambitions were the major concern. The Foreign Office spoke of Sukarno as another Hitler, asserting that his territorial ambitions extended to include the Malayan peninsula, the Philippines, all of New Guinea, and perhaps other parts of Melanesia. At the same time, the British government was reluctant to become deeply involved in the worsening crisis in South Vietnam. This reluctance was even more pronounced after a Labour Government came to office in 1964.

The Americans, by contrast, were becoming more deeply enmeshed in Vietnam and were taking the view that this was the crucial theater for the future of much of Southeast and East Asia. At the same time, they regarded Confrontation as a minor problem. They supported the creation of Malaysia, but did not want to drive Sukarno into the communist camp. They urged Australia and the other Commonwealth countries to use the minimum force to ensure that Sukarno's aims were thwarted. When the Australians asked whether they could expect American support under the ANZUS Treaty if they became involved in a serious conflict with Indonesia, the Americans said that this depended on two considerations. First, they had to show restraint in their handling of Sukarno; and second, they had to support the Americans elsewhere in Southeast Asia, especially in Vietnam.[6] Because of Confrontation, Australia would have to pay a premium for its ANZUS insurance policy, not just against some hypothetical future threat, but against an existing danger.

Australia thus found that it was caught between its two great power allies in two regional conflicts. Each major power was urging Australia to give more support in one conflict, while limiting its involvement in the other. To try to resolve these issues, Australia sought "quadripartite talks" between Britain, the United States, Australia, and New Zealand, but the Americans said that they did not want to give the impression that a "white men's club" was trying to resolve Asia's problems. The American stance also reflected

5 On the history of Confrontation, see J. A. C. Mackie, *Konfrontasi: The Indonesia-Malaysia Dispute, 1963–1966* (Kuala Lumpur, 1974).

6 See especially the "Report of Meeting [of the Australian Cabinet] with Mr. Averell Harriman [U.S. undersecretary of state for political affairs] 7th June, 1963," in CS file C3812, CRS A4940/1, AA.

Washington's long-standing reluctance to share information about American military plans and policies, an attitude which had frustrated Australian leaders ever since the ANZUS Treaty had been signed.

Two undercurrents in Australian-American relations concerning Southeast Asia should be noted at this point. The first was the fear that the United States might withdraw its military forces from Southeast Asia, just as Australia's other great power ally, Britain, was to do in the late 1960s. It might seem strange today, given what we know of the policies of John Kennedy and Lyndon Johnson, but Australians in the early 1960s harbored suspicions that the Democrats would prove "softer" on communism in Southeast Asia than their robust Republican predecessors. In a further irony, it would be a Republican president, Richard Nixon, who would re-ignite these fears after his declaration of what became "the Guam doctrine" or "the Nixon Doctrine" in 1969. Irrespective of who was in the White House, Australian policy was always aimed at strengthening American determination to stay the course in Vietnam and to remain militarily committed to the defense of Southeast Asia.

At the same time, there was a second fear in Australian minds, mostly unspoken and only hinted at even in highly classified documents. This was the possibility that the American political and military leadership could not necessarily be trusted to run a limited war without resorting to the use of its massive technological advantages, which might lead to nuclear war. This might be called the MacArthur factor, for it probably owed much to memories of Douglas MacArthur's advance to the Yalu during the Korean War. For obvious reasons, this fear was seldom uttered aloud, but it was a constant concern, especially during the crises in Laos between 1960 and 1962.[7] It seems to have been part of the reason why the Australian government clung so long to the concept that any intervention in Southeast Asia should be under the aegis of the Southeast Asia Treaty Organization (SEATO) despite that body's manifest weaknesses. Australians thought that an American commander might be better restrained by a multilateral command, such as SEATO, than by a solely American command in Washington.

In the face of these dilemmas, the Australian government tried to please both of its great-power allies. To meet British requests, it sent forces to Indonesia and allowed them to be involved in highly sensitive cross-border operations; but at the same time, in response to American pressure, it kept these forces limited and imposed as much restraint as possible on British tactics. To Vietnam the Australians at first sent only the minimum number

7 See Edwards, *Crises and Commitments*, chap. 12.

of forces that would retain American goodwill. In 1962, as we have seen, Australia committed a small team of army advisers to Vietnam, as well as a squadron of Sabre jet fighters to be stationed in Thailand. The army advisers were supposed not to become involved in combat operations, while the Sabre jets were confined to Thai air space, not operating over Laos or Vietnam. In 1963, Australia rejected American pressure to send transport aircraft and pilots from the Royal Australian Air Force to Vietnam. In 1964, however, the Americans raised the pressure for "more flags" in Vietnam. The Australian embassy in Washington urged a positive response, particularly in order to improve Australia's prospects of American support in the Indonesian-Malaysian Confrontation.[8] The Australian government responded by nearly trebling the size of the team of army advisers, by publicly acknowledging that these advisers would inevitably be involved in combat, and by sending a flight of transport aircraft from the Royal Australian Air Force (soon to become affectionately known as Wallaby Airlines).

The period between August 1964 and February 1965 was the most critical period of confrontation and culminated in the commitment by Australia in January–February 1965 of a battalion of infantry and other combat forces to the border operations on the island of Borneo. This and other actions by Malaysia's allies seemed to have a decisive effect, for from this time on the Commonwealth commanders were confident that they had the situation under control. At the same time, the international focus was rapidly passing to Vietnam, and the Australians were becoming increasingly sympathetic to the American view that this was the critical theater for the future of Southeast Asia. In April 1965, following a number of military and political discussions with the Americans, including military staff talks in Honolulu, the Australian government took what is generally regarded as the crucial step in the incremental involvement in the war by committing a battalion of infantry to Vietnam.

The discussions that led to this commitment began when an assistant secretary of state briefed both the Australian and New Zealand ambassadors in Washington on December 4, 1964.[9] The Americans tended to deal jointly with their two ANZUS partners, but it soon became apparent that the New Zealand and Australian attitudes toward commitment in Vietnam were significantly different. In both Canberra and Wellington, policymakers displayed attitudes to commitment ranging from hawkish to dovish, but the

---

8 Cablegram 1341, Alan Renouf, charge d'affaires, Australian Embassy, Washington, to Department of External Affairs (hereafter DEA), May 11, 1964, DEA file 696/8/4 part 4, CRS A1838, AA.

9 Cablegram 3365, Keith Waller, Australian Ambassador, Washington, to John Gorton, acting minister for external affairs, Dec. 4, 1964, DEA file 696/8/4 part 6, AA.

balance in the two capitals was not the same. No one was more hawkish than Australia's most senior serviceman, Air Chief Marshal Sir Frederick Scherger, who represented Australia at the staff talks in Honolulu. To the amazement of the New Zealanders, Scherger seemed even more anxious than the Americans to see Australian troops committed to Vietnam and went far beyond the terms of his cautious official brief in the discussions. The New Zealanders suspected that Scherger's robust stance was probably related to his close relationship with the Australian prime minister, Sir Robert Menzies.

For their own part, the New Zealanders took their cue from their prime minister, Keith Holyoake, who (in the words of a leading New Zealand historian) was "almost viscerally cautious about embroilment in the Vietnam War."[10] His reluctance apparently stemmed from his awareness that New Zealand had meager military resources, which were already heavily involved in supporting Malaysia against Indonesia's Confrontation. Holyoake and his colleagues were acutely aware that political instability in Saigon prejudiced the success of Western intervention and that any commitment would provoke political controversy at home. They argued these views at length, but eventually decided that their overriding priority was to maintain the American alliance and that the relative enthusiasm displayed by the Australians restricted their freedom of maneuver. As one senior official put it: "We can't afford to be left too far behind Australia and we can't afford not to support the Americans – though I have the gravest doubts about their coming out of this with any degree of success."[11] Nearly a month after Australia had committed its first battalion of about 800 troops, New Zealand announced the commitment of an artillery battalion of about 120 men, who would fight alongside the Australians. Later in the war, New Zealand committed rifle companies of infantry, who were integrated into the Australian battalions.

Although these forces were minuscule compared with those about to be committed by the United States, the two Tasman countries had thus clearly identified themselves in Vietnam as military supporters of their great ally. For the next three years they were under continuing pressure to increase their forces. In early 1966, Australia replaced its initial battalion with a two-battalion task force, enabling it to operate with greater independence

---

10 Roberto Rabel, " 'We Cannot Afford to Be Left too Far Behind Australia': New Zealand's Entry into the Vietnam War in May 1965," *Journal of the Australian War Memorial* no. 32 (Mar. 1999): www.awm.gov.au/journal/j32/rabel.htm. See also Robert Rabel, " 'The Dovish Hawk': Keith Holyoake and the Vietnam War," in Margaret Clark, ed., *Sir Keith Holyoake: Towards a Political Biography* (Palmerston North, 1997), 173–93.

11 Quoted in Rabel, "We Cannot Afford," para. 39.

from the American command. The government also announced that, to maintain the commitment at this level, the task force would include "national servicemen" from the selective system of compulsory military service introduced the previous year. This linked the two critical issues, Vietnam and conscription, on which the protest movement of the late 1960s and early 1970s would be based. Unlike the American "draft," the Australian system of conscription was based on a birthday ballot of twenty-year-old males at a time when the voting age was twenty-one. The leader of the opposition in the Australian Parliament, Arthur Calwell, denounced the system as the "lottery of death"; henceforth opposition to the principles and the operation of the system did much to fuel the growth of the protest movement. New Zealand did not introduce any form of conscription, and accordingly the political controversies over the war were less strident.

By a bitter irony, a major part of the strategic rationale for Australia's involvement in Vietnam evaporated just as that involvement took its lasting and controversial shape. The still clouded events in Jakarta on the night of September 30–October 1, 1965, began the shift of power from President Sukarno to a hitherto little-known general named Suharto. Although accompanied by the massacre of hundreds of thousands of real or supposed communists, the subsequent political transition was carried out slowly and subtly. Not until well into 1966 was it clear that Suharto was in effective control. In August 1966, Confrontation was officially declared to be over, but for some time afterward there were widespread fears that it might be reignited. Only in the latter months of 1966 could policymakers in Australia and elsewhere in the region be confident that Confrontation could now be excluded from their strategic calculations.

By this time Australia's commitment to Vietnam, which had initially owed much to the fear that Confrontation might escalate, had acquired a momentum of its own. Prime Minister Harold Holt, who succeeded Menzies in January 1966, was happy to identify himself with the commitment to an extent that other senior policymakers considered naive. Holt saw the Vietnam commitment not just as a grim necessity of international politics or as a costly premium to be paid on the insurance policy for Australia's security, but as part of a process by which Australia would help the United States to create a stable, prosperous, noncommunist Southeast Asia, which would be in Australia's as well as America's long-term political and economic interests. On the basis of this shared vision of Asia's future, he established a personal and political rapport with the increasingly embattled President Johnson. In June 1966, amid a warm welcome to the White House, Holt adopted Johnson's 1964 campaign slogan by describing himself as "an admiring friend, a staunch friend that will be all the way with LBJ." Even his political supporters cringed at this "blank cheque," but Holt was unapologetic.[12] Johnson returned the compliment by becoming, in October, the first incumbent president of the United States to visit Australia. A little over a month later, Holt won his first general election as prime minister in a landslide after campaigning on the issues of Vietnam and conscription. Immediately after the election victory, he personally initiated another increase in the level of the commitment, not only adding to the number of soldiers in the task force but also contributing a squadron of Canberra bombers and a destroyer to serve in the Gulf of Tonkin. At this point, Australia became the only ally of the Republic of Vietnam other than the United States to send forces from all three armed services.

During 1967, however, the whole atmosphere of the commitment changed. Public opinion began to turn against the war, although a clear majority still favored the commitment. A protest movement started to take shape that included moderates who wanted an end to the commitment and radicals who sought far-reaching changes to Australian society. Divisions began to emerge in sections of the community which had hitherto been firm supporters of the commitment, including the Catholic Church, the ex-service community, and the major metropolitan newspapers. The operation of the selective service system, which compelled a small proportion of twenty-year-old males to serve in Vietnam while their peers enjoyed the benefits of a highly prosperous economy, undermined middle-class support for the government. Some Christian denominations, notably the Methodists, considered the provisions for conscientious objection inadequate. In 1967, "new left" organizations, often inspired by American groups like Students for a Democratic Society, also emerged in Australia. Radical students became prominent on several university campuses, attracting considerable publicity – mostly hostile – when they began collecting money to support the forces of the National Liberation Front in South Vietnam, the Viet Cong against whom Australian soldiers were fighting.

To add to the government's political problems, the rising costs of defense, following a decade of low expenditure, were constraining its economic and political programs. The government was also deeply affected by the announcement that Australia's other "great and powerful friend," Britain, intended to withdraw its forces from the region. In July 1967, therefore, when President Johnson sent two of his senior advisers, Clark Clifford and

---

12 The context of this statement, which has become inextricably linked with Holt in Australian public memory, is discussed in Edwards, *Nation at War*, 111–14.

General Maxwell Taylor, to seek additional support from America's regional allies, the two men met a polite but unhelpful response. Clifford explained that Australia's attitude would have a great impact in Congress, where the president would have to ask for increased taxes to meet the cost of the war. As he put it two days later in Wellington, "one additional New Zealand soldier might produce fifty Americans."[13] In Canberra as in Wellington, these arguments proved unavailing. Holt referred to the impact of defense expenditure on the balance of payments, to the cost of a recent drought, and to the burden of Australia's immigration and foreign aid programs. He argued that Australia could do more for the stability of the region by strengthening its economy than by adding to its Vietnam commitment.

While insisting that they had no more military support to offer, the Australians urged the Johnson administration to stand firm in Vietnam. By a great irony, they seem to have achieved the opposite effect. Before the end of the year Clifford had replaced Robert McNamara as Secretary of Defense. During the Johnson administration's last year, Clifford helped to turn its policy away from escalation toward withdrawal. In an important article published soon after he left office, he said that he had been much influenced by the responses of Australia, New Zealand, and other allies to his visit in 1967. If Australia could send 300,000 troops overseas in World War II but was now so reluctant to send more than 7,000 servicemen to Vietnam, perhaps the danger of a communist victory there had been exaggerated.[14] He had seen that Australia was in fact far from being "all the way with LBJ." The Holt government, renowned then and ever since as a supporter of the Vietnam commitment, had unintentionally helped to turn American policy toward withdrawal.

Little of this was known at the time. Late in 1967, the Johnson administration put immense pressure on Australian ministers and secured a further increase in the commitment. With great reluctance, the Australian government increased the task force from two to three battalions, a move supported by senior Army officers for military reasons. At the same time, it informed Washington that Australia had reached the absolute limit of its capacity.

The commitment had in fact reached its peak, although this was not announced at the time. In early February 1968, at the height of the Tet offensive, Prime Minister John Gorton announced that a ceiling had been placed on the Australian commitment. At the time, Gorton had just come

---

13 Cablegram 667, D. McNicol, Australian High Commissioner to New Zealand, to DEA, Aug. 3, 1967, CS file C1473 part 3 CRS A4940/1, AA.
14 Clark M. Clifford, "A Viet Nam Reappraisal: The Personal History of One Man's View and How It Evolved," *Foreign Affairs* 47, no. 4 (July 1969): 601–22.

to office and his views on the Vietnam commitment were a matter of intense speculation. His apparently off-the-cuff statement appeared in the papers on the same day as the famous photograph of the South Vietnamese police chief, General Nguyen Ngoc Loan, shooting a captured Viet Cong cadre.[15] The coincidence reinforced the perception that Australian policy on Vietnam had reached a turning point; henceforth, debate centered on how soon the troops would be brought home.

In 1969, the new president of the United States, Richard Nixon, adopted a policy of "Vietnamization" under which he began to withdraw American troops on the assumption that the South Vietnamese forces were now better able to fend for themselves. This marked a turning point in Australian public opinion: From this time on, opinion polls showed more support for a withdrawal of Australian forces from Vietnam than for their retention. The government faced political pressures to begin withdrawals at a rate comparable to that of the American forces, but the Nixon administration pressed Australia and the other troop-contributing countries to maintain their forces at full strength. To add to these conflicting pressures, the Australian military leaders were strongly of the view that the task force was a balanced unit, that a partial withdrawal would be undesirable, and that any withdrawal should be on the basis of "one out, all out." The Australians pressed the administration for information on its withdrawal plans, but found that few officials in Washington had any idea of the timetable that Nixon was supposed to have in mind. The Australian government was manifestly displeased with the fact that it had to react to American decisions of which it had minimal prior notice. Finally, after Nixon announced an unexpectedly large American withdrawal in April 1970, the Australian government announced that one of the Australian battalions would not be replaced when its tour of duty ended later that year, reducing the task force from three to two battalions.

In 1971, the government was planning a staged withdrawal of the remaining two battalions and other units, which would have had most of the Australian forces out of Vietnam by late 1972, when the next general election was due. This proposal was overtaken by the cataclysmic effect of the announcement in July 1971 that President Nixon had accepted an invitation to visit China. Although Nixon and his national security adviser Henry Kissinger had separated policies toward Vietnam and China, the Australian Cabinet concluded that this dramatic change in China policy presaged an acceleration of the American withdrawal from Vietnam and decided to speed up the Australian timetable. Prime Minister William McMahon announced

15 *Sydney Morning Herald*, Feb. 3, 1968.

that most combat forces would be home by Christmas, and the last two battalions of the task force were withdrawn in the latter months of 1971.

There had been some occasional tension between the Nixon administration and successive Australian prime ministers over the lack of information on American withdrawal plans, but these were kept within diplomatic channels. Far greater was the stress caused by the fact that in December 1972 Australia elected its first Labor government in twenty-three years. The so-called Christmas bombing of Hanoi and Haiphong, between December 18 and 29, thus coincided with the first days in office of a political party which had opposed the war with increasing vehemence over the previous seven years. In sharp contrast to the 1966 election, Vietnam was now an electoral liability for the outgoing conservative coalition. Immediately upon election, the new government withdrew the last Australian troops in Vietnam – the team of advisers who had been the first unit sent there – and ended the conscription policy. The resumption of American bombing of North Vietnam, and especially the media reports which greatly exaggerated its cost in civilian lives, prompted some of the newly appointed ministers to act as if they were still the leaders of the protest movement that they had been over the preceding few years. One said that the bombing was "the most brutal, indiscriminating slaughter of defenseless men, women, and children in living memory"; another condemned Nixon's and Kissinger's "mentality of thuggery."[16] The new prime minister, Gough Whitlam, was more diplomatically adept, keeping his criticisms of the bombing to a personal letter to Nixon while trying to maintain good Australian–American relations on other issues; but his efforts were totally overshadowed by the actions of his ministerial colleagues. Nixon was infuriated by the reaction from a country that had hitherto been America's staunchest ally in Indochina. He disdained to answer Whitlam's letter and grouped Australia with Sweden, a long-standing public critic of the Vietnam War, as his two least-favored Western governments.

The tensions in Australian–American relations, probably the greatest in the relationship since the signing of the ANZUS Treaty, gradually eased over the ensuing years, being overtaken by domestic crises in both countries, which saw both Nixon and Whitlam leave office in highly controversial circumstances in 1974 and 1975, respectively. Whitlam's fall was not unrelated to the end of the Vietnam War, for his unsympathetic attitude to the admission of South Vietnamese refugees and orphans at the time of the

---

16 These phrases were used by, respectively, Dr. Jim Cairns, minister for trade and industry, and Mr. Tom Uren, minister for urban and regional development; see Edwards, *Nation at War*, 323.

fall of Saigon in April 1975 was widely criticized and prompted influential calls for his removal. These calls were based as much on considerations of humanitarianism as on those of strategy.

By this time, most Australians had lost sight of the strategic circumstances that had led their country into involvement in the Vietnam War. Amid all the division and dissent provoked by Vietnam and conscription, many Australians forgot about the conflicts in Southeast Asia, especially those caused by Indonesia's Confrontation of Malaysia, which had shaped Australian policy in the mid-1960s. Vietnam had taken on such momentum as a symbol in domestic politics that a balanced assessment of its place in foreign and defense policy had become almost impossible. With the benefit of hindsight, it is possible to have some sympathy for the policymakers who faced extremely difficult decisions in 1964–5. The combination of American pressure, the threat posed by "confrontation," and the momentum developed by the "forward defense" policy made it almost inevitable that Australia would make some form of commitment to Vietnam in 1965. That is not to deny that the commitment should have been much more adeptly handled, with greater attention to an exit strategy that would have allowed for an earlier and more graceful withdrawal at a later stage. More criticism is appropriate for those who failed to see that by about 1969–70 the international position had greatly changed, undermining the strategic relevance of the Australian commitment. At this time, the Australian government missed opportunities to withdraw, at least partially, from Vietnam, before the political and social divisions in the Australian community had reached their peak.[17]

Vietnam has come to be regarded in conventional political wisdom as a major strategic error. As with the United States, there was something of a "Vietnam syndrome" in Australian foreign policy in the 1980s, which was countered by the reaction to and outcome of the Gulf War. Future Australian governments, faced with the question of whether to join an American-led coalition in an international intervention, will now have to choose between regarding Vietnam or the Gulf as the appropriate example. The evidence suggests that most governments in Canberra are likely to conclude that the benefits of collective security and of the insurance premium on the American security guarantee still outweigh the costs, but Australians will hope that any such commitments will be handled with greater skill and caution than was the case in the mid-1960s.

17 See especially the exchanges between Canberra and Washington in December 1969 discussed in Edwards, *Nation at War*, 239–40.

11

People's Warfare Versus Peaceful Coexistence

Vietnam and the Sino-Soviet Struggle for Ideological Supremacy

EVA-MARIA STOLBERG

Western historiography on the Vietnam War focuses predominately on America's involvement and its impact on U.S. foreign and domestic policy, with all these facets summarized under the apt heading of America's Vietnam trauma. Because neither the Soviet Union nor the People's Republic of China was directly involved in sending troops into battle, there is no comparable trauma in either country. Instead, Moscow and Beijing preferred to act behind the scenes and let their Vietnamese comrades play the game of trial-and-error in the Sino-Soviet dispute over the future of world communism and its attitude toward the West. Vietnam became an object of prestige in the persistent Sino-Soviet struggle for ideological supremacy.

Shortly after the breakdown of the Soviet Union, in 1992–3, the archive of the former Communist Party of the Soviet Union (CPSU) released documents on this topic, and Russian scholars also published a number of pertinent articles and books.[1] However, a diplomatic scandal provoked by the *New York Times* in late 1993 led to a restriction in access. The most revealing documents are stored behind an "iron curtain" in the Archive of the President of the Russian Federation (APRF), namely, the military and the former KGB archives. An opening of the archives in the People's Republic of China is not to be expected in the near future. From time to time the Party Committee of the Chinese Communist Party (CCP) publishes some documents on China's role in the Cold War as well as on the Korean and Vietnam conflicts, but these documents are selective.[2]

---

1 An excellent Russian study of the Soviet role in the Vietnam War is Ilya V. Gaiduk, *The Soviet Union and the Vietnam War* (Chicago, 1996).
2 The most important publication is the *Dangde wenxian* (Party Documents), a bimonthly journal published by the Zhonggong Zhongyang wenjiansuo (CCP Central Archives, Beijing); further, see the numerous memoirs by high diplomatic and military officials, such as *Zhou Enlai waijiao huodong dashiji, 1949–1975* (A Chronology of Zhou Enlai's Diplomatic Activities, 1949–1975) (Beijing, 1993),

From the founding of the People's Republic of China in 1949, the Sino-Soviet coalition had been characterized by deep divisions that also affected the ideological stance, policy, and strategy of both countries during the Cold War. National interests and security concepts were shaped by their leaders' perceptions of how their own societies could compete and survive in the global environment of the time. In this context, the Vietnam War was a decisive predictor.[3]

After the victorious revolution of the Chinese communists, who came to power in October 1949, Chinese Deputy Premier Liu Shaoqi self-confidently proclaimed one month later at the World Congress of Communist Trade Unions in Beijing that China had set a shining example for Asian peoples, who could not follow the Soviet model because of their different history, culture, and social conditions. "People's warfare" would be the best method for promoting revolution in agricultural societies.[4] Accordingly, Vietnamese General Vo Nyugen Giap appreciated the Chinese communists' victory: "This great historic event, which altered events in Asia and throughout the world, exerted a considerable influence on the war of liberation of the Vietnamese people. Vietnam no longer was in the grip of enemy encirclement, and was henceforth geographically linked to the socialist bloc."[5]

This was not new: In the 1920s, Chinese and Vietnamese communists, under the umbrella of the Communist International (Comintern), favored an alliance of oppressed peoples against Western colonialism, an aim that was strongly supported by the Soviet Union. Stalin's preference for Sun Yatsen's Guomindang (Nationalist Party or GMD) implied that not only the Chinese communists but also the Vietnamese comrades were put under the charge of the GMD united front.[6] This ended with Chiang Kai-shek's break with Moscow in 1927. Loosening its close ties to the Chinese, Vietnam turned toward Moscow, still under the strong influence of Stalin's school, which touted the slogan of "Socialism in One Country," emphasizing the national interests of the Soviet Union. Leon Trotsky, the father of permanent

or by the PLA General Staff: e.g., Wang Xiangen, *Yuanyue kangmei shilu* (A Factual Report of Assistance to Vietnam Against the United States) (Beijing, 1990).

3 For an overall view, see Odd Arne Westad, *Brothers in Arms: The Rise and Fall of the Sino-Soviet Alliance, 1945–1963* (Stanford, Calif., 1998).

4 Eva-Maria Stolberg, *Stalin und die chinesischen Kommunisten 1945–1953: Eine Studie zur Entstehungs-geschichte der soujetisch-chinesischen Allianz vor dem Hintergrund des Kalten Krieges* (Stuttgart, 1997), 249–52.

5 Vo Nguyen Giap, *The Military Art of People's War: Selected Writings of Vo Nguyen Giap*, ed. Russell Stetler (New York, 1970), 87–8.

6 For details, see the excellent study by William J. Duiker, *The Comintern and Vietnamese Communism* (Athens, Ohio, 1965). The author refers to the colonial archives in Paris.

revolution, was eliminated. The internal struggles in Moscow had a profound impact on Chinese and Vietnamese communists.[7] Although Ho Chi Minh developed his own ideas on people's warfare in the 1920s, he was strongly influenced by Mao's strategy after his arrival in Yan'an, the CCP's remote headquarters. Because of the similarities of both societies, this impact weighed heavier than that of faraway Moscow. Moreover, Stalin was generally suspicious of Asian communist leaders such as Mao Zedong and Ho Chi Minh, fearing the "Asian hybrid of Titoism."[8] It should be noted that Vietnamese and Chinese communists found in their struggle against French colonial rule and Japanese occupation, respectively, an arena for practicing people's warfare for the first time. In Maoist terms, people's warfare meant that in the first phase the revolutionary forces would leave the cities in the hands of the superior enemy forces and conduct extensive guerilla warfare in the countryside in order to disperse the enemy forces in a war of attrition. In the course of the longer second stage of strategic stalemate, the revolutionary forces would consolidate and expand their control over the countryside by means of the political mobilization of the rural population. In the third phase, the revolutionary forces would then encircle the cities step-by-step and annihilate the enemy. Mao's pamphlet, "On Protracted War" (1938), established the guiding principles, fed by the ideological pattern of imperialist aggressors such as Japan and France and later applied to the United States. Indeed, these stereotypes cannot be separated from the perception of people's warfare, which on the whole was appropriate to justify the course of the Asian communist parties in domestic and foreign affairs alike.[9]

With no understanding of the dynamics of the liberation movements in Asia, Stalin was willing to concede leadership to China. During the winter of 1949–50, when Stalin and Mao negotiated the Sino-Soviet Pact, both leaders agreed on a division of duties. Indochina and Southeast Asia lay outside Soviet interests and therefore became a "playing field" for communist China.[10] When Ho Chi Minh, during his visits to Beijing and Moscow in January–February 1950, asked for political, economic, and military support for his struggle against the French, Stalin referred him to the Chinese.

---

7 For a discussion, see ibid., 24–7; Huynh Kim Khanh, *Vietnamese Communism, 1925–1945* (Ithaca, N.Y., 1982), 173–8.

8 Quoted from Xiaoming Zhang, "Communist Powers Divided: China, the Soviet Union, and the Vietnam War," unpublished manuscript, dated May, 1, 1999, 2.

9 On Ho Chi Minh's stay in China and the influence of Maoism, see Jiang Yongjing, *Hu Jiming zai Zhongguo* [Ho Chi Minh in China] (Taipei, 1972).

10 Charles B. McLane, *Soviet Strategies in Southeast Asia* (Princeton, N.J., 1966), 261–78; Zhu Yuanshi, "Liu Shaoqi yi-jiu-si-jiu nian mimi fang Su" (Liu Shaoqi's Secret Mission to the Soviet Union in 1949), *Dangde wenxian* (Party Documents), no. 3 (1991): 76–7.

New evidence from Chinese archives shows that Stalin rejected any involvement in the situations in Indochina and Korea.[11] The Chinese attitude was quite the opposite: They were unreservedly willing to supply weapons for Vietnam's war against France, and China later sent military advisers led by General Luo Guibo, later the Chinese ambassador to Hanoi. From August 1950 onward, these advisers instructed the Vietminh in guerilla warfare at training camps in the neighboring Chinese province of Yunnan. However, the Chinese government and general staff were reluctant to send troops. As Pham Le Bong, a Vietminh deserter, reported in 1953, the Chinese promised troops only in the case of a total defeat of the Vietminh. The Chinese did not want to risk open warfare – a policy they followed in the Korean War until the fall of 1950. After the Chinese intervention in the Korean War in October, an open military engagement was not debated in government and military circles for many years. China's intervention in Korea proved to be a heavy burden for its economy and had far-reaching consequences.[12] China's support for Vietnam and North Korea arose not only from its determination to gain ideological leadership in Asia; security policy was important as well. At the beginning of the 1950s, Beijing feared a military confrontation with the "imperialist powers," particularly the United States, along its peripheries, meaning Korea, Taiwan, and Indochina. China was convinced that the conflicts in these regions were interrelated. Beijing felt itself encircled by enemies.[13] Despite its nonintervention in Indochina, it had great interest in strengthening a communist Vietnam, which would then be an ally of its "big brother," China. It is therefore plausible that there was a connection between the Vietminh offensive against the French on October 16, 1950, and the Chinese intervention in Korea one week later.

A change in China's and the Soviet Union's Indochina policies emerged after Stalin's death and the end of the Korean War. The new leadership in Moscow pushed for a peaceful solution to the conflict in Southeast Asia. Chinese Foreign Minister Zhou Enlai also sought a compromise with the Western powers in order to prevent U.S. intervention in Vietnam. China's main purpose in Geneva was to gain power, status, and international prestige

11 Zhai Qiang, "China and the Geneva Conference of 1954," *China Quarterly*, no. 129 (1992): 106; Chen Jian, "China and the First Indo-China War, 1950–1954," ibid., no. 133 (1993): 88.

12 Zhai Qiang, "China and the Geneva Conference," 109; Melvin Gurtov, *The First Vietnam Crisis: Chinese Communist Strategy and United States' Involvement, 1953–1954* (New York, 1965), 12; Peter Parker, *Vietnam – wie es wirklich war: Indochina im Kräftefeld der Grossmächte* (Bern, 1974), 41; Zhai Qiang, "Transplanting the Chinese Model: Chinese Military Advisers and the First Vietnam War, 1950–1954, *Journal of Military History* 57 (1993): 698–715.

13 Chen Jian, "China and the First Indo-China War," 90; Zhai Qiang, "China and the Geneva Conference," 104.

after the previous isolation caused by the war on the Korean peninsula. Because of its inexperience in international affairs, China closed ranks behind the Soviet Union. Communist politics in Geneva were characterized by unanimity. The Vietminh, who – after the victory at Dien Bien Phu (1954) – wanted to expel the French from Indochina and reunite Vietnam under their rule, instead had to accept the country's division, due to Soviet and Chinese pressure.[14] However, the Vietnamese communists immediately asked for China's help in consolidating their regime in the North, obviously with an eye toward later reunification by military means. In June 1955, Vietnamese Defense Minister Vo Nguyen Giap met in Beijing with his Chinese colleague Peng Dehuai, the former commander of the Chinese Volunteer Troops in Korea, and with a representative of the Soviet Military Advisory Group in China. The talks, continued in October, dealt with war planning. To a certain degree, these war preparations resembled the North Korean war plan of 1950. Like the North Koreans, the North Vietnamese pushed for military reunification. The Soviet and Chinese advisers disagreed, which presaged an ideological quarrel on the Sino-Soviet horizon. The policies of the CPSU and CCP leadership therefore deeply affected policy making in the lower ranks. Whereas the Soviet advisers favored peaceful coexistence of the two Vietnamese states and reunification by referendum, the Chinese demanded a protracted war, arguing that the increasing U.S. involvement in South Vietnam was a betrayal of the Geneva accords.[15]

The results of the Geneva conference were half-heartedly accepted by the Vietnamese communists.[16] Following Soviet Premier Nikita Khrushchev's speech on the Soviet Union's new principles of "peaceful coexistence" in international politics at the Twentieth CPSU Congress in February 1956, Soviet Deputy Premier Anastas Mikoyan visited Hanoi at the beginning of April. However, peaceful coexistence in its international scope would mean a permanent division of Vietnam for the sake of an understanding among

---

14 Xiaoming Zhang, *Communist Powers Divided*, 4. According to a report by former Vietnamese Politburo member Hoang Van Hoan, the victory of the Vietminh at Dien Bien Phu was only achieved thanks to Chinese arms supplies. *Beijing Review*, Dec. 7, 1979: 11–12; Jacques Dalloz, *The War in Indo-China, 1945–1954* (London, 1990), 179, 182.

15 Hoang Van Hoan, *Canghai yisu: Hoang Van Hoan geming huiyilu* [A Drop in the Ocean: Hoang Van Hoan's Revolutionary Reminiscences] (Beijing, 1987), 267; Buo Ming, *Zhongguo junshi guwentuan yuanyue kangfa douzheng shishi* (Historical Facts on the Role of the Chinese Military Advisory Group in the Struggle to Aid Vietnam and Resist France) (Beijing, 1990), 126–7; *Jianguo yilai Mao Zedong wengao* (Mao Zedong Manuscripts Since the Foundation of the PRC) (Beijing, 1991), 5:419; Guo Ming, *Zhongyue guanxi yanbian sishinian* (The Development of Sino-Vietnamese Relations in the Last Forty Years) (Nanning, 1991), 65; Pei Jianzhang, *Zhonghua renmin gongheguo waijiaoshi, 1949–1956* (Diplomatic History of the People's Republic of China, 1949–1956) (Beijing, 1994), 94; Stolberg, *Stalin und die chinesischen Kommunisten*, 219–20.

16 William J. Duiker, *The Communist Road to Power in Vietnam* (Boulder, Colo., 1981), 163.

the Soviet Union, the People's Republic of China, and the United States. China, in the years after Geneva, also endeavored to neutralize Cambodia and Laos to prevent them from being drawn into the Southeast Asia Treaty Organization (SEATO) by the United States. In the meantime, some of the more aggressive North Vietnamese preferred to intensify the "contradictions" within South Vietnamese society and therefore created an underground network there for promoting revolution aimed at eventual re-unification. Obviously, the North Vietnamese did not want to become a pawn in the Sino-Soviet contest for ideological hegemony; instead, they showed a dynamism of their own.[17]

During the Eighth CCP Party Congress (May 5–23, 1958), when Mao's proposals for the "Great Leap Forward" and the "People's Communes" were adopted, China's foreign policy underwent a change. Zhou Enlai's strategy born of Geneva was abandoned for the sake of a new revolutionary anti-imperialism that would challenge the status quo in Vietnam. Two years after Khrushchev's speech on destalinization, the Chinese dropped the Soviet model altogether. As early as 1959, Mao understood Khrushchev's "peaceful coexistence" as a direct adoption of John Foster Dulles's conception of "peaceful evolution" and as a corruption of Marxist internationalism.[18] The withdrawal of Soviet experts from China signaled a breach between the two communist powers in the summer of 1960, and the Vietnamese communists believed the time was ripe for armed struggle in South Vietnam. But the final decision was delayed because of the intraparty disagreement on strategy that reflected the larger Sino-Soviet dispute. Whereas Giap felt that revolution in the South would be long and arduous, Le Duan and Nguyen Chi Thanh favored a blitzkrieg strategy and agreed with the Chinese point of view. In the spring of 1961, President John F. Kennedy approved sending four hundred special military advisers to South Vietnam, and China responded. In a talk with North Vietnamese Premier Pham Van Dong in Beijing in June, Mao favored an armed struggle, whereas Zhou Enlai, still imbued with the "spirit of Geneva," preferred a more flexible course, using political and diplomatic approaches along with illegal tactics inside South Vietnam.[19] Wang Jiaxiang, the director of the CCP's Department for Foreign Affairs and later China's ambassador to Moscow, pointed out China's limited re-sources and economic problems, and interceded with Zhou Enlai to show restraint in the Vietnam conflict. Although Wang supported Khrushchev's

---

17 R. B. Smith, *An International History of the Vietnam War*, vol. 1: *Revolution versus Containment, 1955–1961* (Basingstoke, U.K., 1983), 74, 96.

18 Xiaoming, *Communist Powers Divided*, 7.

19 Guo, *Zhongyue guanxi*, 67; Zhou, *Zhou Enlai waijiao huodong dashiji, 1949–1975*, 313.

idea of peaceful coexistence, he did not want to give the impression that he was a "revisionist." Therefore, Wang declared that despite the Soviet Union's official announcements, Khrushchev and his sympathizers would in reality not mind if the Chinese adopted the idea of militant class struggle in foreign policy for the sake of "dragging [China] into the trap of war with America." Wang concluded that China's involvement would be to its enemies' advantage. In case of war, China would not be able to restore its economy, a basic requirement for being a global player. But this economically based argument did not convince Mao, whose word was dogma.[20]

During a visit to Hanoi in May 1963, Chinese President Liu Shaoqi proclaimed in an official speech that the struggle between the revisionists (Khrushchev and the Soviets) and the "true Marxist-Leninists" (the Chinese) actually centered around "whether or not the peoples of the world should carry out revolutions."[21] Ho Chi Minh sided with Le Duan and Thanh, who supported war in the South. In the following months, a campaign was waged against the revisionists, mainly Giap, who was suspected of being a "friend of Khrushchev."[22] Had Wang Jiaxiang, Zhou Enlai, and other experts in foreign policy won that debate against Mao, China would have played the role of just an observer in the Vietnam War. Mao's radical drive for a confrontation with the United States was related to his own vision of class struggle and peoples' warfare in Chinese society. The class-conscious masses should promote them both inside and outside of China. The Vietnam War served as a vehicle for China to forge a national identity. Against this background, in the summer of 1962, the Chinese were willing to deliver to the Democratic Republic of Vietnam (DRV) weapons and munitions free of charge and in such number that it would be sufficient to equip over two hundred infantry battalions. Most of the deliveries were meant to support the underground liberation movement in South Vietnam.[23] Detailed negotiations went on during the next months. Liu Shaoqi had assured Ho Chi Minh when they met earlier in the year that in case of a confrontation with the United States, North Vietnam could rely on China: "We are standing by your side, and if war breaks out, you can regard China as your rear."[24] During the same year, Beijing agreed to send a volunteer army into the DRV if the U.S. Army crossed the seventeenth parallel. A similar promise was made (and kept) by

20 See the memoirs of Wang Jiaxiang's wife: Zhu Zhongli, *Liming yu wanxia: Wang Jiaxiang wenxue zhuanji* (Dawn and Dusk: The Literary Biography of Wang Jiaxiang) (Beijing, 1986), 394–6.
21 Philip B. Davidson, *Vietnam at War: The History, 1946–1975* (London, 1988), 304.
22 Ibid., 305–6.
23 Guo, *Zhongyue guanxi*, 69; Wang, *Yuanyue kangmei shilu*, 25.
24 For details on the Sino-Vietnamese negotiations, see Qiang Zhai, "Beijing and the Vietnam Conflict, 1964–1965," *Cold War International History Project Bulletin* nos. 6–7 (winter 1995–6): 235.

the Chinese in the Korean War. In both conflicts, Mao was determined to clash with the United States.[25] Indeed, it was Mao's military support that made guerilla warfare possible in the South and led, moreover, to a dangerous escalation. From 1956 to 1963, China delivered artillery, aircraft, and warships to the DRV valued at 320 million yuan.[26]

In 1964, the United States began to shift the focus of its Vietnam policy toward Hanoi and away from the South, and declared that it would not accept the increasing infiltration of troops and weapons from the North.[27] Obviously, Mao thought the United States was a paper tiger because in June he pushed North Vietnamese General Van Tien Dung into closer cooperation with China, and at the beginning of July Zhou Enlai and a high-ranking CCP delegation, including Wu Xiuquan, Chen Yi, Yang Chengwu, and Deng Xiaoping, visited Hanoi. The envisaged cooperation took shape in August, shortly after the Gulf of Tonkin incident. China not only sent Soviet MIG-15 and MIG-17 fighter jets to Hanoi but also put its border troops in south and southwestern China on alert.[28]

The U.S. decision to escalate the Vietnam conflict in February 1965 by means of aerial bombing runs over North Vietnam (Operation Rolling Thunder) implied that if Hanoi wished to reunite Vietnam by military measures, it would have to depend completely on its Soviet and Chinese allies. The U.S. threat to escalate the bombing campaign north of the seventeenth parallel would make the deployment of Soviet advanced military technology indispensable. Khrushchev had lost interest in Indochina during the summer and fall of 1964 and wanted to keep the Soviet Union out of the Southeast Asian conflict for fear of a "second Cuban Missile Crisis." The Vietnam War also had an obvious advantage for the Soviets because it concentrated the attention of their rivals – the United States and China – in regions other than Europe and the Soviet Far East, thereby serving Soviet security interests there. However, the Soviet policy of nonintervention in Vietnam was an affront to the North Vietnamese leadership, which drifted further toward the Chinese. In December 1964, the Chinese defense minister visited Hanoi, and a treaty on military cooperation, designating a troop dispatch, was

25 Ibid. On the Korean War, see Stolberg, *Stalin und die chinesischen Kommunisten*, 234–6.

26 Li Ke and Hao Shengzheng, *Wenhua da geming zhong de renmin jiefangjun* (The PLA in the Great Cultural Revolution) (Beijing, 1989), 409.

27 George C. Herring, *America's Longest War: The United States and Vietnam, 1950–1975* (New York, 1986), 117–19.

28 Xue Mouhong and Pei Jianzhang, *Dangdai Zhongguo waijiao* (China's Contemporary Foreign Policy) (Beijing, 1990), 159; Zhou, *Zhou Enlai waijiao*, 413; Chen, "China's Involvement," 364; Qiang Zhai, "An Uneasy Relationship: China and the DRV During the Vietnam War," unpublished manuscript, 4, dated May 1, 1999.

signed.[29] The Chinese promise should be seen against the background of the Sino–Soviet dispute: Soviet reluctance was interpreted as a welcome chance to draw the North Vietnamese completely into the Chinese orbit and to alienate them from China's Soviet rival. Sino–Soviet relations were at a stand-still at that time. After Khrushchev's ouster from power, the Chinese hoped for an improvement in relations, anticipating that Leonid Brezhnev would abandon the Soviet policy of peaceful coexistence.[30] But when Marshal Rodin Malinovsky officially proclaimed that the Chinese should oust Mao just as the Soviet Union had done with Khrushchev, Beijing turned its back. Moreover, Anastas Mikoyan, a Soviet Politburo member, declared that Brezhnev would continue Khrushchev's policy of peaceful coexistence.[31]

The deployment of Chinese ground troops seemed not much more than propaganda. In view of China's socioeconomic problems, such an inter-vention would have meant open confrontation with the United States and was therefore unrealistic. Mao thus told the pro-Chinese American jour-nalist Edgar Snow in an interview that China would enter the war only if the United States attacked the mainland.[32] Mao's statement revealed that peoples' warfare was a consistent element of Maoism, yet would be used ju-diciously, depending on domestic events and national security interests. This was Beijing's view of national liberation struggles in Vietnam and elsewhere. However, this position created a dilemma: Not only the United States, but also the Soviet Union might get the impression that China was the real paper tiger, an image that did not sit well with the Chinese leadership's great concern – Mao's especially – for the international reputation of the People's Republic. Moreover, Asian countries might doubt the credibility of peoples' warfare, and Moscow could take advantage of it, which of course did not happen. Thus, the North Vietnamese came to the understandable opinion that if the United States attacked the DRV, "The Soviets [would do] nothing and the Chinese [would] only talk."[33] Furthermore, it explains the increasing skepticism toward Maoism as a model for Vietnam.

29 Ilya V. Gaiduk, "The Vietnam War and Soviet-American Relations, 1964–1973: New Russian Evidence," *Cold War International History Project Bulletin*, nos. 6–7 (winter 1995–6): 250, citing doc-uments from the Rossiiskii Tsentr Khraneniia: Izucheniia dokumentov novejistorii (former CPSU Archives), fond 4, opis 18, delo 582, 95/462; see also Cold War International History Project at cwihp.si.edu/cwihplib.nsf/Collection.
30 See conversation between Zhou Enlai and Ho Chi Minh, Hanoi, Mar. 1, 1965, in Odd Arne Westad et al., eds., *77 Conversations Between Chinese and Foreign Leaders on the Wars in Indochina, 1964–1977*; Cold War International History Project, Working Paper no. 22 (Washington, D.C., May 1998), 75.
31 Xiaoming, *Communist Powers Divided*, 11–12.
32 "CIA Secret Report on Sino-Vietnamese Reaction to American Tactics in the Vietnamese War," *Journal of Contemporary Asia* 13, no. 2 (1983): 265.
33 Duiker, 47; Qiang, "Beijing and the Vietnam Conflict," 237.

The chief of staff of the People's Liberation Army (PLA) withdrew his promise to send Chinese pilots to North Vietnam; the air force feared U.S. technical superiority.[34] A confrontation with the United States in the air would be a lost cause, in contrast to better conditions for people's warfare in the Vietnamese jungle. The preference for ground combat led to the deployment of a considerable number of Chinese military personnel to North Vietnam. Nearly 320,000 men served there between June 1965 and March 1968. They were not sent into direct combat; rather, they served behind Vietnamese lines by building and repairing roads, bridges, and rail lines. Furthermore, China built a secret harbor on Hainan Island in the South China Sea, from which arms were transported to the National Liberation Front (NLF) in South Vietnam.[35]

As with the Korean War, Mao saw U.S. involvement in regional conflicts along Chinese borders as a direct threat to China's national security. Whereas he could count on Stalin's help during the Korean War, this possibility did not exist during the Vietnam War primarily because of Mao's sharp criticism of Soviet revisionism. During a visit to Beijing in February 1965, Soviet Premier Aleksey Kosygin suggested a united Sino-Soviet policy on Vietnam; Mao countered with the assertion that China's discord with the Soviet Union would continue for another 9,000 years. Kosygin's proposal was viewed as an attempt "to subordinate fraternal parties to the Soviet party and turn them into Russian tools because the Soviet Union sought to dominate the world jointly with the United States."[36] Moreover, Mao wanted to show the world, especially the United States and the Soviet Union, that China was an equal superpower, the third player in the global power game. An official message to Johnson in April 1965 clearly revealed Mao's self-confidence:

Should just such an action [Operation Rolling Thunder] bring on American aggression against China, we will unhesitatingly rise in resistance and fight to the end. China is prepared. Should the United States impose a war on China, it can be said with certainty that, once in China, the United States will not be able to pull out, however many men it may send over and whatever weapons it may use, nuclear weapons included. . . . If the United States bombards China, China will not sit here waiting to die. If they come from the sky, we will fight back on the ground.[37]

This was a flat-out rejection of the Soviet vision of peaceful coexistence.

---

34 Qiang, "An Uneasy Relationship," 5.   35 Ibid., 7–8.
36 Ibid., 13.
37 Barry Naughton, "The Third Front: Defense Industrialization in the Chinese Interior," *China Quarterly* no. 115 (1988): 351–86; *Mao Zedong junshi wenji* (Collection of Mao Zedong's Military Writings) (Beijing, 1993), 6:402.

The Great Leap Forward, the Cultural Revolution, and China's role in the Vietnam War should have made the international community realize that China no longer was the Soviet Union's junior partner. As in the Korean War, when the United States crossed the 38th parallel, Mao was surprised by the Tonkin Gulf incident. In both instances he did not expect a direct attack by the United States. However, it was a justification for the creation of a huge arms industry first in Dongbei (formerly Manchuria, neighboring Korea) and then in the southwestern provinces. Furthermore, this rearming can be explained by Mao's theory of war (especially people's warfare) and peace as a counterpoint to the new spirit of peaceful coexistence in Soviet military theory. In the context of the new phase in the Vietnam War, Defense Minister Lin Biao published a treatise on guerilla tactics that did not apply to the U.S. threat; rather, it was a direct but somewhat late response to the book *Military Strategy* edited by Soviet Chief of Staff Vasilii Sokolovsky and published in 1962. The order for the official Chinese response came directly from Mao.[38] It was at the beginning of the 1960s – after China's break with the Soviet Union – that the chairman developed his own theory of international politics and became the true decision maker on foreign policy in the CCP. It also should be emphasized that despite factional tendencies, the inner circle, including Zhou Enlai, stood behind Mao. Defining Chinese foreign policy, the chairman believed that a broad international united front needed to be formed by the so-called intermediate zones in Europe, Asia, Africa, and Latin America, including China itself, to counter American and Soviet imperialism. Indeed, Mao wanted to establish a "third front."[39] This foreign-policy line functioned as an outlet for domestic issues. Mao was worried about China's future, particularly after his rule ended and a new leadership came to power. He felt that his principles of Chinese revolution, the so-called Maozhuyi (Mao Zedong's ideas), would be betrayed and that the political system would degenerate under younger leaders who, coming under the thrall of peaceful coexistence with the capitalist world, would finally allow China to open up to the West.[40] Therefore, as a dialectic thinker, Mao used the Vietnam War to invoke anti-imperialist emotions among the Chinese population in order to counteract the modernizers – the "revisionists" – within the party and state apparatus and to ensure his place in history. This was the main purpose

---

38 Zhonggong Zhongyang wenjiansuo (CCP Central Archives), *Mao Zedong waijiao wenxuan* (Mao Zedong's Selected Writings on Foreign Policy) (Beijing, 1994), 506–8.

39 See Bo Yibo, *Ruogan zhongda juece yu shijian de huigu* (Recollections of Major Important Decisions and Events) (Beijing, 1993), 1137–9. Bo was Mao's chief secretary.

40 Chen Jian, "China's Involvement in the Vietnam War," 361–3.

of the "Aid Vietnam and Resist America" campaign and of the "Great Proletarian Cultural Revolution." There was an immediate link between the war in Indochina and the increasing radicalization of Chinese domestic policy. As Mao himself admitted in various speeches from 1964 to 1966, the weakness of the permanent revolution in Chinese society often hindered an efficient military involvement in Indochina against large-scale U.S. intervention. China's perpetuation of revolution at home and abroad was an emotionally charged process, whereas Soviet policy appeared for the moment to be much more level-headed.[41]

The envisaged mass mobilization in case of a direct U.S. attack on China itself was wishful thinking indeed. A report from April 1964 compiled by the PLA general staff mentioned serious logistical problems. The transportation system and electrical and water facilities concentrated near the big cities could easily be destroyed by the enemy. Neither the civilian population nor industry was prepared for war.[42] Mao thus initiated the ambiguous project of the third front, wherein each province should develop its own defense facilities in order to divert military attention away from the capital, the major cities, and the coastal regions. The Vietnam War and the U.S. threat thus inadvertently contributed to the industrial development of China's interior provinces. However, Mao and the Chinese leadership, including Zhou Enlai, assumed that the third front would discourage a direct attack on China by the United States.[43]

Soviet policy toward Vietnam changed after Khrushchev's departure in October 1964. In early 1965, the new Soviet prime minister, Kosygin, visited Beijing, Hanoi, and Pyongyang, thereby signaling a revival of the Soviet Union's Asian policy. Kosygin's shuttle diplomacy pursued the revival of communist unity in Asia for two ends: (1) to patch up Sino-Soviet relations, and (2) to deter U.S. military action in Vietnam. During his stay in Hanoi, Kosygin was accompanied by missile specialists, and on February 10, 1965, the Soviet Union and North Vietnam concluded a treaty on military and economic aid.[44] This was striking because only some months before, in December 1964, the North Vietnamese declared that Soviet military and

---

41 Qiang Zhai, "Beijing and the Vietnam Conflict," 238; see also Odd Arne Westad, "History, Memory, and the Languages of Alliance-Making," in Westad et al., eds., *77 Conversations Between Chinese and Foreign Leaders*, 8.

42 Zhou, *Zhou Enlai waijiao*, 455; CCP Central Documentary Research Office, ed., *Zhu De nianpu* (Chronicle of General Zhu De) (Beijing, 1986), 537–9. *Summary of World Broadcasts (SWB), Far East (FE)*, 1779, A2/1; ibid., 1780–3, A2; ibid., 1786, A2.

43 Gaiduk, "Vietnam War and Soviet-American Relations," 250.

44 Gaiduk fails to see the connection between the change in Soviet attitude and the North Vietnamese–Chinese military treaty of December 1964.

civilian experts would not be welcomed in the country.[45] Obviously, Hanoi used the turmoil surrounding the dramatic shakeup in Soviet leadership and the consolidation of power by Brezhnev to exert pressure on the Soviets. The North Vietnamese indeed felt that they were being wooed by both of the communist great powers. It thus was no accident that, when the North Vietnamese and Chinese signed the military treaty, the new Soviet leadership gave up the former policy of denying agency for the National Front for Liberation of South Vietnam (NFLSV) in Moscow. The Soviets wanted to set a counterpoise.[46] The extensive Soviet military assistance to the DRV and NFLSV after 1965 exceeded one billion rubles. Moscow's overall purpose was to undercut Chinese military involvement in Vietnam.[47] Moscow delivered the newest surface-to-air missiles, aircraft, and field artillery. In North Vietnam, Soviet military experts instructed their Vietnamese comrades but – like the Chinese – did not take part in combat. Nonetheless, Vietnam offered an appropriate battlefield testing ground for Soviet military technology. This did not imply that Hanoi would now take the Soviet side in the Sino-Soviet dispute, however. Instead, it secured itself maximum profit by exploiting both allies – the People's Republic of China and the Soviet Union. For example, the Soviet ambassador in Hanoi, Ilya Shcherbakov, pointed out that "the Vietnamese conducted their foreign policy, including their relations with Moscow (but also with Beijing), from a narrow, nationalistic viewpoint. Soviet aid was regarded by Hanoi exclusively from the standpoint of their benefit to Vietnam, rather than for the good of the international socialist cause." Later, in 1968, a Vietnamese journalist revealed in an interview to the newspaper *Pravda*: "What is the Soviet Union's share in the total assistance received by Vietnam, and what is the share of Soviet political influence there, if the latter can be measured in percent? The respective figures are: 75–80 percent and 4–8 percent." The Soviets were not the only ones worried about Vietnamese motivations. According to KGB reports, the Chinese leadership also was concerned about the DRV's increasingly independent foreign policy.[48] Furthermore, in CCP circles the fear was widespread that the Soviets sought to control North Vietnam and were willing to leave the South to the United States. The creation of Soviet-U.S. spheres of influence in Indochina was the last thing the Chinese wanted.[49]

45 Gaiduk, "Vietnam War and Soviet-American Relations."
46 Smith, *International History of the Vietnam War*, 3:54.
47 Xiaoming, *Communist Powers Divided*, 14.
48 *Far Eastern Economic Review*, June 15, 1979, 38–9.
49 Westad, *History, Memory, and the Languages of Alliance-Making*, 10.

By comparing the anti-imperialist propaganda of the Chinese press with that of the Vietnamese and by referring to Chinese arms supplies, U.S. intelligence specialists were convinced that it was China that encouraged North Vietnamese aggression. Furthermore, they argued that during Kosygin's visit the Vietnamese tried to involve the Soviets in the conflict by subtle means.[50] This scenario was plausible because shortly after Kosygin had arrived in Hanoi, the Vietcong on February 7 began its offensive against the South. In the meantime, the Chinese had suspicions concerning Moscow's moderate stance, above all that the Soviets wanted détente with the United States at the expense of the people's revolution in Vietnam and that the superpowers would sell out Asian interests. In a conversation with Ho Chi Minh in Hanoi on March 1, 1965, Zhou Enlai declared:

So in our [the Chinese and Vietnamese] course of revolution, and in our struggle against the United States, the matters of top secrecy should not be disclosed to them [the Soviets]. . . . We oppose the Soviet military activities that include the sending of missile battalions and two MIG-21 aircraft as well as the proposal to establish an airlift using forty-five planes for weapons transportation. We also have to be wary of the military instructors. Soviet experts have withdrawn, so what are their purposes when they wish to come back? We have had experience in the past when there were [Soviet] subversive activities in China, Korea, and Cuba. We therefore should keep an eye on their activities, namely, their transportation of weapons and military training.

And on another occasion the Chinese foreign minister told his North Vietnamese comrades:

The Soviets are now assisting you. But their help is not sincere. I want to tell you my opinion. It will be better without the Soviet aid. This may be an ultra leftist opinion. . . . As you have asked for my opinion, I would like to tell you the following: I do not support the idea of Soviet volunteers going to Vietnam, nor [do I support] Soviet aid to Vietnam. . . . After Kosygin returned from Hanoi, the Soviets used their support of Vietnam to win our trust in a deceitful way. Their purpose is to cast a shadow over the relationship between Vietnam and China, to split Vietnam and China.[51]

Zhou Enlai's words reveal how the atmosphere between Beijing and Moscow was poisoned by suspicion and how Vietnam represented a battleground in Sino-Soviet ideological warfare. China's fight against the Soviet Union seemed to be no less fervent than that against the United States.

Furthermore, Deng Xiaoping promised an aid program for North Vietnam of nearly $1 billion per annum, an exaggerated promise in view of

50 *Hongqi* (Red Flag), Nov. 11, 1965 (English ed. in *Peking Review*, Nov. 12, 1965).
51 Westad et al., eds., *77 Conversations Between Chinese and Foreign Leaders*, 75–7, 87, 91.

China's poor economic situation.[52] It basically was a smokescreen directed against the Soviets. Any Soviet initiative for a new international conference on Indochina like the 1954 Geneva Conference was rejected by the Chinese. The official refusal came much later, in November 1965.[53]

Seeking détente with the United States, Moscow observed that the tough stance of its Chinese rival on the Vietnam conflict created a negative image in the international community, especially in the United States. There was a general impression that China stood in the way of a peaceful solution and that the stubbornness of the Vietnamese politburo was rooted in the "Chinese factor."[54] Although this was close to the truth, it was not the whole story: China's foreign policy under Mao was often oversimplified and misunderstood. Of course, Mao himself and the communist leadership too often steered an ambivalent course in foreign policy. However, the chairman was worried that an escalation of the Vietnam War would expose his country to an immediate threat from the United States. Mao asked Kosygin in February 1965 whether the Soviet Union would come to China's aid in case of attack. The Soviet prime minister's response was noncommmittal.[55]

There was, indeed, a significant divergence in the Soviet and the Chinese approaches to the Vietnam issue. The Soviet thinking was more traditional, namely, that a socialist country such as Vietnam has the right to reunify and a right to exist, especially when it is threatened by a Western capitalist power. But protection by a socialist superpower (either the Soviet Union or China) had to be provided within the framework of coexistence. By contrast, the Chinese saw the Vietnam conflict as part of a larger anti-imperialist liberation movement emerging elsewhere in Southeast Asia – in Indonesia, Malaysia, the Philippines, and Thailand. According to Zhou Enlai, "Southeast Asia was the area in the world where contradictions are most concentrated, struggles most fierce, and revolutionary conditions most ripe." Mao also argued that

in Asia, the United States was occupying Taiwan, turning South Korea and South Vietnam into its colonies, exercising actual control and partial military occupation of Japan, undermining Laotian neutrality and independence, plotting subversion

---

52 Smith, *International History of the Vietnam War*, 3:55.
53 Chinese Foreign Minister Zhou Enlai in an interview with K. S. Karol of *Le Nouvel Observateur*, Nov. 9, 1966, cited by W. R. Smyser, *The Independent Vietnamese: Vietnamese Communism Between Russia and China, 1956–1969* (Athens, Ohio, 1980), 88.
54 Qiang, "An Uneasy Relationship," 3.
55 *Peking Review*, Mar. 26, 1965; William E. Griffith, *Sino-Soviet Relations, 1964–1965* (Cambridge, Mass., 1967), 407–18.

of the Cambodian government, and interfering with other Asian countries . . . that Vietnam constituted a link in Washington's chain of encirclement around China.[56]

In the Chinese view, these armed struggles would succeed not because of Soviet military technology but thanks to guerilla warfare. They thus observed the Soviet arms transfer with suspicion and rejected an international conference on Indochina because that would mean that China was only a power *inter pares*. Another event added fuel to the flames of the Sino-Soviet dispute: On March 4, 1965, Vietnamese, North Korean, and Chinese students demonstrated in front of the U.S. Embassy in Moscow. At first glance the action was directed against the bombing raids on North Vietnam. In actuality, it was a demonstration against Soviet "appeasement" in the face of U.S. policy. After the breakup of the demonstration by Soviet police, the Chinese government officially sided with the students and started a press campaign against the Soviet Union.[57] The incident had far-reaching consequences. The Soviet position on the question of a new Geneva conference on Indochina, which was originally suggested by the Soviets, now hardened due to the further deterioration of Sino-Soviet relations. Foreign Minister Andrei Gromyko and Soviet diplomats informed the Americans that an international conference would not be the right place for negotiations. Instead, the United States should enter into direct talks with Hanoi. So, the Soviets tried to back out of the Vietnam conflict, making it a bilateral problem between Hanoi and Washington.[58] They wanted simultaneously to increase their arms sales to the North Vietnamese. For this they needed Chinese goodwill. The transport of Soviet materiel to Hanoi had to cross Chinese territory. On April 17, 1965, the Soviet Union requested Chinese permission to use airports in southern China and to station Soviet contingents to defend them. The request was denied by the Chinese, who obviously saw that the Soviet Union wanted to force them into a military alliance and make Beijing dependent on Moscow.[59] As a demonstration of its own might, China successfully tested its second atomic bomb on May 14, 1965. This also strengthened Beijing's hand vis-à-vis Hanoi and Washington. The Chinese government wanted to show that the People's Republic was

---

56 Smith, *International History of the Vietnam War*, 3:59, with reference to telegram no. 2600, Mar. 15, 1965, U.S. Embassy, New Delhi; Qiang, "An Uneasy Relationship," 8–9.

57 See a later report in *Peking Review*, Dec. 7, 1979; Harry Harding and Melvin Gurtov, "The Purge of Luo Jui-ch'ing: The Politics of Chinese Strategic Planing," *Rand Corporation Document* R-0548-PR (Santa Monica, Calif., 1971), 26.

58 Smith, *International History of the Vietnam War*, 3:132–3.

59 Ibid., 135.

a power to be reckoned with in Asia. The atomic test took place during a pause in U.S. bombing; bombing soon resumed and Hanoi rejected any discussions with the United States.[60]

In contrast to the official campaign against the United States' "deceitful maneuver" in the Chinese newspaper *Renmin Ribao* (People's Daily), PLA's chief of staff Luo Ruiqing asserted in his appeal for a united front of all social-ist countries against imperialism that China should reach a compromise with the Soviet Union. Obviously, Luo Ruiqing made such a suggestion because he wanted to modernize his army with Soviet aid.[61] But in China, as in the Soviet Union, the hardliners prevailed. In late May 1965, Mao's and Lin Biao's perception of people's warfare regained influence in the PLA. In the Kremlin, Nikolay Podgorny, Khrushchev's former ally, and Mikhail Suzlov, one of the Politburo members who initiated the coup against Khrushchev in the fall of 1964, clashed over policy. Podgorny represented the "economic" faction for which the solution of the economic problems left behind by Khrushchev were more important than foreign military adventures. But Podgornii, like Kosygin, lost influence. The winners of the internal party struggle in the spring of 1964 were Brezhnev and Suzlov, both of whom favored an increase in Soviet military aid to North Vietnam. They feared a loss of Soviet influence resulting from the mounting differences between Beijing and Moscow. In May, this decision led to the delivery of offen-sive aircraft such as Il-28 fighters. At the same time, the Soviet mass media began a campaign to "Assist Vietnam Against U.S. Aggressors."[62] However, the radicals in Beijing did not want to support it. At the end of June the PLA sent troops to North Vietnam and created a divisional headquarters.[63] The radicalization of the CCP and the CPSU provided the North Vietnamese with the necessary moral support to envision an offensive against the South.

The next round in the Sino-Soviet debate over Vietnam began in April 1965. In a secret démarche of April 3, the Soviet Union suggested to Beijing that they should pursue united action. Moscow's plan included the trans-fer of 4,000 military personnel through China to Vietnam, the use of air fields in southwestern China, and a free-traffic corridor through China's airspace. Beijing saw this plan as an attempt to control China and rejected it. United action by both powers never succeeded due to Beijing's pride. Moreover, Sino-Soviet ideological and strategic rivalry hampered any show

---

60 Gaiduk, "Vietnam War and Soviet-American Relations."
61 Ibid., 138.   62 *Peking Review*, Sept. 3, 1965.
63 Union Research Institute, ed., *Documents of the Central Committee of the Chinese Communist Party, 1966–1967* (Hong Kong, 1968), 29–31.

of unanimity toward the United States, and it confused the Vietnamese, leaving them vulnerable.[64]

In the fall of 1965, another round in the domestic Chinese debate on military strategy began. Luo Ruiqing was convinced that the United States wanted only a limited war in Vietnam and thus was not a real threat to China's national security. He pointed out that "weapons do not decide everything," in contrast to Lin Biao's slogan, "Long Live the Victory of People's War!"[65] The radicals experienced a setback when the people's liberation movement in Indonesia failed. It was obvious that people's warfare was impracticable, especially in the case of Vietnam. The result of the internal party struggle was Luo Ruiqing's removal from all his posts in April 1966 and his later purge by the Red Guards during the Cultural Revolution.[66] In the meantime, the United States and the Soviet Union pursued diplomatic initiatives, such as the Shelepin mission to Hanoi, during a second U.S. bombing pause. Simultaneous to the Shelepin mission, Kosygin met with the Indian and Pakistani governments in an effort to isolate China, and Brezhnev visited Mongolia.[67]

Whereas in February 1966 the pragmatic faction in the CCP around Liu Shaoqi and Peng Zhen demanded a less ideological take on the Cultural Revolution, a debate in the CPSU was moving forward on the question of Stalin's rehabilitation and the containment of liberal tendencies in Soviet society (for example, the trial of the writers Siniavskii and Daniel). Zhdanov's old "two camps" concept was revived.[68] The Soviets and Chinese suddenly changed roles. With the re-emergence of Mao and his appeal for a new cultural revolution, the radicals won the upper hand. In the Kremlin, the pragmatic faction around Brezhnev and Suzlov repressed neo-Stalinism. In the summer and fall of 1966, a sharp deterioration in Sino–Soviet relations occurred, illustrated by the storming of the Soviet embassy in Beijing by the Red Guards. The Vietnamese tried to keep themselves out of this conflict. Hanoi did not support the radicalism of the Red Guards, and not only because of the Soviets' extensive aid. Hanoi pursued its own path toward socialism: In contrast to the Maoists in China, the North Vietnamese favored decentralization of the economy.[69] It was not surprising that at a

64 Xiaoming, *Communist Powers Divided*, 14–15.
65 Smith, *International History of the Vietnam War*, 3:262–3.
66 Ibid., 295.
67 Jan M. van Dyke, *North Vietnam's Strategy for Survival* (Palo Alto, Calif., 1972), 192.
68 Kenneth T. Young, *Negotiating with the Chinese Communists: The United States' Experience, 1953–1967* (New York, 1968), 294.
69 For instance, in 1970, the amount of Soviet assistance to Vietnam reached 316 million rubles. Gaiduk, *Soviet Union and the Vietnam War*, 253.

time when the Red Guards beleaguered the Soviet embassy in Beijing, the North Vietnamese leaders Pham Van Dong and Vo Nguyen Giap met with Brezhnev at his seaside resort on the Black Sea. Both sides feared Sino-U.S. rapprochement. At the high tide of the Cultural Revolution and the turmoil caused by the Red Guards, the Chinese were increasingly concerned about border security and thus interested in a U.S. withdrawal from Vietnam. On September 5, 1966, the Chinese openly signaled this wish in a meeting of Chen Yi with a Japanese delegation.[70]

However, the process of finding a peaceful solution to the question of Vietnam was arduous and painfully slow. The change in the Sino-Soviet-U.S. triangle came in 1972 after President Richard M. Nixon's visit to China. In mid-June, Soviet President Podgorny visited Hanoi and pressed the North Vietnamese to negotiate. The Soviet Union now had its own problems to resolve. Credits for wheat imports and arms limitation agreements with the United States dominated Soviet policy. Furthermore, the extensive military shipments to North Vietnam in the preceding years had burdened the Soviet economy, especially in view of the fact that they had no direct security relevance for the Soviet Union.[71] China also favored a peaceful solution to the Vietnam conflict. As the former Chinese PLA representative Zhu Kaiyin revealed in *Xinwen ziyou daobao* (Press Freedom Guardian) on September 29, 1995, Mao reduced military aid to North Vietnam because he believed that the North Vietnamese were wasting Chinese weapons.[72] The most important fact, though, was that thanks to Nixon's visit, China could play the Soviet Union off against the United States. Furthermore, it seemed that the Taiwan question could be solved, but only in cooperation with the United States. The North Vietnamese thus drifted into international isolation.[73] The shifting Soviet and Chinese policies dealt them a heavy psychological blow. Because of their total dependence on the two big Communist brothers for arms and food supplies, they felt abandoned and betrayed. North Vietnam's unpredictability and unmanageability, and its hesitation to clearly take sides with one or the other "big brother" in the Sino-Soviet contest for ideological supremacy, hardly inspired Moscow and Beijing to enthusiasm in their support for the war. Moscow and Beijing had every reason to come to terms with the United States and to favor a cease-fire and political solution in Vietnam. The Sino-U.S. and Soviet-U.S. summits during 1972 showed that neither the Soviets nor the Chinese were

70 *Xinwen ziyou daobao* (Press Freedom Guardian), Sept. 29, 1995, 3.
71 Barbara W. Tuchman, *The March of Folly: From Troy to Vietnam* (New York, 1984), 371.
72 *Xinwen ziyou daobao* (Press Freedom Guardian), Sept. 29, 1995, 3.
73 Tuchman, *March of Folly*, 371.

willing to sacrifice their own national interests, which here meant improved relations with the United States, to support socialist North Vietnam, even as it struggled with the strongest Western power. When on January 27, 1973, a DRV-U.S. peace agreement was signed, it reflected a new world order unthinkable without the Sino-Soviet-U.S. rapprochement of 1972. The Beijing–Washington–Moscow axis and not the fragile Moscow–Hanoi–Beijing alliance became the decisive factor in world politics. It was a critical problem for the Hanoi government that Vietnam had been caught in the fight among the three giants. The Vietnam War demonstrates how far away the Moscow–Hanoi–Beijing triangle was from the official propaganda of "internationalism" and "Communist brotherhood." Each player followed its own nationalistic policy, which evoked mutual mistrust and suspicion and contributed to prolonging the conflict. Furthermore, throughout history all three communist countries exhibited a love-hate attitude toward each other. China was eager to borrow technology from the Soviet Union, just as North Vietnam was from its Chinese neighbor; however, the Asians wanted to preserve their cultural heritage and their national independence. Additionally, the cultural differences between China and Vietnam contributed to the complications in the triangle. Thus, it was not just the United States who lost the Vietnam conflict; the communist powers also failed. Each leg of the Moscow–Beijing–Hanoi triangle struggled to gain a superior position by undermining the policy of the others in this ideological contest.

PART THREE

Recasting Vietnam: Domestic Scenes and Discourses

12

The Center-Left Government in Italy and the Escalation of the Vietnam War

LEOPOLDO NUTI

The purpose of this chapter is to provide an overall assessment of the impact of the escalation of the Vietnam War on U.S.-Italian relations, on Italian foreign policy, and on the evolution of Italian domestic politics. Between 1965 and 1968, the Vietnam War played a large role in U.S.-Italian relations and was the cause of a heated domestic debate that divided not only Italian political parties but Italian diplomats as well, resulting in the resignation of one foreign minister and of one of the country's most important diplomats, the ambassador to the United States.

In order to understand how and why the escalation of the conflict in Southeast Asia had such a disproportionate relevance for Italian domestic and foreign policy, I first look at the origins of the center-left government, stressing the American concern over the impact that the "opening to the left" may have had on the traditional Italian alignment with Washington on foreign policy matters. I also look at how and why the war in Vietnam became an issue in Italian domestic politics. I then briefly tell the story of Italy's diplomatic involvement in attempts to bring about a negotiated settlement of the conflict, from the trip to Hanoi by Florence Mayor Giorgio La Pira to the tangled webs of the "Marigold" and "Kelly" negotiations, and try to explain the reasons for this burst of diplomatic activity on a matter in which Italy had no direct interests. In the conclusion, I suggest that the war might have had a negative impact on the experiment of the center-left by helping to end the isolation of the Italian Communist Party that the opening to the left was supposed to bring about.

THE LONG DEBATE: THE UNITED STATES AND THE OPENING TO THE LEFT

The pattern of postwar U.S.-Italian relations was shaped by the role the United States played both in the liberation of Italy during World War II and, above all, in its reconstruction efforts of the early postwar years, when the threat of a communist takeover spurred the Truman administration to become deeply involved in Italian domestic politics. This commitment reached a first, successful climax with the political elections of 1948, which resulted in a sound defeat of the communist-led Popular Front and persuaded Washington that its assistance could steer Italian politics away from any communist menace and into a firm pro-Western direction. The United States turned into one of the key actors of the Italian political system and started a long-term campaign to stabilize Italian politics, even though its efforts always fell somewhat short of the desired objective. To be sure, Italy's Western alignment was never seriously in doubt, but the parliamentary majority on which it rested began to decay after the political elections of 1953, dangerously exposing the various cabinets to pressures from a still-powerful pro-Soviet left, which controlled about one-third of the electorate.[1]

A possible solution to the problem had slowly developed by the mid-1950s, when the hitherto pro-communist Socialist Party (PSI) began to display some signs of restlessness and led many observers to believe that it was ready to break free from the control of the Italian Communist Party (PCI). If the PSI could be firmly brought into the democratic camp, the Communist Party would be thoroughly isolated, Italy's Western alignment would be made more secure, and possibly some reformist zeal could be infused into the placid policies of the increasingly static cabinets led by the Christian Democratic Party (DC).[2]

This "opening to the left," as it was called, was nevertheless regarded by its opponents as a maneuver that could easily swing Italian politics in an unwanted direction. At the very least, the Eisenhower administration feared a weakening of Italy's Atlanticist foreign policy if the socialists were included in the ruling coalition without a thorough revision of their past record: The combination of PSI neutralism and anti-Americanism with the traditional Italian ambitions to play a relevant role in the Mediterranean, together with the attention displayed by some Italian politicians toward the movement of the nonaligned countries, seemed to the United States a rather dangerous

---

1 On U.S.-Italian relations after World War II, see Ennio Di Nolfo, "The United States and Italian Communism: World War II to the Cold War," *Journal of Italian History* 1, no. 1 (1978): 74–94; Ennio Caretto and Bruno Marolo, *Made in USA: Le origini americane della repubblica italiana* (Milan, 1996); David Ellwood, *L'alleato nemico* (Milan, 1975); Marco Fini and Roberto Faenza, *Gli americani in Italia* (Milan, 1979); and James E. Miller, *The United States and Italy, 1940–1950: The Politics and Diplomacy of Stabilization* (Chapel Hill, N.C., 1984).

2 Italian historian Pietro Scoppola believes that such a development was almost a foregone conclusion after the failure of De Gasperi's attempt in 1953 to modify the Italian electoral system: Pietro Scoppola, *La repubblica dei partiti: Profilo storico della democrazia in Italia, 1945–1990* (Bologna, 1991), 320.

mix that had to be stopped before it could really affect the formulation of Italian foreign policy.

Even inside the PSI there were strong doubts about the best course of action, and a very vocal minority was in favor of maintaining the old alliance with the PCI. The PSI secretary, the aging but very popular Pietro Nenni, tried to steer his party away from its tradition of "united frontism" but had to move very carefully so as not to split his followers. In order to keep the party united, therefore, he shrouded his foreign policy statements in an ambiguous and fuzzy neutralist overtone, and only with great timidity did he dare to gradually reveal a more pro-Western orientation.

Faced with the ambiguity of the PSI's new course, the Eisenhower administration did little to encourage any rapprochement between the DC and the socialists, and actually took several steps to prevent any quick con-clusion of an agreement.[3] Thus, by the time the Kennedy administration took over the problem was still far from solved, and the Italian political system had reached an impasse that seemed bound to last forever. Some of Kennedy's advisers, however, took a strong interest in the matter be-cause of their personal concern with Italian history and politics. They also joined a bureaucratic battle with some of the most conservative sections of the administration in order to change U.S. policy on this issue and to get the "opening to the left" under way. Arthur M. Schlesinger Jr., W. Averell Harriman, and Robert Komer became the key figures in the new admin-istration who pushed for a coalition between the Christian Democrats and the Socialists;[4] their efforts, however, met with strong resistance by those who feared the possible negative repercussions of a DC-PSI collaboration on the future of Italian foreign policy.[5] As for President John F. Kennedy,

---

3 To be sure, there were forces even in the 1950s that saw the "opening to the left" as a real opportunity for the United States: William Colby, *Honorable Men: My Life in the CIA* (New York, 1978), chap. 4: "Covert Politics in Italy"; Alan Arthur Platt, "U.S. Policy Toward the 'Opening to the Left' in Italy," Ph.D. diss., Columbia University, 1973, 137–8.

4 Arthur M. Schlesinger, Jr., *A Thousand Days: John F. Kennedy in the White House* (New York, 1965); Platt, "U.S. Policy Toward the 'Opening to the Left'"; Roberto Faenza, *Il malaffare: Dall'America di Kennedy all'Italia, a Cuba, al Vietnam* (Milan, 1979); Spencer M. Di Scala, *Renewing Italian Socialism: Nenni to Craxi* (New York, 1988); Leo Wollemborg, *Stars, Stripes, and Italian Tricolor: The United States and Italy, 1946–1989* (New York, 1990). See also especially Leopoldo Nuti, *Gli Stati Uniti e l'apertura a sinistra: Importanza e limiti della presenza americana in Italia* (Rome, 1999), which develops the themes I have also sketched in "I socialisti o i missili? La politica estera dell'amministrazione Kennedy e l'Italia," *Italia Contemporanea*, no. 204 (autumn 1996): 443–70; and Leopoldo Nuti, "Missiles or Socialists? The Italian Policy of the Kennedy Administration," in Douglas Brinkley and Richard Griffiths, eds., *John F. Kennedy and Europe* (New Orleans, La., 1999).

5 According to at least one account, the split was repeated even inside the CIA, with the "analysts" in favor of the experiment and the "operatives" against it; see Faenza, *Il malaffare*, 64; for further discussion of the CIA attitude, see also Di Scala, *Renewing Italian Socialism*, 122–3. CIA Director John McCone seems to have supported the "opening," or at least this is what he said to FIAT President Vittorio Valletta during the latter's trip to the United States in May 1962: Piero Bairati, *Valletta* (Turin,

he let his advisers pursue the new approach but never openly intervened in their dispute with the State Department, placing the Italian policy of his administration on a sort of dual track.

A protracted struggle developed between supporters and opponents of the center-left formula: After almost two years it was terminated when a number of factors, both domestic and international, swung the balance in favor of the "opening to the left."[6] By the time the Johnson administration took office, the doubts about the reliability of the PSI had been cast aside (but not completely removed), and support of the center-left formula had become the official position of U.S.-Italian policy.

The participation of the Socialists in the cabinet ultimately depended on the position they would take on the country's foreign policy, and their ambiguous record on this subject made it difficult to forecast with any certainty what impact they might have.[7] A State Department paper described the problem in rather stark terms: "Italian democracy (and American interests in Italy) may be faced with the alternative of one governing coalition which seems to present more opportunity for reducing PCI strength, and another which would be a more cooperative ally of the US in NATO and in foreign affairs in general."[8] It is important to understand that the solution to this dilemma depended on the evolution of the Italian socialists' foreign policy but also on the new trends in the international system that began to take shape in the aftermath of the Cuban Missile Crisis. One of the preconditions for the increasing favor of the Kennedy administration for the new formula therefore was the growing support displayed by the center-left parties for a moderate détente with the Soviet Union. As U.S. ambassador to Italy Frederick Reinhardt noted in the fall of 1962:

There is throughout the greater part of the Italian political spectrum an inherent tendency toward neutralism which has been more in evidence under the present Italian leadership than for some time past.... Yet, the Italian center left

---

1983), 311–12. Head of Counterintelligence James J. Angleton was, on the contrary, quite hostile to the initiative and reportedly went as far as suspecting Arthur Schlesinger of being a Soviet agent: David C. Martin, *A Wilderness of Mirrors* (New York, 1980), 183–4.

6 The climax of this U.S.-PSI rapprochement probably was the famous meeting of John F. Kennedy and Pietro Nenni in the Quirinale gardens during the president's short trip to Italy in June 1963. For a brilliant description of the event, as well of its impact on the other Italian party leaders, see the oral history interview with William Fraleigh, John F. Kennedy Presidential Library (hereafter JFKL). See also Pietro Nenni, *Gli anni del centro-sinistra: Diari, 1957–1966* (Milan, 1982), 288.

7 For a balanced assessment of the PSI's foreign policy, see research memorandum REU-40: Italian Socialist Foreign Policy, Apr. 27, 1962, box WH 12, WH files: subject files: Italy, Arthur Schlesinger, Jr., papers, JFKL. I am grateful to John Orme for his assistance in obtaining the declassification of this document.

8 "Italy: Department of State Guidelines for Policy and Operations," Jan. 1962, box 120, NSF: CO: Italy General, folder State Guidelines, JFKL.

government and its political and press supporters appear to be moving closer to United States views with respect to certain elements of foreign policy than are anti-Communist center and conservative elements, which traditionally support us here. For instance, the center left spokesmen emphasize the dangers of nuclear proliferation, the importance of the development of an Atlantic community, and are more ready to accept United States leadership and control of Western military forces in a multilateral framework. . . . Their support for British entry into the European community has been quite articulate.[9]

Thus, the new international climate that arose after the climax of the Cuban Missile Crisis was very influential in the development of the Italian political system. As relations between the United States and the Soviet Union seemed to improve, the moderate Italian left seemed more inclined to share governmental responsibilities and support U.S. foreign policy. This rapprochement was further enhanced by the PSI's strong dislike for the Gaullist attempts to establish a French-led, presumably conservative European bloc.[10]

Eventually, a center-left government became more palatable to the United States not only as a tool to cut down the PCI's influence but also as a further guarantee of U.S.-Italian alignment within the Western bloc. If foreign policy had been the most divisive issue, and the most difficult obstacle to the conclusion of a compromise between the PSI and the DC, the change in the international scenario erased some of the difficulties and made it easier for the two parties to find common ground.

To be sure, there were still some foreign policy issues that could hamper the development of the center-left, as was the case with the Multilateral Force (MLF) in the last months of the Kennedy administration. The famous Merchant mission in the spring of 1963 seemed to signal a renewed interest in the Kennedy administration for this project, but the Italian opponents of the opening to the left tried to use it as a tool to disrupt the delicate negotiations between the DC and the PSI for the formation of a new majority. They invented an American request that the Socialists accept the MLF as a test of their trustworthiness, clearly hoping that the PSI would refuse and be obliged to abandon the negotiations. In a situation where a protracted debate between the two parties seemed on the verge of failure, the MLF almost became the straw that broke the camel's back. By the end of 1963, however, the Socialists were able to verify that there was no immediate request for their declaration of support for the MLF: If anything,

---

9 Telegram from the Embassy in Rome to the Department of State, Jan. 12, 1963, U.S. Department of State, ed., *Foreign Relations of the United States* (hereafter *FRUS*), 1961–1963, XIII, 854–7.

10 Leopoldo Nuti, "Italy, the British Application to the EEC, and the January Debacle," in Richard Griffiths and Stuart Ward, eds., *Courting the Common Market: The First Attempt to Enlarge the European Community, 1961–1963* (London, 1996).

the Kennedy administration seemed more interested in the positive conclusion of the opening to the left.[11] Even after the formation of the new
government, however, the MLF continued to haunt the coalition and likely
would have split it asunder had the cabinet been called to make a sudden
decision – almost a harbinger of the similar impact that the Vietnam War
would have on Italian politics.[12]

U.S.–ITALIAN RELATIONS IN THE SHADOW OF VIETNAM

Escalation and the Italian Political Parties

The two preconditions that shaped the change in the U.S. attitude toward the center-left in the Kennedy years, namely, the ideological sympathy
among reformist and progressive groups and the evolution of the international system, were both somewhat modified after 1963, and this change
inevitably affected U.S.-Italian relations. To begin with, Italian public opinion was deeply shaken by the Kennedy assassination, and most center-left
politicians doubted that Lyndon B. Johnson might give them the support
they had enjoyed under his predecessor. Even if he were willing to pay any
attention to this issue and back up Italian reformers, he lacked the aura
that surrounded President Kennedy and made him immensely popular with
the masses and with many Italian politicians.[13] Besides, the resignation of
Arthur Schlesinger from the new administration left it without the strongest
ideological supporter of the "opening to the left." It is true that by the time
Johnson became president, support of the center-left had unofficially become U.S. policy, but the balance of forces in Italy was still precarious and
required cautious handling if the experiment was to flourish.

---

11 Riccardo Lombardi to Nenni, Nov. 2, 1963, box 30, folder letters from Riccardo Lombardi,
Archivio Pietro Nenni, Serie C. 1944–1979, Archivio Centrale dello Stato (hereafter ACS); Giovanni
Pieraccini to Nenni, Nov. 15, 1963, box 36, folder 1731, letters from Pieraccini, Giovanni, ibid. In
the first letter, Lombardi, according to information received from the DC, stressed that the creation
of the MLF could not be postponed any further, whereas the second letter stated the exact oppo-
site. See also the two letters from Altiero Spinelli to Nenni, Nov. 8 and Nov. 14, 1963, DEP-I–58,
Fondo Spinelli, Archivio Storico della Comunità Europea. On this issue, see also Leo J. Wollemborg,
Stelle, strisce e tricolore, 175–6.
12 See, e.g., Prime Minister Aldo Moro's remarks to Walt Rostow in July 1964: Airgram A-01 from
Rome to Department of State, July 1, 1964, "PM Moro's View on Domestic and International
Situation," box 196, national security file, country file: Italy, vol. 2, Lyndon B. Johnson Presidential
Library (hereafter LBJL).
13 See, e.g., the conversation between Schlesinger and Nenni in Apr. 1964, as described by Nenni in
Gli anni del centro-sinistra, 347–8. There is no specific study of U.S.-Italian relations in the Johnson
years. For an excellent overall evaluation of U.S.–European relations in this period, see Massimiliano
Guderzo, *Interesse nazionale e responsabilità locale: Gli Stati Uniti, l'Alleanza Atlantica e l'integrazione
europea negli anni di Johnson, 1963–1968* (Florence, 2000).

This decline of ideological support made any evolution of the international system all the more relevant for the success of the center-left. The continuation of a détente between Washington and Moscow would create an ideal climate for the implementation of a dialog between the Socialists and the Christian Democrats, which would not be called on to make any dramatic foreign policy decisions likely to split their fragile alliance. Inside both parties, in fact, were powerful factions that regarded the alliance with their erstwhile enemy as little less than a sellout and were ready to grasp the first opportunity to terminate the experiment and reverse the course of Italian politics.

It should come as no surprise, then, that the Vietnam conflict was regarded with grave concern by the Italian supporters of the new political formula because it threatened to become the issue on which the opening to the left might founder should the cabinet be called to support the U.S. escalation. Divided as it still was among several factions, the PSI would at best be able to give a silent endorsement, but it was much more likely to insist that Italy take a negative stance against U.S. involvement – a position that the large majority of the Christian Democrats would be certain to oppose.

For the adversaries of the center-left, however, U.S. involvement in the Vietnam conflict might provide the right tool to reverse a trend they heartily disliked. Afraid of a rather bleak future if the rapprochement between the Christian Democrats and Socialists succeeded, the Italian Communists promptly began to harp on the theme of U.S. "imperialist" aggression against Vietnam to break out of their growing isolation. The Communist Party had a very easy time using the escalation of the war and particularly the bombing of North Vietnam as a rallying point for a large section of the population and as an instrument to embarrass the Socialist Party and its choice to cooperate with the Christian Democrats. Having overcome many doubts and uncertainties before breaking their old alliance with the PCI, the rank and file of the Italian Socialist Party were in fact vulnerable to communist propaganda and to the familiar tunes of a united front to condemn the "American war of aggression." In short, the war could provide the PCI with the means to unravel the whole process of the "opening to the left" and recreate its old alliance with the Socialist Party.

The war also offered a good opportunity to the right-wing parties (the Neo-Fascists, the Monarchists, and the Liberals) that opposed the center-left. They strongly defended the U.S. role in Southeast Asia and sharply rebuked the government for not being forceful enough in its support of the Johnson administration. Although this criticism had a minor impact on Italian public opinion, it played a significant role in making the government feel uneasy and provided ample ammunition for all those right-wing Christian Democrats who were looking for means to scuttle the boat from inside the majority coalition.

From the very beginning of the escalation, therefore, the key figures in the center-left government found it necessary to express to their American counterparts their reservations about the impact the war might have on Italian politics and, as a consequence, on U.S.-Italian relations. It is true that, as Johnson said to Foreign Minister Amintore Fanfani during the latter's trip to Washington in 1965, U.S.-Italian relations by then "had never been better."[14] Both Rome and Washington were aware, though, that the war in Southeast Asia might become a sticking point in their relationship. "Vietnam," wrote presidential aide Jack Valenti to Johnson in April 1965, "was the one issue that threatened the Moro-Nenni relationship." If the DC Prime Minister Aldo Moro was to take too strong a stance in favor of the United States, it would exacerbate his relations with Nenni and help the Communist Party "make some hay."[15] In December 1965, Foreign Minister Fanfani articulated the problem to Secretary Dean Rusk in the same terms:

He had been tremendously impressed by public and press attitudes in Italy regarding Vietnam. Nenni has abstained, but how about his party? F. said, as the secretary knows, he [Fanfani] has always tried to split the Socialists from the Communists *but the Viet-Nam problem is working against this trend.* The U.S. should imagine itself in a situation where it might take an extreme decision re: Viet-Nam that might cause the Italian government to fall and precipitate a government crisis in Italy.[16]

Both governments, therefore, acted to defuse the issue: Washington by asking only for a rather modest display of support for the cause of containment in Indochina, Rome by more-or-less giving Washington what it wanted and at the same time multiplying its initiatives to try to find a way out.

From 1965 onward, U.S.-Italian meetings turned into a litany of Italian expressions of discomfort at the prospect of any further U.S. involvement in the war. "This war," Socialist leader Pietro Nenni explained to W. Averell Harriman, who had been one of his most influential supporters in the formative years of the center-left and who still encouraged him to pursue a reformist program with more zeal, "is creating many difficulties in Europe,

---

14 Memorandum of conversation, Johnson-Fanfani, "Recent International Developments; Italian-American Relations," May 24, 1965, box 379, conference files 1949–1973, Record Group (hereafter RG) 59, National Archives, College Park, MD (hereafter NA).

15 Jack Valenti memorandum to President Johnson, Apr. 16, 1965, confidential file, CO127, Italy (1965), White House central file, LBJL. Also in *FRUS*, 1964–1968, XII, 228–30.

16 Memorandum of conversation, Dec. 22, 1965, in *FRUS*, 1964–1968, XII, 248–53.

in Italy, and in me."[17] Faced with a vocal leftist opposition within his own party that constantly demanded a firmer stance against the American policy in Vietnam, Nenni was torn between his desire for the success of the political experiment on which he had staked the last years of his political career and the need to prevent any further split inside the PSI, which had already lost a sizeable left-wing faction upon entering the government in late 1963. By 1967, such key figures in the party as Riccardo Lombardi had become very critical of the war and had pressured Nenni to adopt a more determined anti-American position.[18] Nenni was opposed to the conflict and also was convinced that the United States would never be able to achieve a clear victory. He sincerely believed that the only reasonable solution might come from a negotiated settlement, and although he was aware that many road-blocks were being thrown up by Hanoi,[19] he never tired of repeating that the United States should stop bombing the North and negotiate its way out of the conflict. Nenni was also very aware of the heavy blows that the war was inflicting on the image of the United States in European public opinion. In 1967, he explicitly asked Vice President Hubert H. Humphrey – yet another supporter of the opening to the left – to tell Johnson that he should stop the bombing of North Vietnam in order to recapture some of the prestige the United States was quickly losing among the Western Europeans: "Europe does not understand America any longer, America is not under-standing Europe. The root of the discord is the Vietnam War."[20] This belief was shared by the Italian ambassador to Washington, Sergio Fenoaltea. Although in public he felt it necessary to display unwavering support of the United States, in his private remarks Fenoaltea was pessimistic about the

---

17 Nenni, *Gli anni del centro-sinistra*, 512–14. For the U.S. version of the Nenni-Harriman conversation, see Memorandum of Conversation, Feb. 18, 1965, in Declassified Documents Research System (hereafter DDRS), 1975/5592.

18 Lombardi and other PSI members would later join the Russell Tribunal to investigate U.S. war crimes in Southeast Asia. At the first Conference in Stockholm, the only Italian member in the Russell Tribunal was Lelio Basso, who had been a PSI member until 1963 and had left the party to set up the left wing of the Italian Socialist Party for Proletarian Unity (PSIUP). For the minutes of the first conference, see www.homeusers.prestel.co.uk.

19 See, e.g., his remarks to Arthur Goldberg in Nenni, *Gli anni del centro-sinistra*, 649.

20 Pietro Nenni, *I conti con la storia: Diari 1967–1971* (Milan, 1982), entry of Mar. 31, 1967. This grave concern for the moral standing of the United States in world opinion was shared, and expressed many times to President Johnson by Pope Paul VI. Although the pope avoided any clear statement about whether the war was right or wrong, he privately expressed his understanding for the U.S. effort to arrive at a just peace. But the pope warned Washington that the most important priority should remain the preservation of the U.S. image abroad, which was being increasingly tarnished by the bombing of North Vietnam. Clearly, the Catholic Church's anxieties influenced – and also mirrored – large segments of Italian society. For examples of Pope Paul VI's concern, as well as his intimate and frank discussions with Johnson, see *FRUS*, 1964–1968, XII, 640–1, 645–7, 649–66, 667–9.

outcome of the war and feared its repercussions on the Atlantic alliance.[21] This concern about a general loosening of Atlantic ties, moreover, was increased by the contemporary debate about the possible ratification of a nuclear nonproliferation treaty between Moscow and Washington. Whereas most of the parties in the center-left coalition approved of the treaty, they were somewhat nervous about the possibility of a deal between the superpowers that would discriminate against the European allies and were afraid that this might cause a decoupling of U.S. and Western European security.[22] To Moro, the Vietnam conflict and the NPT were two facets of the same nightmare scenario because he was afraid that their joint impact on Italy and the rest of Western Europe would push them toward a more neutralist stance.[23]

The Johnson administration understood its ally's predicament and did not put much pressure on Rome for more vocal support – although Washington would, of course, have preferred a less skeptical partner. Sometimes, however, Italian politicians overstated their case, and when during his Washington trip in 1967 President Giuseppe Saragat harped on the difficulties that the war was creating in Italian public opinion, a tired Johnson snapped back that the conflict was certainly creating worse difficulties for him with American public opinion.[24] By and large, however, the public stance of the Italian administrations was regarded as satisfactory, even if there was a gradual, almost imperceptible devolution from the more benevolent "comprehension" of the American involvement in the war expressed by Moro in his speeches to the Italian senate and chamber of deputies in 1965 to a more lukewarm "consideration" declared by Foreign Minister Fanfani two years later. The occasional gesture of goodwill toward the United States – such as when Moro in 1966 wrote to the prime ministers of the three countries of the International Control Commission (Canada, India, and Poland) to urge their intervention with Hanoi to prevent the North Vietnamese from trying American prisoners-of-war as war criminals[25] – did not hide the Italian population's waning support for the

---

21 Nenni, *I conti con la storia*, entry of Mar. 21, 1967. A less forceful presentation of Nenni's point is Telegram 5110 from Rome to the Secretary of State, Apr. 1, 1967, Memcons, box 438, folder VP's Trip to Europe, vol. III, Lot File Conference Files, RG 59, NA.

22 See the comments on this point by Moro and Fanfani during their talks with Vice President Hubert Humphrey in 1967, in Telegram VIPTO 035 from Rome to the secretary of state, Apr. 1, 1967, Memcons, box 438, folder VP's Trip to Europe, vol. III, Lot File Conference Files, RG 59, NA.

23 See Moro's thoughtful comments to Ambassador Egidio Ortona in late 1967, in Egidio Ortona, *Anni d'America: La cooperazione, 1967–1975* (Bologna, 1989), 55.

24 Ibid., 38.

25 Memo from Secretary of State Dean Rusk to President Johnson, Aug. 2, 1966, in DDRS, 1989/2286; telegram from Department of State to U.S. Embassy in Rome, Aug. 3, 1966, in DDRS, 1988/835.

U.S. position in Vietnam. By late 1967, Moro was clearly aware that his previous declarations of understanding for the United States had become insufficient in dampening the growing unrest in Italian public opinion against the war, and he was engaged in a tireless effort to contrive a position that would still be acceptable to Washington without arousing the wrath of domestic opposition.[26] The other Western European governments, however, were not much more forthcoming in their declarations of support for the war in Southeast Asia, and the Johnson administration was aware that the government in Rome could hardly behave differently because it was constantly being harassed by the left wing's anti-American attacks, which ranged from the denunciation of the United States' campaign of "genocide" to the occasional sensationalist speculation about the inevitable outbreak of World War III.[27]

The Secret Negotiations

The center-left government supported its embattled ally in a less obvious way by working between 1965 and 1968 to advance the chances of a peaceful settlement of the conflict. Given the dramatic impact of the war on Italian politics and society, it should come as no surprise that in those years, Italian diplomacy was very active in trying to bring about a negotiated resolution of the war and was involved in various efforts to mediate between Washington and Hanoi. Indeed, the first Italian suggestion to cooperate was put forward a few days after the beginning of operation "Rolling Thunder" in early March 1965.[28] Over the years Italy had tried several times to play such a mediating role in many controversial issues, trying for instance to bring about a rapprochement between the United States and Egyptian President Gamal Abdel Nasser in 1957–8.[29] These moves had been inspired by the desire to enhance Italy's international standing, by the belief in the country's special interests in the Mediterranean, and by the firm conviction that, having lost all of its colonies and not being tainted by the same colonialist heritage as the other Western European countries, Italy represented a privileged interlocutor for the newly independent countries of the Third World.[30] This set of assumptions prompted some Italian politicians and diplomats

26 Ortona, *Anni d'America*, 55.
27 See, e.g., the special editions of two left-wing dailies, "l'Unità" and "Paese sera," on May 19, 1967, cited by Nenni in *I conti con la storia*, 63–5.
28 Memorandum of conversation, Mar. 5, 1965, in *FRUS, 1964–1968*, XII, 218–23.
29 On this episode, see in particular Alessandro Brogi, *L'Italia e l'egemonia americana nel Mediterraneo* (Florence, 1996).
30 On Italy's postcolonial policy, see Bruna Bagnato, *Vincoli europei echi mediterranei: L'Italia e la crisi francese in Marocco e in Tunisia, 1949–1956* (Florence, 1991).

to share the belief that Italy could also play a useful role in the case of Vietnam.

The first initiative took place at the end of 1965. In September, the Italian foreign minister, Fanfani, discussed the Vietnam situation with Rusk in a private meeting during the twentieth session of the United Nations General Assembly (which soon appointed Fanfani as its chairman). Fanfani twice openly asked Rusk "whether he could pursue any reports of an inclination on the part of Hanoi to negotiate . . . only in an exploratory way." From the minutes Rusk does not seem to have given any clear-cut answer, but Fanfani must have understood this as tacit approval. Shortly afterward, in fact, Fanfani's old friend and the former mayor of Florence, Giorgio La Pira, after some personal contacts with the North Vietnamese embarked on a spectacular trip to Hanoi, where he held several conversations with Ho Chi Minh (whom he had met in France years earlier) and Prime Minister Pham Van Dong. A devout Catholic who wanted to turn Florence into a center for international reconciliation, La Pira had taken a number of controversial initiatives over the years that were not always in line with the "orthodox" course of Italian foreign policy as conceived in Rome. In this case, he might have acted on his own initiative. Nevertheless, given his close relationship with Fanfani and the latter's attitude during his meeting with Rusk, it is quite likely that Fanfani consented to the trip and perhaps that Fanfani had approached Rusk precisely with this project in mind.

Back from North Vietnam, La Pira discussed the gist of his talks with Fanfani. It was La Pira's impression that the North Vietnamese were willing to accept a cease-fire on the basis of the status quo, and obviously Fanfani hastened to pass the information to the U.S. representative to the United Nations, Ambassador Arthur Goldberg.[31] Washington did not immediately dismiss this opening, probably in order to placate one of its most important allies. After a few days, however, Johnson's closest advisers reached the conclusion that the whole operation was just one more example of North Vietnamese propaganda.[32] Eventually, the whole thing came to naught because excerpts of the Italian-American correspondence on this subject were leaked to the *St. Louis Post-Dispatch*; Hanoi then forcefully denied that the DRV ever mentioned an intent to make any peace overtures during its conversations with the former mayor of Florence.[33]

---

31 Letter from Fanfani to Goldberg, Nov. 20, 1965, in DDRS, 1986/890. The United States, however, had already learned what these conversations were about from a confidential source. See telegram from the U.S. Embassy in Moscow to Department of State, Nov. 22, 1965, reprinted in *FRUS*, 1964–1968, XII, 246.

32 Ibid., doc. no. 120.   33 Wollemborg, *Stelle, strisce e tricolore*, 223–5.

Fanfani and La Pira resented what they thought was the explicit sabotage of their efforts: In an interview with a right-wing Italian magazine, La Pira vented his rage with some scathing comments about U.S. foreign policy that would have been embarrassing enough for the Italian government even if the interview had not taken place in Fanfani's own house and in the presence (if not at the instigation) of Mrs. Fanfani. The result was a stormy debate in the Italian media and in parliament that prompted Fanfani – who had caused a similar uproar a few weeks earlier on the issue of Italian recognition of the People's Republic of China – to resign as foreign minister.[34] The government, however, decided to support Fanfani and persuaded him to withdraw his resignation. A few weeks later, though, the second Moro cabinet fell apart because of a purely domestic debate over public education. But the whole La Pira–Fanfani episode had been instrumental in hastening the cabinet's demise because it had revealed a clear foreign policy division inside the coalition, with the right wing sharply attacking the "naive" attempts of the foreign minister to mediate between the belligerents.[35]

Italy found itself at the center of another negotiation attempt soon thereafter. At the end of June 1966, Giovanni D'Orlandi, the Italian ambassador to Saigon and dean of the diplomatic corps there, was approached by Janusz Lewandowski, the Polish delegate in the International Control Commission set up by the 1954 Geneva conference. Lewandowski told D'Orlandi that in recent conversations in Hanoi he had persuaded the North Vietnamese leadership to explore the possibility of a peace settlement that did not include immediate reunification of Vietnam nor the establishment of a socialist system in the South. He believed that the two of them possessed a wonderful opportunity and should explore it with all the necessary secrecy and precautions. D'Orlandi quickly referred the proposal to Fanfani, who instructed him to inform the U.S. ambassador to Saigon, Henry Cabot Lodge.[36]

---

34 For the U.S. point of view, see Intelligence note 643, "Possible Implications of Fanfani's Resignation," Thomas L. Hughes, director, Bureau of Intelligence and Research, to Dean Rusk, secretary of state, Dec. 28, 1965, in DDRS, 1977/361.

35 See also Fanfani's own recollections in "Fanfani ricorda il contributo italiano alla pace," *Politica Internazionale*, no. 1 (1973): 147–9.

36 Telegram from U.S. Embassy in Saigon to Department of State, June 29, 1966, in *FRUS*, 1964–1968, IV, 468–70. The historical debate about who actually started the negotiations is still far from conclusion: See the new evidence from Eastern European sources as presented by James G. Hershberg, "Postmen, Advocates, Peacemakers or 'Crooks'? New Evidence on Polish Mediation Efforts and the Vietnam War, 1965–1967," paper presented at the conference "America's War and the World: Vietnam in International and Comparative Perspectives," German Historical Institute, Washington, D.C., Nov. 19–22, 1998.

The proposal reached Washington on June 29, and in a few days the trilateral negotiations, code-named "Marigold," were under way.[37] D'Orlandi enjoyed an excellent reputation among his colleagues in South Vietnam, and Lodge regarded him as a trustworthy channel should the Johnson administration decide to pursue this particular track: "You could be guaranteed of devoted help actuated by the deepest feelings of friendship for the U.S. as well as absolutely accurate reporting with considerable insight into the implications of everything that is said."[38] Initially, D'Orlandi's value was acknowledged by Johnson himself, who told a friend in confidence that, even if he did not think much of it, this was "the most realistic, the most convincing, the most persuasive peace feeler I've had since I've been president."[39] From the beginning, however, the Johnson administration held serious doubts whether the messages conveyed by Lewandowski represented Hanoi's real point of view or were simply Polish attempts at manipulation. The White House also was suspicious that for the North Vietnamese this was not a real negotiation to end the war but an attempt to discover the basis of the American negotiating position.[40] After a prolonged stalemate, Lewandowski, D'Orlandi, and Lodge began work on a compromise formula, and the United States, although aware of the risks involved in the initiative, undertook to demonstrate its desire to move forward by submitting a "possible agreement formula." Once agreed on, the U.S. proposal was transmitted to Hanoi through Lewandowski on December 1, and it briefly looked as if it could really form the basis for a major diplomatic breakthrough. However, while a secret meeting with North Vietnamese representatives to be held in Warsaw was being discussed, the United States resumed bombing Hanoi.[41] By December 14, the Polish foreign minister, Adam Rapacki, informed the United States that he wished to terminate the negotiations, squarely placing the blame for their failure on the American resumption of bombing. The United States tried to shift some of the blame by insisting that the failure

---

37 The story of Marigold is fairly well known. Most of the documents, even if in an incomplete version, were published by George Herring, ed., *The Secret Diplomacy of the Vietnam War: The Negotiating Volumes of the Pentagon Papers* (Austin, Tex., 1983), 210–370, and are printed in *FRUS, 1964–1968*, IV. A detailed chronology prepared by the Johnson administration – "Marigold: A Chronology" – is reproduced in DDRS, 1996/1642. From the Italian angle the story has been told by one of the members of Giovanni D'Orlandi's staff: Mario Sica, *Marigold non fiorì: Il contributo italiano alla pace in Vietnam* (Florence, 1991).
38 Telegram from U.S. Embassy in Vietnam to Department of State, July 2, 1966, in *FRUS, 1964–1968*, IV, 481–3.
39 Editorial Note, ibid., 473. In his memoirs, Johnson presented a more disparaging assessment of the initiative. See Lyndon B. Johnson, *The Vantage Point: Perspectives of the Presidency, 1963–1969* (New York, 1971), 252.
40 "Marigold: A Summary," p. 1 – DDRS, 1996/1641.
41 Robert Dallek, *Flawed Giant: Lyndon Johnson and His Times, 1961–1973* (New York, 1998), 389.

was actually due to Poland's attempt to put forward new terms and conditions. The negotiations ended with acrimonious bickering over who was responsible for their collapse.[42] Then, on December 24, the United States unilaterally decided to suspend for an indefinite period bombing within ten miles of Hanoi's center, and tried to reopen negotiations through the Polish channel. Hanoi did not answer, which provoked Johnson's angry remarks about the absolute lack of reciprocation from the North Vietnamese.[43]

When Frederick Reinhardt, the U.S. ambassador to Rome, reviewed the whole story with Fanfani in early January 1967, they agreed that the Polish attempt to blame the United States for the failure of the talks was not acceptable because the United States had constantly repeated that any termination of the bombing was conditional on the actual beginning of direct negotiations. Reinhardt then told Fanfani that, for the time being, Ambassador D'Orlandi should not take any further action.[44] The Italians, however, were not so easily deterred: Shortly afterward, Fanfani told Undersecretary of State Eugene Rostow that he had been approached directly by Hanoi and that subsequently Ambassador Reinhardt had expressed his government's acute interest in this new approach, provided that the interlocutor could be quickly identified and his credentials firmly established.[45] By February the picture was made even more complicated by press leaks that led to the disclosure of large portions of the Marigold story; on being informed of Johnson's February 12 decision not to recommence bombings, however, Fanfani hastened to inform Rusk that Italian diplomacy remained willing to provide its services should they become necessary.[46] Rusk then informed Fanfani that bombing was being resumed and thanked him for his help, implicitly suggesting that, even if he remained on the alert for any serious signal coming from Hanoi, for the time being the Marigold channel should be considered closed. In April, however, further conversations between Reinhardt and D'Orlandi seemed promising enough to the U.S. Department of State that it authorized Reinhardt to attend a trilateral meeting with D'Orlandi and Lewandowski in order to explore any possible new approaches.[47]

---

42 "Marigold: A Summary," p. 4 – DDRS, 1996/1641. On the recriminations about the failure of the negotiations, see also Hershberg, "Postmen, Advocates, Peacemakers, or 'Crooks.'" See also James G. Hershberg, with the assistance of Leo W. Gluchowski, "Who Murdered 'Marigold'? New Evidence on the Mysterious Failure of Poland's Secret Initiative to Start U.S.–North Vietnamese Peace Talks, 1966," Cold War International History Project, Working Paper no. 27 (Washington, D.C., 2000).

43 Telegram from Department of State to U.S. Embassy in Poland, Dec. 23, 1966, in *FRUS, 1964–1968*, IV, 968–9; Johnson's comments are in ibid., 986–7.

44 "Marigold: A Chronology," 58, in DDRS, 1996/1642.

45 Ibid., 68.   46 Ibid., 80.

47 Ibid., 88.

Although it is difficult to say whether the Marigold negotiations ever really had a chance of getting off the ground, it is important to underscore their relevance from the angle of U.S.-Italian relations. Even if Fanfani had been a bit too sanguine about the outcome of the initiative, and even if Italian eagerness to be useful sometimes might have been counterproductive, the Marigold channel demonstrated to Washington the reliability of its Italian partner and the fact that Italian diplomacy could play a serious role in exploring possible paths to a negotiated settlement of the war. A later American assessment confirms that the initiative was viewed favorably by the United States.[48]

Italy's sensitivity to the war in Vietnam was confirmed by an episode that followed the collapse of the Marigold negotiations. During a parliamentary debate on foreign policy in April 1967, Fanfani took a stand on the U.S. involvement in Vietnam that was somewhat less supportive than the one adopted by Moro two years earlier because he supported the cessation of the bombing without a clear indictment of Hanoi's responsibility for the war. Fanfani's statements would probably have gone unnoticed if Fenoaltea had not interpreted them as a weakening of Italian support for the United States. Skeptical as he was about a positive outcome to the war, the Italian ambassador nevertheless believed that the Italian foreign minister should display firm public support for the country's most important ally: On April 30, he handed in his resignation, which in turn prompted yet another virulent debate in the media, in parliament, and even within the diplomatic corps. Fanfani tried to persuade Fenoaltea to reverse his decision, but the ambassador eventually confirmed his resignation.[49] The turbulent episode revealed a certain malaise inside the Italian diplomatic corps. Edgardo Sogno, the ambassador to Rangoon and a maverick figure within the corps, sent a series of telegrams to the Ministry of Foreign Affairs in which he expressed his contempt for the government's conduct. Sogno declared that he was ashamed of his own country and indirectly blamed Fanfani for his relentless support of the Marigold negotiations, which, according to him, never had a chance of success because they were a mere ruse devised by Hanoi to suit its own purposes. But above all he decried the fact that the

fantastic image of an Italy working for peace, projected in Parliament on the screen of an impossible negotiation for the benefit of pacifists, communists and morons,

---

48 Vietnam Negotiations, May 8, 1968, in Herring, ed., *Secret Diplomacy*, 532.
49 Ortona, *Anni d'America: La cooperazione*, 9–12. See also Sergio Fenoaltea, *Italia Europa America* (Milan, 1980).

has been paid by presenting to the country and to world opinion a peaceful face of Hanoi which does not exist and, to the detriment of our ally, an intransigent image of America which is a slander.[50]

Sogno's blunt words were an exception in the guarded language of Italian diplomats. And yet it was clear that many among them did not agree with Fanfani's and D'Orlandi's optimistic evaluation of the negotiations and shared Sogno's and Fenoaltea's doubts about the conduct of their own government.[51] Nevertheless, once the crisis subsided with the appointment to Washington of Egidio Ortona, who had been in the U.S. capital for most of his career, the Italian government gradually resumed its efforts at mediation.

In late 1967, a new channel was opened to explore possible negotiations. In September and November, D'Orlandi met twice with Phan Van Su, the North Vietnamese ambassador to Prague, and after some debate it was agreed that Su would travel to Rome to meet with Fanfani.[52] In December, during his visit to Rome, President Johnson made clear to the Italian leaders that the United States, although seeking "negotiations at the earliest possible moment," would not consider another interruption of the air campaign unless under the conditions outlined in the San Antonio formula.[53] In the meantime, Fanfani had been approached in Rome by Romanian diplomats who asked him to consider several signals coming from North Vietnam. On January 23, 1968, Ortona informed Rusk about Fanfani's talks in Rome, and Rusk's vague acknowledgment was then communicated to the Romanians.[54] The talks were to take place under the most unlikely circumstances: By the end of the month, the most important North Vietnamese/Vietcong military offensive of the whole conflict had been unleashed, and the war seemed to be on the verge of yet another major escalation. Nevertheless, while the Tet Offensive was in full swing, Fanfani cabled Ortona from Rome that a representative from the Hanoi government (Su) had asked to meet with him; in the following days, with American consent, Fanfani had a few conversations with two envoys from North Vietnam. By late February, the so-called Killy explorative talks took

---

50　Telespresso da Edgardo Sogno (Rangoon) al Ministero degli Esteri, June 19, 1967, box 114, folder 2385/I , Archivio Nenni, serie goveno, ACS.

51　The doubts were strengthened by the somewhat cryptic attitude taken by Italy during the Six-Day War in early June 1967, which to many observers seemed to place both Israel and its enemies on the same level. One might also add, however, that the domestic criticism of the Italian mediating efforts was unwarranted by the more benign appraisal given by the United States itself. See note 48 to this chapter.

52　"Killy: Italian–North Vietnamese Track," Feb.–Mar. 1968, in Herring, ed., *Secret Diplomacy*, 817–18.

53　Record of meeting, Dec. 23, 1967, in *FRUS, 1964–1968*, XII, 285–7.

54　Ortona, *Anni d'America: La cooperazione*, 73–5.

place in Rome, with D'Orlandi and a U.S. envoy, Daniel I. Davidson, special assistant for the Far East, who was one of Harriman's closest aides.[55] The U.S. diplomats had the impression that Fanfani tried to convey the seriousness of the initiative by making "a more positive translation" into English of the Italian notes he had taken during his talks with Su.[56] Fanfani also added that "he was prepared to drop the matter entirely if the U.S. desired," explaining to the Americans that his major concern here was that a further escalation of the war "would help the Communist vote in Italy."[57] Persuaded that the initiative was worth exploring, Davidson recommended to Washington the continuation of the dialog between D'Orlandi and Su, even though once again the secrecy of the talks had been blown by a press leak, this time by an Italian left-wing newspaper.[58] Initially, Hanoi's reaction to the leak was unusually mild, but after a new pointless round of talks between Su and D'Orlandi on March 1, and in spite of a renewed expression of American interest in continuing negotiations, by mid-March operation Killy had clearly come to a dead end.[59] A secret internal memo by the Italian Foreign Ministry, however, described the contacts as a continuation of the earlier Italian efforts and, underlining the North Vietnamese interest in the Italian channel, was relatively optimistic regarding the possible future role of an Italian mediation: The Tet Offensive and the American response had produced a military stalemate, which in turn made negotiation all the more necessary and, indeed, possible.[60]

The new situation created by Johnson's March 31, 1968, speech and by the subsequent declarations from both sides about their willingness to start direct negotiations completely changed the international landscape in which the Italian attempts at mediation had taken place. The war was unlikely to escalate further, and direct talks between the two belligerents were going to take place. This clearly reduced the need for any third-party mediation and basically ended Italy's role in the conflict, even if the Italian Foreign Ministry still envisaged a possible role in accelerating the peace process and facilitating the conclusion of an accord.[61]

---

55 Ibid., 77.
56 "Killy: Italian–North Vietnamese Track," Feb.–Mar. 1968, in Herring, ed., *Secret Diplomacy*, 819.
57 Ibid., 821.   58 Ibid., 822–3.
59 Ibid., 825.
60 Ministero Affari Esteri, DGAP – Uff. 5, "Alcune considerazioni sull'attuale situazione in Vietnam," Mar. 12, 1968, box 114, folder 2385/II, Archivio Nenni, serie governo, ACS.
61 Ministero Affari Esteri, DGAP – Uff. 5, "Appunto – alcune considerazioni sui più recenti sviluppi," Apr. 6, 1968, box 114, folder 2385/II, Archivio Nenni, serie governo, ACS.

CONCLUSION

There is a remarkable symmetry between the escalation of the Vietnam conflict and the progress of the center-left government in Italy. By the spring of 1968 both had reached their apexes and wound down in the following years: Whereas the Tet Offensive in early 1968 marked the beginning of the end of American involvement, the 1968 elections in Italy ended in an overall defeat for the Italian Socialists and spelled the end of the attempt to bring about a vigorous social-democratic left. Having overcome their former divisions and merged, the Italian Socialists in the 1968 elections garnered only 19 percent of the overall vote, less than what they had achieved in the previous elections as two separate parties (the PSI and the PSDI). The negative outcome led to some rancorous quarrels and eventually to a renewed split between the two parties, which can be regarded as the symbol of the unimpressive achievements of the opening to the left. The Italian political scene soon was dominated by the entirely new issue of opening a dialog between the Christian Democrats and the Communist Party, which made a vigorous comeback.

To view the Vietnam War as one of the factors in the limited success of the center-left governments would certainly be excessive. The bases of the limited accomplishments of the *apertura* were mostly domestic and were related to such factors as the economic recession, which made the implementation of costly, badly needed social reforms more difficult; the strong opposition of the Italian conservatives to any attack on their privileges; and the cultural backwardness of a democratic left that was still torn between the contrasting aspirations to modernize and to dismantle the capitalist system. Yet, the parallel escalation of the Vietnam War did have an impact on the evolution of the center-left and even aided the forces that were working to prevent its success.

To begin with, the image of the United States changed from the good-hearted, selfless liberator of World War II dispensing chocolate bars to starving, half-naked little Italian children to one of a brutal mass murderer cruelly dropping its high-tech explosives on the embattled North Vietnamese and their starving, half-naked little children. This perception of the United States as a merciless aggressor prevented the transformation of the cultural mind-set of the Italian Socialists – and more generally of the Italian left-wing electorate – that the opening to the left was meant to achieve. The ultimate goal of the operation, in fact, was to engender nothing less than the mutation of the Italian left, persuading it to abandon its old myths and shibboleths and turning it into a modern social democracy – an objective that implied discarding the anti-Americanism that the Italian Socialists had espoused in the early years of the Cold War. Eventually, this moderate leftist party would attract to its ranks that large portion of the electorate that sympathized with the PCI but did not truly believe in the Soviet myth, leaving the Communist Party with only a tiny nucleus of hard-core Stalinists and rendering it a largely irrelevant force in Italian politics.

But none of this happened. The Vietnam War reinforced all the suspicions about the United States that the pro-Soviet Italian left had carefully cultivated in the previous years and also was skillfully exploited by the PCI to maintain a powerful link with the more moderate leftist groups. To be sure, this was not a uniquely Italian phenomenon: The Vietnam War, as Donald Sassoon has written, became "the rallying call of the radical left throughout Western Europe and North America."[62] And yet, although most of the leaders of the West European socialist parties – from Harold Wilson to Willy Brandt – remained loyal to their Atlantic ally and uttered few, if any, criticisms of the escalation of the war, many Italian Socialists acted quite differently. Some, for instance, became involved in the activities of the Russell tribunal and sharply condemned U.S. involvement. Far from becoming a "normal" social democratic party with a large base safely anchored to a stable pro-Western perspective, the Italian Socialists were pulled in very contradictory directions and gradually became a marginal political force until their brief revival in the late 1970s and early 1980s. What was worse, from the American perspective, was that the resurgence of anti-American feelings engendered by the war in Vietnam was not limited to the Italian left. By the end of the 1960s, the United States had squandered a large portion of its huge reservoir of public sympathy and goodwill it had accumulated in Italy during World War II and its immediate aftermath.

---

62 Donald Sassoon, *One Hundred Years of Socialism: The West European Left in the Twentieth Century* (London, 1997), 344.

13

Auschwitz and Vietnam

West German Protest Against America's War During the 1960s

WILFRIED MAUSBACH

Thomas Nipperdey, in an ironic twist on Leopold von Ranke's famous dictum, once remarked that "All of German history is intermediate to Hitler."[1] The 1960s certainly were. In West Germany, public discourse throughout the decade was imbued with references to the country's troubled past. Nearly every important event in the Federal Republic's political, social, and cultural life was discussed against the background of National Socialism. Although some issues grew immediately out of this period, like the Eichmann and Auschwitz trials or the suspension of the statute of limitations with regard to atrocities committed during the Third Reich, others did not, like the *Spiegel* affair, the Multilateral Nuclear Force (MLF), the Emergency Laws, and – last but not least – the Vietnam War.

This chapter will show how the Vietnam War was perceived in the Federal Republic, given the atmosphere, and how the war in turn became a symbolic weapon in an assault on the collective identity of West Germans. In other words, and more provocatively: This chapter's premise is that West German students were protesting not so much against the current American actions in Southeast Asia as against past German atrocities in Europe. For them, Vietnam represented an opportunity to break away from their parents' generation of perpetrators and assuage their inherited national guilt.

It is obvious, then, that I am concerned more with the specifics of the West German protest movement than with its similarities to other social movements that had sprung up worldwide during the 1960s.[2] There was, to be sure, extensive cross-fertilization across national boundaries. However,

---

1 Thomas Nipperdey, "Unter der Herrschaft des Verdachts," *Die Zeit*, Oct. 17, 1986, 12.
2 Carole Fink, Philipp Gassert, and Detlef Junker, eds., *1968: The World Transformed* (New York, 1998); Doug McAdam and Dieter Rucht, "The Cross-National Diffusion of Movement Ideas," *The Annals of the American Academy of Political and Social Science* 528 (1993): 56–74; George Katsiaficas, *The Imagination of the New Left: A Global Analysis of 1968* (Boston, 1987).

interviews with student activists from different countries show, and some sociologists point out, that national and historic contexts must be taken into account.[3]

In contrast to most social-movement research, I do not aim here at generally applicable social-scientific explanations. Nevertheless, I use the concept of a generation gap as the point of departure and argue that a strikingly different set of experiences led the students of 1968 to challenge the way West Germans saw themselves by trying to reconstruct their recollections of the past.[4] As Charles Maier has observed, "Memory itself becomes not a simple act of recall but a socially constitutive act. The German version of these trends is the invocation of 'history,' less as a record than as a problematic constituent of identity."[5] Thus, student activists in Berlin, Bonn, Frankfurt, and Munich wanted to forge a new identity, an identity that internalized the horrors of the past and would therefore be able to respond to present evils.

I

In the 1950s, Cold War culture reigned in West Germany as it did in the United States. Its main ingredients were anticommunism and consumerism. The common notion of a nation suppressing its past is certainly too simple,[6] but it is nevertheless true that Germans dealt with their recent past in an administrative rather than a personal way.[7] Exculpatory arguments were

---

3 Ronald Fraser, *1968: A Student Generation in Revolt: An International Oral History* (New York, 1988), 4–5; Heinz Bude, *Das Altern einer Generation: Die Jahrgänge 1938 bis 1948* (Frankfurt am Main, 1997), 19–21; Sidney Tarrow, *Democracy and Disorder: Protest and Politics in Italy, 1965–1975* (Oxford, 1989), 3.

4 See, e.g., Lewis S. Feuer, *The Conflict of Generations: The Character and Significance of Student Movements* (New York, 1969); Klaus R. Allerbeck, *Soziologie radikaler Studentenbewegungen: Eine vergleichende Untersuchung in der Bundesrepublik Deutschland und den Vereinigten Staaten* (Munich, 1973); and Norbert Elias, *The Germans: Power Struggles and the Development of Habitus in the 19th and 20th Century*, trans. Eric Dunning and Stephen Mennell (New York, 1996), 229–97. See also Karl Mannheim, "The Problem of Generations," in *From Karl Mannheim*, ed. Kurt H. Wolff, 2d ed. (New Brunswick, N.J., 1993), 351–98.

5 Charles S. Maier, *The Unmasterable Past: History, Holocaust, and German National Identity* (Cambridge, Mass., 1988), 169.

6 Hermann Lübbe, "Der Nationalsozialismus im deutschen Nachkriegsbewusstsein," *Historische Zeitschrift* 236 (1983): 579–99; Hermann Graml, "Die verdrängte Auseinandersetzung mit dem Nationalsozialismus," in Martin Broszat, ed., *Zäsuren nach 1945: Essays zur Periodisierung der deutschen Nachkriegsgeschichte* (Munich, 1990), 169–83; Manfred Kittel, *Die Legende von der "Zweiten Schuld": Vergangenheitsbewältigung in der Ära Adenauer* (Berlin, 1993); Robert G. Moeller, "War Stories: The Search for a Usable Past in the Federal Republic of Germany," *American Historical Review* 101 (1996): 1008–48; Jeffrey Herf, *Divided Memory: The Nazi Past in the Two Germanys* (Cambridge, Mass., 1997), 267–333.

7 Norbert Frei, *Vergangenheitspolitik: Die Anfänge der Bundesrepublik und die NS-Vergangenheit* (Munich, 1996); Detlef Garbe, "'Äusserliche Abkehr, Erinnerungsverweigerung und 'Vergangenheitsbewältigung': Der Umgang mit dem Nationalsozialismus in der frühen Bundesrepublik," in Axel Schildt and Arnold Sywottek, eds., *Modernisierung im Wiederaufbau: Die westdeutsche Gesellschaft der 50er Jahre* (Bonn, 1993), 693–716; Peter Graf Kielmannsegg, *Lange Schatten: Vom Umgang der Deutschen mit der nationalsozialistischen Vergangenheit* (Berlin, 1989).

widespread, Adolf Hitler often appeared as the person solely responsible for events between 1933 and 1945, and high school history textbooks barely mentioned the Holocaust.[8] Things began to change, however, in the second part of the 1950s. The herald of this change was the publication in 1955 of the paperback edition of *The Diary of Anne Frank*, which sold 700,000 copies by the end of the decade. A theater adaptation attracted an audience of nearly two million, and more than twice as many people flocked to the 1959 cinematic version.[9] By that time moviegoers had already seen a dubbed version of Alain Resnais's documentary *Night and Fog*, with its blunt portrayal of Nazi atrocities; the film soon became a standard fixture in classrooms across West Germany. Moreover, a wave of anti-Semitic incidents at the turn of the decade eventually triggered a reevaluation of textbooks, compelling editors to add materials on the Holocaust and, for the first time, to include the perspectives of its victims.[10]

Another trajectory of Holocaust awareness was the major trials of concentration-camp personnel and their superiors. If the 1958–9 trial of two Sachsenhausen SS sergeants elicited little public interest, the proceedings against Adolf Eichmann in Jerusalem triggered a full-blown media blitz in 1961. This set the stage for the spectacular trial of Auschwitz personnel in Frankfurt from 1963 to 1965.[11]

Still, the abundance of information on Nazi crimes did not satisfy the younger generation. The more they learned about their nation's past, the more they noticed the lack of a sense of guilt among their elders. It is telling that one of the most influential books of the time, originally published in 1967, bore the title *The Inability to Mourn* rather than *The Inability to Remember*.[12] Toward the end of the Auschwitz trials Martin Walser wrote in *Kursbuch*, an important journal of the critical intelligentsia, that the meaning of the proceedings in Frankfurt had long moved from the realm of judicial prosecution to become an enterprise of elucidation for a population that

8 Falk Pingel, "Nationalsozialismus und Holocaust in westdeutschen Schulbüchern," in Rolf Steininger, with Ingrid Böhler, eds., *Der Umgang mit dem Holocaust: Europa – USA – Israel* (Vienna, 1994), 221–32; Martin Kolinsky and Eva Kolinsky, "The Treatment of the Holocaust in German History Textbooks," *Yad Vashem Studies* 10 (1974): 149–216; Ludwig von Friedeburg and Peter Hübner, *Das Geschichtsbild der Jugend* (Munich, 1964).

9 Ulrich Brochhagen, *Nach Nürnberg: Vergangenheitsbewältigung und Westintegration in der Ära Adenauer* (Hamburg, 1994), 434; Alvin Rosenfeld, "Popularization and Memory: The Case of Anne Frank," in Peter Hayes, ed., *Lessons and Legacies* (Evanston, Ill., 1991), 243–78.

10 Harold Marcuse, "The Revival of Holocaust Awareness in West Germany, Israel, and the United States," in Fink, Gassert, and Junker, eds., *1968*, 421–38, esp. 422–3; Werner Bergmann, *Antisemitismus in öffentlichen Konflikten: Kollektives Lernen in der politischen Kultur der Bundesrepublik 1949–1989* (Frankfurt am Main, 1997), 235–77.

11 Jürgen Wilke et al., *Holocaust und NS-Prozesse: Die Presseberichterstattung in Israel und Deutschland zwischen Aneignung und Abwehr* (Cologne, 1995).

12 Alexander Mitscherlich and Margarete Mitscherlich, *The Inability to Mourn: Principles of Collective Behavior*, trans. Beverley R. Placzek (New York, 1975).

seemed incapable of acknowledging what had happened. However, Walser feared that the stark description of cruelty and the language the media used in reporting it might in fact facilitate repression: "We have nothing to do with these events, these atrocities, and we know this for a fact." Walser was worried that the lawyers, who could only prosecute personal crimes, would eventually remove the deeds so far from their national context that only pure brutality would be left.[13] He and many of his generation yearned for a concept of guilt that could be ascribed individually but be accepted collectively.

There was a wave of literary works during this period that were concerned with moral steadfastness, among them Max Frisch's *The Firebugs* (1958), Siegfried Lenz's *Zeit der Schuldlosen* (1961), and Günther Grass's *Tin Drum*, in which Oscar Matzerath, a dwarf, drums against the brown order. Some dramas, inspired by the Auschwitz and Eichmann trials, echoed this theme. Rolf Hochhuth's play *The Deputy* (1963) indicted Pope Pius XII, who looked the other way in spite of credible information on the Holocaust as it was happening.[14] Peter Weiss's play *The Investigation* (1965) sought to prove the complicity of supposedly innocent bystanders whose behavior nevertheless made Auschwitz possible.[15]

For many in the up-and-coming generation, though, it was impossible to talk to their parents about National Socialism, much less elicit an admission of guilt from them. Detlev Claussen recalls being confronted with Nazi medical experiments for the first time in high school in 1963: "I came home very upset and talked about it. Without explanation, my father responded by talking about the Communists after 1945. He simply refused to deal with the Nazi past. The East is now, the past is past, he was saying in effect."[16] But that was about to change.

II

When Chancellor Ludwig Erhard proclaimed in his 1965 inaugural speech that the postwar period had come to an end, he was right in more ways than

---

13 Martin Walser, "Unser Auschwitz" (1965), reprinted in Carsten Seibold, ed., *Die 68er: Das Fest der Rebellion* (Munich, 1988), 12–24, here 13.

14 Werner Bergmann, "Die Reaktion auf den Holocaust in Westdeutschland von 1945 bis 1989," *Geschichte in Wissenschaft und Unterricht* 43 (1992): 327–50, esp. 349. The controversy surrounding Pope Pius XII was recently re-ignited by John Cornwell, *Hitler's Pope: The Secret History of Pius XII* (New York, 1999). See also George O. Kent, "Pope Pius and Germany: Some Aspects of German Vatican Relations, 1933–1943," *American Historical Review* 70 (1964): 59–78; and Michael Phayer, "Pope Pius XII, the Holocaust, and the Cold War," *Holocaust and Genocide Studies* 12 (1998): 233–56.

15 See Robert Cohen, "The Political Aesthetics of Holocaust Literature: Peter Weiss's *The Investigation* and Its Critics," *History and Memory* 10/2 (1998): 43–67.

16 Quoted in Fraser, *1968*, 87.

one.[17] At home, the consensus forged by the necessities of dealing with the consequences of the war and of rebuilding the country began to unravel. Abroad, confrontation within the communist camp and a strong desire for détente in the West called into question the anticommunist attitude that had provided a shield against the past as well as the cornerstone of a new identity for many West Germans. Détente enabled the younger generation to begin to question the Federal Republic's firm Cold War identity. What they tried to inject was a sense of guilt and collective responsibility. The new postwar generation insisted on a radical renunciation of the half-heartedness that had hitherto characterized their elders' dealings with the past.[18]

Student activists in the 1960s took up the general mood of antimilitarism and fear of war that had characterized German society in the 1950s, when this mood had found expression in considerable opposition to German rearmament and in protests against the inclusion of the Bundeswehr in NATO's nuclear strategy.[19] From 1960 on, there were Easter peace marches against war in general and against nuclear weapons in particular. They were organized by the nonpartisan Campaign for Disarmament (*Kampagne für Abrüstung*), which was the rallying point of extraparliamentarian opposition until the mid-1960s.[20] Its protests, however, were essentially concerned with residual problems left over from West Germany's largely successful reclamation of sovereignty in the 1950s.[21] Rearmament raised the question of military equality, including at least some participation in the control over nuclear weapons, a problem that the Kennedy administration tried to solve by proposing the MLF. The second residual problem was the far-reaching emergency powers left to the Allies as long as the German Basic Law remained silent about this matter. Attempts by the *Bundestag* to enact relevant legislation provoked considerable domestic opposition. Unrestricted German sovereignty aroused suspicion not only abroad but in some segments of

17 *Verhandlungen des Deutschen Bundestages:* 5. Wahlperiode, Stenographische Berichte, vol. 60 (Bonn, 1965), 17.

18 See Bernhard Giesen, *Intellectuals and the German Nation: Collective Identity in an Axial Age*, trans. Nicholas Levis (New York, 1998), 148–51.

19 See Wolfgang Kraushaar, *Die Protest-Chronik 1949–1959: Eine illustrierte Geschichte von Bewegung, Widerstand und Utopie*, 4 vols. (Hamburg, 1996); and Detlef Bald, *Die Atombewaffnung der Bundeswehr: Militär, Öffentlichkeit und Politik in der Ära Adenauer* (Bremen, 1994).

20 Frank Werkmeister, *Die Protestbewegung gegen den Vietnamkrieg in der Bundesrepublik Deutschland 1965– 1973* (Marburg a.d. Lahn, 1975), 49–62; Karl A. Otto, *Vom Ostermarsch zur APO: Geschichte der ausserparlamentarischen Opposition in der Bundesrepublik 1960–1970* (Frankfurt am Main, 1977); idem, ed., *APO: Ausserparlamentarische Opposition in Quellen und Dokumenten 1960–1970* (Cologne, 1989), 23–4, 104–9; Werner Balsen and Karl Rössel, *Hoch die internationale Solidarität: Zur Geschichte der Dritte-Welt-Bewegung in der Bundesrepublik* (Cologne, 1986), 116–20.

21 Lothar Rolke, *Protestbewegungen in der Bundesrepublik: Eine analytische Sozialgeschichte sozialen Widerspruchs* (Opladen, 1987), 195–7.

German society as well. This domestic, historically founded mistrust mush-roomed when the Federal Republic's most valued and trusted ally broke the internalized taboo of nonaggression with mostly tacit but frequently quite vocal support from the government in Bonn.

Given the Campaign for Disarmament's preoccupation with war, it is hardly surprising that early criticism of American actions in Southeast Asia focused on the dangers of an expanded conflict. Particularly alarm-ing was Operation Rolling Thunder, the program of sustained bombing of North Vietnam that began in mid-February 1965.[22] On March 7, an annual gathering of Social Democratic Party delegates in Frankfurt "noticed with consternation that by bombing North Vietnamese cities on February 7, 10, and 12, and March 2, the United States had abandoned the policy of limiting conflicts that since the Korean War had been one of the strongest guarantees for keeping the Cold War from turning into a hot war."[23] Rolling Thunder also elicited a declaration by the Easter peace marchers: "Facing defeat, the United States has expanded the war in Vietnam, pursuing escalation that is regarded by all military experts as the most certain road to a new world war.... The war in Vietnam has to end before its rubble buries us all."[24] Behind these fears lay the experience of World War II, of Allied air raids, and of pulverized German cities, an experience, then, of victimization. One motto of the Easter peace marchers read: "Dresden, Würzburg, Vietnam – terror bombers on the attack."[25] At first students were no exception to this line of thought. "For years I'd had nightmares about the terrible bombing of Dresden at the end of World War II. I could see the houses burning still. And that's why I identified with the Vietnamese – the campaign against the war was a kind of working-through of my personal history," recalled a former student at the Free University of Berlin.[26] A leaflet by the Socialist Students

22 Robert D. Schulzinger, *A Time for War: The United States and Vietnam, 1945–1975* (New York, 1997), 170–4; Brian VanDeMark, *Into the Quagmire: Lyndon Johnson and the Escalation of the Vietnam War* (New York, 1991), 212–21; James Clay Thompson, *Rolling Thunder: Understanding Program and Policy Failure* (Chapel Hill, N.C., 1980).

23 Guillaume to Parteivorstand der SPD, "Entschliessungsantrag der Jahresdelegiertenversammlung des Unterbezirks Frankfurt a.M.," Mar. 7, 1965, box 1, Willy-Brandt-Archiv (hereafter WBA), SPD/Parteivorsitzender, Verbindungen mit regionalen Parteiorganisationen (ausser Landesverbände und Bezirke), Archiv der sozialen Demokratie (hereafter AdsD), Bonn.

24 Quoted in Zentralrat der Freien Deutschen Jugend (FDJ), Zentrale Arbeitsgruppe (ZAG), "Übersicht und Informationen über den Verlauf und den Umfang der Ostermärsche der Atomwaffengegner 1965 in Westdeutschland," Apr. 21, 1965, file 117146, DY 24, Stiftung Archiv der Parteien und Massenorganisationen der DDR im Bundesarchiv (hereafter SAPMO-BArch), Berlin.

25 Ibid.

26 Quoted in Fraser, *1968*, 100. The importance of World War II experiences for the generation of 1968 has been stressed by Elisabeth Domansky, "A Lost War: World War II in German Memory," in Alvin H. Rosenfeld, ed., *Thinking About the Holocaust: After Half a Century* (Bloomington, Ind., 1997), 233–73.

League (SDS) warned as early as the summer of 1964, after the Gulf of Tonkin incidents, of a dangerous internationalization of the conflict, and in April 1965 the SDS reiterated that "this would put peace at immediate risk not only in Asia but in Central Europe as well."[27] After the bombing raids on North Vietnam intensified in 1965, two SDS leaders, who also headed the official student government organization (AStA) at the Free University, signed an antiwar declaration sponsored by East Berlin. Trying to justify this treasonous deed to the student parliament, one of them explained that their primary motivation had been "that America might be forced to cause a worldwide war in which even nuclear weapons could be used. Therefore, we felt that we could not subscribe to the clichés propagated in Germany about the war in Vietnam, namely, that it is a struggle between communism and capitalism."[28]

But for both politicians and the public in West Germany, this struggle still was the main determinant of global politics. When Lyndon Johnson, five days after President John F. Kennedy's death, promised that the United States would "keep its commitments from South Vietnam to West Berlin,"[29] Germans were eager not to question this assertion. Chancellor Erhard assured Johnson and the American public that "Viet-Nam was important to most Germans because they regarded it as a kind of testing ground as to how firmly the United States honors its commitments. In that respect there existed a parallel between Saigon and Berlin."[30] McGeorge Bundy, Johnson's national security adviser, took the same line with members of Congress, emphasizing "that the defense of Berlin, right now, is in Vietnam."[31] But student activists and antiwar protesters in Germany would not buy it. When Saigon's ambassador to the Federal Republic reiterated the analogy at a roundtable discussion at the Free University of Berlin, student leader Rudi Dutschke stormed the panel, challenging "His Excellency" with American intelligence findings indicating that 80 percent of the rural

---

27 SDS LV Berlin, leaflet "Vietnam," Aug. 12, 1964, folder: BV II Gruppen, Teil I 1964/65 SDS, B1, Archivbereich "APO und Soziale Bewegung," ZI 6, Free University Berlin (hereafter AASB); "Resolution zur Vietnam-Frage," Apr. 5, 1965, folder: SDS, Horlemann Vietnam 1966, ibid.
28 Speech by Wolfgang Lefèvre before the Konvent, Oct. 26, 1965, folder: SDS Vietnam Horlemann 1966, B1, AASB; see also Tilman Fichter and Siegward Lönnendonker, *Kleine Geschichte des SDS: Der Sozialistische Deutsche Studentenbund von 1946 bis zur Selbstauflösung* (Berlin, 1977), 89.
29 Address before a joint session of the Congress, Nov. 27, 1963, in *Public Papers of the Presidents of the United States: Lyndon B. Johnson*, vol. 1 (Washington, D.C., 1965), 8.
30 Memorandum of Conversation, June 4, 1965, U.S. Department of State, ed., *Foreign Relations of the United States* (hereafter *FRUS*), 1964–1968, II (Washington, D.C., 1996), 718; see also Knappstein to Auswärtiges Amt, "Besuch des Bundeskanzlers in USA," here: Öffentliche Erklärungen, May 28, 1965, folder: 2066, B 136, Bundesarchiv, Koblenz (hereafter BAK).
31 Congressional reception, Feb. 12, 1965, congressional briefings on Vietnam, box 1, Lyndon B. Johnson Library, Austin, Tex.

population in South Vietnam supported the National Liberation Front.[32]
The Social Democratic University League (SHB) felt the parallel was inap-
propriate and an insult to their country.[33] Helmut Gollwitzer, professor of
theology at the Free University of Berlin and a prominent supporter of the
protest movement, emphasized: "The freedom of Berlin and the freedom
of the West is not defended but endangered in Vietnam." He warned that
the brutalization of American policy would eventually undermine democracy in Germany. "The future of the young is once again sacrificed for the
blindness of the older generation, but the one difference from 1933 is that
this time the young are not enthusiastically joining in with the madness but
are rising against the blindness and the folly."[34]

"Once again" – these two words inspired most of the protest. Whereas
the historian Golo Mann, in reviewing the German edition of Arthur
Schlesinger's *The Bitter Heritage*, fatalistically recommended "a polite and
sad silence" as "the most dignified bearing," student activists felt it was "unprincipled to remain silent: He who keeps quiet agrees."[35] A leaflet by the
Vietnam Solidarity Committee in West Berlin declared: "All citizens who
keep quiet are tacitly tolerating the U.S. war, and they become implicated in
just the same way as those who remained silent in spite of Hitler's crimes."[36]
What was unfolding was a struggle over the controlling political analogies
in the discourse of the Federal Republic.

III

Early protest in West Germany against the Vietnam War was driven by moral
and humanitarian motives. Its point of reference was a mixture of general war
weariness and German suffering during the bombing raids of World War II.

---

32 Ulrich Chaussy, *Die drei Leben des Rudi Dutschke: Eine Biographie* (Berlin, 1993), 146–7. In a cable to
    Washington, the American Mission in Berlin mentioned neither this particular incident nor Dutschke
    but rather reported that the South Vietnamese ambassador "was occasionally able to impress some of
    the audience with forceful and dignified answers to polemical 'questions,' " and that "the SDS, which
    styles itself the 'democratic left', gave a depressingly fascistic performance." Calhoun to secretary of
    state, subject: Vietnamese Ambassador at the Free University of Berlin, Dec. 7, 1966, POL 17
    VIET S – GER W, box 3020, Record Group (hereafter RG) 59, National Archives, College Park,
    Md. (NA).
33 Gerhard Bauss, *Die Studentenbewegung der sechziger Jahre in der Bundesrepublik und Westberlin*
    (Cologne, 1977), 172; *Beschlüsse und Stellungnahmen des Sozialdemokratischen Hochschulbundes (SHB)*
    (Bonn, 1966).
34 Helmut Gollwitzer, "Rede bei der Vietnam-Demonstration in Westberlin," Oct. 21, 1967, folder:
    SDS, B III, AASB.
35 Golo Mann, "Irrtümer in Vietnam," *Der Spiegel* 21, no. 20 (1967): 166; "Beschlussprotokoll der 20.
    ordentlichen Delegiertenkonferenz des SDS," Nov. 3, 1965, folder: BV 20. DK 1965, AASB.
36 Richard Lindt and Peter Biesold, "Solidarität mit Vietnam," Apr. 1965, file 117747, DY 24,
    SAPMO-BArch.

However, the all-encompassing struggle with the past in the first half of the 1960s soon shifted this perspective. Increasingly, identification with the sufferings of the Vietnamese people was inspired by a view that saw Germans not as victims but as perpetrators. Thus, the new categorical imperative that Hitler, according to Theodor Adorno, had imposed on mankind, namely, "to arrange their thoughts and actions so that Auschwitz will not repeat itself, so that nothing similar will happen," attained an exceptional significance for German protesters.[37]

The first order of the day, however, was to break up the East–West mind-set of the public and to provide information on the true nature of the war. The Berlin chapter of the SDS was particularly suited for the latter task because it had been appointed at a September 1964 delegates' conference to study the situation in Vietnam. In early 1965, it established a working committee that organized a panel discussion with representatives of the U.S. mission in Berlin, published a news digest from American, French, and German sources, and showed U.S. and North Vietnamese propaganda films about the war. Moreover, the students put together an exhibition with pictures gathered in East Berlin, partly from the North Vietnamese embassy and partly from representatives of the National Liberation Front of South Vietnam. The exhibition was made available to SDS chapters throughout West Germany.[38] The primary goal of all these activities was to disprove the American contention that the conflict in Southeast Asia derived essentially from aggression from the north[39] and to portray the confrontation instead as a civil war in which the United States had intervened on the side of the villain.[40]

All these efforts, however, did not produce any tangible results. As Daniel Cohn-Bendit recalled: "It started with bombings on Vietnam. And again bombings on Vietnam. And helplessness, total helplessness. Marching left

---

37 Theodor W. Adorno, *Negative Dialectics*, trans. E. B. Ashton (New York, 1973), 365.

38 Siegward Lönnendonker and Jochen Staadt, "Der Krieg in Vietnam, in: Die Bedeutung des Sozialistischen Deutschen Studentenbundes (SDS) für die ausserparlamentarischen Protestbewegungen im politischen System der Bundesrepublik in den fünfziger und sechziger Jahren. Vorläufiger Abschlussbericht für die Zeit vom 1. Februar 1987 bis zum 31. Juli 1990," unpublished manuscript, 2–12; Jürgen Horlemann, "Einladung – Open House: Vietnam," Mar. 25, 1965, folder: SDS, Vietnam Material, B IV; Jürgen Horlemann to Hartmut Schauer, Aug. 10, 1965, folder: BV II Gruppen, Teil I 1964/65 SDS, B1, AASB.

39 U.S. Department of State, *Aggression from the North: The Record of North Viet-Nam's Campaign to Conquer the South* (Washington, D.C., 1965). For U.S. efforts to spread this gospel in Europe, see Caroline Page, *U.S. Official Propaganda During the Vietnam War* (London, 1996), 53–7.

40 See also Jürgen Horlemann and Peter Gäng, *Vietnam – Genesis eines Konflikts* (Frankfurt am Main, 1966); Robert Havemann, "Vietnam und wir," *Neue Kritik* 7, no. 35 (1966): 15–18; "Kampagne für Abrüstung, Vietnam-Report," Sept. 15, 1966, folder: SDS Vietnam Materialien, B IV, AASB.

and right, saying: stop it, stop it! – and nobody stops, and it doesn't stop."[41] Here it was again: silence in the face of a catastrophe. Tilman Fichter and Siegward Lönnendonker, the chroniclers of the German SDS, have observed that "the disgust about the German bourgeoisie after Auschwitz, which remained silent about the American genocide in Vietnam, left its mark on the convictions of the antiauthoritarians."[42] This "second silence" discredited the bourgeoisie once and for all, and it marks the beginning of student radicalization in Germany. As Hans-Jürgen Krahl, Adorno's last assistant in Frankfurt and a leader of the SDS, emphasized: "Auschwitz presents us with a new situation in our discussions of strategy because it suggests new qualities of obliviousness and ahistoricity in the consciousness of the masses; with this I mean... the destruction of the bourgeois individual, ... and one shouldn't speak of idle talk here, because we all know that we began our revolutionary protests in the FRG basically because we mourn this destruction of the bourgeois individual and not because we are genuine socialists, and that we derived our categories of emancipation from this as well."[43]

Some student activists now felt that they had to go beyond humanitarian protest. Bernd Rabehl, a leading SDS figure in Berlin, proclaimed, "He who, after Auschwitz, takes action only by indulging in moralistic rhetoric based on the contradiction that the crimes perpetrated in Vietnam cannot, for a second, be tolerated and yet cannot, for the time being, be effectively prevented, of course fails to notice that he belongs to Johnson's brain trust."[44] Falling back on Marxist theories that had been discussed within the SDS in the early 1960s, students developed an explanatory framework for the American engagement in Southeast Asia. It interpreted the Vietnam War as an exemplary struggle in which the capitalist world tried to stabilize its power by proving the pointlessness of emancipatory efforts throughout the Third World.[45] These efforts, however, were at the same time the only hope for a socialist alternative in the West, an alternative that, given the moral abdication of the bourgeoisie, would finally take seriously Adorno's new categorical imperative. These students expected that the spread of liberation

---

41 "Die Linke lebt – ein Fernsehdialog," in Rudi Dutschke, *Die Revolte: Wurzeln und Spuren eines Aufbruchs* (Reinbek, 1983), 264–313, here 283.

42 Fichter and Lönnendonker, *Kleine Geschichte des SDS*, 142.

43 H. J. Krahl, "Beiträge zum Hochschul–teach–in SDS–SHB," 1969, file 332, Zsg 2, BAK.

44 Uwe Bergmann et al., *Rebellion der Studenten oder Die neue Opposition* (Reinbek bei Hamburg, 1968), 166.

45 Rüdiger Griepenburg and Kurt Steinhaus, "Zu einigen sozioökonomischen und militärischen Aspekten des Vietnamkonflikts," *Das Argument* 8, no. 36 (1966): 44–61; Kurt Steinhaus, "Thesen zum Krieg in Vietnam," *Neue Kritik* 7, no. 34 (1966): 3–4; idem, *Vietnam: Zum Problem der kolonialen Revolution und Konterrevolution*, 2d ed. (Berlin, 1967).

movements throughout the Third World would disrupt the reproductive process of capitalism, rendering impossible the consumerist strategies that had deprived the proletariat of its revolutionary potential.[46]

This conceptual framework was meant to transform the hitherto merely moral protest and add a domestic dimension to it. It was presented in May 1966 at a supposedly scientific congress in Frankfurt, the first anti-Vietnam event with countrywide participation. According to its SDS organizers, the congress was not to be a "mere verbal spectacle about the pros and cons of American intervention" but should "lead the political protest to socialist convictions."[47] The conveners of the congress found a congenial keynote speaker in Herbert Marcuse, an icon of the Frankfurt School and professor of sociology at the University of California at San Diego. Marcuse agreed with the view that Third World liberation movements were the principal agents of change in a capitalist world system, and he recommended "a solidarity of reason and sentiment."[48] Taking a similar line prior to the congress, Dutschke elaborated on the duties of the protest movement resulting from the crucial role of the Third World: "This is the dialectic of 'true poverty' that has to be completed on a global scale by a 'dialectic of correct understanding' in the capitalist centers to achieve what Marx . . . has called the alliance of thinking and suffering mankind. The struggle of the Vietcong . . . must be turned into conscious understanding through rational discussion and principally illegal demonstrations and activism back home."[49]

The latter, however, was still a matter of contention within the SDS. Its federal executive wanted to broaden the protest and slowly train a larger movement in socialist ideas. The local chapters in Munich and Berlin, however, had no patience for such a course. In Munich, SDS members would rather have lost a few fellow travelers than stick with merely moral protest, and they called for socialist praxis.[50] In Berlin, identification with the Vietnamese Liberation Front was so strong that a leaflet even implied resistance at home: "What has been neglected up to now, the opportunity to recognize ourselves in the condemned who defend themselves success-fully, and thus not simply write them off amid cries of despair, this is what

---

46 See Lönnendonker and Staadt, *Der Krieg in Vietnam*, 18.
47 Helmut Schauer and Hartmut Dabrowski, "SDS–Rundschreiben 4–65/66," Apr. 1, 1966, folder: 19. o. DK des SDS, AASB.
48 Herbert Marcuse, "Die Analyse eines Exempels," *Neue Kritik* 7, no. 36/37 (1966): 37.
49 Bergmann et al., *Rebellion der Studenten*, 69; see Ingo Juchler, *Die Studentenbewegungen in den Vereinigten Staaten und der Bundesrepublik Deutschland der sechziger Jahre: Eine Untersuchung hinsichtlich ihrer Beeinflussung durch Befreiungsbewegungen und –theorien aus der Dritten Welt* (Berlin, 1996), 116–88.
50 Gruppe München SDS and Vietnam–Referat, "Vietnam–Arbeit Winter 1965/66 und Sommer 66," n.d., folder: BV 21. DK 1966 SDS, AASB.

finally must be accomplished."[51] Provocation was meant to reveal the terror of the system and to furnish proof of its vulnerability, as the Vietcong did in Indochina. Activism, then, was treated as equivalent to enlightenment. A secret CIA report described this as "the idea that the more [Dutschke] and his followers demonstrated and challenged the system, the more the governing elements in society would 'unmask' their true character by resorting to naked force."[52] That, of course, was a self-fulfilling prophecy. Nevertheless, the establishment's reaction to provocation reinforced the students' mistrust regarding developments in West Germany. In his introductory remarks to the Frankfurt congress, SDS leader Hartmut Dabrowski observed that Bonn was not only supporting a fascist regime in South Vietnam but also might be trying to establish authoritarian and even fascist rule in Germany.[53]

Along with this radicalization in theory came a radicalization in rhetoric. Activists began comparing the American conduct of war in Southeast Asia with Nazi behavior in the 1930s. The link most often used in this regard was a remark reported in the press by South Vietnamese Prime Minister Nguyen Cao Ky that he admired Hitler.[54] The implied message was that Americans (with West German support) were fighting under the swastika in Vietnam. Protesters pointed out that Washington was using Vietnam as a field of experimentation for new weapons in much the same way Nazi Germany had done during the Spanish Civil War.[55] In a declaration supporting the international congress on Vietnam held in Berlin in 1968, a group of well-known writers and intellectuals proclaimed: "Vietnam is our generation's Spain. We must not burden ourselves with guilt by remaining quiet or noncommittal in the face of the revolutionary struggle of the Vietnamese people."[56] By that time, however, the dominant analogy no longer was Guernica but the epitome of inhumanity: Auschwitz.

---

51 "Informationen über Vietnam und Länder der Dritten Welt," no. 1, May 1966, reprinted in Siegward Lönnendonker and Tilman Fichter, with Claus Rietzschel, eds., *Freie Universität Berlin 1948–1973: Hochschule im Umbruch (Dokumentation)*, vol. 4: *Die Krise 1964–1967* (Berlin, 1975), no. 528, p. 308. See also Lönnendonker and Staadt, *Der Krieg in Vietnam*, 43–54; Juchler, *Studentenbewegungen*, 118–21.

52 Report no. 0613/68: "Restless Youth," Sept. 1968, folder: Youth and Student Movements–CIA, box 12, Walt W. Rostow file, national security file, Lyndon B. Johnson Library, Austin, Tex. See also Bergmann et al., *Rebellion*, 75–7.

53 Hartmut Dabrowski, "Vietnam – Analyse eines Exempels: Rede zur Eröffnung des Kongresses (Auszüge)," *Neue Kritik* 7, no. 36/37 (1966): 29–30.

54 See, e.g., the "Appell für den Frieden in Vietnam," *Die Zeit*, Dec. 9, 1966, reprinted in Otto, ed., *APO*, 120–2; Dabrowski, "Vietnam – Analyse eines Exempels (Schlusserklärung)," *Neue Kritik* 7, no. 36/37 (1966): 38–40.

55 Wilhelm Bauer, "Positionen in Vietnam," *Neue Kritik* 6, no. 29 (1965): 6–8; Georg W. Alsheimer, "Amerikaner in Vietnam," *Das Argument* 8, no. 36 (1966): 2–4.

56 Quoted in Juchler, *Studentenbewegungen*, 258.

IV

Although the term *genocide* had been used as early as 1965 and then increasingly after 1966 to characterize American actions in Vietnam, it was not until 1967 that direct references to Auschwitz became prevalent. Again, Marcuse's thinking had an impact on students. Marcuse essentially divided the history of mankind into the categories of barbarity and socialism, with Auschwitz and Vietnam used as metaphors for the former.[57] In 1966, he remarked, "There are photographs that show a row of half-naked corpses laid out for the victors in Vietnam; they resemble in all details the pictures of the starved, emaciated corpses of Auschwitz and Buchenwald."[58] The following year he wrote in a letter to Max Horkheimer, "I see in America today the historic heir to fascism. The fact that the concentration camps, the murders, the tortures take place outside the metropolis ... doesn't change the nature of it."[59] German intellectuals chimed in. The lyricist Erich Fried published a collection of poems in 1966 titled *und Vietnam und*, in which he repeatedly invoked Auschwitz.[60] This provoked a discussion in the respected journal *Der Monat* on whether, following a famous dictum about Auschwitz by Adorno, it was possible to write poems about Vietnam.[61] In February 1967, the journal *Das Argument* carried the headline "Auschwitz, Vietnam, and no end to it." Inside, philosopher Günther Anders wrote in outrage about the Pentagon asking American GIs to learn Vietnamese idioms. "I know what the Nazis perpetrated in Auschwitz. However, I fear that they, when compared to those hypocrites who formulated and distributed those Vietnam maxims, were gentlemen of horror. I have never heard ... of crematorium workers being required to use Yiddish in order to coax the Jews into the gas chambers."[62] Ten months later, the journal printed a collection of aphorisms by Anders in which he claimed that the Vietnamese, charred by napalm, resembled the Jews cremated in Auschwitz.[63] Other political intellectuals expressed similar views, including Peter Weiss, whose

---

57 See Zvi Tauber, "Herbert Marcuse: Auschwitz und My Lai?" in Dan Diner, ed., *Zivilisationsbruch: Denken nach Auschwitz* (Frankfurt am Main, 1988), 88–98.

58 Herbert Marcuse, *Eros and Civilization* (Boston, 1974), xx.

59 Marcuse to Horkheimer, June 17, 1967, in Wolfgang Kraushaar, ed., *Frankfurter Schule und Studentenbewegung: Von der Flaschenpost zum Molotowcocktail 1946–1995*, 3 vols. (Hamburg, 1998), 2:262.

60 Erich Fried, *und Vietnam und*, exp. ed. (Berlin, 1996).

61 See Peter Härtling, "Gegen rhetorische Ohnmacht: Kann man über Vietnam Gedichte schreiben?" *Der Monat* 19, no. 224 (1967): 57–61; Harald Hartung, "Poesie und Vietnam: Eine Entgegnung," ibid., no. 226: 76–9.

62 Günther Anders, "Vietnam und kein Ende," *Das Argument* 9, no. 42 (1967): 4.

63 Günther Anders, "Der amerikanische Krieg in Vietnam oder Philosophisches Wörterbuch heute," *Das Argument* 9, no. 45 (1967): 360; see also Günther Anders, *Visit Beautiful Vietnam: ABC der amerikanischen Aggressionen heute* (Cologne, 1968).

play *Viet-Nam Discourse* premiered at the Studio Theater in Munich in 1968.[64]

The proceedings of the International Russell Tribunal in Stockholm lent additional credibility to these accusations. Evoking memories of the postwar Nuremberg trials, the tribunal charged the United States with genocide.[65] Protesters in Germany were quick to seize on results of the tribunal's first session as early as May 1967. "Was it 5 or 6 Million Jews?" asked a brochure in Frankfurt am Main, pointing out that newspapers in the United States were already speculating whether a million or just half a million Vietnamese had died in the war. "Such deliberations alone indicate that what is still called war has for a long time inhabited the dimension of extermination. The tribunal in Stockholm has begun to mark out this dimension."[66] In Berlin, a student newspaper printed a special issue with a headline claiming that U.S. generals would have been sentenced to be hanged in Nuremberg.[67] On May 25, 1967, the AStA at the Free University hosted a roundtable discussion on the tribunal with international experts.[68] A SDS-dominated Vietnam Committee distributed a resolution to the audience of about 1,000 students that commended the tribunal's verdict for calling a spade a spade but also warned students not to leave it at that. "A soothing of the conscience remains ineffective and abstract if the inquiries of the tribunal do not move every one of us to break through the powerlessness of mere protest and indignation."[69]

While student activists were spreading the news from Stockholm, the German public was shocked by other news coming from Brussels. There, a department store had burned down, killing hundreds of customers. The

64 Peter Weiss, *Diskurs über die Vorgeschichte und den Verlauf des lang andauernden Befreiungskrieges in Viet Nam . . . (Schauspiel)* (Frankfurt am Main, 1968); see also Hyeong Shik Kim, *Peter Weiss' "Viet Nam Diskurs": Möglichkeiten und Formen eines Engagements für die Dritte Welt* (Frankfurt am Main, 1992). Weiss had already published his views on the topic in 1966; see Peter Weiss, *Vietnam!* (Berlin, 1966).

65 Wolfgang Abendroth, "Das Arbeitsergebnis der ersten Session des Russell–Tribunals in Stockholm," *Blätter für deutsche und internationale Politik* 12 (1967): 589–92; Betrand Russell and Jean–Paul Sartre, *Das Vietnam–Tribunal* (Reinbek bei Hamburg, 1968); Jean–Paul Sartre, "Entwurf einer Erklärung über den Begriff Völkermord: Rede bei der Sitzung des Russel–Tribunals in Roskilde (Dänemark)," *Neue Kritik* 9, no. 47 (1968): 68–85; John Duffett, ed., *Against the Crimes of Silence: Proceedings of the International War Crimes Tribunal* (New York, 1970). For reactions in Washington to the tribunal, see William Conrad Gibbons, *The U.S. Government and the Vietnam War: Executive and Legislative Roles and Relationships,* 4 vols. (Princeton, N.J., 1995), 4:431–4; Tom Wells, *The War Within: America's Battle over Vietnam* (Berkeley, Calif., 1994), 141–3; and Fredrik Logevall, "The Swedish–American Conflict over Vietnam," *Diplomatic History* 17 (1993): 429–31.

66 Büro für Vietnam, Information & Nachrichten 1, June 1967, RZ 2822, Dokumentationsstelle für unkonventionelle Literatur, Bibliothek für Zeitgeschichte, Stuttgart (BfZ–Doku).

67 Berliner Extrablatt, Sondernummer, May/June 1967, RZ 3104, BfZ–Doku.

68 Leaflet, folder: 00120, BfZ–Doku; Lönnendonker and Staadt, *Der Krieg in Vietnam,* 80.

69 "Resolution des Vietnam–Komitees an der Freien Universität Berlin," folder: 00106, BfZ–Doku.

discrepancy in the public's reaction to the events in Belgium and Vietnam invited yet another provocation by a splinter group of the Berlin SDS, the so-called *Kommune I.* The group had formed in the fall of 1966 and was notorious for spontaneous actions without caring much about theory. In December 1966, after burning effigies of Johnson and East German leader Walter Ulbricht in front of the posh Café Kranzler on Berlin's Kurfürstendamm, they wrote, "Too often we had demonstrated in an or-derly, well-mannered, and unsuccessful manner. We were fed up with posing as an advertisement for democracy, a democracy that used our demonstra-tions as formal confirmations of a no longer existing content, a democracy that accepted us in false tolerance as long as we remained uninfluential. We realized that we were unable to reach anybody with these dated forms of demonstrations. . . . Our protest creates only a false solidarity with Vietnam, which evaporates in two hours, throwing everybody back into isolation be-cause of the ineffectiveness of their protest. Thus, it becomes impossible to convey any connection between the personalized violence in Vietnam and the institutionalized violence here."[70] In late May 1967, while students heard about the first results of the Vietnam Tribunal, the Kommune decided to make Berliners aware of Southeast Asian reality by ironically commenting on the catastrophe in Brussels. They disseminated several cynical leaflets whose repulsiveness served to expose the cynicism of the public toward Vietnam. One of the leaflets claimed that the burning department store had conveyed to a European metropolis for the first time "this crackling Vietnam feeling." Another one read, "Our Belgian friends have finally gotten the knack of letting the public really partake in the funny hustle and bustle in Vietnam; they set a department store on fire, three hundred prosperous citizens lose their exciting lives, and Brussels becomes Hanoi. . . . Burn, ware-house [*sic*], burn!"[71] While prosecutors indicted the authors of these lines on charges of instigating arson, authorities in Berlin helped the movement to draw the longed-for parallel to the violence in Vietnam.

On the evening of June 2, 1967, several thousand students gathered out-side the German Opera to protest the presence of the despotic Shah of Iran,

70 Kommune I, "Quellen zur Kommune–Forschung, Entwurf III," folder: D 0895, BfZ–Doku. See also Jens Hager, *Die Rebellen von Berlin. Studentenpolitik an der Freien Universität*, ed. Hartmut Häussermann, Niels Kadritzke, and Knut Nevermann (Cologne, 1967), 96–101; and Claussen, *Die drei Leben des Rudi Dutschke*, 149–51.

71 Leaflets nos. 7, 8, from May 24, 1967, reprinted in *Freie Universität Berlin 1948–1973*, 4: doc. nos. 708, 709, p. 442. See also excerpts from the reports by expert witnesses in the ensuing lawsuit against the authors of the leaflets, "Auszüge aus den gutachterlichen Äusserungen zum Prozess gegen Langhans/Teufel wegen Aufforderung zur Brandstiftung," folder: 00135, BfZ–Doku; and Peter Szondi, "Aufforderung zur Brandstiftung? Ein Gutachten im Prozess Langhans/Teufel," *Der Monat* 19, no. 227 (1967): 24–9.

who was on a state visit to West Berlin. Clashes ensued when police pushed the crowd away from the opera, and in the resulting confusion the student Benno Ohnesorg was shot to death by a plainclothes police officer. James Tent, in his history of Berlin's Free University, has aptly called this incident "the spiritual crossroads for the German student movement."[72] A few left-leaning groups suddenly found themselves transformed into an academic mass movement, the radicalism of Free University students spread to campuses all over West Germany, and loosely linked protest groups were welded together in an impressive extraparliamentarian opposition. What's more, the vanguard of the movement was now convinced that it had to do away with the system. At the headquarters of Berlin's SDS on the Kurfürstendamm, a young woman had an uncontrollable fit of crying on the night of the shooting, shouting out, "This is the Auschwitz generation, and there is no arguing with them."[73] The woman, Gudrun Ensslin, was on her way into the terrorist scene. Her later companion, Ulrike Meinhof, who only two years earlier had acknowledged John F. Kennedy's "enlightened anticommunism," now wrote: "Thus the students learned to appreciate the police baton as the manifestation of a violence that is latently inherent in the system they live in, not as a flaw but as a pillar of the system."[74] The SDS declared, "The postfascist system in the FRG has become a prefascist system."[75] Consequently, students turned from enlightening activism to resistance. Yet again they found confirmation in the thinking of Marcuse, who returned to the Free University in July 1967 to explain once more his argument that there was a natural right to resist the repressive tolerance of advanced capitalist societies. "The fact is," he said, "that we find ourselves up against a system that from the beginning of the fascist period to the present has disavowed through its acts the idea of historical progress, a system whose internal contradictions repeatedly manifest themselves in inhuman and unnecessary wars and whose growing productivity is growing destruction and growing waste. . . . We must resist if we still want to live as human beings, to work and be happy. We can no longer do so in alliance with the system." But Marcuse also gave hope: "If in this sense Vietnam is in no way just one more event of foreign policy but rather connected with the essence of the system, it is perhaps also a turning point in the development

---

72 James F. Tent, *The Free University of Berlin: A Political History* (Bloomington, Ind., 1988), 323.

73 Quoted in Stefan Aust, *The Baader Meinhof Group: The Inside Story of a Phenomenon*, trans. Anthea Bell (London, 1987), 44.

74 Ulrike Marie Meinhof, *Deutschland Deutschland unter anderm* (Berlin, 1995), 84, 122–3.

75 "Erklärung des Bundesvorstandes des Sozialistischen Deutschen Studentenbundes, Niederlage oder Erfolg der Protestaktion," reprinted in Lutz Schulenburg, ed., *Das Leben ändern, die Welt verändern! 1968: Dokumente und Berichte* (Hamburg, 1998), 54–8, here 55.

of the system, perhaps the beginning of the end."[76] Among student activists in West Berlin and the Federal Republic, Vietnam no longer was a mere example of the imperialist strategies of Western capitalism, and it also ceased to be a mirror of past German atrocities. Auschwitz was about to return to the country where it originated. To avert this, the Vietcong had to be victorious, and its struggle had to be supplemented by resistance back home. Dutschke wrote: "To us, this means nothing but to definitely support the Vietnamese liberation struggle through our own emancipatory process in the intensifying political fight against *our* existing order."[77] Accordingly, the delegates' conference of the SDS in September declared:

After the SDS succeeded in enlarging and driving forward the opposition movement, it is now primarily necessary to expose as indirect support of the colonial counterrevolution bourgeois-liberal positions such as the plea for a "more humane" war, a sham democratization through reforms, and a negotiated compromise that would result in an end to the revolution. This presents us with considerable opportunities to convey the international revolutionary importance of the struggle of the Vietnamese people to ever-growing parts of the radical democratic opposition and to mobilize this opposition for a consciously anti-imperialist and anti-capitalist commitment. Thus, the fight against U.S. imperialism and its support by the Federal Republic becomes more and more a progressive element of the revolutionary movement in West Germany itself.[78]

It should not come as a surprise, then, that Dutschke denied that the antiwar demonstrations in Germany on October 21, 1967, were part of the international day of protest against the Vietnam War. Instead, he claimed, they were meant as part of the power struggle at home.[79] In 1967, the old analogy between Berlin and Saigon acquired a whole new dimension. "Isn't," asked a student newspaper, "Berlin in Vietnam or vice-versa since June 2?"[80]

V

By 1968 a vocal opposition of peace marchers, students, scholars, writers, and artists had succeeded in destroying the traditional Berlin–Saigon analogy.

---

76 Herbert Marcuse, "The Problem of Violence and the Radical Opposition," in Herbert Marcuse, *Five Lectures: Psychoanalysis, Politics, and Utopia* (Boston, 1970), 83–108, quotations 94, 87. See also Bernd Rabehl, "Repressive Toleranz: Der SDS und das Problem der Gewaltfreiheit," in Andreas Gestrich, Gottfried Niedhart, and Bernd Ulrich, eds., *Gewaltfreiheit: Pazifistische Konzepte im 19. und 20. Jahrhundert* (Münster, 1996), 139–42.

77 Rudi Dutschke, "Zum Verhältnis von Organisation und Emanzipationsbewegung: Zum Besuch Herbert Marcuses," reprinted in Kraushaar, *Frankfurter Schule*, 2:255 (original emphasis).

78 "Beschlussprotokoll der 22. o. Delegiertenkonferenz des SDS," n.d., folder: BV 22. DK 1967 SDS, AASB. See also Bauss, *Studentenbewegung*, 192–3.

79 Bergmann et al., *Rebellion*, 82–4.

80 Monika Steffen, "Tiere an Ketten – SDS und Horkheimer," *Diskus* 17, no. 5 (1967): 11, reprinted in Kraushaar, *Frankfurter Schule* 2:263.

According to a United States Information Agency (USIA) survey, 65 percent of West Germans in 1968 denied that the American presence in Vietnam could be compared to America's presence in Berlin.[81] Ironically, however, the analogy meanwhile had, through numerous detours, found its way back into the German discourse on the Vietnam War. It was now employed by opponents of the war and thus was charged with a wholly different meaning.

The attitude of West German protesters toward the American war in Vietnam was shaped primarily by their confrontation with their own nation's past. As Norbert Elias has observed, "The rising generations saw themselves burdened . . . with the stigma of a nation that had a tendency toward barbaric acts of violence."[82] The upshot of this burden was, as Horst Mahler, a prominent member of the movement, once remarked with a reference to Hegel, an "anxiety for the well-being of humankind (*Herzklopfen für das Wohl der Menschheit*)."[83] When the United States, West Germany's indispensable ally, the guarantor of West Berlin's freedom, and a role model for many in the younger generation, seemed to revive barbarism in Southeast Asia, activists in West Germany felt an almost existential need to rise against the carnage. They bestowed the sense of sympathy that they had found lacking in their parents' attitudes toward the victims of the Holocaust on the Vietnamese liberation movement. Thus, they invoked Vietnam as a present representation of Auschwitz. This was meant, first, to confront their parents with the past; second, to redeem themselves of the burden of guilt; and third, to appeal to their compatriots to stop the evil this time.

When the opposition's efforts at information met with a stoically unmoved public, student activists resorted to provocation as a means of enlightenment. This set in motion a mutually reinforcing confrontation with authorities. Again, it was Germany's totalitarian past that produced an extraordinary sensitivity to the establishment's reactions. Protesters suspected that the ruling elite wanted to dismantle liberal freedoms and gradually return to authoritarian or even fascist methods. The *Spiegel* affair in 1962, plans to introduce emergency legislation (commonly referred to in opposition circles as "National Socialist laws"), and – last but not least – the establishment of a Grand Coalition in the fall of 1966 seemed to support this view. So did the violent reaction of police, most of the press, and state prosecutors to the provocations of the activists. When personalized violence

81 "Some Recent West German Public Opinion Indications on Issues Relating to German–American Relations," Sept. 11, 1968, S–36–68, box 5, Office of Research Special Reports, 1964–82, RG 306, NA.

82 Elias, *Germans*, 229.   83 Quoted in ibid., 262.

returned to Germany on June 2, 1967, leading opposition groups concluded that Germany's transformation into a fascist system had already taken place. The Auschwitz metaphor was, repatriated from Vietnam, so to speak, and resistance became the order of the day.

The International Vietnam Congress, held at the Technical University in West Berlin on February 17–18, 1968, manifests the purest expression of this transition from protest to resistance and from the perception of the war as an example of American politics to its perception as an example of successful liberation movements that had to be supplemented in the industrialized world.[84] In calling on students to attend the congress, organizers emphasized that it was crucial to "take up the struggle against the oppressors in our own country." They warned against a merely symbolic understanding of their actions and urged their fellow students "to commence the coordinated battle against imperialism on European soil."[85] The symbolic protest that to a certain extent had violated norms with the intention to stir the public conscience now was replaced by the movement's self-deception of having an actual function in the struggle against imperialism. But again this delusion stemmed from the students' feeling that they were witnessing a recurrence of the past. As one student at the Vietnam Congress explained: "If we want to understand the liberation struggle in Vietnam correctly, it means that we have to get rid of this government," otherwise, he continued, "we will perish in a concentration camp one day."[86] Three days later, Dutschke appeared at a hearing in West Berlin's House of Representatives only to exclaim: "Your liberalism has vanished long ago in the authoritarian state apparatus of fascism."[87] When the establishment held a pro-American rally the following day, students observed that civil servants had gotten an hour off, just as on the occasion of Hitler's speeches thirty years earlier. Some even asked, "When will students have to wear stars?" referring to the physical identification of Jews under the Nazis' Star of David Decree.

If the Vietnam Congress in Berlin marked an important watershed in the evolution of the movement, it also proved to be its climax. Soon thereafter the movement dissolved. This was due to a number of reasons. The

---

84 Klaus–Uwe Benneter, *Februar 1968: Tage, die Berlin erschütterten* (Frankfurt am Main, 1968); Bernd Rabehl, *Am Ende der Utopie: Die politische Geschichte der Freien Universität Berlin* (Berlin, 1988), 256–68.

85 "Aufruf an die deutschen Hochschulen zum Vietnamkongress am 17./18.2.1968," reprinted in *Freie Universität Berlin 1948–1973*, vol. 5: *Gewalt und Gegengewalt (1967–1969)*, comp. and ed. Siegward Lönnendonker, Tilman Fichter, and Jochen Staadt (Berlin, 1983), 274. See also Michael Bühnemann, "Vietnamkongress an der TU," *Anrisse*, no. 64, Feb. 7, 1968, 8, DZ 426, BfZ–Doku.

86 Der Senator für Inneres (Abteilung IV), *Bericht über die auf der "Internationalen Vietnam–Konferenz" am 17. Februar 1968 in West–Berlin gehaltenen Reden* (Berlin, 1968), 25.

87 For this and the following, see *Freie Universität Berlin 1948–1973*, 5:75–8.

duty for revolutionary action proclaimed by the Congress in Berlin sent students on a search for a revolutionary subject, and they became lost in groundwork as well as in theoretical disputes. Countless so-called K-groups of Marxist-Leninist, Maoist, Trotskyist or some other outlook sprang up, hardly distinguishable from each other but equally reluctant to join forces.[88] With the assassination attempt on Dutschke in April 1968, the movement lost its leading figure. Some students were disillusioned that short-lived up-risings all over the world did not produce a revolutionary situation or a general mass following. Others were deterred by recurring violence and went back to their books. What's more, the national and international sit-uation was in a state of flux. Peace negotiations on Vietnam would finally ensue, and the Soviet invasion of Czechoslovakia distracted attention from Southeast Asia. At home, the Grand Coalition was voted out of office and a new reform government under Chancellor Willy Brandt promised to "dare more democracy."

It goes without saying that West German protesters of the 1960s, or those of later years for that matter, did not bring about an end to the war in Vietnam. That, however, was never their primary goal. Instead, they took aim at the cultural, political, and social fabric of their own country. They succeeded in reconstructing the social frames of memory in the Federal Republic of Germany. Conservatives acknowledged as much when, after returning to power in 1982, they lamented that Germans had come to terms with Hitler but now had to come to terms with the coming to terms with Hitler that had led to the student rebellion of 1968.[89] The movement failed to alter West Germany's political economy. In conjunction with the aforementioned success, this failure produced a legacy of terrorism led by people who were still driven by the triad of Auschwitz, Vietnam, and Bonn. Their despair was still perceptible at a recent meeting in Zurich, where one of them remarked in resignation that, after Auschwitz, Willy Brandt should have felt the need to demonstrate against the war in Vietnam in front of the American embassy.[90]

---

88 See Gerd Koenen, *Das rote Jahrzehnt: Unsere kleine deutsche Kulturrevolution 1967–1977* (Cologne, 2001), 257–315; Hildegard Weiss, *Die Ideologieentwicklung in der deutschen Studentenbewegung* (Munich, 1985), 29–31; and Gerd Langguth, *Die Protestbewegung in der Bundesrepublik Deutschland 1968–1976* (Cologne, 1976), 46–50.

89 See Claus Leggewie, "A Laboratory of Postindustrial Society: Reassessing the 1960s in Germany," in Fink, Gassert, and Junker, *1968*, 277–94.

90 See Markus Wehner, "Über die Toten spricht man nicht: In Zürich trafen sich ehemalige Terroristen der RAF und der Roten Brigaden," *Frankfurter Allgemeine Zeitung*, May 28, 1997, 5.

14

The World Peace Council and the Antiwar Movement in East Germany

GÜNTER WERNICKE

During the Cold War, interstate relationships assumed the form of a bloc confrontation that took primacy over all other fields of international competition and all other levels of social discord, including activities – which transcended these blocs – to prevent a third (nuclear) world war. Peace movements can be traced historically as social phenomena linked in intricate ways with the action-reaction cycles of foreign and security policies that evolved in each decision-making apparatus. Cold War history presents a complexity of such shifts. Within that overall analysis, the Vietnam War both highlighted and catalyzed some major changes in that flow.

There still has been no critical history of the World Peace Council (WPC) (earlier: World Council for Peace), and there are few case studies. Research into the East German peace movement is limited to "opposition movements."[1] In this chapter, I draw on archival research and characteristic examples to illustrate the main concerns of the WPC, focusing on the WPC's response to the Vietnam War in terms of its own international composition and political objectives; the paradoxical status of the German Peace Council (GPC) of the German Democratic Republic (GDR); and solidarity with Vietnam in the GDR, how it was organized, and why it garnered the support it did.

THE WORLD PEACE COUNCIL

The WPC was founded in April 1949 at two parallel congresses held in Paris and Prague under the same symbol: Picasso's dove. The German Committee

---

1 Cf. Erhard Neubert, *Geschichte der Oppositon in der DDR 1949–1989* (Berlin, 1997); Thomas Klein, Wilfriede Otto, and Peter Grieder, *Visionen: Repression und Opposition in der DDR (1949–1989)*, 2 pts. (Frankfurt an der Oder, 1996).

of the Partisans for Peace soon followed. Forged in the postwar antifascist spirit, the WPC aimed to be an international voice for peace. It evolved as an international alliance backed by communist parties in East and West, with aims substantially formulated around the foreign policy of the Soviet bloc, although leaving room for other international peace networks to participate. Ultimately, however, the peace movements in both camps were immured within their blocs, and in the quest for concerted action, these proved more often than not to be almost insurmountable obstacles. Only when the conflict in Vietnam escalated did the WPC build again on the moral outrage of the immediate postwar years and seek common ground for effective international cooperation.

Vietnam was to be a litmus test for the WPC. Its desire to be a substantial player in the world peace movement was sometimes at odds with Soviet foreign-policy priorities and with the basic strategies of the communist movement, itself never homogeneous. The WPC experienced a minor watershed in its attitude toward Western peace groups around 1964–5, and the pacifist response was more than verbal. Attentive observers sought explanations: "The reasons go back to the shifting alignments in the Cold War and particularly the Sino-Soviet rift. The WPC and its Soviet line supporters find themselves under considerable pressure from the Chinese and their allies, which is why they are willing to take a new look at the independent movements."[2]

Vietnam brought to a head the Sino-Soviet controversy that had created a stalemate within the WPC. It also coincided with the rise of other national independence movements, which openly challenged the original pacifist aspirations of the WPC in that support for the anti-imperialist cause implied accepting a belligerent phase of struggle.

In the Marxist view of historical development, peace and socialism are inextricably linked because socialism sets out to replace that very imperialist system that inevitably breeds war. This dilemma was compounded, in the analytical logic of East European governments, by the conclusion that imperialism sought to destroy their countries by means of the arms race, either militarily or economically, and by political isolation (containment, rollback). Almost by definition, well-intentioned neutrality in the Western camp was perceived as an objective threat to the survival of socialism (and hence peace). In divided Germany, this was not only a theoretical concern but also a pervasive political experience.

---

2 Tony Smythe, report on the Annual General Assembly of the International Peace Bureau held at L.O-skolen, Sormarka, Norway from 23–27 August 1964, 7, box 93, War Resisters International, International Institute for Social History, Amsterdam.

The unhealthy structure of the East European peace councils (which were not founded on grassroots organizations) and their dual tasks as both peace and party functionaries led to a very official campaigning technique that operated "by the ton," that is, collecting signatures, holding mass meetings, and inviting more and more people and organizations to world assemblies. In the mid-1960s, concerned activists in the ranks of the WPC stepped up their calls for a reform of method and rhetoric, and for true campaigning independence.

This is symptomatic of a basic dilemma that confronted the WPC once the new "establishment" in the nominally socialist countries had taken its toll on the postwar idealism from which the movement had grown. The predicament concerned both political content and presentation. There was a perceived need to attract committed peace activists outside communist circles and to use a language not automatically associated with Moscow. Winning noncommunist public figures for the movement was intended to demonstrate political openness, and yet any objections to measures proposed by the Soviet Union risked isolating the critics or paralyzing the organization. This fundamental problem repeatedly exacerbated the complicated relationship with independent Western peace groups. Tension within the WPC was especially evident as worldwide protest against the Vietnam War crystallized into organized movements.

THE PEACE COUNCIL OF THE GDR

In functional terms, the GPC was part of the WPC and reflected the contradictions described above. By the time of the Vietnam War it was also an auxiliary of the GDR's governing communist party (Sozialistische Einheitspartei Deutschlands, or SED) sent out into the international arena to pursue the cause of diplomatic recognition while still playing some part in promoting official foreign policy among the domestic population. This should not be underestimated, nor should the key role played by the GPC in international peace structures as a result of Germany's division, a focal issue for various organizations seeking to counter the threats of bipolarity. Germany offered a bridge between the East-dominated WPC, under direct or indirect communist leadership, and diverse Western peace movements. The unresolved German question embraced many controversies that defied easy labeling as communist or noncommunist.

In 1962, the Politburo of the Central Committee of the SED decided to restructure the GPC, henceforth known as the Peace Council of the GDR. A special Christian Working Group, with various denominations represented, was set up within the GPC. In the same year, the Politburo decided to introduce new articles of association for the Afro-Asian Solidarity Committee (AASK), an organization within the National Front, and in July 1965, the Vietnam Committee was established as an integral part of this. In two ways, this Politburo intervention determined the role that the Peace Council was able to play in Vietnam and Indochina in general a few years later. On the one hand, the political remit now imposed on the Peace Council increasingly channeled its activity into the international arena, where the GDR was fighting for diplomatic recognition. On the other hand, the GPC was expected to participate in the Vietnam solidarity campaign at home under the aegis of the AASK, following the logic that anti-imperialist struggle would ultimately serve the cause of world peace. Sociopolitical influences of this kind took various, often absurd forms. The primarily political reorganization "recommended" by the Politburo was triggered by a number of factors and was typical of the undeniable conflicts in which peace committees in Eastern Europe sometimes found themselves. Kurt Hälker, responsible at the time for international relations at the GPC and simultaneously GPC delegate to the Vietnam Committee, referred to it in a recent interview as "crazy":

It caused us a lot of problems. Defending that was a feat of acrobatics. We weren't even convinced of it ourselves. It was a tragedy. The peace movement was a melting pot. A broad policy of alliance really was put into practice. There were voices within the peace movement which were critical, too. There were various different factors you might consider, and you have to. After all, they wanted pluralism, if they wanted to be serious about the alliance policy. I don't believe that was convenient. And there were contradictions in the party, too.[3]

Hälker confirmed that by the late 1960s the GPC was acting primarily as a committee for the international recognition of the GDR, whereas the Vietnam Committee was responsible for the solidarity movement within the republic. Both functioned internationally as official representatives of the GDR's Vietnam solidarity movement. "That was a kind of a division of labor."[4]

THE WPC AND VIETNAM

The conflict in Indochina had been a major theme in WPC activity after the Korean War, but in the 1950s (after Geneva) and early 1960s it paled before

---

3 Author's interview with Hälker, June 26, 1997.
4 Author's interview with Hälker, Sept. 28, 1998.

the need to counter direct confrontation between the power blocs, especially in Europe, and to press for peaceful resolution of the German question.

However, the Sino-Soviet dispute cast its shadow over more and more issues. After the WPC conference in Stockholm in December 1961, the undermining effects grew increasingly apparent. Understandably, the Chinese sought to use the National Liberation Front (NLF) and the Democratic Republic of Vietnam (DRV) for their own purposes, following the row about the nuclear test ban treaty in 1963 and disagreement over the Sino-Indian border. Behind this Chinese strategy, supported by its Albanian friends, was a clear attempt to split the communist-led WPC, especially on the part of its Asian adherents, and bring them under Beijing's control.

WPC president John D. Bernal complained about the divisive tactics of the Chinese committee: "The trend of their arguments, expressed in harsh language, is that the intention behind this sincere attempt to improve W.C.P. organisation and procedure is to stifle democracy."[5] However, the growing problems within the ranks of the WPC were also rooted in contradictions emerging in the organized world communist movement, especially between the Chinese and Soviet parties, which began in the late 1950s and escalated after 1960.

The first major consequence was a split in the Japanese peace movement in 1963–4. This caused problems for sections such as the GPC because its participation in events like the Japanese commemoration of Hiroshima and Nagasaki now hinged on the political sensitivities of the SED as well as on diplomatic restrictions (namely, visa rejections by several NATO countries and the policy of the Allied Trades Office in West Berlin). The GPC shared a view widespread in the WPC that its presence was necessary "to prevent circles under Chinese influence misusing delegates for a policy which aims to damage the WPC." However, the Politburo was adamant, and in the summer of 1964, the GPC announced that it would not be going to Japan.[6] The rift was now very deep. In fact, when the WPC met in Warsaw in the fall of 1963, it was Devi Prasad and the pacifists of War Resisters International who attempted to mediate between the camps.[7]

5 Bernal, memorandum on World Council of Peace organization and procedure, May 26, 1964, in folder E.3.4, box 63, J. D. Bernal papers, add.8287, Cambridge University Library (hereafter CUL).
6 Heinz Willmann to Gen. Heinz Stadler, Büro Norden, May 30, 1964, in IV A 2/2.028/100, DY 30, Stiftung Archiv der Parteien und Massenorganisationen der DDR im Bundesarchiv (hereafter SAPMO-BArch). Norden added a handwritten note to the letter from Willmann to Norden. See Heinz Willmann to Prof. Albert Norden, Betr.: DDR-Delegation zu Konferenzen in Japan, July 1, 1964, ibid.
7 Bericht des Bundesvorsitzenden über die Tätigkeit der IdK im vergangenen Jahr, in Protokoll der Jahreskonferenz der Internationale der Kriegsdienstgegner am 10. und 11. Oktober 1964 in Schweinfurth, 8, in 226.1080, DZ 9, Bundesarchiv Berlin (hereafter BArch Berlin).

The rift persisted, and Eastern European peace councils now tried to isolate the Chinese. These tussles began to paralyze the organization in the mid-1960s. The GPC, a strong supporter of Moscow, stated in a draft to the SED Central Committee (just before the WPC Presidium met in Berlin on December 6–9, 1964): "The attitude of the Chinese leadership to date has caused an extreme exacerbation of the situation in the World Peace Council and often crippled its work. The onslaughts from the Chinese side are conducted variously with such vehemence that there was a threat that the movement would split, as it did in some countries."[8] The Chinese campaign, supported by several Asian organizations, overshadowed all subsequent WPC meetings until the mid-1970s because its delegates sought to "correct" the line of the Soviet-dominated WPC.

Until the mid-1960s the WPC had functioned primarily, in Rüdiger Schlaga's apt words, as "a bridge with two-way lanes, across which information was transported into both systems."[9] It then underwent an internal crisis that dampened the impact of its broad coalition policy, almost whittling it down to the formal status of a primarily diplomatic relationship that increasingly reflected Soviet foreign policy.[10] Inevitably, these symptoms disfigured the WPC, leaving some irreparable scars as activists wrestled with their conscience. A prime example of this was Bernal, scientist, communist, and president of the WPC, who experienced its suction into the Soviet undertow and attempted to steer a constructive course. In December 1963, his own conflict broke to the surface in a personal letter to the Italian Communist Senator Velio Spano, who had questioned WPC strategy at a meeting in Warsaw. Various Western organizations, including the Continuing Committee of the International Confederation for Disarmament and Peace (ICDP), had been invited to the meeting, which was postponed – it seems – under pressure from Moscow due to tensions with the Chinese and forthcoming talks at the top party level. Bernal wrote:

When you complain of the lack of a clear political perspective, I feel that that lack is absolutely intrinsic. We cannot have a political perspective that follows either the

---

8 Sekretariat des Friedensrates der DDR, Entwurf: Vorlage für das Sekretariat des ZK, Betr.: Präsidiumssitzung des Weltfriedensrates in Berlin vom 6. bis 9. Dezember 1964, Nov. 16, 1964, 4, in IV A 2/2.028/98, DY 30, SAPMO-BArch.

9 Rüdiger Schlaga, *Die Kommunisten in der Friedensbewegung – erfolglos? Die Politik des Weltfriedensrates im Verhältnis zur Aussenpolitik der Sowjetunion und zu unabhängigen Friedensbewegungen im Westen (1950–1979)* (Münster, 1991), 323.

10 Albert Norden to Walter Ulbricht, Nov. 19, 1964, in IV 2/2.028/98, DY 30, SAPMO-BArch; Zur Lage im Weltfriedensrat: Notizen für die Problemdiskussion in Helsinki, May 20–24, 1965 (Streng vertraulich!), ibid.

Russian or the Chinese line; nor is any simple compromise between them possible. What I envisage at the moment in the next year or two of what I imagine will be an extended and uneasy political truce, is some kind of holding operation in which we would try to damp down quarrels and preserve at any rate the framework of unity.[11]

Bernal's concerns were triggered not only by the rift between the communist spearheads; he also was deeply troubled about the growing tendency in the West, in response to the Cold War, to divide the peace movement into "aligned" and "nonaligned" camps:

If we are to have peace in this world, it must be between people of whom some are communists and others are not. The idea that it should be possible to have a world peace movement from which communists are excluded easily passes on to another, which is self-contradictory; that of having an anticommunist peace movement.... The essence of an effective federation of peace organisations – neither "aligned" nor "non-aligned" – is that all should support one general peace policy, but that each should be free to interpret how to operate it in the context of the conditions in its own country.[12]

With Western members of the WPC, especially in Britain, struggling to prove their peace credentials, creeping anti-imperialism was bound to raise eyebrows among potential allies. This new orientation sparked much controversy in the WPC, which was clearly reflected in the Vietnam solidarity movement. For the Presidential Committee, Bernal pressed the Soviet Peace Committee to recognize the growing willingness for different sections of the peace movement to work together at an unprecedented level in opposing U.S. policy in Vietnam: "But I think this unity is being greatly endangered by the way we are handling the immediate situation in Vietnam, and the corresponding tendency to turn the World Council of Peace into another version of the Afro-Asian Solidarity Movement, that is directed mainly against imperialism and particularly against the United States. It means a changing of the whole character of the world peace movement." Concerned that the WPC might eventually split over this issue, Bernal pointed out that

a movement against imperialism is not in itself necessarily a peace movement. It might become so, but only after the defeat of imperialism, and that means only after war. It has been one of the fixed ideas of the world peace movement since its inception that the peoples can actually stop war by influencing the governments that lead towards war, not by opposing them by military means. I am

11 J. D. Bernal to Senator Velio Spano, Dec. 18, 1963 (Private and confidential!), in folder E.17, box 67, Bernal papers, MSS.add.8287, CUL.
12 J. D. Bernal, co-operation for world peace, 5–6, in folder E.11.6.3, box 65, ibid.

seriously afraid that this principle will be lost sight of in discussions, and we may move to a position further back than when the Movement was formed in 1948.[13]

Certainly, there were realists in the WPC and in the Soviet establishment who saw that the Chinese "revolutionism" fanning Vietnamese resistance to a peaceful compromise could jeopardize a broader international campaign against escalating U.S. aggression. They also thought that explicit support for the Vietnamese position would "damage the Movement and make it appear more clearly one of the Communist states versus the rest," which ultimately meant "throwing away our allies among the liberals and many working-class elements in Western countries." Projecting the WPC as a "strictly revolutionary body" would merely reflect the opposing political aims of either the Soviet Union or China and would appear either as a sellout to the Chinese or as a betrayal of Third World liberation movements. Bernal wanted at all costs to resist "a policy of unifying our enemies and dividing our friends."[14] There were increasing calls for "some new thinking at the top level" in the WPC if it was not to become a "League against imperialism or a protagonist on the Soviet side in the dispute between the communist parties, with the Chinese and their supporters trying to create rival organisations."[15]

In the GDR itself, Politburo member Albert Norden (also a member of the WPC Presidium) directed Ulbricht's attention to the "Chinese" problem along with other flaws he saw in the WPC, such as the lack of an "orientation toward large-scale mass action," the absence of "united leadership," and differences between Bernal's London office and the secretariat in Vienna (transferred to Helsinki, 1968).[16]

In 1964, the presidential committee was already committed to the campaign against the Vietnam conflict waged by the United States in the wake of the Gulf of Tonkin affair. Bernal testified to this in a letter to Homer A. Jack, executive director of the U.S. Committee for a Safe Nuclear Policy (SANE), reiterating the WPC's priorities for Vietnam: "(1) end hostilities, (2) negotiate a peaceful settlement. In this instance we have made a third demand, namely strict implementation of the 1954 Geneva Agreements."[17] Bernal's own approach was symptomatic of the differences

---

13 Bernal to Alexandr Korneichuk, June 11, 1965, 1–2, in folder E.17, box 67, ibid.
14 Ibid., 2–3.
15 "G.S. *[Gordon Schaffer]* to J.D.B., "Some personal impressions" (Personal and confidential!), in folder E.3.5, box 63, ibid.
16 Albert Norden to Walter Ulbricht, Nov. 19, 1964, 1–2, in IV 2/2.028/98, DY30, SAMPO-BArch.
17 J. D. Bernal to Dr. Homer Jack, Executive Director, SANE, New York, March 17, 1964, in folder E.17, box 67, Bernal papers, add.8287, CUL.

between London and the pro-Moscow perspective in Vienna: The Soviet Union was unhappy about Vietnamese persistence and Chinese support for both the DRV and the NLF, openly welcomed by Vietnamese delegations to every conference and during all their visits abroad, notably to the GDR. The Soviet Union's priorities now were nuclear disarmament, détente with the United States, and the establishment of a European security system.

Certainly, the movement that began as a protest against the Vietnam War was becoming something much broader, unprecedented in postwar history in size and concerted energy. In the summer of 1966, the Swedish Peace and Arbitration Society launched an initiative for a Stockholm Conference on Vietnam, which heralded a new fusion of efforts by peace organizations of very different inspirations. In the run-up to this conference, both the secretariat and the presidential committee of the WPC were encouraged by the opportunity, so long anticipated, to forge a broad spectrum of unity around "opposition to the war in Vietnam," motivated by "a variety of grounds, varying from those based on purely humanitarian considerations, stirred by the atrocities that the war has produced, and wishing to see a rapid end to it irrespective of the political conditions of the settlement, to those who wish primarily to reach a settlement that secures the genuine independence of the Vietnam peoples." There was a determination to dispense with tired old practices: "Quibbling about details of policy in a settlement" would be "worse than useless." In any case, the document continued, "We must not assume that the main business is to issue resolutions or manifestos. That has been done too often in the past. Its aim is to produce action to put an end to the war, and this may come more from the actions of the delegates to the conference acting in their several countries along the general lines which are hammered out at the conference itself."[18]

Romesh Chandra, WPC general secretary after 1965, saw this commitment as a realistic first step toward overcoming bloc mentality in the international peace movement, and he appealed for wholehearted, long-term cooperation. He underlined the "fundamental task in this new period to coordinate as far as possible the actions of all the different peace forces, and to bring about a common liaison with these other peace organisations. We believe that the Stockholm Conference is the first step in this direction" and that cooperation "will enable us to increase our activities in all fields and, of course, particularly on the most urgent question of the struggle of the people of Vietnam against U.S. aggression. . . . This does not mean for

18 Notes for discussion at World Conference on Vietnam (first draft), 12, in folder E.15.6, box 66, ibid.

an instant that we are giving up or are in any way reducing the independent activities of the World Council of Peace."[19]

In July 1967, more than four hundred opponents of the war arrived in Stockholm from all over the world. They included eminent American campaigners such as Dr. Benjamin Spock, Sidney Lens, Homer A. Jack, Alfred Hassler, and David McReynolds. A continuation committee was set up to fight across the globe for peace in Vietnam. The new spirit of alliance was articulated in a declaration of support – disputed yet ultimately unanimous – for the Stockholm Liaison Committee from the WRI and the ICDP. Other organizations that chose to play a role included the International Fellowship of Reconciliation, the International Peace Bureau, the Christian Peace Conference, the Quakers, the Women's International League for Peace and Freedom, and Amnesty International.

THE GDR AND VIETNAM SOLIDARITY

Immediately after the Stockholm Conference, the Peace Council of the GDR and the AASK and its Vietnam Committee met to evaluate the event in the presence of the DRV ambassador and the NLF's Berlin representative. Otto-Hartmut Fuchs of the Berlin Conference of Catholic Christians in European States referred to the conference and its structures as a possible "model for action."[20] The Central Committee of the SED expressed its satisfaction in witnessing at last "a worldwide campaign run jointly by the major international pacifist organizations and the World Peace Council,"[21] and it undertook to make a priority of enabling representatives from the GDR to take part in future meetings in the Stockholm Conference process.

Just before the Helsinki Congress in April 1965, Bernal had convened an extraordinary meeting of the WPC Presidium in Stockholm on stepping up international protest in support of the Vietnamese people. The East German government and the SED Politburo had given it backing. The SED Secretariat adopted a draft submitted by the GPC and asked it to propose that the WPC send a high-profile delegation to Hanoi to establish permanent

---

19 Meeting of the W.C.P. Presidential Committee, Prague, February 25–27, 1967, Romesh Chandra, Secretary General, Report on the Activities, Programme of Work and Organisational Problems of the World Council of Peace, 9, 11, in 27.131, DZ 9, BArch.

20 O. H. Fuchs, Berliner Konferenz Katholischer Christen aus Europäischen Staaten, Bericht über die Tätigkeit der BERLINER KONFERENZ im Zusammenhang mit der "Weltkonferenz über Vietnam" (Stockholm 6./9.Juli), in 111.549, ibid.

21 Friedensrat der DDR, Vorlage für das Sekretariat der SED, betr.: Teilnahme einer Delegation des Friedensrates und des Vietnam-Ausschusses der DDR an der Stockholmer Vietnam-Konferenz vom 6.–9.7.1967, May 29, 1967, 3, in J IV 2/3 A-1464, DY 30, SAPMO-BArch.

representation and a working party to South Vietnam to investigate the use of poison gas and chemical weapons against civilians. In addition, it was to organize regional conferences to strengthen world protest.[22] The Politburo, which had acquired decision-making powers in this matter in 1966, now attached priority to assisting the DRV and, later, the NLF. A document issued on June 17, 1968, by the SED's Department of International Relations, drawing on a note from the GPC's own international department, refers to the "principles underlying the international policy of the SED and the GDR, on the basis of proletarian internationalism" in stating that assistance would include "enabling volunteers to go to Vietnam should the government of the DRV so request." It also mentions aid provided by the GDR before 1964, including a gift of 63 million marks in 1956 and donations worth 6.3 million marks by 1964, then consignments of goods from 1964 to 1968 worth 417.5 million convertible marks. Military assistance was mentioned without further details. On June 29, 1966, the Council of Ministers agreed to accept 2,500 trainees and 950 students from Vietnam. From the Vietnam Committee's foundation in July 1965 to April 1968, East Germans donated 75 million marks, of which 30 million came through the trade unions (1965: 2.5 million; 1966: 19.5 million; 1967: 34 million; 1968: 19 million).[23]

1968, which began with the Tet Offensive, was a crucial year in the anchoring of the GDR's commitment to Vietnam and in the creation of the structures that were to organize solidarity. By June 1968, the Vietnam Committee chaired by Health Minister Max Sefrin had established links with Vietnam solidarity committees in Belgium, Britain, Japan, the Netherlands, Scandinavia, West Berlin, and West Germany. The committee aimed to mobilize the East German population by using "convincing political action to explain the problems of the struggle of the Vietnamese people" and by showing how "this relates to our own anti-imperialist struggle."[24] It initiated a series of campaigns such as "Blood for Vietnam," "Medical Supplies for Vietnam," and "Fertilizer for Vietnam." In addition, the Politburo now unconditionally endorsed plans adopted by the Council of Ministers on June 18, 1968, to meet a request from the DRV for military supplies worth

22 Friedensrat der DDR to Hager, Mitglied Politbüro des ZK der SED, Betr.: Ausserordentliche Beratung des Präsidiums des Weltfriedensrates in Stockholm, Apr. 12, 1965, 2, in J IV 2/3 A-1171, DY 30, ibid.

23 Abteilung Internationale Verbindungen, Information über die politische und materielle Unterstützung durch die DDR für das vietnamesische Volk, June 17, 1968, 6–7, in 243.1204, DZ 9, BArch. The 1968 figure is through April.

24 Willi Zahlbaum, Sekretär AASK-Vietnam-Ausschuss to Gerd König, Abt. Internationale Verbindungen des ZK der SED, June 14, 1968, 7, in 57.282, DZ 9, BArch.

27 million marks and other goods worth 13.5 million marks. In August 1969, the Politburo endorsed corresponding figures of 16 million and 10 million marks for 1970 (November 1970: 15.5 million and 12.5 million marks; November 1972, in response to a request from the governing Communist Party in North Vietnam: 21 million and 15.5 million marks).[25]

This pronounced increase in East Germany's commitment was prompted by the GDR's deep identification with the Vietnamese struggle. There were a number of reasons for this, and they were not merely ideological. There was, for example, the fact that West Germany was providing political and moral support to the United States and "development aid" to South Vietnam,[26] which inevitably prompted the GDR to express its disapproval and its solidarity with North Vietnam. Besides, both the DRV and the NLF endorsed the GDR's stand in warning against the danger of neofascist resurgence in West Germany and explicitly criticized the West German government for enacting its new emergency legislation. On June 4, 1968, the South Vietnamese Committee for the Defense of World Peace issued a statement on this issue that echoed the sensibilities of the East German government: "Together with progressive peoples throughout the world, the people of South Vietnam most roundly condemn the dangerous maneuver of the West German authorities in adopting 'emergency laws' which threaten humanity with another war disaster."[27] This unambiguous position paved the way for a community of interest between North Vietnam and a GDR frustrated by the cautious response of both the Soviet and French peace committees to its requests that more attention be paid to solving the German question. This was the issue to which the GPC was primarily

25 Politbüro des ZK der SED, Reinschriftenprotokoll Nr. 25 (June 18, 1968): 7. Unterstützung der DRV auf militärischem Gebiet im Jahre 1969, Anlage Nr. 4, June 18, 1968, 6: 39–40, in J IV 2/2/1174, DY 30, SAPMO–BArch; Wunschliste der DRV: Umlauf des Briefes vom Generalsekretär Pham van Dong, Apr. 8, 1968, in J IV 2/2 A-1309, ibid.; Politbüro des ZK der SED, Reinschriftenprotokoll Nr. 32 (Aug. 19, 1969): 9. Beschluss über die Unterstützung der DRV auf militärischem Gebiet im Jahre 1970, Anlage Nr. 4, Aug. 19, 1969, 4: 27–28, in J IV 2/2/1240, ibid.; Politbüro des ZK der SED, Reinschriftenprotokoll Nr. 48 (Nov. 3, 1970): 10. Beschluss über die Unterstützung der DRV im Jahre 1971, Anlage Nr. 3, Nov. 3, 1970, 6: 15, in J IV 2/2/1308, ibid.; Politbüro des ZK der SED, Reinschriftenprotokoll Nr.52 (Nov. 24, 1970): 7. Beschluss zum Ersuchen der Regierung der DRV an die Regierung der DDR um materielle Hilfeleistung im Jahre 1971, Anlage Nr. 8, Nov. 24, 1970, 5: 46–51, in J IV 2/2/1312, ibid.; 14.11.1972, Politbüro des ZK der SED, Reinschriftenprotokoll Nr. 48 (Nov. 14, 1972): 8. Beschluss zum Ersuchen der Regierung der DRV an die Regierung der DDR um materielle Hilfeleistung im Jahre 1973, Anlage Nr. 7: 9. Beschluss über die Unterstützung der DRV im Jahre 1973, Anlage Nr. 8, Nov. 14, 1972, 5: 56–63, in J IV 2/2/1422, ibid.

26 For further details, see Alexander Troche, "Berlin wird am Mekong verteidigt": Die Ostasienpolitik der Bundesrepublik in China, Taiwan und Südvietnam 1954–1966 (Düsseldorf, 2001), 241–433; and Stanley R. Nelson and James R. Collns, Allied Participation in Vietnam (Washington, D.C., 1975), 164–5.

27 Südvietnamesisches Komitee zum Schutze des Weltfriedens (der NLF Südvietnams), Erklärung über die Annahme der Notstandsgesetze durch den Bundestag der westdeutschen Regierung, June 4, 1968, 2, in 155.769, DZ 9, BArch.

dedicated, and at WPC meetings it repeatedly appealed for more resolute backing to enable the GDR to break out of its diplomatic isolation. The moral support between Vietnam and the GDR was mutual, and the GDR was clear in endorsing the basic demands of the DRV and NLF. In the spring of 1968, representatives from North and South Vietnam indicated to the Peace Council that, although the GDR was showing uninterrupted solidarity with Vietnam, the opening of talks seemed to have dampened the commitment of some other peace organizations, and despite a WPC appeal to send delegations to Paris to put pressure on the negotiators, its sections had not responded; nor were the British and Swiss peace commit-tees, for example, lobbying their governments to remove visa restrictions on Vietnamese delegations seeking to enter their countries.[28] In a letter to the SED Central Committee, Albert Norden described this ebb deplored by the Vietnamese, claiming that WPC activity had been largely paralyzed.[29]

In the GDR's view, this raised another issue on which consensus reigned with the Vietnamese. Evaluating the WPC presidial meeting in Nicosia in June 1968, GPC general secretary Werner Rümpel argued that it was important and correct – especially regarding Vietnam – to strive for the broadest possible unity in action with other peace movements, but lamented a tendency in the WPC to seek "'breadth' at any price and with an un-limited readiness to compromise." He singled out Ivor Montagu (Britain), Yves Farge (France), Walter Diehl (West Germany), and Isabelle Blume (Belgium), who in his view all cherished a "number of illusions about the role and politics of the right-wing social democratic leadership in West Germany," and in practice were guilty of "a certain support for the impe-rialist policy of penetrating [socialism] to weaken it from the inside," just as they tended to overestimate the role of students and intellectuals.[30]

In this context, the ambivalent attitude of the political leadership of the GDR and its Peace Council toward the new peace forces who were play-ing an active part in the movement against the Vietnam War was vividly illustrated in February 1968, when an International Vietnam Congress was hosted in West Berlin.

Those images of 1968 are difficult to forget, even for East Germans. Ernesto Che Guevara's message to Latin American revolutionaries was: "Make two, three, many Vietnams" and the chants of "Ho, Ho, Ho

28 Friedensrat der DDR, n.d., Gespräch mit den Delegationen aus der DRV, der NLF Südvietnams und Laos, in 228.1987, DZ 9, BArch.
29 Albert Norden to ZK der SED, in IV A 2/2.028/98, DY 30, SAPMO-BArch.
30 Werner Rümpel, Bericht über die Tagung des Präsidiums des Weltfriedensrates vom 6.–8.6.1968 in Nicosia, June 17, 1968, 4, in 57.282, DZ 9, BArch.

Chi Minh" became symbols for a worldwide student and youth movement that began to rock the foundations of the system. In West Germany, this protest movement was increasingly linked with opposition to the Emergency Laws. The fire that swept through American campuses also ignited mass protests at universities in West Germany and West Berlin during 1966 and 1967, and in the GDR, too, this mood caught the popular imagination. It inspired the official solidarity movement and fueled public consciousness to a degree that should not be underestimated.

In 1966, the West European Students' Committee for Peace in Vietnam was set up. It tried to coordinate the campaigns underway in all West European countries, with the exception of the Spanish and Portuguese dictatorships. The West German League of Socialist Students (Sozialistischer Deutscher Studentenbund, or SDS) decided at a delegates' conference in September 1967 in Frankfurt am Main – attended by representatives of the Soviet Students Council, the Central Council of the GDR's Free German Youth (Freie Deutsche Jugend, or FDJ), and the American SDS (Students for a Democratic Society) – to expand its actions against the Vietnam War.

There already were criticisms, above all from the SED and FDJ, about the activists' radical mood and resistance to authority. This wariness grew after the first direct action taken during preparations for the tribunal against conservative media mogul Axel Springer's publishing house in West Berlin, when on February 2, 1968, stones shattered the windows of six Springer offices in the city. Rudi Dutschke was one of the best-known leaders of the antiauthoritarian wing of the SDS in West Berlin at the time. In late 1967, he began to implement his vision of a new International and proposed holding the Vietnam Congress in February 1968, hoping to unite hundreds of the war's opponents at this border between the two systems. Talks were held between the FDJ and the SDS, warily monitored by the Politburo, where Norden defined the terms. In January 1968, the Politburo "supported" the Central Council of the FDJ's decision not to participate in the congress and sent it instructions accordingly. One major reason for the East German leadership's reluctance to sanction this congress was the fear that the conference would be used, under the cover of solidarity and unity, "to challenge the strategy and tactics of the socialist countries."[31] A specific problem was the planned participation of the American SDS (seen as a key component in the distrusted New Left), the Cuban Communist Party (relations were strained at the time, partly because the latter had played

---

31 Probleme im Zusammenhang mit der vorgesehenen Vietnamkonferenz in Westberlin, Jan. 23, 1968, 1, in IV A 2/2.028/107, DY 30, SAPMO-BArch.

a key role in setting up the Organización Latinoamericana de Solidaridad, or OLAS, which favored guerrilla warfare), and a range of "left sectarian, Trotskyist and Maoist youth and student organizations." West German SDS emissaries agreed at a discussion on January 19 (which they had requested and designated informal) to a number of FDJ demands relating to the conference, granting the FDJ, the Komsomol, and the South Vietnamese NLF representative in the GDR the right to speak. Cooperation nevertheless ceased. There had even been demands to postpone the conference in order to acquire firmer control, and failing this there were ideas for counteractivities in East Berlin, a big mass meeting or demonstration with effective press coverage expressing the GDR's solidarity with the Vietnamese struggle before the conference opened on February 17–18.[32]

The GDR leadership was equally ambivalent about a demonstration against the U.S. war in Vietnam planned for Sunday, February 18, already banned by the West Berlin Senate.

Concerned about sympathy among their own GIs, the American authorities advised their military police to use force if demonstrators appeared outside the barracks in Dahlem, as originally planned. On the eve of the conference, Bishop Kurt Scharf held a crisis meeting with Bernd Rabehl of the German SDS, the West Berlin police, and the governing mayor of West Berlin. There was a compromise, but the ban was not lifted. That night, forty-six students – including Peter Brandt, son of the West German foreign minister – were arrested for hanging posters. The threat of open confrontation grew.

On February 17, about 5,000 people, mostly students, met in the main auditorium of the Technical University of Berlin under the Vietcong flag and Guevara's slogan from the OLAS Conference in Havana: "It is the duty of a revolutionary to make revolution." Dutschke passionately called for Western opposition groups to join forces with revolutionary liberation movements. Speaker after speaker described the conference as the fuse that would ignite organized political resistance. The counterstrategy would include a second front in the centers of capitalism via an open campaign to "Smash NATO!" Hans-Jürgen Krahl of the West German SDS justified this demand by arguing that NATO had become a weapon "in the

---

32 Politbüro des ZK der SED, Reinschriftenprotokoll Nr. 3: 4. Informationen des Genossen A. Norden über die Absicht der Durchführung einer internationalen Vietnam-Konferenz in Westberlin, Jan. 26, 1968, 2, in J IV 2/2/1152, DY 30, SAPMO-BArch; Erich Rau, Entscheidungsfrage zur internationalen Vietnamkonferenz in Westberlin am 17.–18.2.1968, Jan. 30, 1968, in IV A 2/2.028/107, ibid.; Information über ein Gespräch mit Initiatoren der Westberliner Vietnamkonferenz, Jan. 30, 1968, in ibid.

struggle against social revolutionary movements in the Third World."[33] Action was needed to infiltrate the armed forces and to target bases, shipments of American arms, and West European branches of American companies. The participants ignored the Berlin Senate, and the dawn of a new era of resistance was celebrated with a protest demonstration whereby 20,000 people marched on the Deutsche Oper, where a rally took place, accompanied by minor skirmishes with the police. When students affixed posters of Rosa Luxemburg, Karl Liebknecht, and the NLF flag to a crane, they were torn down and burnt by members of the Junge Union, the youth organization of the Christian Democratic Union (CDU), disguised as construction workers. Dutschke saw this provocation as the prelude to violence and warned the protesters not to rise to the bait: "Those who are burning our flags and tearing down our posters now will be the first to hoist the red flag over Springer's tower block!"[34]

In the seclusion of the university auditorium a revolutionary utopia had been forged, and the spirit of a revolutionary surge caught hold. But it did not carry the masses: The East Germans present did not feel that these were the forces that would end the Vietnam War, even if the representatives of the DRV and NLF, who had also come across from their East Berlin embassies, enthusiastically welcomed the proceedings. The subsequent reports of the Peace Council and the Politburo failed to mention this event, which spoke volumes for the official East German evaluation.

As the year progressed, Vietnam became a safety valve. In fact, it may well have saved the WPC from being split in two by the Warsaw Pact invasion of Czechoslovakia. The loud protests of peace forces worldwide at the sight of Soviet tanks in Prague were soon drowned out by a louder outcry against the Vietnam War.

The Prague Spring of 1968 marked the watershed, despite the attempts by the WPC to polish its image in the 1970s. This event decisively shattered the original consensus on which it had been built in 1949. It sealed the WPC's fate as an instrument subject to the overriding influence of Soviet foreign policy.

The Prague Spring also marked an irreparable fraying of the fabric of communist power in eastern Europe. Lastly, Prague demonstrated, despite all the declarations of unity at the communist party conferences in 1969 and 1976, that the alleged homogeneity of the communist movement no

33 *Internationaler Vietnam-Kongress Februar 1968 Westberlin: Der Kampf des vietnamesischen Volkes und die Globalstrategie des Imperialismus*, reprint (Berlin, 1987), 143.
34 Cited in Gretchen Dutschke, *Wir hatten ein barbarisches, schönes Leben: Rudi Dutschke – Eine Biographie* (Cologne, 1996), 187.

longer could withstand public scrutiny. Polycentrism became a reality. Certainly, growing tensions and even animosity between the Chinese and Soviet communist parties had limited the commitment of protest campaigns in the nominally socialist countries, as did the complex relationship between the Workers' Party of Vietnam and the NLF. However, the real test of the WPC's unity came with the appearance of tanks on the streets of Prague. According to Hälker, this could easily have put an end to the WPC, and Vietnam became, in his words, the "principal cement" holding the WPC together after the Peace Council of the GDR had made its own attempt to "cement" the Presidium at its crisis meeting in Lahti (Finland) in November 1968.[35] Interestingly, at a meeting of the WPC Secretariat on September 3 in Helsinki, the GDR's representative was the only person to defend the invasion, whereas the other East European peace committees were conspicuous by their absence.[36] Secretary Chandra and coordinating president Blume were particularly insistent that the "invasion by armed troops" and a "rapid withdrawal of the occupying forces" be seriously discussed.[37] The rift in the WPC's structure did not heal with time, even though a compromise was reached. The WPC rallied from its death bed with an appeal to step up international action for peace at a time when the campaign to end the Vietnam conflict was mobilizing many sections of the community, despite the subduing effects of the Paris talks and President Richard Nixon's announcement of a Vietnamization policy.

In the GDR, solidarity with Vietnam grew by leaps and bounds after the autumn of 1968, like a pressure valve enabling the population to let off steam or at least channel it constructively while reassuring themselves of basic ideological principles.

Attending the meetings of the Stockholm Conference on Vietnam remained a priority in the Secretariat of the Central Committee until 1972. These meetings had grown in size and input: By May 1969, there were participants from fifty-six countries and twenty-four international organizations. At the height of the movement, the World Assembly for the Peace and Independence of the Indo-Chinese Peoples in Versailles in March 1972 attracted 1,200 delegates from eighty-four countries and thirty-two organizations. This was due at least in part to the commitment of the WPC and of Chandra, who traveled widely in order to mobilize support for

---

35 Author's interview with Hälker, Sept. 28, 1998.
36 Information über die Situation im Weltfriedensrat im Zusammenhang mit den Massnahmen des 21. August, 93–5, in IV A 2/2.028/98, DY 30, SAPMO-BArch.
37 Isabelle Blume (WPC) to Walther Friedrich (GPC), Erklärung der koordinierenden Präsidentin des Weltfriedensrates und des Generalsekretärs, Aug. 24, 1968, in 466.2422, DZ 9, BArch.

an end to the war. On September 5, 1970, the Executive Committee of the Stockholm Conference, composed of eleven international and eleven national organizations, held a meeting in the GDR. East Germans also played an active part in the work of the International Commission for the Investigation of U.S. War Crimes in October 1970, after it was set up in March at the 5th Stockholm Conference.[38] The British philosopher and pacifist Bertrand Russell, who had come to the WPC Congress in Helsinki in July 1965 to demand an end to the American war of aggression in Vietnam and plead for worldwide action to halt the U.S. policy of experimental human slaughter, became the venerable eminence of this esteemed International War Crimes tribunal. Experts from the GDR made a notable contribution to its widely acknowledged findings. The tribunal played an active role in recording the war crimes through various media. The documentary films made by East German directors Walter Heynowski and Gerhard Scheumann were highly acclaimed and were used by the Vietnam movement worldwide to mobilize public opinion.

This appeal to basic humanitarian concerns fell on fertile soil in the GDR, even if interspersed with the customary sloganeering (and probably because it was a refreshing contrast to constantly repeated platitudes). It reflected a genuine and widespread identification with intrinsic socialist values. 1968 was, for example, the first year of Christmas Solidarity Concerts on the radio (and later television), and children donated some of their Christmas presents to children in Vietnam. In 1968, donations collected from citizens exceeded 40 million marks.[39] The solidarity movement conducted most of its activities under the aegis of the Vietnam Committee – which improved its standing in the eyes of the Peace Council in 1969, when the GPC's deputy general secretary, Richard Zänkner, was asked to join.[40] Until the war ended, the movement continued to raise awareness of the plight of the Vietnamese people and Indochina, and through this structure the relatively unsullied East German sense of solidarity found public expression.

In the early 1970s, Vietnam was a potential key to drawing the world's very diverse peace movements closer together. The WPC had emerged as an accepted factor, recognized for its often selfless contributions, and a symbol

---

38 Friedensrat der DDR to Gen. Stadler, Bericht über die 5.Stockholmer Vietnam-Konferenz, Apr. 6, 1970, in IV A 2/2.028/100, DY 30, SAPMO-BArch.

39 Vietnam-Ausschuss beim Afro-Asiatischen Solidaritätskomitee der DDR, Information über wichtige Aktionen der Bevölkerung der DDR zur Unterstützung des kämpfenden vietnamesischen Volkes im Jahre 1968, Dec. 11, 1968, 2–5, in 457.2385, DZ 9, BArch.

40 The chairman was Max Sefrin, and the secretary was Willi Zahlbaum. The Secretariat included the Ministries of Material Procurement and Foreign Trade and Investment, and representatives of professional and mass organizations.

of the committed input of the GDR, as commentators regularly observed. The GDR continued to provide material and technical resources for the Stockholm movement; given the very small amount of hard currency at the GDR's disposal, its support was an indication of the leadership's continuing priorities. After 1973, and especially after 1975, the GDR turned its attention to the reconstruction efforts in the now reunited socialist Vietnam.

By 1975, government aid to Vietnam from the GDR had totaled 1.5 billion marks; of this sum, 442 million had been collected in the form of private donations. This figure does not include the cost of industrial training or student fees for young Vietnamese who came to the GDR. Additional material aid worth 10.93 million marks was announced after the fall of Saigon in April 1975;[41] the following month, the promised aid was increased to 50 million marks.[42] The GDR played a major role in this reconstruction effort until its own demise.

However, the GDR was increasingly concerned about a preference for militant forms of action, favored above all by the Vietnamese (DRV and NLF) and American elements in the Stockholm movement, rather than campaigns to collect signatures of protest. The GDR gradually distanced itself from the Vietnamese call to claim "sole, complete freedom of decision" in the solidarity movement and to ignore the coordinating services of the Stockholm Conference. This was articulated in internal reports and openly challenged by the Soviet Union and the GDR.[43] The GDR also began to criticize the rather self-centered activism of Chandra, who tended to disregard previously determined strategies and resist ideas from the East European peace committees. Meanwhile, the Soviet Union and the GDR hoped to link the Stockholm movement, which had "never had a truly mass basis because it was not allied with the international and national mass organizations," more closely to the broader anti-imperialist movement. They saw the International Indochina Conference planned for Versailles in February 1972 as a "test case for holding a world meeting of anti-imperialists."[44]

The World Assembly for the Peace and Independence of the Indochinese Peoples, actually held in March, brought together 1,200 delegates from

41 Politbüro des ZK der SED, Reinschriftenprotokoll Nr. 17 (Apr. 22, 1975): 23: Materielle Hilfe für die befreiten Gebiete in Südvietnam, Anlage Nr. 15, Apr. 22, 1975, 9: 97–9, in J IV 2/2/1558, DY 30, SAPMO-BArch.

42 Politbüro des ZK der SED, Reinschriftenprotokoll Nr. 19 (May 6, 1975): 2. Zusätzliche Solidaritätsleistung für Vietnam, Anlage Nr. 1, May 6, 1975, 1, 9, in J IV 2/2/1560, ibid.

43 Friedensrat der DDR, Werner Rümpel (GPC), Information über Fragen der Zusammenarbeit zwischen dem Friedensrat der DDR und dem Sowjetischen Komitee zum Schutze des Friedens (Konsultation am 26. und 27.2.1970 in Moskau), March 3, 1970, 5–6, in 206.994, DZ 9, BArch.

44 Röhmer, Generalsekretär AASK, Information über die Internationale Indochina-Konferenz (10.–13.2.1972) in Versailles/Frankreich, Dec. 23, 1971 (Streng vertraulich), 1, in 458.2389, ibid.

eighty-four countries and thirty-two organizations. It was certainly a highlight in the international solidarity movement, in which the Stockholm
Conference on Vietnam was a major influence, continuing to hold its own
conferences until the mid-1970s, although they lost the momentum that
they had at the beginning of the decade.

CONCLUDING REMARKS

The détente that began to take hold in Europe and between the United
States, the Soviet Union, and China, the Conference on Security and Cooperation in Europe (CSCE) process, and, in particular, the completion of
the Vietnam negotiations in Paris inevitably shifted the focus of the international peace movement, including the WPC.

The international movement against the Vietnam conflict was not homogeneous but pluralistic. The primarily communist-led WPC managed to
play its part productively without staking a claim to leadership. In Hälker's
assessment, although the WPC generally "chipped in everywhere and promoted everything," it also recognized that the Vietnam issue was "a specific,
quite fundamental question within the world peace movement," in whose
ranks the GDR made "a committed and constructive contribution" acknowledged across the globe.[45]

In the GDR itself, there was a division of labor. Both the Vietnam Committee and the Peace Council were steered through directives from the SED
leadership. Despite the repetitive crudeness of much official campaigning
and the popular wariness vis-à-vis the regular experience of party doctrines
donned or feigned for political occasions, the plight of the Vietnamese
touched a chord. The widespread spontaneous solidarity that was extended
by many ordinary East Germans was borne of a basic humanitarianism and a
desire to do something concrete in opposition to American policy in Southeast Asia. The reports that reached East Germans each evening on television, whether from the GDR or West Germany, showed defoliated forests,
napalm-scorched villages, and women and children scarred with burns.
These images required no declaration of political principle. Among the
older generation, moreover, memories of World War II were revived. East
Germans were outraged by the use of conventional and chemical weapons –
especially napalm and agent orange – by a large, powerful country against
a small, impoverished people. This solidarity was relatively consistent across
the social spectrum and was expressed publicly in the countless donation

45 Author's interview with Hälker, Sept. 28, 1998.

drives and petitions organized by various associations in conjunction with the Vietnam Committee.

These fundamental values reflected the theoretical premises on which the nominally socialist states were founded. By the same token, the leading communist parties of these states derived from their basic Marxist tenets an assumption that their role was to lead the world peace movement. Given that these parties exerted a direct influence on their national peace structures, this creed imported an essentially sectarian strand that tainted efforts by the World Peace Council to cooperate with other peace movements.

This same leadership role led in the GDR to a constellation of party-oriented structures that included not only the Peace Council but also the AASK under the umbrella of the National Front. In their response to the Vietnam War, we see reflected a complex cluster of shifts and contradictions so characteristic of the WPC's history, governed as it was by several ideologically determined factors: (1) the relationship between regional/local conflicts/wars and the overall aims of each national alliance or network of peace/antiwar groups as components of the international peace movement; (2) the specific relationship between the Vietnam War and the ideological roots of different sections of the peace movement, and its interaction with ideological/political attitudes to the issue of war/peace; (3) the impact on attitudes toward the Vietnam War of changing priorities as part of shifting conflicts within systems and between the blocs; (4) internal differentiations and debates within the international peace movement and their impact on the Vietnam focus.

15

All Power to the Imagination!

Antiwar Activism and Emerging Feminism in the Late 1960s

BARBARA L. TISCHLER

The importance of women's efforts in the United States and throughout the world to end the war in Vietnam has been subsumed into a paradigm that suggests that many women activists abruptly fled the antiwar movement in the late 1960s to take up the new feminist cause, abandoning the antiwar cause that had initially ignited their activist energies. This teleological approach tends to diminish the positive effects of organizational, theoretical, and personal lessons learned and insights experienced in the antiwar movement to the emergence of a highly structured, theoretically nuanced, and personally impassioned movement of, by, and for women, whose constituent groups, however diverse and disconnected, shared the idea of liberation from male authority.

In an era of revisionist 1960s scholarship that seeks to reexamine some of the assumptions about activism throughout the world, it is important to reflect, not simply on the origins of the feminist movement in the civil rights and antiwar movements, but also on the importance of women's roles in the movement to end the war in Vietnam as a self-contained historical phenomenon *and* as an inspiration to the new feminist movement in the United States and throughout the world. This task is by no means a simple or straightforward one. Women's struggles within the antiwar movement, even when these struggles were not specifically dismissed as "trivial," have often been seen as an adjunct to those of male activists. Like soldiers on the battlefield, soldiers in the movement saw women as ornaments (at worst) or auxiliaries whose purpose was to make life on the barricades less arduous.

In 1979, historian Sara Evans published *Personal Politics: The Roots of Women's Liberation in the Civil Rights Movement and the New Left*, a path-breaking study of the origins of the new feminist movement. Locating the spirit that activated many women in the United States to construct a movement of their own in the struggles for civil rights and against the devastating war in Southeast Asia, Evans sought historical continuity as well as transcendence for the new feminism. Her narrative evoked women's contradictory feelings of de-historicized isolation rooted in the imperatives of the historical moment as well as an emerging, if not perfectly defined, sense of connectedness to the "usable past" of earlier women activists that would be posited in the 1970s by social historians as the stuff of real history.

Evans's work on the roots of contemporary feminism is an example of scholarship about the 1960s that eschews the top-down focus of more traditional historical writing. Recognizing the limitations of "great man," "great woman," or even "great movement" theories of historical development, she and others writing for both scholarly and popular audiences offered analysis and remembrances of the loosely structured but symbolically powerful activism of this period. Simply put, women proved themselves to be able and active participants in both the civil rights and antiwar movements in the United States. In performing the tasks required of them and recognizing the limitations of the post–World War II version of the proper "woman's sphere," women activists acquired essential organizational skills and sharpened their analytical approach to advocacy. In doing so, women perceived the need for action *as women* and were consequently prepared with the skills and the ideological framework to become their own advocates.

The civilian antiwar movement can be analyzed in the context of a generic spirit of activism around the world. Although that movement is often identified with the activities of white, middle-class college students whose leaders were primarily male, it also provided an opportunity for people of color and women to voice their opposition to the war itself and to an antiwar movement that seemed increasingly resistant to hearing their individual voices. Describing the importance of Vietnamese women to the struggle against the U.S. military establishment, a female member of the Black Panther Party connected the accomplishments of revolutionary women in Vietnam to the need for women's revolutionary activity in the antiwar movement:

The Vietnamese women are out there fighting with their brothers, fighting against American imperialism, with its advanced technology. They can shoot. They're out there with their babies on their backs . . . and they're participating in the revolution wholeheartedly, just as the Vietnamese men are participating in the revolution, in the national liberation struggle. The success of their national liberation struggle is just as much dependent upon the women continuing in the struggle as it is dependent on the Vietnamese men.[1]

---

1 Interview cited in G. Louis Heath, ed., *Off the Pigs! The History and Literature of the Black Panther Party* (Metuchen, N.J., 1976), 342.

Women whose revolutionary activity was truly a life and death matter provided inspiration for women who were beginning to conceptualize the liberation struggles of others as part of their own struggle for liberation and identity.

As early as 1965, women were actors in the drama of war and peace that was enacted on the public stage after the passage of the Gulf of Tonkin Resolution and the beginning of Operation Rolling Thunder in February 1965. After the announcement of B-52 bombing missions over Vietnam, Helga Alice Herz, a Holocaust survivor and founding member of Women Strike for Peace (WSP) in Detroit and a member of the Women's International League for Peace and Freedom (WILPF), committed suicide on a Detroit street corner. Following the example of Buddhist monks in Vietnam and a few Americans who immolated themselves in protest of the repressive regime of South Vietnamese Prime Minister Ngo Dinh Diem, Herz left a letter in which she exhorted Americans to "decide if this world shall be a good place to live for all human beings or if it should blow itself up into oblivion."[2] Herz's personal protest did not go unnoticed. A month after her death, North Vietnam's *Vietnam Courier,* an English-language biweekly that had been devoted exclusively to coverage of the war since its inception in April 1964, observed that Herz's dramatic protest proved the existence of antiwar sentiment in the United States. The paper also printed a letter from the Vietnamese Women's Union, which observed that the war "stains the honour and tradition of the freedom and equality-loving American people." Shortly after Herz's death, WSP members Mary Clarke and Lorraine Gordon traveled to Moscow for a commemoration of the twentieth anniversary of the end of World War II. After meeting with representatives of South Vietnam's National Liberation Front, the two women continued their journey, spending three days in Hanoi in an impromptu and unauthorized citizen visit in a country that was under constant attack by the United States. They stayed in private homes in an effort to keep news of their trip out of the press. They visited bomb shelters and hospitals and held informal talks with North Vietnamese leaders. Before their return to the United States, Clarke and Gordon laid the groundwork for future meetings between American and North Vietnamese women, accepting the suggestion of Prime Minister Pham Van Dong that Jakarta, Indonesia, would be a good choice for a future meeting.[3]

---

2 Amy G. Swerdlow, *Women Strike for Peace: Traditional Motherhood and Radical Politics in the 1960s* (Chicago, 1992), 130.

3 Mary Hershberger, *Traveling to Vietnam: American Peace Activists and the War* (Syracuse, N.Y., 1998), 2–6.

On December 22, 1966, four women activists accepted an invitation from
the Vietnamese Women's Union to travel to Hanoi to see for themselves
the results of the war and American bombing and to bring information
back to the antiwar movement in the United States. Barbara Deming was a
member of an A. J. Muste socialist group; Grace Mora Newman, an activist
from the Bronx, was the sister of Dennis Mora, of the "Fort Hood Three"
who had refused orders to fight in Vietnam and was facing a long prison
term for his actions; Patricia Griffith was active in WSP in Ithaca, New.
York; and Diane Nash had been active in the Freedom Rides, CORE (the
Congress of Racial Equality), and SNCC (the Student Non-Violent Coordinating Committee). At Hanoi's Thong Nhat Hotel, the Americans met
representatives from Beheiren, the Japanese antiwar movement, trade union-
ists from Moscow, West German antiwar activists, and a camera crew from
Cuba. They visited villages, hospitals (where the effects of fragmentation
bombs were dramatic and disturbing), schools, and factories. Before returning to the United States, the women were allowed to visit two American
prisoners, who presented them with notes to their families and messages
urging an end to the war.[4] It might be argued that the women's visit served
the propaganda needs of the North Vietnamese. Nevertheless, the destruction wrought by American bombs was real, and the information brought
back to the American antiwar movement by these women provided valuable evidence of the necessity of their actions to end the war. Although
the American women who traveled to Hanoi did not place their trip in a
specifically feminist context, their independent action *as women* flew in the
face of commonly held assumptions in society at large and in the New Left
that women needed to follow the direction of male leaders. Clearly, women
could contribute to antiwar activism, even playing major roles frequently
assigned only to men.

The decentralized, multifaceted, indeed multicultural and countercultural, civil rights and antiwar movements exerted a powerful influence on
the collective conscience of their time and provided a forum in which
women found not only a framework for the feminist movement but also a
stage for activism and organizing in their own right. It is important to examine aspects of the antiwar movement that helped to frame the late-1960s
feminist consciousness by looking at women's analysis of the war from both
a civilian and military perspective.

In the effort to end the war in southeast Asia, young American women
also worked alongside male participants in the movement. With an acute

4 Ibid., 76–8.

awareness of "generation gap" politics that demanded their participation in a war over which they had no control, young men and women, according to historian Ruth Rosen, "expressed contempt for the military and economic 'establishment,' vowed to change 'the system,' and favored direct action over the stodgy, hierarchical, bureaucratic ways of the adult world."[5] Rosen argues that women in the college cohort of the mid-1960s faced not one generation gap but two. They were part of the "Baby Boom" generation, the largest bulge in the birth rate in recent American history with the power of numbers and relative affluence on their side but little political power with which to articulate a "youth agenda," even if such an agenda had existed in a clearly articulated form. In addition to being young and legally disempowered,[6] women faced the infantilization of their sex. Protected by families and the state from the privileges and demands of adult status and responsibility, white middle-class "girls" were presumed to be spending their teenage and young adult years waiting for the husband who would continue to protect them from the real, grown-up world.

Many white women who had grown up with a "good girl" image of themselves at first found it difficult to develop an independent analysis of their status within the antiwar movement. Margery Tabankin, an antiwar activist student at the University of Wisconsin from 1965 to 1969, described this dynamic:

Part of being a woman was this psychology of proving I was such a good radical, "better than the men." We felt we were motivated by something higher because we didn't have to go to war ourselves. Most guys didn't take women seriously, however. They were things to fuck. . . . You went through this intense experience [at demonstrations], and you went back and had sex. [However] It [sex] was much more on men's terms.[7]

For women raised to value their ability to serve men, sexually and personally (Tabankin remembered that she had been so taken with organizer Tom Hayden that she even did his laundry when he visited Madison to give a speech), it could be difficult to break the pattern of gender subordination. Creating another model for participation in the antiwar movement, a model based on comradeship and equality rather than sexual servility, involved

5 Ruth Rosen, "The Female Generation Gap: Daughters of the Fifties and the Origins of Contemporary American Feminism," in Linda K. Kerber, Alice Kessler-Harris, and Kathryn Kish Sklar, eds., *U.S. History as Women's History: New Feminist Essays* (Chapel Hill, N.C., 1995), 315.

6 Neither men nor women who had reached the age of 18 could vote in presidential elections until 1972. Women of all ages faced restrictive laws relating to credit and their legal status as property holders as well as discrimination in employment and other aspects of society and culture based on pervasive and long-held assumptions about their ability to function as fully responsible adults.

7 Myra MacPherson, *Long Time Passing: Vietnam and the Haunted Generation* (New York, 1985), 552.

radical changes in men's attitudes about women and women's attitudes about themselves.

The call for women's liberation within the antiwar movement in the United States was illustrated at the Jeanette Rankin Brigade protest in Washington, D.C. in January 1968. New York's Radical Women, not content to accept the traditional women's role in protesting the killing of the men in their lives, sought to transform the event into a call for women power. Shulamith Firestone called for women's unity, not simply as people who opposed the war, but as women thinking for themselves. She wrote in the pamphlet for the "Burial of True Womanhood" march that women

have refused to hanky-wave boys off to war with admonitions to save the American Mom and Apple Pie. You have resisted your roles of supportive girl friends and tearful widows, receivers of regretful telegrams and worthless medals of honor. And now you must resist approaching Congress playing these same roles that are synonymous with powerlessness. . . . Until we have united into a force to be reckoned with, we will be patronized and ridiculed into total political ineffectiveness. So if you are really sincere about *ending* this war, join us tonight and in the future.[8]

The "Burial" action revealed deep fissures among members of the antiwar movement: male activists for whom women's issues were not on the metaphorical radar screen; "politico" women who denigrated women's issues as frivolous in their efforts to be taken seriously as political thinkers by themselves and their male colleagues; and women activists who increasingly defined themselves as feminists could no longer be assumed to share the same faith in movement coalition politics that had fueled the antiwar movement just a few years earlier.

In trying to make sense of the antiwar movement beyond the borders of the United States, it is instructive to note the extent of participation in the movement itself. While it is tempting to speak of a "generation in revolt," that phrase does not adequately describe students and young people, at least not in the United States. While involvement in the antiwar movement was widespread and increasing, especially after Tet and then again after the invasion of Cambodia in April 1970, it is far from clear that the antiwar movement ever captured the attention of the majority of young Americans. But, as activist Abbie Hoffman noted, political action that takes the form of cultural rebellion is hardly the stuff of majoritarian politics.

In contrast, the French movement was not only a protest against the war, it was a transformative critique of capitalism, unemployment, commercialism,

8 Shulamith Firestone, "The Jeanette Rankin Brigade: Woman Power?" in Judith Hole and Ellen Levine, eds., *The Rebirth of Feminism* (New York, 1971), 117.

and state (not to mention, American) power in the postwar world. According to author Raymond Boudon, "while in Germany, in the United States, or in Holland, student activism always involved a minority of students, it was almost impossible in May and June of 1968 to find a French student who was against *le mouvement*." Indeed, the protests that began at Le Sorbonne and Nanterre and spread beyond the universities and to less radical cohorts whose members were activated by issues such as employment pointed to the growing contradiction "between the liberal elitist orientation of the university and the rapid changes in the characteristics of the student body."[9] Protests in France were all-encompassing, they included and were activated by the energies of women, and they contributed to the emergence of a class-conscious but more powerfully gender-conscious feminist movement in that country. Even though Charles de Gaulle's conservative government did not lose power in the election of 1968, and there is evidence that the protests of that spring actually pushed the electorate a bit further to the right, for a brief moment, the existing order was, according to historian Arthur Marwick, "brought to a halt by the combined action of students and workers."[10] Throughout Italy in the "hot autumn" of 1968, students and workers articulated their grievances against the government, the Pirelli Tire Company (to name only one example of industrial strife), and the Catholic Church. One protest often served as inspiration for another in what many, especially in the American Left, came to see as a revolutionary moment.

Very soon, women's powerful and critical voices emerged that articulated a theory of political reform and revolution that not only assumed the validity of a women's perspective, but asserted the *superiority* of women's theoretical understanding, basic assumptions about the world, and modes of action that could be seen as antimale. In June 1968, Valerie Solanis published the "S.C.U.M. [Society for Cutting Up Men] Manifesto" in "The Berkeley Barb." She cast her argument in blatantly sexual terms and asserted, in effect, that the presence of men was detrimental to the development of a true revolutionary politics because men were capable of little more than antirevolutionary philosophizing:

There's no reason why a society...should have a government, laws or leaders.... The male's inability to relate to anybody or anything makes his life pointless and meaningless (The ultimate male insight is that life is absurd.), so he

---

9 Raymond Boudon, "Sources of Student Protest in France," in Philip G. Altbach and Robert S. Laufer, eds., *The New Pilgrims: Youth Protest in Transition* (New York, 1972), 297–8.
10 Arthur Marwick, *The Sixties: Cultural Revolution in Britain, France, Italy, and the United States, c.1958–c.1974* (New York, 1998), 584.

invented philosophy and religion. Being empty, he looks outward, not only for guidance and control, but for salvation and for the meaning of life. Happiness is impossible on this earth, so he invented Heaven. . . . A woman not only takes her identity and individuality for granted, but knows instinctively that the only wrong is to hurt others and the meaning of life is love. . . . No genuine social revolution can be accomplished by the male, as the male on top wants the status quo, and the male on the bottom wants to be the male on top. . . . The male changes only when forced to do so by technology, when he has no choice, when "society" reaches the stage when he must change or die. We're at that stage now; if women don't fast get their asses in gear, we may very well all die.[11]

The language here is one of frustration and disgust: Men have failed to end the war or to create a more humane society. For the women of S.C.U.M., there was no structural or organizational alternative but to challenge men to move out of the way.

Even with the appearance of Solanis's "Manifesto" in 1968, women activists tended to participate in organizations with another primary purpose, rather than activists in their own cause. The antiwar movement benefited from the expertise, organizational experience, and courage of women on many college campuses and in the larger world. However, the extent to which "women's issues" became contested terrain between men and women (and even among women) cannot be underestimated. Women who were radicalized by the antiwar movement found themselves marginalized by their comrades in struggle in that same movement. It is interesting not so much that the new feminism emerged out of women activists' frustration, but rather that so many women remained active in the antiwar movement into the 1970s even as they moved toward theorizing and founding a movement of their own.

Among the prominent student organizations that committed themselves to the antiwar movement, Students for a Democratic Society (SDS) was perhaps the most visible and the most influential in terms of setting the stage for feminist activism. Kirkpatrick Sale has underscored the importance of SDS to the women's movement, and, indeed, most other late 1960s alternative movements: SDS, Sale writes, was

the seedbed for the women's liberation movement – sometimes, to be sure, as much by inadvertence as intention – and supplied many of that movement's initial converts, and it played a part both formally and informally in other kinds of political broadening such as high-school organizing, GI resistance, trade-union agitation, the

---

11 Valerie Solanis, "S.C.U.M. Manifesto," *The Berkeley Barb*, June 7–13, 1968, 4, quoted in Judith Clavir Albert and Stewart Edward Albert, eds., *The Sixties Papers: Documents of a Rebellious Decade* (New York, 1984), 463–4.

Venceremos Brigades to Cuba, and "radical caucuses" in the professional societies of almost every branch of the academy.[12]

SDS faced challenges from women to consider issues of participation and leadership, but with no theoretical analysis of the role of women in radical politics, the group was ill-equipped to hear these challenges and act on them. The Port Huron Statement, the organizing statement of SDS written primarily by Al Haber in August 1962, articulated a generational perspective on materialism, democracy, and the role of the university as an instrument of social reform, but the document said nothing at all about women. The group's dramatic increase in size and scope after the introduction of ground combat troops into Vietnam in February 1965 fixed its sights firmly on the struggle to revolutionize American society. Efforts to raise women's issues as a distinct political agenda were met with the assertion that women's concerns were peripheral to the broader political agenda: ending the war. Nevertheless, as early as December 1965, the SDS National Council included a workshop on "Women in the Movement" that produced a statement asserting that "the problem of participation by women is a special problem – one that reflects not only inadequacies within SDS but one that also reflects greater societal problems, namely the problem of the role of women in American society."[13] Although SDS women were not able to get the National Council to address the problem of women in the movement, their analysis was broad-ranging and cultural, refined in the same fire as that in which SDS had shaped its critique of the war, racism, imperialism, and American society itself.

The resolution passed by the SDS National Council in December of 1967 subsumed women's issues under the broader rubric of "building the anti-imperialist movement in this country,"[14] much to the dissatisfaction of women who were coming to see women's liberation as distinct from anti-imperialism or the struggle to end the war. This same resolution placed the responsibility of taking the initiative to "discourage male supremacism in interpersonal relationships with both men and women."[15] The tone of this resolution, later reprinted in *New Left Notes*, was particularly offensive to women activists because it appeared to trivialize the issue of male supremacism by making it simply an issue between and among individuals.

---

12 Kirkpatrick Sale, *SDS: The Rise and Development of Students for a Democratic Society* (New York, 1973), 9–10.

13 Ibid., 252.

14 Cited in Alice Echols, *Daring to Be Bad: Radical Feminism in America, 1967–1975* (Minneapolis, 1989), 121.

15 Ibid., 122.

Further, it placed the burden of dealing with sexism on women rather than on SDS as a whole.

In 1968, the SDS national convention endorsed the concept of equal pay for equal work for women, but a more comprehensive statement about women's liberation sparked, according to historian Mari Jo Buhle, a "raucous denunciation similar to what Socialist women had endured [earlier in the century] when they dared to compare women's liberation with that of the Proletariat."[16]

As the national SDS organization was debating relatively bland statements of support of women's rights and struggling with dissent within its own ranks, individual women leaders subsumed the feminist critique of the organization into a broader analysis of women in American society. In March 1968, Naomi Jaffe and Bernadine Dohrn argued powerfully against the pervasive sexism in mainstream consumer culture while also taking aim at the movement that defined women through men:

Over the past few months, small groups have been coming together in various cities to meet around the realization that as women radicals we are not radical women – that we are unfree within the Movement and in personal relationships, as in the society at large. We realize that women are organized into the Movement by men and continue to relate to it through men. We find that the difficulty women have in taking initiative and in acting and speaking in a political context is the consequence of internalizing the view that men define reality and women are defined in terms of men. We are coming together not in a defensive posture to rage at our exploited status vis a vis men, but rather in the process of developing our own autonomy.[17]

As Jaffe and Dohrn articulated an institutional perspective rooted more in revolutionary struggle than in women's liberation, the women who were forming their own groups emanating out of SDS were less complacent about the gap between SDS policy and practice. In early 1969, one SDS woman wrote:

We were still the movement secretaries and the shit-workers; we served the food, prepared the mailings and made the best posters; we were the earth mothers and the sex objects for the movement men. We were the free movement "chicks" – free to screw any man who demanded it, or if we chose not to – free to be called hung-up, middle-class, and up-tight. We were free to keep quiet at meetings – or if we chose not to, we were free to speak up in men's terms.... We found ourselves unable to influence the direction and scope of projects. We were dependent on the male for direction and recognition.[18]

16 Mari Jo Buhle, *Women and American Socialism* (Urbana, Ill., 1983), 324.
17 Naomi Jaffe and Bernadine Dohrn, "The Look Is You," *New Left Notes* (Mar. 18, 1968), 5, cited in Albert and Albert, eds., *The Sixties Papers*, 228.
18 Sale, *SDS*, 526.

Even as she decried sexism in the movement and in society, Dohrn did not accept the centrality of women's issues in a revolutionary context. In March, she responded, "Most of the women's groups are bourgeois, unconscious, or unconcerned with class struggle and the exploitation of working class women."[19] The rift was becoming pronounced for many women activists as the very movement that had espoused freedom and creativity, especially in terms of individual expression and sexuality, now trivialized their concerns as less than central to the real issue of class struggle and bringing an end to the Vietnam War. Increasingly, women activists who spoke out came to feel that there was no return to the mainstream of radical politics.

Women in SDS and throughout the antiwar movement began to challenge the premise that a broad-ranging attack on American capitalism and imperialism would mitigate the need for ending male supremacy. They refused to accept the idea that women's issues were marginal, but this refusal came at no small price. Women often had to choose between continuing alliances with men and the need to raise critical issues that the Movement had failed to acknowledge. Women themselves were often split on the issue of "which was more important – ending the war or ending sexism." Worst of all, women who spoke out in support of women's issues were attacked with a discourse filled with sexist and near-pornographic images. Coming from comrades in the struggle to end the war and create a new society, this was painful indeed. Activist Ellen Willis reflected on this experience:

It's hard to convey to people who didn't go through that experience how radical, how unpopular and difficult it was just to get up and say, "Men oppress women. Men have oppressed *me*. Men must take responsibility for their actions instead of blaming them on capitalism. And, yes, that means *you*." We were laughed at, patronized, called frigid, emotionally disturbed man-haters and – worst insult of all on the left! – apolitical.[20]

A similar theme emerged in the connection of the personal to the political in the open letter written by "A Berkeley Sister," "To A White Male Radical." This essay stresses the importance of personal connection in political relationships. In this instance, the woman veteran of the movement is willing to go her own way to avoid becoming oppressed by the very activists who had so recently struggled with her in the antiwar cause that,

19 Ibid.
20 Ellen Willis, "Radical Feminism and Feminist Radicalism," in Sohnya Sayres, Anders Stephanson, Stanley Aronowitz, and Fredric Jameson, eds., *The '60s Without Apology* (Minneapolis, 1984), 94.

for so many men, was defined in specifically masculine terms:

I . . . will not accept your ridiculous role of self-reliance; it is inhuman, counterrevolutionary and opposed to the goals of Women's Liberation. Your reluctance to be close and open when all is said and done indicates that you make a rather limited socialist after all. Refusing vulnerability you are refusing friendship. Refusing acts of sharing you seem so sadly alone. Long ago, earlier feminists wanted to be tough like you. Only fifty years later did they realize how they had assumed the role of the oppressor. Like many Blacks they had silently slipped into the oppressor's habits and therefore truly failed. That is why you are an enemy.[21]

As Sara Evans noted, women who moved tentatively toward their own organization "kept trying to find a way to be equal within the very insurgency that had built the very foundation for their growing self-consciousness."[22]

For many women antiwar activists, membership in a movement in which they faced the constant risk of marginalization when they connected the movement to stop the war and the movement for political revolution to the movement to achieve personal and societal liberation created increasing personal and organizational tension and was increasingly difficult to maintain. Yet, for others, the connections remained powerful, as they saw the struggle for women's liberation in a larger revolutionary context. Writing in response to Robin Morgan's "Goodbye to All That," in which she railed against male activists for their oppression of women and, worse yet, for their lack of understanding and support for women's issues, Genie Plamondon, Minister of Communication of the White Panther Party, wrote of the need to stay the antiwar, revolutionary course:

I'm gonna raise my head and my *fist* in anger and love, and join my brothers and sisters in demanding and working and fighting for *Freedom now* – *by any means necessary* – I'm not going to join any women who want a "genderless society" – they can have their own genderless tribe, I'm not down on that – I love to fuck, I love being a woman, and I love *men* – oh yes I do – Nor am I going to join any woman, any body, who wants to "take over the movement" – bullshit – I align myself with all revolutionary people who are dedicated to serving the people and liberating the planet from *all* oppressive forces – the White Panther Party is dedicated, Rising Up Angry is dedicated, the Young Patriots and Young Lords are dedicated, the Weathermen are dedicated, the Vietnamese are dedicated, the Koreans the Cubans the Chinese and Africans are dedicated – and we are all *revolutionaries*, we are all for *change* – on the planet and within ourselves, anybody not prepared

---

21 A Berkeley Sister, "To A White Radical" in *The Berkeley Tribe* (May 15–22, 1970), 8, quoted in Albert and Albert, eds., *The Sixties Papers*, 518.

22 Sara M. Evans, *Personal Politics: The Roots of Women's Liberation in the Civil Rights Movements and the New Left* (New York, 1979), 189.

to change will *die*, and I won't waste my time saying goodbye. . . . *Seize the time outlaws!!!!!*[23]

Plamondon's perspective came to be one of a minority of women who began their revolutionary activities in the antiwar movement and found their path to personal and women's liberation in a revolutionary, and not specifically a feminist, movement context.

Women did not always lobby for recognition of their issues from within established movement groups, preferring instead to stage antiwar events with a women's focus. For example, in February 1966, women at Berkeley held a rally and protest at the Army induction center in Oakland four days after two army nurses were killed in a helicopter crash in Vietnam. Making the connection between their own need for a separate movement and that of African-American activists in SNCC, the women declared that "parallels can be drawn between treatment of Negroes and treatment of women in our society as a whole."[24] In June of the following year, the same theme emerged at the Women's Liberation Workshop at the SDS national convention. Workshop participants formulated an analysis of women's position in the United States, in the movement, and in their closest working and personal relationships with male colleagues:

As we analyze the position of women in capitalist society and especially in the United States we find that women are in a colonial relationship to men and we recognize ourselves as part of the Third World. Women, because of their colonial relationship to men, have to fight for their own independence. This fight for our own independence will lead to the growth and development of the revolutionary movement in this country. Only the independent woman can be truly effective in the larger revolutionary struggle. We seek the liberation of all human beings. The struggle for liberation of women must be part of the larger fight for human freedom. We recognize the difficulty our brothers will have in dealing with male chauvinism and we will assume full responsibility in helping to resolve the contradiction. Freedom now! We love you![25]

Even though women remained active in SDS and other movement groups for a few more years, by 1967, the die had been cast for activist women who perceived that the tension between mainstream movement participation and articulating grievances of their own could no longer be resolved.

23 Genie Plamondon, "Hello to All That," in *The Berkeley Tribe* (Mar. 6–13, 1970), 13, quoted in Albert and Albert, eds., *The Sixties Papers*, 522–3.
24 Cited in Charles DeBenedetti, *An American Ordeal: The Antiwar Movement of the Vietnam Era* (Syracuse, N.Y., 1990), 146.
25 *New Left Notes* (July 10, 1967), cited in Evans, *Personal Politics*, 190–1.

In Europe, feminism can also be analyzed in terms of its emergence from larger efforts worldwide to create a fundamentally new social order. George Katsiaficas has analyzed the student movement (which encompassed but also transcended antiwar protest) in international terms:

In February, 1968, for example, students in France were heard chanting "Solidarity with SDS," the New Left organization in Germany which was under attack. The next month, 400 German SDS members formed a prominent contingent at a demonstration in London. After the French students erupted in May, police battled 5,000 students in Rome who gathered to burn De Gaulle in effigy. In June and July, there were four days of street fighting in Berkeley when police attacked demonstrations in solidarity with the striking workers and students of France. On June 15, 10,000 Japanese students blockaded the center of Tokyo to show their solidarity with French students. In Santiago, Chile, thousands of students attacked the U.S. Embassy on October 4 in support of students in Mexico and Uruguay, who themselves identified with the May 1968 student revolt in France.[26]

This spirit of solidarity and cooperation arose in the New Left in opposition to the hierarchical and authoritarian spirit in which governments conducted themselves. Women's voices were powerful among those who offered a new paradigm of cooperation, community, and egalitarianism.

Women were not content to accept the notion that their personal concerns were any less important because they spoke to issues of self-esteem, sexuality, and female equality. The founding of the National Organization for Women in Washington, D.C. in 1966 was accompanied by a statement that revealed the international perspective of the women's movement: "The time has come for a new movement toward free equality for all women in America, and toward a truly equal partnership of the sexes, as part of the world-wide revolution of human rights now taking place within and beyond our national borders."[27] Within a few months a new journal, *Donna e Societa*, began publication in Italy.

In France, women began forming their own groups after May 1968. One of the most important of these called itself "*politique et psychoanalyse.*" Founded by Lacanian psychoanalyst Antoinette Fouque, this organization sought a way to reconcile the personal and the political, a synthesis of psychoanalysis and materialism, or Freud and Marx. Early feminist actions, such as the placing of a wreath dedicated to the *wife* of the unknown soldier at France's memorial to patriotism and sacrifice, intentionally placed women at the center of the historical stage. With the war in Vietnam still raging and the bureaucratic structure against which students had protested in 1968 still

26 George Katsiaficas, *The Imagination of the New Left: A Global Analysis of 1968* (Boston, 1987), 41.
27 NOW Circular, Oct. 1966, cited in Marwick, *Sixties*, 679–80.

largely in place, French media sources frequently marginalized and trivialized women activists. But, in calling the protesters members of the "*Mouvement de Liberation des Femmes*," cynical critics gave the movement its name.[28]

French feminists set in motion a process of theorization of feminist discourse. Transcending purely personal responses to oppression that emerged from the consciousness-raising process to develop a theory that could serve as a call for action, feminist thinkers such as Simone de Beauvoir began to speak in distinctly theoretical terms. According to historian Arthur Hirsch, feminists argued that women's subordinate position in society is not

a natural condition. Rather, the inequality of the sexes is the result of a social mode of domination of women known as patriarchy or phallocracy. The near universal prevalence of this domination is not an argument for its biological necessity but rather an indication of its deep-rooted pervasiveness in all previous and contemporary social systems, including both capitalism and socialism. . . . Ultimately, the goal of feminism is to abolish sex roles altogether and create an egalitarian society in which individuals are not defined by their gender or sexual preference.[29]

As a representative statement of the radical movement, this is a far cry from radical Mark Rudd's "Get me a chick to do some typing!" comment at Columbia in 1968. French feminists struggled within the *mouvement*, only to determine that theirs was a struggle that needed a voice of its own. With de Beauvoir's help, abortion became a prominent feminist issue in France, particularly with the "Manifesto of the 343," a declaration by prominent women that they had had illegal abortions. The issue became one of many important specifically feminist debates in the early 1970s. Although feminists themselves might not always agree on the extent to which they should participate in mainstream politics or focus on specifically radical women's issues, French feminists succeeded in making the personal part of the political and intellectual agendas of recent decades. Nevertheless, the persistent focus on the personal as the starting point for political action tended to drive a wedge between traditional movement activists and new feminists who refused to accept the hierarchies of the left any more than they were willing to accept hierarchy and patriarchy in society at large. By the 1970s, feminists could find themselves as estranged theoretically from their former comrades in the movement as from mainstream society. According to American activist Ellen Willis,

a genuine alliance with male radicals will not be possible until sexism sickens them as much as racism. This will not be accomplished through persuasion, conciliation,

28 Arthur Hirsch, *The French New Left: An Intellectual History from Sartre to Gorz* (Boston, 1981), 214–15.
29 Ibid., 215.

or love, but through independence and solidarity: radical men will stop oppressing us and make our fight their own when they can't get us to join them on any other terms.[30]

Women were beginning to see themselves as participants in an independent movement and not as an adjunct, auxiliary, or subordinate part of any other male-dominated radical organization.

In the Federal Republic of Germany, as in France, the student movement sought to separate itself from the material prosperity but deadening cultural conformity of the late 1950s. As the 1960s progressed, individuals in the German student movement also parted company with the analysis that dictated that the international class struggle took precedence over more personal concerns. In an assertion of the "politics of the self" (*Politik in der ersten Person*), activist Helke Sander in 1968 "harshly criticized male student activists' sexist behavior and asserted that the private sphere is political," thereby placing the individual at the center of the countercultural analysis. Animated by the slogan "All Power to the Imagination," German women struggled to bring their concerns, under the banner of sexual politics, to the realm of pubic debate.[31] In the longer term, German feminist theorists contributed to the New Subjectivity movement in literature with consciousness-raising texts (*Verständigungstexte*) whose purpose, according to Sabine von Dirke, was to "present an authentic experience rather than a highly stylized literary product."[32]

In England, too, new cultural and intellectual currents flourished, inspired in part by feminist theoretical contributions to the new cultural and political discourse. Just as feminism emerged out of a critique of patriarchy, the alternative universities, publications, and theoretical treatises emerged out of a critique of bureaucracy and antidemocratic societal organization. For example, Sheila Rowbotham contributed articles with a feminist theoretical perspective to "Black Dwarf," an underground newspaper that presented itself as anti-imperialist and antiwar. London's anti-university included courses on literature and psychology in which women writers were the object of serious study taught by Juliet Mitchell, one of the school's founders. By the 1970s, the Center for Contemporary Cultural Studies in Birmingham became a major locus of feminist scholarship and activism. The Center, despite its importance in British cultural studies circles, underwent its own internal struggles around the importance of feminist ideas. The eleventh issue of the

30 Ellen Willis, "Up from Radicalism: A Feminist Journal," *US #2* (New York, 1969), 115.
31 See Sabine von Dirke, *All Power to the Imagination: The West German Counterculture from the Student Movement to the Greens* (Lincoln, Neb., 1997), 67–8.
32 Ibid., 90.

Center's journal *Working Papers* was published as *Women Take Issue*, whose purpose was to highlight feminist scholarship and women's issues as central to the Center's work. On a more mundane level, from child care to struggles over equal pay, English feminists brought the personal into public view.

Britain's *History Workshop* was instrumental in raising working-class women's issues:

At a Ruskin workshop on working-class history in the autumn of 1969, female participants became frustrated by the meeting's exclusive preoccupation with male workers and by men's dominant position in the group. The women decided to hold their own informal session on women's history, a move greeted with "a gust of masculine laughter." Initially, the breakaway group met to plan a workshop that would be about women, but their discussions gradually became broader, and they ended up planning the first national women's liberation conference in Britain. Five hundred people – four hundred of them women – attended sessions at Ruskin in February, 1970.[33]

Women activists who had started their careers protesting the inequities of society and the brutality of the Vietnam War continued to concern themselves with these important issues, but their perspective had changed. An analysis of class oppression had given way for many to an understanding of radical politics through the lens of gender.

Women's activism and the emergence of a feminist analysis could be found in some unlikely places. The war and the countercultural zeitgeist in the United States in the late 1960s brought out an activist impulse, even an imperative to act, among women who might otherwise have pursued their careers and their lives with few political reference points. Popular actress Jane Fonda and singer Holly Near, along with actor Donald Sutherland, participated in the "political vaudeville" show known as FTA, which toured the country for nearly a year in 1971 and was released as a film in 1972. FTA, "Free the Army," "Free the Americans," "Fun, Travel and Adventure" (the name of a popular GI antiwar newspaper published at Fort Knox, Kentucky), or, in military parlance, "Foxtrot, Tango, Alpha," were all stand-ins for what came to be the political statement "Fuck the Army!" Performed on and near military bases and in coffeehouses throughout the United States and in Japan, the Philippines, and elsewhere in the Pacific Rim, the FTA show satirized military life as well as U.S. foreign policy.[34]

In 1971, Jane Fonda was hardly the American woman most likely to become active in the struggle to end the Indochina War. Daughter of actor Henry Fonda, she had won an Academy Award for her role in *Klute* and had

33 Dennis Dworkin, *Cultural Marxism in Postwar Britain* (Durham, N.C., 1997), 193.
34 "The Show the Pentagon Couldn't Stop," *Ramparts* (Sept. 1972), 29–32.

earned a reputation for her jet-setting lifestyle rather than political activism. Inspired by the intractability of the war itself, Fonda became interested in the peace movement and sought ways to support it. In February 1971, she helped to organize three days of war crimes testimony sponsored by Vietnam Veterans Against the War called the Winter Soldier Investigation. Later that year, she announced the formation of the FTA troupe to perform a show written by Jules Feiffer and directed by Mike Nichols. Hoping to provide an alternative to the apolitical entertainment offered by more traditional Hollywood stars, Fonda declared that, "It has become disconcerting for many of us in Hollywood to see that Bob Hope, Martha Raye, and other companies of their political ilk have cornered the market and are the only entertainers allowed to speak to soldiers in this country and in Vietnam." Apparently, the army brass agreed with this assessment. When the FTA troupe proposed to present its debut performance at Fort Bragg, North Carolina, the commanding officer Lt. General John J. Tolson III declared the show to be "detrimental to discipline and morale."[35] Five hundred GIs attended the show off base. Their reactions were mixed, many saying that they had hoped to see the sexy "Barbarella" character rather than the newly politicized Fonda.

Coming to political consciousness at age thirty rather than as a young student and acquiring her analytical perspective quickly, often while fly-ing from one protest to another, Fonda seemed eager to compress all of her political energy into support for as many radical causes as she could find in the early 1970s, telling *Life* magazine, "I never felt politics touched my life. But, as a revolutionary woman, I'm ready to support all struggles that are radical."[36] Fonda and husband Tom Hayden helped to organize the Indochina Peace Campaign, supported the Black Panthers and United Farm Workers, and campaigned for George McGovern. Fonda's strident, somewhat naïve commentary on the progress of the Vietnamese revolution gave her the nickname "Hanoi Jane" that prompted threats against her life and the appearance of anti-Jane bumper stickers.

In 1972, Fonda traveled to Hanoi to film the effects of the bombing on the people of North Vietnam. According to Mary Hershberger:

Although the Pentagon denied it was bombing the dikes, Fonda filmed bomb craters directly on the dikes on the Red River and, like foreign journalists who visited Hanoi that year, and the Swedish ambassador, Jean-Christophe Oberg, she became convinced that the bombings were deliberate. If public protests did not halt

35 "Left Face," *The New Republic* (Mar. 31, 1971), 9.
36 " 'Nag, Nag, Nag': Jane Fonda Has Become a Nonstop Activist," *Life* (Apr. 23, 1971), 51.

them, they could do enormous direct harm to the Vietnamese caught in the path of flooding as well as igniting typhoid and dysentery that massive flooding would bring in their wake.[37]

From her political activist phase in the 1970s Fonda returned to acting with a renewed political consciousness, as in the 1978 film, *Coming Home*. Even when she retreated from the politics of revolution to the economics of fitness with her workout books, tapes, and videos, Jane Fonda has continued to be a very public American woman who remains an advocate of women's issues. In the early 1970s, Fonda found her own variety of feminist consciousness through her activism on behalf of the antiwar movement.

Often, new feminist activism first took the form of publishing position papers in which the mainstream radical had little interest. The result was a variety of new feminist newspapers. For example, the alternative paper, *off our backs*, first appeared in 1970. Its seed money of $400 had been raised the previous year to start a GI antiwar coffeehouse. According to the editors,

the name *off our backs* was chosen because it reflects our understanding of the dual nature of the women's movement. Women need to be free of men's domination to find their real identities, redefine their lives, and fight for the creation of a society in which they can lead decent lives as human beings. At the same time, women must become aware that there would be no oppressor without the oppressed, that we carry the responsibility for withdrawing the consent to be oppressed. We must strive to get off our backs, and with the help of our sisters to oppose and destroy that system which fortifies the supremacy of men while exploiting the mass for the profit of the few.[38]

Drawing on their experience in the antiwar movement as well as their radical political language and perspective, the women of *oob* made connections with women from all over the world, including Vietnam, to promote the cause of women's liberation. *oob* went through its own growing pains, factionalism, and splits, but it survived into the 1990s as a vehicle for radical feminist expression.

It should come as no surprise that women who participated in the antiwar movement often describe the experience in transformational terms. The female Harvard graduate who described her search for credibility as a "girl" in a male-dominated movement commented that the war and the movement to stop it "changed my life – in the way I questioned everything, in the sense

37 Hershberg, *Traveling to Vietnam*, 208.
38 See Carol Anne Douglas and Fran Moira, "*Off Our Backs*: The First Decade (1970–1980)," in Ken Wachsberger, ed., *Voices for the Underground*, vol. 1: *Insider Histories of the Vietnam Era Underground Press* (Tempe, Ariz., 1993), 107–30.

of involvement in something greater than myself, and in the sense of my outrage."[39] Whether or not that sense of outrage led individual women into feminist groups, it was a major contributing factor in keeping women connected to the revolutionary enterprise in one form or another.

The new feminism has drawn its inspiration and sustenance from myriad sources, a few of which were described here. No linear tale of "progress" from one movement to another, the story of the new feminism is a complex tapestry of interconnections and apparent disconnections. When viewed from a feminist perspective, the experiences of the women described here make sense in both a national and a world context. Even unwitting sisterhood can be powerful, and, as Evans suggested in 1979, this sisterhood has the potential to realize that power in varieties of activism both highly visible and as yet unrealized.

39 MacPherson, *Long Time Passing*, 543.

16

Vietnam

Many Wars?

LLOYD C. GARDNER

The history of "America's Longest War" remains highly contested territory –
and will undoubtedly continue so far into the future. When compared to the
overarching narrative of World War II, even with all of its subtexts, Vietnam
has no epic tale to relate, only episodes. Studs Terkel, perhaps the most
famous chronicler of the voices of America in our time, entitled the book
of interviews he did about the World War II era, *The Good War*. "There was
a time of good feeling," veterans told him. "The country felt it had done
something worthwhile. The guys came back feeling they had accomplished
something."[1]

Soldiers returning to "the world" from 'Nam – as they put it – often
felt contradictory emotions about what they had experienced. For many,
satisfaction for duty done as citizen-soldiers mixed with puzzled resentment
at the antiwar movement. While still feeling troubled and confused about the
ultimate purposes of a war that America seemed unable to win, they resented
the stereotype of the veteran strung out by post-traumatic stress syndrome.
And while the legend of veterans reviled and spat upon conveniently serves
political and ideological needs of various pressure groups, it is certainly
the case that for the first time the nation's ambiguous feelings about the
war have colored the veterans' perceptions of how they should feel about
themselves.

Some who went to Vietnam with antiwar sympathies found their views
altered by what they witnessed. Al Gore arrived in Vietnam an out-and-
out critic fresh from Harvard. He had enlisted upon graduation to protect
his father, Senator Albert Gore, whose antiwar positions were not popular in Tennessee and threatened his reelection prospects in 1970. The
younger Gore's memory tells us a great deal about the continuing ambiguities

---

1 Studs Terkel, *"The Good War," An Oral History of World War Two* (New York, 1984), 308.

surrounding the war today – as it moves from personal recollection to public monument:

When I actually went there and got to know some of the South Vietnamese, who were genuinely terrified of what would happen to them if they lost their freedom in a takeover by the North, my easy assumptions about the nature of the conflict were challenged by the reality of it. It was so much more subtle. I still think that the policy was a mistake, but I think that it was much more complicated than either proponents or the opponents of that policy thought.[2]

A new factor has entered into contemporary perceptions of Vietnam: the collapse of the Soviet Union. When President Ronald Reagan described the war as a noble endeavor in an ultimately victorious Cold War over the evil empire, it was hardly a popular view – especially in academic circles. Today, that view has received more attention. There has always been the argument, moreover, that the war could have been won – but for a failure of nerve. Commenting on what befell his lot as Richard Nixon's chief adviser on foreign affairs and Vietnam, Henry Kissinger wrote:

Too many of our young were in rebellion against the successes of their fathers, attacking what they claimed to be the overextension of our commitments and mocking the values that had animated the achievements. A new isolation was growing. Whereas in the 1920s we had withdrawn from the world because we thought we were too good for it, the insidious theme of the late 1960s was that we should withdraw from the world because we were too evil for it.[3]

Almost no issue concerning the war and its history is free of controversy. And none is likely to be settled by the opening of "enemy" archives, Russian, Chinese, or North Vietnamese. Having spent a good deal of time over the past two years working closely with activist veterans in the construction of New Jersey's Vietnam Educational Exhibit, I am more keenly aware than ever that Vietnam was not simply one war, from the highest policymaking level down to the individual soldier's experience.

Over the course of seemingly endless meetings to discuss the narrative for the exhibit, what representations to illustrate trends in American society during the turbulent "sixties decade," what space to give to Vietnamese history, and how to explain the agony of the war and its no less frustrating aftermath in the MIA/POW controversy, there finally emerged a series of compromises often dictated more by deadlines than agreement. When the exhibit opened, however, grudging acquiescence that opposition views had

---

2 Louis Menand, "After Elvis: Is There a Future for a Politician Whose Ideas Are Almost as Big as His Ambitions?" *The New Yorker*, Oct. 26, 1998, 164–7.
3 Henry Kissinger, *White House Years* (Boston, 1979), 56–7.

to be represented gave way to an acknowledgment of diversity. Perhaps this "good will" blossomed out of Senator John McCain's dedicatory remarks that reminded the largely veteran audience that the exhibit was not intended to settle questions about Washington's policies, or to honor a cause he continued to believe was the right one, but to present the war experience in all its complexity and to honor those who answered the call to service.

Still, it is difficult to fit Vietnam into the narrow idea of a "battle" – like Custer's last stand – a sacrifice that bought time for newly emerging nations in an ultimately successful struggle with the "Evil Empire." It is difficult, indeed, to see the Cold War as an uninterrupted continuum from the end of World War II to the collapse of the Berlin Wall. But that is another matter for discussion elsewhere. American servicemen, it should be remembered, had been sent into battle by leaders who insisted that the decision *in Vietnam itself* would determine the outcome of the Cold War. Perhaps policymakers escalated the stakes in order to convince themselves, or perhaps they were genuinely convinced, as Ambassador Henry Cabot Lodge put it in the discussions over whether to send the first 100,000 troops to Vietnam, that to withdraw would be "worse than a victory for the Kaiser or Hitler in the two World Wars."[4]

Yet Vietnam still stands out as the war without a Pearl Harbor to clarify and codify its meaning. How, then, did events in a country far off the map of national awareness in 1945 ultimately provide such a challenge to what American leaders expected of themselves and what they believed others expected of them? To begin with, the victories that ended World War II dealt only with the military defeat of the Axis powers. There were many "hidden" wars going on simultaneously, conflicts that had other objectives, conflicts with implications for the origins of direct American involvement in Vietnam, and the ultimate contradictions that arose as a consequence.

Resistance to German and Japanese expansionism constituted the core conflict of what we call World War II. But when that core exploded over the world, it set off secondary and tertiary conflicts too often missed in both popular and scholarly reflections on the outcome of the war. Moreover, even within the core conflict there were important distinctions to be found. There was, for example, the second Russo-German war being fought for geopolitical supremacy in Central Europe – a continuation of the same struggle that went back, some would argue, to Napoleon. And there also was the Anglo-German-Italian war being fought, in large part, over the

4 See the review of David M. Barrett, ed., *Lyndon B. Johnson's Vietnam Papers* (College Station, Tex., 1997), by Edwin E. Moise, on H-Diplo, Nov. 13, 1998, H-Diplo@H-Net.MSU.EDU.

general challenge to the British Empire in the Mediterranean. In the Far East, there was the Anglo-Japanese war waged within specific territorial domains of the British Empire. And there was also the Sino-Japanese war over rightful leadership in Asia, cultural as well as political. There was the American war against the Axis Tripartite Pact, in Europe to defeat Germany's bid to dominate the continent, with all that implied for the wider world, in Asia to rebuff Japan's effort to shut out Western influence. And, finally, there was also an internal struggle over how to wage a successful campaign for the "American Century" – a panoramic, futuristic vision which came to the Western Hemisphere with the early explorers.[5]

In the Depression decade that preceded Pearl Harbor, the New Deal proposed reforms and partial self-containment as the answer to a world divided into pre-Orwellian ideological and economic blocs, autarkic icebergs that congested the sea lanes of international commerce. Secretary of State Cordell Hull put the situation the United States faced this way: "Why dammit, these nations have told us again and again what they mean to do.... If they succeed, we will have to transact our business with the rest of the world through Tokyo and Berlin."[6]

But the congestion was not limited to economics. Even most New Dealers saw Roosevelt's experimentation in intranationalism as a risky venture politically and did not place faith in it except as a temporary set of necessary measures until the world was made healthy again – whatever America's role would have to be in that effort. Robert Coover's outlandish Cold War novel *The Public Burning* has as one of its principal characters a mythic "Uncle Sam" who tutors Vice President Richard Nixon on the golf course at Burning Tree from time to time and in his daydreams. Sounding very much like the Tennessean Cordell Hull, "Uncle Sam" holds forth at considerable length on his obsession with "staying young." "To him," Coover's Nixon relates in one conversation, "a closed frontier was like a hardened artery and too much government, too much system, too much political theory, was a kind of senility. It was what made him hate socialists." "This here's a country of beginnings, of projects, of vast designs and expectations," Uncle Sam declares, rolling off a few cartwheels in front of Nixon. "It's got no past; all it has is an onward and prospective look!"

---

5 One cannot overlook other wars, for example, the genocidal war against the Jews or the internal ethnic and political purges within the Stalinist empire. My intention here, however, is not to deconstruct World War II into a recitation of individual experiences akin to *Saving Private Ryan* but to pay attention to the Vietnam War's relation to the various conflicts that made up that world conflagration.

6 Quoted in Lloyd C. Gardner, *Economic Aspects of New Deal Diplomacy* (Madison, Wis., 1964), 169.

Irrepressible New Deal troubleshooter Tommy "The Cork" Corcoran, no less a mythic character in his own right, recalled for Studs Terkel how Roosevelt's instructions in the precedent-shattering third term campaign bespoke a new vision. "Tommy, cut out this New Deal stuff," FDR told him. "It's tough to win a war." FDR did not want arguments over the New Deal to cloud the issue of America's future. Talking privately with an intimate friend in 1943, the president ruminated on Woodrow Wilson's advice that the public had limited tolerance for liberal reform about one-third of the time and reverted to conservatism the other two-thirds. "He wants to get out of domestic problems," Margaret Suckley wrote in her diary, "and help to carry on international ones."[7] After the 1940 election, Tommy the Cork wound up in Asia. "I was put into the China war." He was an idealist, he told Terkel, but "I believed in arithmetic." Leaping forward from recollection to the present, he admonished the interviewer:

Detaching Southeast Asia from the communist philosophy is the most important thing we've got. I have a hunch that we're the repository of the civilized forces that are left in the world. I was in a completely new world over there, with the Chinese and Singapore and Malaya and the rest of it. It was the great adventure of my life.[8]

Bolstered by the miracle of American war production which in a short time lifted the country out of "The Depression Blues," Roosevelt still worried about obstacles to a "completely new world over there," not only the wide divergence of objectives with the Soviet Union, but divisions within the West over the vexed "colonial question."

At an informal dinner in June 1944, Roosevelt rambled on about the stakes in the colonial question, revealing his concerns about a war after the war between metropolitan powers and the peoples who inhabited their nineteenth-century conquests. All the signs were there for anyone to see, as he pointed out to his guests:

In regard to the Far East in general, which means the yellow race, which is far more numerous than the white, it will be to the advantage of the white race to be friends with them and work in cooperation with them, rather than make enemies of them and have them eventually use all the machines of western civilization to overrun and conquer the white race.[9]

Roosevelt even blamed prewar "appeasement," and sometimes the war itself, on craven British and French desires to protect their empires at almost

7 Geoffrey C. Ward, ed., *Closest Companion: The Unknown Story of the Intimate Friendship Between Franklin Roosevelt and Margaret Suckley* (Boston, 1995), 251.
8 Terkel, *The Good War*, 318–19.
9 Diary entry, June 28, 1944, quoted in Ward, ed., *Closest Companion*, 314.

any cost. "Don't think for a moment, Elliott," Roosevelt supposedly confided to his son, "that Americans would be dying in the Pacific tonight, if it hadn't been for the shortsighted greed of the French and the British and the Dutch. Shall we allow them to do it all, all over again?"[10]

It seemed clear all along to postwar American leaders that the West's interests could not be protected by bowing to European "colonial" attitudes. At the 1945 Potsdam meeting with Stalin, Truman apparently thought he had the solution within his grasp. He was tremendously "pepped up" by news of the successful atomic test in New Mexico, recorded Secretary of War Henry L. Stimson, and was now confident "of sustaining the Open Door policy" in China – the previously elusive (and illusive) objective of American efforts in Asia for the past fifty years.[11]

Returning to Washington, Truman met with French leader Charles de Gaulle and discouraged the latter's overtures for a bilateral security treaty. That world of entangling alliances was no more. France, the president said, would do well to seek its security in the new world organization. Furthermore, "The United States possessed a new weapon, the atomic bomb, which would defeat any aggressor. What the whole world needed most was economic re-establishment." That point driven home in the plainspoken "American" Truman favored, he had some pointed questions for de Gaulle. What about the communists in his government, what about those obstacles American businessmen were finding in attempting to cooperate with French industrialists?[12]

At approximately the same time as Truman was querying de Gaulle about French internal matters, Ho Chi Minh was preparing to address the Vietnamese with words taken from the American Declaration of Independence. In the Netherlands East Indies, similar scenes were about to occur.[13] Asian nationalist leaders of both rightist and leftist views looked to Washington for aid in throwing off their former masters, whether the Christian Syngman Rhee in Korea or the Communist Ho Chi Minh. Indeed, both Ho and the "puppet" emperor Bao Dai appealed to Truman to intervene to prevent a French return to Indochina.

10 Elliott Roosevelt, *As He Saw It: The Story of the World Conferences of F.D.R.* (New York, 1946), 115. Roosevelt's dramatic revelations of his father's distrust of wartime allies made it a highly controversial book, but even if the younger Roosevelt put words into FDR's mouth, the sentiments were genuine enough.

11 Excerpts from Henry L. Stimson's diary for July 16 and 17, 1945, quoted in Gar Alperovitz, *The Decision to Use the Atomic Bomb, and the Architecture of an American Myth* (New York, 1995), 273.

12 Lloyd C. Gardner, *A Covenant with Power: America and World Order from Wilson to Reagan* (New York, 1984), 88–9.

13 I am grateful to Wim Van Den Doel of Leiden University for sharing his thoughts about 1945 nationalist demonstrations in Jakarta and their relationship to the general problem of American postwar policy in Southeast Asia.

Truman paid no attention to the messages. Historians and policymakers alike have pondered Roosevelt's failure to follow through on his apparent intention to insist upon rapid decolonization by one means or another. Had he done so, it is argued, Truman would have followed suit. Various answers are given, some stressing FDR's fading energy as he confronted the immense tasks of peacemaking, others the unreliability of Nationalist China as a stabilizing power, but the answer often given is that the postwar situation in Europe prohibited challenging France, especially, out of fear of weakening French resolve against communism. As matters developed, of course, France was weakened most by its long and frustrating war to maintain its position in Indochina.

Americans constantly chafed, nevertheless, at their inability to persuade France to make a genuine offer of independence, but worried more about turning the area over to the pro-communist Ho Chi Minh and his Viet Minh cadres. Secretary of State Dean Acheson implied that he might – under great duress – see Ho as an Asian Tito, but the idea held little appeal. Moreover, whatever his original intentions, Ho's orientation was now all the more toward communist systems of economic organization. It would not do to see that "system" as the wave of the future for former colonial areas. Not only would it change economic patterns in those areas, it could cause instability in Europe, struggling already with the dollar gap, as traditional markets and dollar earnings disappeared. Vietnam – the country Roosevelt once claimed to be peopled by small, peace-loving farmers – thus threatened to disturb the world with its revolution.[14]

In the midst of their conversations on the progress of the Korean War at Wake Island, Truman and his aides took turns with General MacArthur in denouncing French policy in Indochina. MacArthur set things going by saying he was "puzzled" as to why the French with their numerical superiority couldn't win. "They are opposed by half of what the North Koreans had. I cannot understand why they do not clean it up." Admiral Radford said the reason was the French had no support among the local Vietnamese. "The rest of Southeast Asia – Burma, Siam – is wide open if the Chinese Communists pursue a policy of aggression." The place to stand was in Indochina. But the French were making a mess of things. The admiral added that recently some French ships stopped at Hawaii, but they were not anxious to go to Indochina and were dragging their feet. "They would have stayed in Pearl Harbor for six months if I had invited them,"

---

14 See Andrew J. Rotter, *The Path to Vietnam: Origins of the American Commitment to Southeast Asia* (Ithaca, N.Y., 1987), 141.

Radford groused. All this French-baiting seemed to rev up the president:

This is the most discouraging thing we face. [We] have worked on the French tooth
and nail to try and persuade them to do what the Dutch had done in Indonesia but
the French have not been willing to listen. If the French Prime Minister comes to
see me, he is going to hear some very plain talk. I am going to talk cold turkey to
him. If you don't want him to hear that kind of talk, you had better keep him away
from me.[15]

Worse still, lamented Secretary of State John Foster Dulles in 1954 during
secret testimony to the Senate Foreign Relations Committee, the French
Communists were being very clever. They had indicated that they would be
glad to have the three states of Indochina – Laos, Cambodia, and Vietnam –
stay in the French Union and not be independent. "They would love to
have three Communist states in the council in the French Union . . . as a
means of taking over France and the French Union."

Once the French were out of the way, Washington believed it could go
about replacing their outdated visions of empire with a world order that
would re-integrate the economies of Southeast Asia with the industrial nations to re-establish world prosperity – and, not incidentally, prevent nationalist fervor from being directed against the West, as Roosevelt had warned.

The Korean War did not turn out the way Truman and MacArthur
imagined it would at the Wake Island Conference, of course. Increasingly,
Vietnam became linked to the stalemated outcome of the Korean War, as
a dangerous continuation of that struggle in another area. Fear of another
Korea took several different forms. John Foster Dulles, especially, saw the
stalemate on the divided Korean Peninsula as prelude to a broad Chinese
advance in Southeast Asia and as a very dangerous precedent. He wanted
to offer the former colonial nations something better than a prospect of
political division. Dulles blamed the predicament on Truman's failure to
carry out the very first "commitment" – Roosevelt's vow to take Indochina
away from France. "Our government," he wrote in a private memorandum
to use against those who criticized American acquiescence in the Geneva
accords and terms for a cease-fire,

allowed itself to be persuaded in this matter by the French and the British and
we acted to restore France's colonial position in Indochina. The French only
maintained their position by bloody massacres which started the colonial war, which
the Communists subsequently took control of.[16]

---

15 "Substance of Statements Made at Wake Island Conference on Oct. 15, 1950," in U.S. Department of
   State, *Foreign Relations of the United States* (hereafter *FRUS*), *1950: Korea* (Washington, D.C., 1976),
   957–8.
16 Draft memorandum, July 9, 1954, John Foster Dulles papers, Mudd Library, Princeton University.

Failure to honor Roosevelt's supposed pledge to redeem France's grave errors thus became an object lesson for all future policymakers. The situation the United States found itself in after the 1954 Geneva Conference posed the prospect of a confrontation with the Peoples' Republic of China in large measure to protect the "workshop of Asia," Japan, for the West. Involvement in Vietnam thus became also a war for an American-sponsored "Co-Prosperity Sphere" to relieve Japan's economic difficulties as its transition from a semi-feudal society relying on militarist solutions to a modern "liberal" capitalist state was made complete. And there were enormous difficulties to face, starting with the American-imposed restrictions on Sino-Japanese trade. But while Japan's economy grew more secure, the political situation in Vietnam itself began to deteriorate.

Dulles's successor, Dean Rusk, rethought the Korean example and concluded that it was, in fact, a good model for Vietnam. Korea had proven the virtues of fidelity to a freely given American commitment. Korea really ought to be set alongside Greece and the Berlin crisis, he insisted, as Cold War victories. Another Korea was, to his mind, a very good solution for Vietnam. When Under Secretary of State George Ball expressed concern about the woeful political skills of the Saigon generals, Rusk retorted: "You don't understand that at the time of Korea that we had to go out and dig Syngman Rhee out of the bush where he was hiding; there was no government in Korea either, and we were able to come through."[17]

American presidents from Truman to Ford cited previous commitments and obligations to justify an effort challenged by dissenters ranging from the New Left in America to the old right in France, Charles de Gaulle. As it eventually became apparent, however, the *commitment* that mattered was to ourselves and not to any particular government in Saigon. On several levels, Vietnam was always a war of abstractions. On the verge of a fateful decision to send General William Westmoreland the first 100,000 men to South Vietnam – in fulfillment of a supposed promise President Dwight D. Eisenhower had made to aid Saigon against its enemies – someone at the conference table wondered aloud about the fitness of the regime to receive such support. Eisenhower's post-Geneva letter to Diem, frequently cited as evidence of a long-standing commitment to South Vietnam's independent existence, did indeed contain a proviso conditioning such aid on satisfactory progress toward developing a stable government. Henry Cabot Lodge, who had presided over American interests in Saigon in 1963 when Ngo

17 From George Ball's oral history at the Lyndon Baines Johnson Library in Austin, Texas (hereafter LBJL), I, 33.

Dinh Diem was overthrown, now declared that such unfulfilled expectations could not be allowed to hinder efforts to thwart the hovering threat
of "neutralism." "We may face a neutralist government at some time in the
future and . . . in those circumstances the US should be prepared to carry on
alone."[18]

General Maxwell Taylor, another past steward of American interests in
Saigon, even argued that should South Vietnamese fecklessness end in the
regime's collapse, "I would favor going against the north anyway." An attack
on North Vietnam, like the "Rolling Thunder" bombing campaign, would
be aimed at reviving morale in the South. Its main purpose "would be to give
Pulmotor treatment for a government in extremis and to make sure that the
DRV [North Vietnam] does not get off unscathed in any final settlement."
In such discussions words like "credibility" and "national security" took on
almost talismanic stature. Arguments against involvement were useless in the
face of such self-enchantment.

When Dean Rusk became the steward of American foreign policy in
1961, the Vietnam War had ceased to be about the precedent Ho's victory
would set or about Japan's economic future, limited objectives that could at
least be reasonably debated, and was now conceptualized in policy thinking as a total conflict between the "city" and the "country." Communist
opportunities, it was argued by Walt Rostow and others, were actually by-
products of an improperly managed modernization process. Vietnam, it
could be argued, became in some ways about the globalization of the Great
Society or, as one disenchanted National Security Council aide would put
it, about a *Pax Americana technocratica* and overcoming the final obstacle
to its realization. Techniques for "curing" poverty at home might not be
applicable to the situation in Southeast Asia, but the approach had many
things in common. And, from the opposite side, Lyndon Johnson could
see no way he could be successful in the War on Poverty at home if he
appeared to be losing Vietnam to the enemy. The enemy was China, which
represented the "country," and its hatred for the West. Here was a new
stage, it seemed, for the playing out of ancient enmities, present once
even in the United States when Populist agitation appeared to threaten
good order. The crossovers between the Vietnam War and the War on
Poverty were often quite remarkable, as in the case of Robert McNamara's
effort to have the Pentagon open a front in the latter with Project 100,000,
a scheme for inducting into the army men who would have previously

---

18 Memorandum for the president, July 20, 1965, Lyndon Baines Johnson papers, box 43, NSC
Histories, National Security Files, LBJL.

been denied "an opportunity to improve themselves and serve their country."[19]

Former Secretary of State Dean Acheson, on the other hand, minced no words about what the Vietnam War meant to America's enemies:

The Communist Chinese minister of defense, Marshal Lin Piao, in a speech on Sept. 3, [1965] referring to North America and Western Europe as the "cities of the world" and to Asia, Africa, and Latin America as the "rural areas," declared that "contemporary world revolution also presents a picture of the encirclement of cities by the rural areas."[20]

Secretary of Defense Robert McNamara portrayed the conflict in similar terms on several occasions, amending his views in his memoirs to suit his latter-day doubts. Thus he includes in his account of the decisions that led to full-scale intervention reasons why he thought the battle must be fought. The decision to start bombing, and all that followed, made sense only, he wrote in a memorandum to the president, if they were in support of a long-range policy to contain communist China – a view he says he came to regard as a "totally incorrect appraisal" of Beijing's supposed threat to American national security. And yet such views accurately reflected the attitudes of almost all the senior officials in government at the time. After the fall of Saigon, McNamara thought the reason for such obtuseness could be found in the "lack of expertise and historical knowledge [which] seriously undermined U.S. policy."[21]

McNamara's assertion that the lack of expertise and historical perspective was the cause of the tragedy in Vietnam has been challenged by numerous commentators, including several serving in the government when the decisions were made. He did not include in his memoirs portions of the memo he sent President Johnson on the need to contain communist China. In these missing sentences, McNamara avers that the Chinese were attempting to construct a coalition in Asia against American interests. "This understanding of a straightforward security threat is interwoven with another perception – namely, that we have our view of the way the U.S. should be moving and of the need for the majority of the rest of the world to be moving in the same direction if we are to achieve our national objectives. . . . Our ends cannot be achieved and our leadership role cannot be played if some powerful and

19 Lloyd C. Gardner, *Pay Any Price: Lyndon Johnson and the Wars for Vietnam* (Chicago, 1995), 296.
20 *Detroit News*, Jan. 19, 1966.
21 McNamara, draft memorandum, Nov. 3, 1965, Gardner, *Pay Any Price*, 514–28; and his later assessment in Robert McNamara, *In Retrospect: The Tragedy and Lessons of Vietnam* (New York, 1995), 218–19.

virulent nation – whether Germany, Japan, Russia or China – is allowed to organize their part of the world according to a philosophy contrary to ours."[22]

Even if McNamara had availed himself of the special expertise on Vietnam that did exist in the government, reasoned counterargument from lower levels of government would have had even less persuasive power than the generalized dissents voiced by George Ball and Clark Clifford in the debates over whether to send the first 100,000 troops. National Security Adviser McGeorge Bundy wrote in a similar near-apocalyptic vein. Historians of the future might designate the 1960s as the decade when "our civilization fashioned so painfully since the Reformation could be said to have reached its end." If that happened, it would likely not be because of nuclear cataclysm, but as a result of a new polarization of the world between the poor, the restless, and the nonwhite peoples, led or pushed by China, as opposed to Europe and North America. If that happened, "we will find ourselves in a virtual state of siege."

> The West, of course, still can survive as a political grouping and even as a culture. We will still maintain overwhelming military power in the sense that we could at any time reduce the land mass of Asia and of Africa to ashes. But this would provide us with slim comfort....
>
> In the last analysis, the West must preserve (or at least not willingly and voluntarily default) its access to, communications with, and benign influence on the peoples of Asia and Africa. We have much that is worthwhile to offer and much to gain. Our society and theirs can be enriched and nourished by the two-way flow of ideas and goods and peoples. China has chosen to slam its doors, at least for the present. We and the other peoples of the world cannot afford to see any more doors close, for every door that closes quickens the pace of rich-poor, colored-white, North-South division of the world.[23]

And yet again in similar fashion, Robert McNamara told a reporter in an interview why Lyndon Johnson's decisions were necessary:

> If the U.S. withdrew from SVN, there would be a complete shift in the world balance of power. Asia goes Red, our prestige and integrity damaged, allies everywhere shaken (even those who publicly ask us to quit bombing, etc.). At home, he foresees as a result of these calamities, a bad effect on economy and a disastrous political fight that could further freeze American political debate and even affect political freedom.

22 McNamara, draft memorandum, Nov. 3, 1965, Gardner, *Pay Any Price*, 514–28.

23 Unsigned memorandum, Feb. 1965, Johnson papers, boxes 28–29, international travel, National Security Files, LBJL. The memo has notes in McGeorge Bundy's handwriting, but the basic themes were common enough in Bundy's day and in that of his successors, Walt Rostow and Henry Kissinger.

On the other hand: If the U.S. achieved in SVN the objectives stated by LBJ in Baltimore, there would then be substantial political and economic and security gains. Way then open to combine birth control and economic expansion techniques in gigantic arc from SVN to Iran and Middle East, bringing unimaginable developments to this region, proving worth of moderate, democratic way of growth for societies.[24]

For some policymakers, America's "secret ally" in this war was to be the Soviet Union. In the Johnson administration, the primary advocate of seeking a successful end to the war through Moscow was Averell Harriman, who believed that he could move the Kremlin to intercede with Hanoi by talking about their common interests in containing the Chinese threat. Some in the State Department were encouraged by Aleksey Kosygin's recent speeches recalling statements by Roosevelt and Eisenhower about the value of Soviet-U.S. "wartime collaboration." Sent to Moscow at his own insistence, Harriman had two lengthy conversations with the Soviet premier on July 15 and 21, 1965. At both, Kosygin warned him that the United States was playing China's game:

You are responsible for tensions in the area and the peoples of the East are turning against you. You have only your puppets there and by your actions and resistance to national liberation movements you only prove the Chinese point that war is inevitable.[25]

Koysgin then interrupted Harriman's efforts to explain Johnson's readiness to accept Vietnamese self-determination "once the war is over" with a derisive outburst, "You don't believe what you are saying." Taking this as a slur on LBJ's motives and his own honesty, Harriman appealed to the Soviet leader to believe in Johnson's sincerity just as Stalin had accepted his word during the war because he, Harriman, had "come to the Soviet Union in the 20's in order to help the Soviet people." It was a marvelous moment in the Cold War, surely, with Harriman asking current Russian leaders to accept Stalin's validation of his credentials!

Had the minutes of these conversations appeared in the press, the public rationale for the American intervention in Vietnam would have suffered a perhaps fatal blow. The second conversation, which ranged over issues of nuclear disarmament and the future of Germany as well as Vietnam, brought out a different side of the Russian position. There were still ritual condemnations of American policy and the same ironic warnings about pursuing a pro-Chinese policy, but this time there were words about prospects for

24 Quoted in William Appleman Williams et al., eds., *America in Vietnam* (New York, 1985), 246–8.
25 Memorandum of conversation, July 15, 1965, *FRUS, 1964–1968*, III, 147–52.

direct negotiations. He had no authority to negotiate for the Vietnamese "comrades," he began, but as he had "previously said, the Vietnamese comrades do not exclude a political settlement, even one bypassing the Chinese." Kosygin had hinted at significant differences between Hanoi and Beijing. What might this mean for future US/DRV discussions, Harriman wondered? "In all confidence," said the Russian leader, "I can only repeat that our Vietnamese comrades do not rule out a political settlement. That is all I can say but this, it seems to me, is very important. Naturally, this would be on the basis of the retention of the 17th parallel."[26]

Nothing came of this strange interlude in the Cold War, but Harriman did not give up. When Lyndon Johnson announced a partial bombing halt on March 31, 1968, the long-time special ambassador sought out Anatoly Dobrynin. Over drinks in his Georgetown home, Harriman explained that Johnson had asked him to be his chief negotiator at the promised peace talks. "I . . . went after him pretty hard," he reported to the White House, "on the necessity of the Soviet Union taking real responsibility" for a successful outcome of the talks. Then, and later, he stressed the opportunities before the United States and Russia if they could contain their allies' propensity for irrational actions, a point he also urged on Richard Nixon's advisers during the interregnum after the election of 1968.[27]

Nixon eventually took a bolder step. He ended the American-Chinese diplomatic imbroglio with a dramatic trip to the Great Wall. It was a three-way ploy. He hoped to confront Hanoi with the need to offer the United States a "decent interval" and, at the same time, to persuade Chinese leaders that the United States no longer wanted a military confrontation while removing the Chinese threat in the minds of Americans conditioned by previous argument to accept the war as a necessary step in containing an expansionist Beijing.

Nixon's arrival at this position had been announced with quiet understatement when *Foreign Affairs* featured his article "Asia After Vietnam."[28] From the opening sentence it was a stunner. "The war in Vietnam has for so long dominated our field of vision," he wrote, "that it has distorted our

---

26 John C. Guthrie, Minister-Counselor, to Dean Rusk, July 26, 1965, with enclosed memorandum of conversation, Johnson papers, boxes 220–1, country file: Russia, LBJL. Unfortunately, *FRUS* editors did not include the transcript in *FRUS, 1964–1968*, III, where the record of the first conversation can be found. However, they did put together a very important editorial note on 179–80 on key elements of the conversation and the reaction in Washington.

27 Gardner, *Pay Any Price*, 464, 532, 541.

28 "Asia After Vietnam" originally appeared in *Foreign Affairs*, Oct. 1967. It is reprinted in Lloyd C. Gardner, ed., *The Great Nixon Turn-Around: America's New Foreign Policy in the Post-Liberal Era* (New York, 1973), 74–92.

picture of Asia. A small country on the rim of the continent has filled the screen of our minds; but it does not fill the map." The United States could not continue the role of world policeman, nor could the world continue to risk a nuclear holocaust because the superpowers became involved in what were essentially local contests.

If another world war – a nuclear holocaust – was to be prevented, it would be necessary to "minimize the number of occasions on which the great powers have to decide whether or not to commit themselves." The most famous sentence in the article read, "Taking the long view, we simply cannot afford to leave China forever outside the family of nations, there to nurture its fantasies, cherish its hates, and threaten its neighbors."

In yet another section of the article, the putative Republican candidate discussed the Asian awakening from centuries of stagnation and poverty:

Poverty that was accepted for centuries as the norm is accepted no longer. In a sense it could be said that a new chapter is being written in the winning of the West: in this case, a winning of the promise of Western technology and Western organization by the nations of the East. The cultural clash has had its costs and produced its strains, but out of it is coming a modernization of ancient civilizations that promises to leap the centuries.

Nixon's inability to leap over the legacies of the Vietnam War, including his own earlier views, stymied not only his efforts to end the war, but, in the end, contributed to the failure of détente or what he called the "structure of peace." His deeply flawed legacy leaves one with more questions than answers. Reformulated in the aftermath of the collapse of the Soviet Union, what might be called the "Truman Doctrine" thread posits American involvement in Vietnam as a necessary and self-sacrificing response to a worldwide challenge in the larger, more recognizable conflict designated as the Cold War. As such, it becomes familiar territory and not the strange and bewildering version of the American "mission" to the world that confused and divided the nation internally and provoked or mystified both advocates and critics of the American Century worldview. The Vietnam War as one Cold War "episode" inscribes the "Fall of Saigon" not as an event portending the final end of the colonial era, but as a lost battle in an ultimately successful struggle with an "evil empire." Even the term "Fall of Saigon" resonates well with memories of earlier heroic narratives from the World War II era, such as Bataan and Corregidor.

Hopefully, raising such questions will open discussion on the "Truman Doctrine" thread and the many other threads of explanation that need to be incorporated in an overview of America's war and the wider world.

Perhaps the most important thread of all, the Vietnamese thread, has been neglected quite simply because the American effort largely ignored the Vietnamese Revolution except as it could be made part of American history. Asked in 1966 to explain the causes of the war and reasons for the deepening American involvement, Secretary of State Dean Rusk told the Senate Foreign Relations Committee:

I think it is very important that the different kinds of revolutions be distinguished. We are in no sense committed against change. As a matter of fact, we are stimulating, ourselves, very sweeping revolutions in a good many places. The whole weight and effort of the Alliance for Progress is to bring about far-reaching social, economic changes. . . .
    I do believe there is a fundamental difference between the kind of revolution which the Communists call their wars of national liberation, and the kind of revolution which is congenial to our own experience, and fits into the aspirations of ordinary men and women right around the world.[29]

Therein, in Secretary Rusk's heartfelt testimony on America's aspirations for Vietnam, is a good starting point for understanding the vast extent of the tragedy that continues to challenge our understanding of the postmodern Thirty Years' War.

29 Williams et al., *America in Vietnam*, 258.

Index

357

Greece, 47, 349
Griffith, Patricia, 324
Gromyko, Andrei, 252
Grosvenor, Charles H., 57
Group of Ten, 165
Guam, 213, 227
guerrilla warfare, 35–8, 40, 92, 203,
  239–40, 244, 252, 313
Guevara, Ernesto Che, 311, 313
Guibo, Luo, 240
Gulf of Tonkin, 53, 94, 98, 191, 211,
  231, 244, 247, 285, 306
Gulf of Tonkin Resolution, 323
Gulf War, 144, 235
gunboat diplomacy, 42
Guomindang (Nationalist Party), 37,
  238

Haber, Al, 329
Hague, The, 166, 183
Hainan Island, 246
Haiphong, 234
Halberstam, David, 159
Halifax, 79
Hälker, Kurt, 302, 315, 318
Hamilton, Alexander, 73–4, 84
Hanoi, 6, 100–1, 113, 115–16,
  118–19, 177, 180, 182–3, 186, 189,
  207, 209–10, 217–18, 234, 240–1,
  243–4, 248–50, 252–6, 259,
  267–76, 293, 308, 323–4, 338, 353,
  354
Harkort, Günther, 168
Harriman, W. Averell, 261, 266, 276,
  353–4
Harrison, William, 109
Hart, Frederic, 16, 139, 141–2, 145
Hassler, Alfred, 308
Ha-Tinh, 38
Havana, 313
Hawaii, 47–50, 347
Hay, John, 48–9
Hayato, Ikeda, 189
Hayden, Tom, 325, 338
Heath, Perry, 59
Hegel, Georg Wilhelm Friedrich, 296
Helsinki, 306, 315–16

Helsinki Congress (1965), 308
Herring, George, 81, 357
Hershberger, Mary, 338
Herz, Helga Alice, 323
Heynowski, Walter, 316
Higginbotham, Don, 78
Hilsman, Roger, 183, 187
Hiroshima, 303
Hirsch, Arthur, 335
Hitler, Adolf, 226, 279, 281, 286, 287,
  290, 297–8, 343
Ho Chi Minh, 6, 27–8, 39, 76, 86,
  100, 202, 209, 239, 243, 250, 270,
  312, 346–7, 350
Ho Chi Minh Trail, 209
Hoar, George F., 48
Hobsbawm, Eric, 13
Hochhuth, Rolf, 282
Hoffman, Abbie, 326
Holland, 165, 327. *See also*
  Netherlands, the
Hollywood, 221, 338
Holocaust, 21, 145, 154, 281–2, 296,
  323
Holt, Harold, 230–2
Holyoake, Keith, 229
Honolulu, 228–9
Hope, Bob, 338
Horkheimer, Max, 291
Howett, Catherine M., 135
Hull, Cordell, 344
Humphrey, Hubert H., 114, 168,
  267
Hunt, Michael, 13, 33

Ia Drang, battle of, 91, 99
imperialism, 13, 21, 29, 31, 42, 44, 59,
  60, 225, 247, 253, 295, 297, 300,
  305–6 322, 329, 331
Inability to Mourn, The (book), 281
Inchon, 107
India, 7, 67, 95, 268
Indochina, 5–7, 13, 28, 29, 30–5,
  37–8, 40–1, 96–7, 101, 116–18,
  120, 177–9, 181, 186–7, 196–7,
  200, 202–3, 205–6, 211, 218–19,
  223, 234, 239, 240–1, 244, 248–9,